NEW
THOUGHTS ON
OLD
AGE

The Contributors

RUTH AISENBERG

ISABEL BANAY

J. SANBOURNE BOCKOVEN

ROBERT N. BUTLER

M. ELAINE CUMMING

NANCY DURKEE

STEPHEN DURKEE

OTTO F. EHRENTHEIL

ROBERT KASTENBAUM

SIDNEY LEVIN

OGDEN R. LINDSLEY

SALLY O'NEILL

KENNETH POLLOCK

CHARLES L. ROSE

ROSALIE H. ROSENFELT

EUGENIA S. SHERE

PHILIP E. SLATER

MARGARET WALLACE

FREDERICK E. WHISKIN

NEW
Thoughts on
OLD
AGE

Edited by
ROBERT KASTENBAUM, Ph.D.
Director of Psychological Research
Cushing Hospital, Framingham,
Massachusetts

SPRINGER PUBLISHING COMPANY, INC.
NEW YORK

PREFACE

Facts about aging have been emerging at an accelerated tempo during the past few years. Some of these facts concern the human problems of growing old in present day society; other facts concern the nature of biological and behavioral changes that occur with advanced age. Previous notions about the nature of "old age" and how one is to live with it no longer seem quite adequate—that is to say, our ideas about aging tend to emulate their subject matter.

Welcome as new facts may be, it is naive to assume that they will automatically improve our understanding and practical management of age-related phenomena. A torrent of facts can as easily bewilder as elucidate, causing us to feel dissatisfied with our old ideas without providing a clear sense of new direction. New thoughts as well as new facts are required.

This book expresses the thoughts and experiences of a number of people, mostly social scientists and clinicians, who believe that new frames of reference and new practical approaches must be developed. The quest for fresh understanding takes various forms: new theoretical formulations derived from systematic positions in the social sciences, clinical explorations involving problems and procedures that had received scant prior attention, and reconsiderations of facts and experiences already known.

Although a number of new *facts* will be found in these pages, the general intent is to prepare the way for the development of new *views* that will enable us to consider aging on a firm intellectual and emotional footing. This book might therefore be regarded not as a detailed compendium of all the raw facts on aging, but rather as the thinking of a set of companions who are eager to share their experiences and to recruit the reader in the quest for an improved understanding of "old age."

We do not assume that the term "old age" itself has a well-defined meaning, or that the right questions have yet been asked, let alone the right answers obtained. In taking an approach that often ignores, or is critical of, favorite verbalisms about "old age," the contributors do not fear that they are depriving anyone of necessary defenses against the feared "grim realities." On the contrary, they believe that the "realities" are not oppressingly "grim" if we face old age squarely and investigate its phenomena with imagination and zest.

We wish to share our experiences, our questions, and our tentative conclusions with all those concerned with human aging—the educator, the social worker, the physician, the nurse, the psychologist, the housing administrator, the public official and every other person curious about the enigmatic process known as "aging."

The book is divided into five major sections. Section I presents theoretical perspectives on old age from the standpoint of four different orientations: disengagement theory, operant conditioning, psychoanalysis and developmental theory. Section II is concerned with psychological and social characteristics of people who live to an advanced age. Section III reports a variety of clinical experiences with elderly patients, including assessments of institutionalization as a remedy, and such relatively new explorations as speech therapy with the aged, and an investigation of wine as a stimulant of interpersonal behavior. How people interpret "old age" is considered in Section IV, which includes studies of the attitudes of both young and elderly adults, and an examination of cross-cultural viewpoints toward aging. Section V deals with a much-neglected topic: the organization of experience in later life (as distinguished from the older person's external behavior). It explores the meaning of time in the organization of experience, reading and artistic expression as other ways of organizing experience, and some consequences of a breakdown in the ability to organize experience. Each section is preceded by an introductory note.

Many of the contributors have been associated in one way or another with Cushing Hospital, an institution operated by the Commonwealth of Massachusetts and devoted exclusively to the care of old people. The population of approximately 650 patients (mean age: 81) is served by departments of nursing, medicine, dentistry, social service, speech therapy, psychology and occupational therapy, and by its own kitchen, laundry, pharmacy, electrical and maintenance shops and police and fire departments. Clergymen representing the major faiths are in attendance, and a volunteer service is in operation. Cushing Hospital does not fit easily into any one institutional category, since it possesses features of a hospital, nursing home, rehabilitation center and community. During the past three years or so it has also developed a strong research orientation. Some of the work reported here was made possible in part by a research grant from the National Institute of Mental Health (MHO-4818: "Drug Effects on Cognition and Behavior in Elderly Patients"). A number of research and training projects are in progress, including a recently initiated "Training Program for Work with the Aged and Dying" supported by a five-year mental health project grant (MH-01520) from the Research Utilization Branch of NIMH. Further information about the hospital is given, from various points of view, in several chapters of this book.

The book is by no means limited to an "institutional view" of old age, either in content or attitude. One might cite, for example, the studies of non-institutionalized veterans of the Spanish-American War (Chapter 5) and of elderly psychologists (Chapter 8), and the critical examinations of institutionalization in Chapters 15 and 16. Physiological and medical factors are incorporated in a number of papers, but chiefly as these contribute to an understanding of aging in its psychosocial aspects. There is no intention here to minimize biological factors, but, rather, to put the spotlight on the aging human as a *person*.

The chapters are printed here for the first time, except for five that are reprinted, sometimes with minor editorial changes. We are grateful to the following publications and authors for their permission to reprint the following articles:

"Depression in the Aged," by Sidney Levin; "Cultural Attitudes toward the Aged," by Philip E. Slater; "The Reluctant Therapist," by Robert Kastenbaum. Reprinted by permission from *Geriatrics,* April, 1963 issue.

"Further Thoughts on Disengagement Theory," by Elaine Cummings. Reprinted by permission of UNESCO from *International Journal of Social Relations,* Spring, 1963 issue.

"The Life Review," by Robert N. Butler. Reprinted from *Psychiatry: Journal for the Study of Interpersonal Processes,* February 1963 issue, by special permission of the William Alanson White Foundation, Inc., ©.

To thank Janet Lei Reidy for her secretarial assistance would be a wholly inadequate remark unless one appreciates how much is involved in being that many-splendored wonder, a "good secretary." To the contributors and all my colleagues I am delighted to express sincere appreciation for the time and effort they have given "above and beyond the call of duty."

ROBERT KASTENBAUM

June 1, 1964
Framingham, Massachusetts

CONTRIBUTORS

Ruth Aisenberg, Ph.D. Senior Research Associate in Psychology, Cushing Hospital, Framingham, Massachusetts.

Isabel Banay, C.P.H. (London). Chief Psychiatric Social Worker, Cushing Hospital, Framingham, Massachusetts.

J. Sanbourne Bockoven, M.D. Superintendent, Cushing Hospital, Framingham, Massachusetts.

Robert N. Butler, M.D. Research Psychiatrist, National Institute of Mental Health, U.S.P.H.S., Bethesda, Maryland.

M. Elaine Cumming, Ph.D. Sociologist, New York Department of Mental Hygiene, Syracuse, New York.

Nancy Durkee, B.S. Psychologist, Cushing Hospital, Framingham, Massachusetts.

Stephen Durkee, M.A. Chairman, Department of Art, State Teachers College, Framingham, Massachusetts.

Otto F. Ehrentheil, M.D. Staff Physician, Veterans Administration Hospital, Boston, Massachusetts; Assistant Professor in Medicine, Tufts University; Instructor in Psychiatry, Boston University, Boston, Massachusetts.

Robert Kastenbaum, Ph.D. Director of Psychological Research, Cushing Hospital, Framingham, Massachusetts; Lecturer in Psychology, Clark University, Worcester, Massachusetts.

Sidney Levin, M.D. Associate Visiting Psychiatrist, Beth Israel Hospital, Boston; Associate in Psychiatry, Harvard Medical School, Boston; Instructor, Boston Psychoanalytic Society and Institute, Boston, Massachusetts.

Ogden R. Lindsley, Ph.D. Director, Behavior Research Laboratory, Harvard Medical School (at Metropolitan Hospital, Waltham, Mass.).

Sally O'Neill, R.N., M.S. Director of Nurses, Cushing Hospital, Framingham, Massachusetts.

Kenneth Pollock, B.A. Graduate Student in Psychology, Columbia University; Research Assistant, Bio-Metrics Research Unit, State of New York, New York.

Charles L. Rose, M.S.W. Research Social Worker, Veterans Administration Outpatient Mental Hygiene Clinic, Boston, Massachusetts.

Rosalie H. Rosenfelt, A.M. Principal Psychologist, Cushing Hospital, Framingham, Massachusetts.

Eugenia S. Shere, Ph.D. Professor of Clinical Psychology, University of Bar-Ilan, Tel-Aviv, Israel (formerly Psychologist, Cushing Hospital).

Philip E. Slater, Ph.D. Associate Professor of Sociology, Brandeis University, Waltham, Massachusetts; Research Consultant, Cushing Hospital, Framingham, Massachusetts.

Margaret Wallace, M.S. Speech Therapist, Cushing Hospital, Framingham, Massachusetts.

Frederic E. Whiskin, M.D. Director, Norfolk County Court Clinics, Boston; Psychiatrist, Cushing Hospital, Framingham; Assistant in Psychiatry, Harvard Medical School, Boston, Massachusetts.

CONTENTS

THEORETICAL PERSPECTIVES

One might insist that attempts to achieve a clear perspective on human behavior are *always* confounded by an indwelling methodological bias, namely, that man is the measurer as well as the measured. But this bias imposes much stricter limitations in the study of old age than it does, for example, in the study of adolescence. No one was in a better position to appreciate this problem than Granville Stanley Hall, an indefatigable student of human behavior who, in his 78th year, wrote that ". . . ever since I published my *Adolescence* in 1904 I have hoped to live to complement it by a study of senescence. The former could not have been written in the midst of the seething phenomena it describes, as this must be. We cannot outgrow and look back upon old age . . . and therefore lack the detachment that alone can give us a true and broad perspective."(1)

Having despaired of achieving "a true and broad perspective," Professor Hall proceeded to write a lengthy, pioneering book on his elusive topic. The contributors to this section of the present volume share both Hall's cautious aforethought and his subsequent disregard of caution in attempting to formulate systematic relationships out of the "seething phenomena." Four theoretical perspectives are brought to bear upon human aging, each representing early stages in the development of a systematic approach. The dearth of systematic theoretical work in this area is well illustrated by the fact that disengagement theory, the oldest approach, was introduced as recently as 1957, and not presented in elaborated form until 1961. Learning, psychoanalytical, and developmental orientations have been active generators of research for many years, but have seldom been applied to improving our understanding of later life.

It is hoped that these chapters will be of value not only for the specific ideas presented but also for the stimulation of fresh thinking on all aspects of human aging.

Reference

1. Hall, G. S. *Senescence*. New York: Appleton, 1922, vii-viii.

New thoughts on
the theory of
disengagement

1

M. Elaine Cumming

The usefulness of a theory depends upon its ability to explain the present and predict the future. In this chapter, I shall simplify and elaborate, in a discursive way, the "disengagement" theory of aging that Henry and I developed with our colleagues between 1957 and 1960 (1,2). I hope in this way to make it better able to describe and predict both the range and the limits of the aging process. In its original form, the theory was too simple; it had only enough detail to account for the main outlines of the process of growing old. By adding new elements and elaborating the basic propositions in more detail, I hope to be able to suggest a little of the complexity and diversity that we see among men and women in old age.

The general theory of disengagement

Disengagement theory was developed during a five-year study of a sample of aging people in an American city. These were 275 adults between the ages of 50 and 90 years; they were in good health and had the minimum of money for independence. Briefly, the theory proposes that under these conditions normal aging is a mutual withdrawal or "disengagement" between the aging person and others in the social system to which he belongs—a withdrawal initiated by the individual himself, or by others in the system. When disengagement is complete, the equilibrium that existed in middle life between the individual and society has given way to a new equilibrium characterized by greater distance and a changed basis for solidarity.

Engagement is essentially the interpenetration of the person with the society to which he belongs. The fully-engaged person acts in a large number and a wide variety of roles in a system of divided labor, and feels an obligation to meet the expectations of his role partners. There are variations, however, in the type of engagement. It is possible to be *broadly* engaged in a number of social systems that exert little influence over the remainder of society, and it is possible to be *deeply* engaged in the sense of having roles whose function is to make policies that affect a large number of others. It is possible to be *symbolically* engaged by epitomizing some valued attribute—by being a famous scientist, poet or patriot.

A few men have roles that combine all three types of engagement and carry with them the extreme constraints that must accompany such a number and variety of obligations; presidents and prime ministers are among them. Very roughly, the depth and breadth of a man's engagement can be measured by the degree of potential disruption that would follow his sudden death. However, the death of someone who has an important symbolic engagement with his society can result in both loss and gain because the survivors can rally around the symbols he embodied and thus reaffirm their value. For many Americans, Dag Hammarskjold's death brought into sharp focus the need for world order.

In its original form, disengagement theory concerned itself with the modal case which, in America, begins with departure of children from families, and then, retirement for men or widowhood for women. It did not take account of such non-modal cases as widowhood before the marriage of the last child or of work protracted past the modal age of retirement. Most importantly, it did not, and still does not, concern itself with the effects of the great scourges of old age, poverty and illness. This discussion will modify and elaborate the theory somewhat and suggest some characteristics of aging people that might make an important difference to their patterns of disengagement. Like the original statement, this modification has the status of a system of hypotheses. Some of the elements are close to being operational as they stand; others are still too general for testing.

Before proceeding further, an asymmetry in the earlier discussions of the theory must be dealt with. Disengagement has been conceived as a mutual withdrawal between individual and society, and therefore the process should vary according to the characteristics of both. In earlier statements, the different ways in which the environment retreats—retirement, loss of kin or spouse, departure of children, and so on—were considered, but the only individual difference discussed in any detail was that between the sexes. Eventually, if the process is to be described adequately, we must have typologies of withdrawal and retreat. I am going to suggest here that deeply-rooted differences in character are a good starting point because it is reasonable to suppose that they color all of life, including the disengagement process.

Temperament and disengagement

In its original form disengagement theory did no more than suggest an ultimate biological basis for a reduction of interest or involvement in the environment. Variations in the process were attributed to social pressures, especially as they are differentially experienced by men and women. A vital difference in style, however, can be expected between people of unlike temperaments, no matter what their sex. Combining biological and social variables within the framework of disengagement theory, it might be possible to suggest a wider variety of styles of inter- action in old age than would otherwise be possible.

A proposed temperamental variable, basically biological, is the style of adaptation to the environment. It seems well established that humans must maintain a minimum of exchange with the environment, or a clear anticipation of renewing exchange with it, in order to keep a firm knowledge both of it and of themselves (11). There appear to be different modes of maintaining this relationship, which can perhaps be called the "impinging" mode and the "selecting" mode (3).

The impinger appears to try out his concept of himself in inter- action with others in the environment; he uses their appropriate re- sponses to confirm the correctness of his inferences about himself, the environment and his relationship to it. If the feedback from others suggests that he is incorrect, the impinger will try to bring others' responses into line with his own sense of the appropriate relationship. Only if he fails repeatedly will he modify his concept of himself.

In contrast, the selector tends to wait for others to affirm his assump- tions about himself. From the ongoing flow of stimulation he selects those cues that confirm his relationship to the world. If they fail to come, he waits, and only reluctantly brings his own concepts into line with the feedback he is getting. The selector may be able to use sym- bolic residues of old interactions to maintain his sense of self more efficiently than the impinger, and thus be able to wait longer for suitable cues.

We assume that temperament is a multi-determined, biologically- based characteristic, and therefore that the temperamental types are normally distributed in the population with few people at the ex- tremes. We also assume that the modal person can both impinge and select as the occasion demands, although perhaps favoring one style rather than the other. A normal person will shift to the alternate pat- tern when it becomes necessary either for appropriate role behavior or for the prevention of "diffusion feelings" (after Erikson, 5). If there are no complicating ego problems, a pronounced selector will probably be known as "reserved," "self-sufficient" or "stubborn," and a pro- nounced impinger as "temperamental," "lively" or "brash." We would expect the impinger, as he grows older, to experience more anxiety about loss of interaction, because he needs it to maintain orientation. The selector, being better able to make use of symbols, may have less difficulty with the early stages of disengagement.

This raises a problem of the difference between the *appearance* of engagement and the *experience* of it. This problem is enhanced by a tendency to contrast disengagement with activity (6). In fact, activity and engagement are not on the same dimension. A disengaged person often maintains a high level of activity in a small number and narrow variety of roles, although it is doubtful if it is possible to be at once firmly engaged and inactive. In any event, the opposite of disengagement is engagement, a concept different from, though related to, the concept of activity.

The result of confusing these two variables is that *active* people are judged to be *engaged*. They may, however, be *relatively disengaged impingers*. They may also, depending upon the type of activity, be exceptionally healthy or restless. There is no real way to judge because the issue has not been put to the test. Unfortunately, many of the populations used for gerontological studies are volunteers and thus can be expected to include a disproportionately large number of impingers. For example, Marc Zborowski reports that a group of volunteers reported little change, over time, of their recreational activities and preferences (13). The author concludes from this that the subjects are not disengaging, using the concept (in Havighurst's sense) as the opposite of active (6). Zborowski's finding is unexpected only inasmuch as disengagement theory would predict a *rise* in recreational activities after retirement among a population that might include numerous disengaged impingers. In contrast to this report is a careful study of a *general population* of older people in New Zealand among whom only 10% belonged to, or wanted to belong to, recreational groups, and only 9% of those not working would seek work if the restrictions on their pensions would allow them (10).

The disengaging impinger can be expected to be more active and apparently more youthful than his peers. His judgment may not be as good as it was, but he provokes the comment that he is an unusual person for his age. Ultimately, as he becomes less able to control the situations he provokes, he may suffer anxiety and panic through failure both to arouse and to interpret appropriate reactions. His problem in old age will be to avoid confusion.

The selector, in contrast to the impinger, interacts in a more measured way. When he is young he may be thought too withdrawn, but as he grows older his style becomes more age-appropriate. In old age, because of his reluctance to generate interaction, he may, like a neglected infant, develop a kind of marasmus. His foe will be apathy rather than confusion.

These are not, of course, ordinary aging processes; the extreme impinger and the extreme selector are almost certain to get into trouble at some crisis point because they cannot move over to the opposite mode of interacting when it is adaptive to do so. In general, in an achievement-oriented society the impinger may be more innately suited to middle age, the selector perhaps to childhood and old age.

In summary, some biologically-based differences among people may be expected to impose a pattern upon their manner of growing old. I shall now return to the theory, with this variable in mind, and at the same time suggest other concepts that it might profitably include.

The outset of disengagement

Disengagement probably begins sometime during middle life when certain changes of perception occur, of which the most important is probably an urgent new perception of the inevitability of death. It is certain that children do not perceive the meaning of death and it is said that "no young man believes that he will ever die." It is quite possible that a vivid apprehension of mortality—perhaps when the end of life seems closer than its start—is the beginning of the process of growing old. Paradoxically, a sense of the shortness of time may come at the height of engagement. Competition for time may draw attention to both its scarcity and its value. There may be a critical point beyond which further involvement with others automatically brings a sense of "there is not time for all that I must do" which, in turn, leads to evaluations of what has been done compared to what was hoped for, and then to allocations and priorities for the future. Those who have never been very firmly engaged should feel less sense of urgency than those who are tightly enmeshed with society—all other things, including temperament, being equal.

Accompanying the need to select and allocate is a shift away from achievement. Achievement, as Parsons says (9), demands a future; when confidence in there being a future is lost, then achievement cannot be pursued without regard to the question, "Shall it be achievement of this rather than of that?" Such a question is the beginning of an exploration of the meaning and value of the alternatives. In American life, where achievement is perhaps the highest value, its abandonment has always been tinged with failure. We would, therefore, expect the relinquishing of achievement to be a crisis, and, indeed, general knowledge and some research tell us that in middle life competent men with a record of achievement may feel sudden painful doubts about the value of what they have done (7). Once any part of achievement is given up, some binding obligations are gone, and even if they are replaced with less demanding ties, a measure of disengagement has occurred.

Disengagement may begin in a different way, somewhat as follows: the middle-aged person who has not undergone an inner period of questioning reaches a point where losses, both personal and public, begin to outrun his ability to replace them. A friend dies, a business closes, his children move far away. For the healthy, aging impinger these losses may be replaced; for the selector they may not, and an awareness of their permanence may be a turning point. With each loss, the aging person must surrender certain potential feelings and actions and replace them with their symbolic residues in memory. In a sense, this substitution of symbols for social action changes the quality of the self. Even if the role partners themselves are replaced, they often cannot substitute for the lost relationship that was built up over the years.

The most crucial step in the disengagement process may lie in finding a new set of rewards. The esteem that achievement brings can be replaced by the affection generated in socio-emotional activity. The approval that comes from meeting contracted obligations can be replaced by the spontaneous responses of others to expressive acts. The inner rewards of weaving the past into a satisfactory moral fabric can partly replace the public rewards of achievement. Nevertheless, in America today there is a net loss because achievement is more highly valued than meaning or expression and because its symbols are more easily calibrated. To be rich is to be recognized a success; wisdom is often its own reward.

Finally, and perhaps most importantly, freedom from obligation replaces the constraint of being needed in an interlocking system of divided tasks. The fully engaged man is, in essence, bound; the disengaged man is free—if he has resources and health enough to allow him to exercise that freedom. The ability to enjoy old age may be the ability and the opportunity to use freedom (4).

No matter how important the effects of the perception of time and the shift in rewards, the essential characteristic of disengagement is that, once started, it tends to be self-perpetuating. If the search for meaning becomes urgent, and the impulse toward seeking out others becomes less rewarding, there will be a tendency not to replace ties broken by loss.

Once withdrawal has begun it may become more difficult to make new contacts. Not knowing quite how to behave under strange circumstances inhibits exploration, and this difficulty, in turn, can reinforce the disengaging process; for example, many elderly people refuse to fly in airplanes, not because they are afraid but because they do not know airport etiquette! A sense of strangeness cannot, of course, in itself lead to withdrawal; any middle-aged adult feels discomfort if he finds himself in an unknown situation without a role.

Prisoners of war must be helped to re-engage after long periods of isolation from their culture. For the aging, such diffusion feelings enhance a process that is already under way—a process made inevitable by man's mortality.

Thus, empirically, we see aging people interacting less and in fewer roles. Modally, ties to kindred become more salient, while distant, impersonal, and more recent ties become less important and finally disappear. This process of reduction and simplification leaves the individual freer from the control that accompanies involvement in a larger number and greater variety of roles. The broadly engaged person thus receives fewer of the positive and negative sanctions that accompany and guide all interactions and control the style of everyday behavior. Therefore, idiosyncratic personal behavior becomes possible. At the same time, ideas, removed from the scenes in which they can be tested out, become more stereotyped and general. (When the Kansas City respondents were asked, "What do you think of the younger generation?", the middle-aged people gave concrete examples of youthful behavior that they found compelling or unattractive while the older people answered in sweeping generalizations, usually negative.)

It seems possible that those who have been deeply engaged in roles that influence considerable areas of society or those who have rare and valuable skills will remain engaged longer than those less deeply involved with the affairs of their generation. This is because the values that inform major decisions are slower to change than everyday norms, and those who have been consciously enmeshed with them may, in old age, symbolize their continuity. Those who have been successful mathematicians, politicians, and poets can count on society remaining closer to them than those who have not influenced or represented their fellow men.

As the number of groups to which an aging person belongs is reduced, his membership in those remaining becomes more important because he must maintain a minimum of stimulation. The memberships of old age—kinship, friendship, and perhaps church—are all marked by a high level of agreement among members and by many explicit common values. In such groups, it is very difficult to deviate far from the common viewpoint. Thus, the more the elderly person disengages from a variety of roles, the less likely is he to take on new ideas. The conservatism of old age is partly a security measure, related to the need to maintain harmony among the remaining companions.

As withdrawal of normative control is an essential aspect of disengagement theory, it must be asked why old people should enter a spiral of decreasing conformity when middle-aged people, except in extreme cases, are able to endure prolonged interpersonal disruptions and quickly reconstitute contact with the norms. Moving from one city to another is an interpersonal crisis, but it does not often set in motion a process that leads to a new orientation to life. The difference seems to be that, for the aging, a combination of reduced biological energy, the seduction of freedom, preoccupation with the accumulated symbols of the past, and license for a new kind of self-centeredness cannot be resisted. Furthermore, all this is *expected* of the older person, and so the circle is further reinforced.

In contrast, if the middle-aged person feels that he is in a situation of reduced social control, he has both the energy and the opportunity to seek new constraints, and if he retreats too far from conformity he is confronted by sanctions. In some ways, an aging person is like an adolescent; he is allowed more freedom and expressiveness than a middle-aged adult. Later, when he is very old, he is permitted the dependency and individuation of the small child.

In this view, socialization is the encouragement of children to abandon their parochialism and individuation and to accept conformity to the demands of the major institutions of society, while disengagement is a permission to return again to individuation. For the old person, then, the circular process of disengagement results in the social tasks getting harder and the alternatives more rewarding, while for the young person, the social tasks remain rewarding and the alternatives are felt as alienation. Were it not for the value placed on achievement, the chains that the adult so willingly allows to bind him might be put off at least as readily as they are taken on.

Society's withdrawal

Disengagement theory postulates that society withdraws from the aging person equally as much as the person withdraws from society. This is, of course, just another way of saying that the process is normatively governed and in a sense agreed upon by all concerned. Everyone knows how much freedom from constraint is allowable and where the line between the oddness of old age and the symptoms of deviance lies. There seem to be deeply-rooted reasons, in both the culture and the social structure, for this withdrawal process.

In the first place, the organization of modern society requires that competition for powerful roles be based on achievement. Such competition favors the young because their knowledge is newer. Furthermore, the pressure of the young on the highest roles cannot be met by an indefinite expansion of the powerful roles. Therefore, the older members must be discarded to make way for the younger. In America, a disproportionately large number of young adults will soon be competing for jobs that are becoming relatively fewer as industry moves toward complete automation. If Americans are to remain engaged in any serious way beyond the seventh decade, as many observers insist they must, roles must be found for them that young people *cannot* fill (9). Only an elaboration of available roles can accomplish this because it is impossible for a society organized around standards of achievement and efficiency to assign its crucial roles to a group whose death rate is excessively high. When a middle-aged, fully-engaged person dies, he leaves many broken ties and disrupted situations. Disengagement thus frees the old to die without disrupting vital affairs.

Finally, at the end of life when one has outlived one's peers, social withdrawal consists in failure to approach. The young withdraw from the old because the past has little reality for them. They cannot conceive of an old person in any but a peripheral role. Thus, they approach him with condescension, or do not approach at all because of embarrassment. This gulf between generations is a by-product of a future-oriented society; when it changes, America will have changed. In the meantime, it seems clear that the older person may find it more rewarding to contemplate a moment of past glory than to try to make new relationships, especially with the young. In the intimate circle, no such effort is needed; the only real social problem for the very old, given health and enough money, may be the lack of such a circle.

Disengagement from roles

Whether disengagement is initiated by society or by the aging person, in the end he plays fewer roles and his relationships have changed their quality.

Socialization insures that everyone learns to play the two basic kinds of roles that are known as instrumental and socio-emotional. The instrumental roles in any given social system are those primarily concerned with active adaptation to the world outside the system during the pursuit of system goals. Socio-emotional roles are concerned with the inner integration of the social system and the maintenance of the value patterns that inform its goals.

Men, for reasons at once too obvious and too complex to consider here, must perform instrumental roles on behalf of their families, and this, for most men, means working at an occupation. Although men play socio-emotional roles, in business and elsewhere, they tend to assign the integrative tasks to women when they are present. In patriarchal societies, a man conceivably can live his whole adult life without playing a socio-emotional role if, in both his family and in his work, others are willing to integrate social systems around him. A married woman, on the other hand, in addition to the socio-emotional role she plays in her family as a whole, must be instrumental in relationship to small children. Very few women, and perhaps only those among the wealthiest, can totally avoid instrumentality. Thus, women are in the habit of bringing either kind of role into salience with more ease than men.

Whether there is any inherent quality that makes it easier to play one role than another is obscure, although the impinging temperament may predispose toward socio-emotionality. Empirically, we see a spectrum that includes goal-directed men, all of whose roles are instrumental (officers in the regular Army whose wives tremble when they shout); men who play socio-emotional roles in some circumstances (comforting the baby when he falls); men who seek out socio-emotional roles (in America, perhaps the personnel man); women who play instrumental roles whenever the situation allows it (club presidents); women who shift from instrumental work roles to socio-emotional family roles; and women who play socio-emotional roles almost all the time (the helpful maiden aunt living in a relative's household).

Most married couples with children, no matter what secondary roles they may hold, have a basic division of labor in which the husband plays a core instrumental role vis-a-vis his family by working, and the wife a core socio-emotional one by maintaining their home and caring for their children. By the time the children have left home and the husband has retired, the original division of labor has lost much of its basis.

A man has no clear-cut role upon retirement. He may still play an instrumental role relative to his wife, but it loses its public label; there is no special place to go to perform it, and there is no paycheck that is the obvious consequence of his daily round. He must bring his capacities for integrative activity into salience much of the time and perhaps even share the instrumental roles that remain available with other retired men. For these reasons disengagement theory proposes that it is more difficult for a man to shift to socio-emotional roles and integrative activities than it is for him to assume new instrumentalities, both because it is a less familiar mode for him and because he is in danger of competing directly with his wife and possibly with his grandchildren for roles within kinship or friendship circles. Therefore, the theory predicts that retirement will bring a period of maladjustment to many American men.

A man's response to retirement may be colored by the type of work role from which he withdraws. If his role has been part of a "true" division of labor, such that he can see the contribution that he is making to the functioning of society, he is likely to have considerable ego involvement in his work—it is to him as children are to a woman, a persistent palpable achievement. If, on the other hand, the division of labor is such that the outcome of his contribution is invisible to him, he will tend to be alienated from the meaning of his work and will find his rewards in his personal relationships with his fellow workers. In the first case, his instrumental role has three facets: he can see his contribution to the larger society, to his immediate working group, and to his family. In the second case, he can see a contribution only to the primary groups, work and family. Men in these two situations may react quite differently to retirement. The first might be expected to suffer more sense of loss immediately upon retirement—as women do when children first depart—but eventually to take much satisfaction from recalling his contribution to social goals and perhaps seeing others build upon it. The second may be relieved at leaving a meaningless work role but eventually suffer from lack of the symbolic connection with his own past, especially if he is a selector and accustomed to depending upon symbols for his orientation and sense of self.

Disengagement from central life roles is basically different for women than for men, perhaps because women's roles are essentially unchanged from girlhood to death. In the course of their lives women are asked to give up only pieces of their core socio-emotional roles or to change their details. Their transitions are therefore easier. This point is strikingly made by Peter Townsend who has described how working class women in London pass smoothly through the roles of daughter, mother, and grandmother (12). The pattern in America may be somewhat less straightforward, but the disjunction for women still seems far less acute than for men. The wife of a retired man can use her integrative skills to incorporate him in new groupings. She must, if she is tactful, become even more integrative through abandoning to him the more adaptive of her domestic tasks. Similarly, the problems raised by widowhood are more easily resolved than the problems raised by retirement. Moreover, the loss of status anchorage that women suffer at the time of a husband's death is less severe than the loss of status suffered at retirement because widowhood, unlike retirement, has no tinge of failure in it. It is the blameless termination of a valued role. Furthermore, the differential death rate that leaves about 20% of American women living without a conjugal bond by age 60, provides a membership group for them. This does not mean that women go out and "join" a group of widows. My impression is that they re-establish old bonds, or move closer to other women who have lost their husbands or never married. They probably tighten their ties to their children as well. Men, in contrast, have difficulty finding membership to compensate for work associations.

In general we might say that a woman's lifelong training to a role that is primarily socio-emotional but nevertheless includes adaptive skills leaves her more diffusely adaptable than a man's working career leaves him, because he does not automatically need integrative skills. Integrative skills are, in a sense, the *lingua franca* wherever people interact with one another. Adaptive skills, in contrast, tend to be more functionally specific and less easily transferred. The disposition toward the instrumental role can remain after retirement, but the specific skills lose relevance. Only rarely does a woman find herself with no membership group that can use her integrative contribution.

Finally, a retired man loses suitable role models—that is, role partners with whom he can try out patterns of adaptation and learn alternatives. He must seek out other retired men who are themselves tinged with failure in his eyes, or learn from women. Women, again because of the differential death rate, have more models, and these are more familiar. For both men and women, however, the roles of old age must be learned from others who are themselves relatively free of constraints —unlike children who are taught the roles they anticipate filling by adults who are as fully engaged and constrained as they will ever be.

Among married couples, a crucial event after retirement may be a shifting of the representative role from the man to the woman. While he works, a husband endows his family with its position in society, but after he enters the socio-emotional world of women and leisure, his wife tends to represent their conjugal society at kinship gatherings and social affairs, even in church activities. In this regard, also, men are more freed by retirement than women are by widowhood.

If these differences between men and women are important, there should be a visible contrast in their ability to cope with the discontinuities of the disengagement process. Two obvious examples that appear related, on the one hand, to women's abilities in finding roles in social systems and, on the other, to the sudden freedom from con-

Table 1. Proportion of homeless* men and women in a time sample of applicants to two relief agencies

	Whole group	Under 60 years	60 years and over
Men: number	227	185	42
% homeless	27.7	27.6	28.6
Women: number	144	100	44
% homeless	6.3	6.0	6.8

*Excluding migrant workers, and those temporarily stranded away from home. These data are from a study of the division of labor among the integrative agents of society financed in part by NIMH Grant M4735; principal investigator, Elaine Cumming.

straint of retirement, are presented. In Table 1 we see the relative proportions of men and women in a study sample who, when seeking help from a public relief agency, were found to be homeless as well as in need of money. At no age are men who are in economic distress as able as women to maintain membership in a domestic unit. Indeed, there is no female counterpart in America to "the homeless man." In Table 2, we see that among a cohort of men and women over 60 years of age entering a mental hospital for the first time, one-third of the non-married men had been living in shelters and old people's homes,

Table 2. Living arrangements of one hundred consecutive first admissions, aged sixty and over, to a mental hospital

| | Men (43 admissions) | | Women (57 admissions) | |
	Married (16)	Unmarried (27)	Married (16)	Unmarried (41)
Domestic unit	81.3%	44.4%	87.5%	63.4%
Hospital or nursing home	12.5%	18.5%	12.5%	26.8%
Shelter or home for aged	6.2%	37.1%	0.0%	9.8%

I am grateful to Mary Lou Parlagreco and John Cumming for permission to use these data from an unpublished study.

whereas less than one-tenth of the non-married women had come from such institutions. Women without husbands appear able to accommodate themselves to both the households of others and the hospital environment more readily than men without wives. The differences mentioned above are statistically significant at better than the one per cent level of confidence. At the age that disengagement is postulated to occur, 65-75, the rate of suicide among women drops and continues to drop, while among men it rises persistently.* This finding leads to the speculation that women go from a little too much constraint to just the right amount of freedom while men go from too much of the one to too much of the other. In spite of this dramatic difference, it is unlikely that men who survive the transition crisis of retirement are as disadvantaged as these data make them seem; they are more likely to resemble Charles Lamb, who says of his sudden and unexpected retirement:

* See *Summary of Mortality Statistics: United States, 1957*. Washington, D.C.: National Office of Vital Statistics.

"For the first day or two I felt stunned—overwhelmed. I could only apprehend my felicity: I was too confused to taste it sincerely. I wandered about, thinking I was happy, and knowing that I was not. I was in the condition of a prisoner in the old Bastille, suddenly let loose after a forty years' confinement. I could scarce trust myself with myself. It was like passing out of Time into Eternity—for it is a sort of Eternity for a man to have all his Time to himself. It seemed to me that I had more time on my hands than I could ever manage. From a poor man, poor in Time, I was suddenly lifted up into a vast revenue; I could see no end of my possessions; I wanted some steward, or judicious bailiff, to manage my estates in Time for me. And here let me caution persons growing old in active business, not lightly, nor without weighing their own resources, to forego their customary employment all at once, for there may be danger in it. I feel it by myself, but I know that my resources are sufficient; and now that those first giddy raptures have subsided, I have a quiet home-feeling of the blessedness of my condition." (8)

Changes in solidarity

I have discussed disengagement as it affects temperamental types, as an inner experience, as a social imperative and as a response to changing roles. Perhaps the most economical way of describing it is in terms of shifting solidarities that may have roots in middle life. In general, aging brings change from solidarity bonds based on differences of function, and hence of mutual dependency, to bonds based on similarities and common sentiments. The post-retirement part of a man's life can be considered, therefore, in terms of a two-stage shift in the nature of his relationships with his wife, his kinsmen, and the rest of the world that starts with departure of children and retirement. The "organic solidarity" of a divided labor that marked his conjugal life is weakened because after retirement he no longer has a clearly marked, publicly recognized, instrumental role; therefore, the "mechanical solidarity" of common belief and sentiments that must precede and accompany the division of labor becomes more salient. The man and his wife as a unit are no longer functioning as a factory for making adults from children, and hence are now related to other segments of society through common characteristics. Thus, both men and women abandon the mutual obligations and power problems of a divided labor among themselves as well as between themselves and society. They move into a more equalitarian relationship with each other and with the world—a relationship in which solidarity is based almost entirely upon a consensus of values and a commonality of interest. Most importantly, the new segmental solidarity is marked by an essential redundancy of the parts. Loss of a member from a system of divided labor disrupts the system. Loss of a member from a group of peers diminishes the society but does not disrupt it.

The second stage of old age comes when the old person is no longer able to carry out the minimum adaptive behavior necessary to maintain health, cleanliness or propriety. At that point, someone else must enter the conjugal society to perform adaptive functions for both man and wife, and thus they return to the asymmetrical social condition of infants in that their contribution to the solidarity lies not in what they *do* but what they *are*—members by birthright of a family. A very old person with no family ties has the pathos of an orphaned child and society deals with him accordingly. This terminal dependency excludes all other social relations. Indeed, among the extremely aged, "collective monologues" such as Piaget describes among children may replace conversation; as Durkheim (4) says, "Society has retreated from the old person or, what amounts to the same thing, he has retreated from it."

Summarizing the shift in solidarity in more concrete terms, we may say that men at work are tied together by sentiments about the work itself and women by sentiments about children, schools and domestic matters. After work ceases, the bonds between a man and those he worked with must literally be reforged if they are to survive, because they must have new substance. After children leave home, while much must be rewrought between women, it is less than for men because they still have in common the roles of spouse and mother, although the latter may be somewhat attenuated.

Among kindred there are values and sentiments arising from many common experiences and, therefore, it is easy for solidarity to persist after disengagement. In other words, it is the diffusely-bonded solidarities that survive and the specifically-bonded ties that wither. If a specific bond involves some divided labor the attachment is stronger, but once the conditions of mutual dependency are removed, it is weakened. In diffusely-bonded relationships, of which kinship is the prototype, common sentiments, values and traditions inevitably form around many activities and events. For this reason, such stable solidarities persist through role changes, and become the salient relationships of old age. The energy to forge such strong links as exist between siblings or very old friends because of common history, common experience and interlocking membership, may be lost as soon as biological energy begins to fade.

It should be noted that there are certain "atemporal" roles available to men that do not become outmoded and can be the basis of a divided labor until extreme old age. The clergyman's role, for example, is concerned with persistent values; it resists obsolescence because it ties society to its timeless values. The clergyman is the instrumental leader in his family, but with the larger society as the social system of reference, he performs an integrative function in an important socio-emotional role. Such roles seem to perform for the whole society the function that women perform for the family—they maintain the pattern of values that inform the goals, and they reduce the tension generated by the effort of adaptation.

The implications

In this discursive account of disengagement theory, I have raised more problems than I have begun to solve. The additions to the theory are untidily grafted onto the original formulation without regard to whether or not they contradict it or shift its focus. The next task is to formalize the propositions and wherever possible cast them in terms that can be tested, but this is another undertaking for another time. Given the choice, I have taken what is for me the pleasanter alternative of thinking widely rather than rigorously, and in doing so I have drawn attention to the theory's need for greater rigor.

References

1. Cumming, E., Dean, L. R., and Newell, D. S. Disengagement, a tentative theory of aging. *Sociometry*, 1960, *23*, No. 1.
2. Cumming, E., and Henry, W. E. *Growing Old*. New York: Basic Books, 1961.
3. Cumming, J., and Cumming, E. *Ego and Milieu*. New York: Atherton Press, 1962.
4. Durkheim, E. *Suicide*. Glencoe, Ill.: The Free Press, 1951, 157-159.
5. Erikson, E. H. *Childhood and Society*. New York: W. W. Norton, 1950.
6. Havighurst, R. Successful aging. *Gerontologist*, 1961, *1*, 8-13.
7. Henry, W. E. Conflict, age, and the executive. *Business Topics*, Michigan State U., no date.
8. Lamb, C. The superannuated man. In C. Tibbetts and W. Donahue (eds.), *Aging in Today's Society*. New York: Prentice-Hall, 1960, 99-100.
9. Parsons, T. Toward a healthy maturity. *Journal of Health and Human Behavior*, 1960, *1*, No. 3.
10. McCreary, J. R., and Somerset, H. C. A. *Older People of Dunedin City: A Survey*. Wellington, New Zealand, Department of Health, 1955.
11. Solomon, P., *et al. Sensory Deprivation*. Cambridge, Mass.: Harvard U. Press, 1961.
12. Townsend, P. *The Family Life of Old People*. Glencoe, Ill.: The Free Press, 1957.
13. Zborowski, M. Aging and recreation. *Journal of Gerontology*, 1962, *17*.

Prolegomena to a psychoanalytic theory of aging and death

2

Philip E. Slater

Life is impoverished, it loses in interest, when the highest stake in living, life itself, may not be risked.—Sigmund Freud

Psychoanalytic ideas concerning aging and death fall into two categories. First, considerable attention has been given to psychological reactions to the imagined, actual, or desired deaths of others, and to feelings about one's own death. This involves examination of the kinds of meanings that death may have in the fantasy life of the individual. If as Fenichel argues, one's own death is at bottom inconceivable, there can be no such thing as a normal fear of death, and it becomes appropriate to interpret the fear of or desire for death as a mask for a variety of other impulses and anxieties. Thus fear of death is sometimes interpreted as fear of orgasm, and the desire for death as a longing for libidinal union with a lost love object (3, pp. 208-209).

It has often seemed unreasonable to critics of psychoanalytic theory that fear of so basic and profound an issue as self-extinction should be regarded as an epiphenomenon, but the bases for this view should be made perfectly clear. Fear of death is not at all primitive, elemental or basic. Animals have no such fear, nor do small children. It depends upon the rather advanced and sophisticated awareness of the self as a separate entity, altogether detached from the natural and social environment. For the individual who feels blended with the world and his society, his own death has little meaning. It is only when he comes to view himself as a unique, differentiated entity with an existence which is separable and apart from other men and objects that he can begin to have anxiety about the termination of that existence. The concept of immortality and that of individuality have a joint nascence, as I have indicated elsewhere (29). When a fear of death begins to make itself felt, therefore, we have the choice of viewing it either as a sign of developmental maturity or a symptom of some other concern, such as those to which Fenichel refers.

The second category pertains to the actual nature of death and the aging process, and hence could just as appropriately be called a theory of life. It is with this category that we will be primarily concerned in this chapter.

Vicissitudes of libido

Central to all psychoanalytic ideas about aging and death is the concept of libido. Unfortunately, this is one of the looser terms in the psychoanalytic lexicon, and its complexity is compounded by the fact that it has been several times redefined to suit the needs of a new theoretical framework. Finally, it is often utilized in interpretive contexts that border on the metaphorical, so we cannot be certain with what degree of literalness the terms which characterize the concept should be applied.

Let us therefore make a brief effort to arrive at a clear-cut and utilitarian definition of libido before considering its implications for a theory of death. Freud defined libido as the "mental representation of the sexual instinct," (14, p. 119) and throughout his life he strove to maintain this specifically sexual and biological definition against tendencies to diffuse and generalize the notion to cover all forms of psychic interest (11, p. 38; 14, pp. 131 ff.).

Yet it has always been a difficult concept to keep in bounds. Let us consider briefly some of the connotations which have been attached to it:

1. It is sometimes used as if it referred to a purely psychic phenomenon, indistinguishable in practice from the idea of *interest*. Freud uses it in this sense in "Mourning and Melancholia," referring to "loss of interest in the outside world . . . loss of capacity to adopt any new object of love . . . turning from every active effort that is not connected with thoughts of the dead." (10, p. 153).

2. It is sometimes used to denote simple sexual arousal or *excitation*. Freud says, for example, that genital tumescence is the somatic analogue and prototype of libidinal cathexis, and suggests that "for every . . . change in the erotogenicity of the organs there is a parallel change in the libidinal cathexis in the ego." (11, p. 41). Thus, genital tumescence would be seen as producing a concentration of libido.

3. A third element in the concept is the idea of *energy*. Thus Freud speaks of "damming up" libido, and of "transposing" the consequent mental tension "into active energy which remains directed towards the outer world . . ." (15, p. 114). The use of the word "cathexis" is, of course, associated with this construction, and Freud often uses the term "sexual energy" as an explicit synonym for libido (11, p. 33).

4. Closely related to the idea of energy is that of plasticity: the capacity of libido to increase, decrease, and change its spatial location.

References are made to measuring the amount or quantity of libido, to storing it up, and to a "reservoir" into which the libido "streams" from various organs (12, pp. 23-4; 15, p. 114, 119).

But how are we to understand Freud when he says that "libidinal cathexes are sent out on to objects and . . . also once more withdrawn, like the pseudopodia of a body of a protoplasm?" (12, pp. 23-4). Is some substance actually extruded from the organism or is this a purely metaphorical statement? We must bear in mind that no one has as yet isolated anything—be it process, charge, or chemical balance—which could usefully be labelled "libido." Freud gives the clearest clue when he argues that "the future may teach us how to exercise a direct influence, by means of particular chemical substances, upon the amounts of energy and their distribution in the apparatus of the mind." (12, p. 79). What is at issue here is the distribution of some sort of energy in the brain itself.

Taylor, in a summary of the remaining differences between computers and the human brain, notes that the brain cell "does not treat [the inputs it receives] all as being equivalent. The point on the cell body at which the connections arrive makes a big difference, so that some signals are given greater importance than others." Furthermore, "the brain is bathed in fluids which can raise or lower the 'firing threshold' of whole blocks of cells. . . ." But "the methods by which it judges relevance remain completely mysterious." (37, pp. 39-40).

"The exact way in which feeling becomes attached to data is crucial . . . it can become attached to fortuitous elements in the situation and even to words. . . . In a practical physiological way, we know absolutely nothing about how this takes place. We can suspect it is connected with the changing chemical patterns in the brain. . . ." (37, p. 43).

In other words, there is nothing at all incompatible between Freud's libido theory and what is now known about the brain. Some mechanism must exist to endow some pieces of data with more interest than others, and it would seem logical that this should be connected in some way with stimulation of the pleasure centers of the brain (24). For the moment we may perhaps content ourselves with observing that when we talk about libido flowing here and there—out onto social objects, back onto the ego or a part of the body—we are referring to the differential energizing of brain cells. We are saying that some messages or connections are being given priority over others, and that these priorities are in turn determined by the strength of their connection with the pleasure centers of the brain. When we say that libido "flows" onto an object, or that the individual "libidinally cathects" an object we are saying that cell connections in the brain which are associated with that object have been activated, or that some chemical adjustment has taken place whereby inputs relating to the object are given higher priority, and that this adjustment has occurred because of the expectation of greater stimulation of the pleasure centers. When we speak of transference in the psychoanalytic sense, then, we are referring to the fact that when connections are established between new stimuli and highly charged old stimuli, some of the "priority charge" from the old will attach itself to the new. Furthermore, there will be a tendency for the brain constantly to institute search operations for such connections, since the "storage cells" involving these early objects are replete with such "priority charge." We must assume, however, that this search process involves a number of inhibitors. We note, first of all, that it follows the course of least resistance, following pathways already determined by the characteristics of the original object and seeking resemblances to the new one (cf. 5).

We would also assume that ambivalence toward the original object inhibits the permanent transfer of this "priority charge." In general, we would expect, for example, that stimuli emanating from the mothering one (in most cases, the actual mother) are given the highest priority for many years, since the largest inputs of erotic gratification come from this source. This will be particularly true in a society like ours, less marked in societies in which feeding, holding, caressing, etc. are shared by many persons, or in which the amount of erotic stimulation is minimal. Psychoanalysts use the term "maternal fixation" to refer to the persistence of this priority far beyond the age when it is appropriate.

Paradoxically, however, such persistence seems to be acute not merely when the amount of gratification received by the child from this source is high, but primarily when it is combined with painful experiences as well. The more unhappy a relationship, the more the individual seems to be unable to move beyond it. The truly idyllic childhood seems often to be the easiest left behind, while the miserable child grows up to a nostalgic and regressed adulthood.

We cannot in the limited context of the present chapter attempt to unravel the many variables which affect this constellation, and we perhaps should not, in any case, add too many stories to an essentially speculative structure. Let us merely suggest that for some reason, unclear to us at the moment, it seems that painful experiences with a high priority object act to inhibit the transfer of this "priority charge," while the relative absence of such experiences permits it to move more freely to new connections. Perhaps the expectation of painful input from the new experience prevents the transfer, forcing the individual back into the same old patterns, endlessly repeated. In this view, then, the term "repetition-compulsion" gives improper emphasis to the process. It is not so much a compulsion to repeat as a compulsive inability for the brain to cathect a new pathway.

The most striking example of this phenomenon is found in mourning. As Freud implies in "Mourning and Melancholia," it is when there is strong hostility toward the lost object that mourning becomes difficult and slow (10, pp. 157 ff; cf. also 23).

Freud's discussion is also illustrative of the way in which a purely internal structural arrangement can be given externalized definition. "The testing of reality, having shown that the loved object no longer exists, requires forthwith that all the libido shall be withdrawn from its attachments to this object. Against this demand a struggle . . . arises— . . . man never willingly abandons a libido position. . . . This struggle can be so intense that a turning away from reality ensues, the object being clung to through the medium of a hallucinatory wish-psychosis." (10, p. 154). It is of the utmost importance that this "psychosis" is precisely the same no matter whether it is an object or a part of one's own body that is in question. What perseverates is the structure of libidinal priorities in the brain, and it matters not at all what they refer to in reality. The "phantom limb" experiences of amputees are precisely the same as the hallucinations of the bereaved. Indeed, the use of the term "phantom" in the above phrase serves to remind us that the very idea of ghosts, which is practically universal, is an expression of this phenomenon. A majority of contemporary primitive societies, not to mention all of those which played a part in the development of our own civilization, hold the belief that the spirits of the dead hover around the living for a time, and are dispersed only at the conclusion of funerary rites or a prescribed mourning period, or upon finally being told or magically compelled to depart. These ancestral shades are simply the "phantom limbs" of the society, persisting until they have been decathected by their loved ones, i.e., until the mourning process has fulfilled its course as described by Freud:

"Each single one of the memories and hopes which bound the libido to the object is brought up and hyper-cathected, and the detachment of the libido from it accomplished." (10, p. 154).

In other words, the priority system must be restructured by *consciously* reassessing its structure piece by piece in this fashion.

Introversion and libido

But there is still another variable, apparently unrelated to the foregoing, which affects the way in which "priority charges" are shifted from one series of cell connections to another. It seems to be independent of pathology—a more generalized variation in over-all speed or rate at which cathexes are transferred. Freud called it "adhesiveness of libido," and viewed it as one of the "fundamental characteristics of the mental apparatus." (6, pp. 343-344). He speaks separately of an attitude which he calls "exhaustion of the capacity for change and development," but makes no clear distinction between them, if, indeed, one can be made. Those with high adhesiveness of libido, he says, "cannot make up their minds to detach libidinal cathexes from one object and displace them to another," while in those with low "adhesiveness" these cathexes are "evanescent," and never to be counted upon. "Loss of plasticity" he discusses in similar terms, referring to an exaggeration of normal "psychical inertia," and stating that "all the mental processes, relations and distributions of energy are immutable, fixed and rigid. One finds the same state of affairs in very old people, when it is explained by what is described as force of habit, the exhaustion of receptivity through a kind of psychical entropy. . . ." (6, pp. 344-345).

From this description it would seem appropriate to consider "adhesiveness of libido" and "loss of plasticity" as one and the same process, perhaps manifested in slightly different ways. Once again the inability to shift priority charges is the fundamental problem. This phenomenon also seems to be identical with that to which the term "introversion" is classically and most correctly applied, from Jung to Eysenck (2,17). Even the terms "shallow-broad" for extravert and "deep-narrow" for introvert seem to describe aptly the different nature of the priority systems of the two.

This entire issue is of particular importance to us in connection with the processes of aging and death, since there is considerable evidence that the degree of introversion of the population increases with age. As yet it is uncertain whether this increase is due to actual changes in individuals or more rapid attrition among extraverts, although what data exist suggest the latter (32). If a certain circularity of reasoning may be forgiven, this leads to the paradoxical notion that one must age in order to live.

We thus have a continuum which we might call "steepness of mental priority hierarchy," equivalent to Freud's "adhesiveness of libido." At one end we find introversion (steep, adhesive), associated with greater age and a greater capacity for survival. Its pathological manifestations involve inability to change, to shift cathexes, to adapt to alterations in the gratificatory economy of the environment. At the other end we find extraversion (level, non-adhesive), associated with youth and a lesser capacity for survival. Its pathological manifestations take the form of impulsivity, and are most prominently expressed in the "psychopathic personality."*

---

* Here the problem is compounded by a deficiency in early mothering: all social stimuli are equally important (or unimportant) because no object was ever the

But why should extraversion reduce survival potential? Does life make a value judgment between two different kinds of normality, or between two different kinds of pathology? Is a given degree of inability to adapt "better" than a comparably defective impulse control?

This is, of course, a false issue. Biological survival is not concerned with individuals, and if natural selection is eliminating extraverts, it is not with a speed that would enable us to detect it. As far as individuals are concerned it is not a question of whether, but *when* they die. If the extravert dies as a consequence of his impulsivity it is just as surely true that the introvert dies of his rigidity. The only difference lies in the fact that the first kind of error tends to produce a sudden death, the latter a slow one.* Hence, the value judgment is made not by "nature," but rather implicitly, unconsciously, and altogether automatically by the individuals themselves, choosing between a brief, untrammeled existence and a long, controlled one.

We are now in a position to understand rather more fully what concepts like "sublimation" and "delay of gratification" mean. For note that we have linked a "flat" priority system with impulsivity—with the inability to postpone gratification. To find the reason for this we must turn back to psychosexual development and the child's relation to the mother.

Clearly the ability to delay gratification is indissolubly linked with the idea that objects are differentially gratifying. One will not be willing to undergo such a postponement if all objects are viewed as equally rewarding. The underlying principle of postponement is one of relinquishing an available but lesser immediate gratification for a more distant but greater one. This is usually described in terms of libidinal *aim,* but we might suggest that initially it is a question of libidinal object. In any case, delay of gratification cannot be separated from the concept of a libidinal hierarchy.

But the establishment of such a hierarchy, as well as its steepness, comes from the nature of the child's experience with the mother. Insofar as a single individual provides a) intense gratification, and b) far more gratification than any other object, a steep hierarchy will develop. The child will be willing to forego immediate gratifications because of the confidence in the availability of a more complete one—

---

source of much gratification. This accords well with our knowledge of the modal background of the psychopathic personality. Maternal deprivation seems consistently to lead to shallow and impermanent attachments in adulthood. The phenomenon of romantic love, on the other hand, which seems clearly to be rooted in the persistence of intense oedipal fantasies, is an example of "adhesiveness" and seems to be found primarily in cultures in which nurturance is concentrated in the mother.

* A good analogy would be the relative speed with which an impulsive and a rigid businessman go bankrupt.

the love, protection, and caresses of the mothering one. This ability does not develop in the psychopathic personality, because the first condition is not present. It is somewhat more marked in populations which grow up under familial conditions such as those which characterize the middle classes in most Western countries, and somewhat less marked in societies in which there is "diffusion of nurturance" among a large number of caretakers of approximately equal importance.

The highest development in steep priority hierarchies, occurring most strongly in Western societies, is the so-called Oedipus complex, and it is for this reason that it is always so closely tied, in psychoanalytic thinking, to superego development. For it is around this period in child development that the libidinal priority system which has already evolved and is fully functioning begins to achieve an organization, and a primitive conceptual statement. Increased concentration of libidinal interest in the organs specifically designed for discharge of sexual tension, together with increased understanding of marriage as involving some sort of possessive exclusiveness and a dawning awareness that such possession is achieved by virtue of the adequate performance of adult roles, generates the fantasy that through appropriate task behavior and relinquishing of childish pleasures the child can obtain total possession of the mother, and hence of a completeness of gratification superior to any heretofore imagined.*

Normally the emergence of this fantasy is articulated with the progressive cathexis of other objects, increasingly distant from the original one though cathected via channels of associative resemblance, so that by the time adulthood is achieved, much of the energy bound up in the fantasy is available to attach itself to new and unrelated objects. This is the ideal developmental pattern outlined by Flugel (5).

But occasionally, as Freud has described so tellingly, the fantasy remains in its original form, unconscious and clinging to its original object (8). A man with a priority system organized around such an oedipal fantasy may build his entire life and career on it. Underneath his ceaseless striving, his harsh self-imposed deprivations and his unflinching determination, lies the romantic and totally unconscious assumption that one day, in this world or the next, somewhere, somehow, by having achieved fame, glory, power, wealth or whatever, he will win access to exclusive possession, as an adult male, of the woman who was devoted to him as a helpless child. As the years go by, this woman becomes withered and old, and ultimately dies, but as Freud emphasizes so repeatedly, nothing changes or ages in the unconscious,

---

* The situation is a little different with female children, since these other changes are typically associated with a transfer of libidinal cathexis from the mother to the father, after the manner Flugel describes (5).

and as a fantasy she remains beautiful, ageless and eternal. Indeed, our hero may "delay gratification" with the same eternal permanence, and pursue his fantasy right into the grave. The fascination of poets with the beauties of bygone ages, and with unavailable and lethal women in general, testifies to the intensity and pervasiveness of this fantasy.

Now, in terms of the theory of libidinal priority hierarchies, this agelessness of the fantasy mother, who remains young and beautiful while her real counterpart fades and dies, is simply a metaphorical representation of the unchanging mental system: connections involving the concept "mother" still have inordinately high priority, even though they involve imagined gratifications which are no longer sought in interactions with the actual mother, indeed, perhaps not in any real relationship at all, but only stand as a kind of ultimate fantasy prize to be awarded when the tasks, which the individual has for this reason been able to cathect, are finally performed.

From this view, the peculiar concept of "sublimation" appears to be nothing more than the most extreme case of this kind of gratification postponement. For as we have noted, the more concentrated and intense the original libidinal gratification, the more steep will be the hierarchy, and hence the more permanent can be the delay (yet cf. 26; 20, pp. 1-2).

We have argued that the vicissitudes of libido are governed by a principle which directs mental energy toward the increase of erotic stimulation. These vicissitudes are therefore entirely internal, although their consequences are external. Three problems now arise: 1) How does this help us to understand aging and death? 2) How can we relate this priority concept to the notion of narcissistic withdrawal of libido from objects under conditions of illness and pain—a notion which is crucial to Freud's libido theory? 3) Thus far we have avoided, through use of the ambiguous word "gratification," confrontation of the hoary question of tension-reduction vs. stimulus-seeking as underlying motivational models. Can we accept Freud's tension-reduction model, along with its handling of stimulus-seeking behavior? It is an explanation which has failed to convince most critics, yet one which lies at the very root of his theory of the death instinct. We will take these questions up in order.

First, aging and death from our viewpoint might be seen as a response to an increasing divergence or incongruity between the internal priority system and external reality. In its simplest form this is expressed in the fact that as an individual grows older he experiences major interpersonal losses with increasing frequency, but the phenomenon occurs more subtly and more persistently in relation to his entire repertoire of habits, skills and interests.

Yet such a view is hardly adequate, since fantasies are never lost, but can be retained indefinitely, and for many individuals the incongruity between their libidinal priority system and external reality is extensive throughout their lives. Clearly this notion in itself is of little help in understanding these processes. Let us therefore turn to the remaining two questions, in the hope that they may throw additional light on this issue.

Pain and libido

"It is universally known, and seems to us a matter of course, that a person suffering organic pain and discomfort relinquishes his interest in the things of the outside world, insofar as they do not concern his suffering. Closer observation teaches us that at the same time he withdraws libidinal interest from his love-objects: so long as he suffers, he ceases to love. The banality of this fact is no reason why we should be deterred from translating it into terms of the libido-theory. We should then say: the sick man withdraws his libidinal cathexes back upon his own ego, and sends them forth again when he recovers. 'Concentrated is his soul,' says W. Busch, of the poet suffering from toothache, 'in his jaw-tooth's aching hole.' " (11, p. 39).

We would say of this tendency that the normal priority system has somehow been superseded by another principle which is semi-orthogonal to it. Regardless of the flatness or steepness of the priority hierarchy, regardless of the particular distribution of libidinal interest across the many mental connections, pain or other bodily discomfort is a signal for a concentration of libidinal interest in the affected organ. We are thus dealing here with a quantitative rather than qualitative variation—with the extent to which libido is diffused over many connections or contracted into a few. The priority system says that $a > b$ (i.e., a is selectively energized, correctly or incorrectly, as having greater potential for gratification than b) $> c > d > \ldots$ $n\text{-}1 > n$. Its steepness or flatness concerns *how much* $a > b$, etc. What we are now discussing is the size of n, the diffusion or concentration of this energy.

Now it may be objected that our assumption of concentration of libido in the affected organ is gratuitous, that all we can actually observe is a *loss* of libidinal interest in other objects. How can we say that there is an accretion in the ego or anywhere else? We can see that the sick or wounded individual is enormously preoccupied with his internal state, but have we any grounds for calling this libidinal, even in the sense in which we have employed this term? What is the anticipated gratification in the poet with the toothache? Is it simply the cessation of the pain or discomfort?

We can best understand the libidinal nature of this process from making a few simple observations. If a man bumps a leg on a chair his automatic and immediate reflexive response will be to rub the injured part. If he cuts his hand he will rapidly put it to his mouth and suck the wound, unless he has been rigidly trained from early childhood not to (as is often the case in our society). In a purely physiological sense this is not necessarily functional behavior, and doctors must often interdict such instinctive reactions, particularly with children, lest they exacerbate the injury. It may even increase the pain, as when a man rubs a fracture; or create a new one, as when a tongue is rubbed raw on a broken tooth. What, then, is the basis of this response? Why does an animal lick its wounds?

It seems clear at the outset that what is involved here is a kind of primitive caress. The organism attempts to give pleasure to its discomfited part. In these gestures we observe the same fusion of sensuous eroticism on the one hand and solicitous nurturance on the other which we normally associate with the care of an infant.* Certain peculiarities of language also express this relation, such as the verb "to nurse," which means at once to give a child the breast and to care for the ill. We talk of "nursing a cold," and almost all folk remedies involve either ingestion of some substance through the mouth or titillating the skin in some way. We speak of "dressing a wound," and the French make the connection even more dramatic with the verb *panser,* which means not only to "dress a wound" but is also used in relation to the grooming of horses. How is it that this complex of rubbing, brushing, washing, petting, and pampering comes to be applied to illness and injury in the same way as to babies and pets?

Let us consider another phenomenon. We observe that although animals and humans may seek to "retire from the field to lick their wounds," humans, at least, are usually unable to achieve such withdrawal. The moment an individual falls ill there is a tendency for others to cluster around and take care of him. This is mitigated somewhat in our own society by our magical fears of contagion, but is institutionalized in the practice of hospitalization. In some nonliterate societies in which the belief in contagion is less virulent, a severely ill man may draw 30 or 40 people into a small dwelling. The process of treating the sick person, furthermore, again recalls the care of the infant. He is relieved from all normal responsibilities and permitted the total passivity and dependency of the infant. He is "nursed back to health," by being put to bed, fed, and generally cared for as if he were helpless.

---

* It is perhaps tedious to point out, as has so often been done, that the language of infant care is also the language of love-making.

With the onset of this illness, let us note, he has become "narcissistic," withdrawing his libidinal interest from those around him. They, on the other hand, seem to be unusually interested in him—we may even say that they have "hypercathected" him. Most important of all, when the illness is over, when he has been "nursed back to health," we discover that his "narcissistic" behavior has vanished, that he has recathected those around him, and diffused his "libido" into the world again.

We may perhaps be forgiven for suspecting that *post hoc* is *propter hoc*—that the collectivity attempts, through nurturant behavior, to seduce the individual into energizing those mental connections which involve the seeking of pleasure from other people. I am suggesting, in other words, as I have elsewhere (30), that people spontaneously respond to narcissistic withdrawal on the part of one of their number with behavior designed to terminate it.

Furthermore, it is not unreasonable to suppose that the animal which licks its wound is not only attempting to reverse the sign of the impulse, or offset it, but is also automatically applying to a part of its body the same principle as the group applies to its injured member. In both cases a contraction of libido occurs and an effort is made by those systems from which libido has been withdrawn to bring about its re-diffusion throughout the system. The human organism is, after all, merely one link in a long chain of organic structures, and we may assume that there are important biological principles which operate through all of these. It seems reasonable to imagine that energy of the kind we have called libido serves to bind structures of all kinds, and hence can be said to exist quite independently of specific organisms, a point to which we shall return later.

We have consistently compared treatment of ill or injured substructures with the treatment of infants, and we might now observe one additional parallel, namely, that the infant is also outside of the system and in the process of being drawn into it. Life begins with erotic stimulation—the individual is, as it were, seduced into the world through pleasurable stimulation. Initially, for the human infant, this is linked to tension-*reduction* through the allaying of hunger pangs, but soon becomes an end in itself, and an avenue to social existence. As we know from the studies of Spitz, this seduction is vital for human existence: the child must be eroticized in order to live, just as the wound must be eroticized in order to heal (33,34).

With most mammals this relationship is even more dramatic. The mother animal will in most cases wash her offspring by licking them all over and, if this stimulation is for any reason omitted, they will usually fail to begin breathing. The sexual basis of this process is sharply underlined in Birch's study of female rats who were prevented from licking their genitals by placing large collars around their necks until just prior to parturition (27, pp. 27 ff.). When they had their litters they neither licked their own genitals nor their off-spring, and the latter died. This would seem to be rather strong evidence of the importance of sexuality in the economy of social interaction—one might even say it is the medium of exchange, just as Parsons has suggested that pleasure is the money of the organism (25, pp. 18 ff.).* The neonate will not live until it receives erotic stimulation from the mother, and the mother will not perform this social function until she has associated the neonate with erotic self-stimulation.

One cannot help being reminded here of Grace Stuart's analysis of narcissism as resulting from a lack of erotic stimulation. Of particular interest is her notion that the selfish, self-indulgent behavior of the narcissist is in reality an awkward attempt at therapy—i.e., through nurturing and gratifying his own ego, the individual tries to cure the disease by removing its cause (35). Presumably this would be successful insofar as the cause is immediate, and unsuccessful insofar as the condition is a more chronic one arising from earlier deprivations. We note, with reference to the former possibility, that people often advise one who shows signs of becoming ill to "take care of himself," or "pamper the flesh a little."

One may even wonder if the ejaculation of semen which occurs when a man is hanged, or undergoes an equivalent agony, does not evolve from a similar process. The trauma is at once so violent and so consciously experienced that the usual libidinal forces are activated with a comparable intensity. The brain engages in a rapid and desperate search operation to determine what connections should be energized, but in vain. The genital then performs its function as a specialized organ for tension discharge (4), and the accumulated energy is orgasmically expended in a final and useless adjustive response. The mythological equivalent of this autonomic gesture may be found in Freud's paper, "The Theme of the Three Caskets"; for, as Freud notes, this theme is essentially one of wish-fulfillment: "Just where in reality he obeys compulsion, he exercises choice, and that which he chooses is not a thing of horror, but the fairest and most desirable thing in life." (13, p. 254). We might add to this, with the hanged man in mind, that the wish serves to make a libidinal cathexis out of the reality of its utter disappearance.

But, as I have remarked in more detail elsewhere (30, p. 344), it is not only the individual himself who makes such attempts to ward off death through libidinal cathexis. One frequently finds the community in which the individual moves behaving in the same way. A death

---

* It is perhaps in this sense that we should view the fact that all of the orifices of the body are eroticized.

almost always activates collective behavior of some kind or another—
a drawing together, a social integration—as well as some sort of loving
behavior toward the corpse. In most societies the corpse is in some
fashion nurtured like an infant: it is bathed, dressed, decorated, gar-
landed; sometimes held, rocked in the arms, kissed.

We thus find an analogous process occurring at several different system levels to the extent that we might wonder whether it would not
be useful to consider all of these responses as part of the *same* process
—as a generalized biological phenomenon transcending the individual
organism and appearing at all levels of organic structuring. It is certainly in this sense that Freud and Ferenczi initially conceived of libido, although this has largely been expunged from the theory.

We can only be rather vague in describing this process at so abstract
a level, and it is difficult to avoid somewhat anthropomorphic language. But it would seem crudely correct to say that 1) units of living
matter show a pronounced tendency to de-energize their attachments
with other units of living matter under stress, and 2) units of living
matter show a pronounced tendency to hyper-energize their connections
with those units showing the above tendency.

I have elsewhere discussed these phenomena as they appear at the
societal level, and need only summarize my observations here. They
begin with the notion that a great deal of familiar yet puzzling social
behavior can be accounted for if we assume two antithetical tendencies operating in all human beings. The first I have called libidinal
diffusion, i.e., a force driving libido toward an increasing number of
increasingly remote objects, along more and more circuitous paths to
tension reduction. The other I have called libidinal contraction, i.e.,
a force driving and concentrating libido in progressively smaller and
more proximate collectivities, and along more direct and simple channels of gratification. These concepts were utilized to explain a variety
of ambivalent social attitudes toward such manifestations of libidinal
contraction as illness, death, psychosis, narcissistic leadership, romantic
love, and incest (30).

In essence, this theory is simply a restatement of Freud's later instinct theory in which he distinguishes between "Eros" and the "death
instinct." Thus Freud refers to what I have called "libidinal diffusion"
("Eros") as a "complicating" force which causes "a more and more
far-reaching coalescence of the particles into which living matter has
been dispersed" (9, pp. 55-56) and the establishment of "ever greater
unities." (12, p. 20). The "death instinct," on the other hand, drives
"organic matter back into the inorganic state" and "aims" to "undo
connections." (12, p. 20).

To understand the way in which libido forms the raw material of
social structure, let us return to Parson's analogue of pleasure as the

currency of the body, "a way of imposing order on still lower level processes." (25, p. 18). Just as money creates orderly activity by centralizing and unifying the motivational basis of that activity, so the pleasure principle creates orderly structures through similar unification of motivation. Each structure borrows libido from the one below it in the structural scale.

The mechanism which effects this transfer is the prevention of total tension discharge. So long as libido is diffused over several objects, such complete discharge is impossible, and the interactions which maintain the connections among the various segments of the structure will continue.

Consider, for example, the operation of this principle on the human level. According to psychoanalytic theory, the early incestuous attachments of the individual are never entirely abandoned. While in the healthy individual the bulk of this libidinal involvement is transferred to other unrelated objects, fragments always remain, largely unconscious and never eradicated, generating residual tensions whose discharge is relegated to the realm of dreams and fantasy. The incest taboo, of course, enforces this transfer, pushing the libido outwards—diffusing it, in other words. In the absence of such a taboo, one could conceive of the possibility of total libidinal quiescence. That is, if all of the sexual energy of an individual were tied up in one object, then it could be utterly discharged through that object, and the "goal" of the "death instinct" would be achieved. The incest taboo and a host of comparable social norms effectively see to it that this never occurs, for so long as an individual cathects more than one object he will be unable to achieve a total absence of libidinal tension. Such tension can be diverted into a variety of socially useful responses—in particular the formation of new cathexes, which serve to link together and bind large numbers of people in libidinal networks, and which further ensure the permanence of this same tension. Any tendency toward short-circuiting this network arouses anxiety in all those participating in it, and activates pressures toward re-diffusion of the contracted libido (30).

Tension reduction and death

For Freud, death was the ultimate cessation of tension—the quiescence toward which all living matter moved. Both he and, more elaborately, Ferenczi, saw life as a state of tension thrust upon living matter by some overwhelming catastrophe of stimulation which not only initiates all of the turmoil, but continually drives the organic material farther and farther from its goal, like a panic-stricken child lost in the forest (4). The increasing circuitousness of the paths to gratification prolong tension and thereby life itself. Hence, death is a kind of orgasm—an escape from stimuli and motion. An individual who experiences a longing for death as a conscious wish is thus expressing, from this viewpoint, a longing for closure—for an end to the ceaseless unfinality of human experience, in which every ending is but another beginning, and every simplicity hides another complexity.

Yet while we know that such feelings arise (for even sleep represents libidinal contraction of this kind, a cathectic withdrawal or turning away from even pleasurable stimuli, and the necessity of shutting off input and discharging tension generated by the accumulated stimuli of the day has been demonstrated by the striking results which occur when people are prevented from dreaming), it is by no means clear why or when stimulation becomes nonpleasurable to the point where a tension-reduction theory of this sort seems to make clinical sense.

Freud confronts this problem rather briefly in his paper on narcissism: "Of course curiosity will here suggest the question why such a damming-up of libido in 'the ego should be experienced as 'painful.' There I shall content myself with the answer that 'pain' is in general the expression of increased tension, and thus a *quantity* of the material event is, here as elsewhere, transformed into the *quality* of 'pain' in the mind. . . ." (11, p. 42).

Since very mild stimulation can be subjectively experienced as pain, however, while very intense sexual stimulation is not, this hardly seems a solution to the problem, as Freud himself seems partially to recognize. Yet Freud was reluctant altogether to abandon the simple tension-release theory of pleasure, partly perhaps for the good reason that, with little complication of a very simple-minded theory, one can get rather farther than one expects without the aid of an additional construct to handle stimulus-seeking. One can posit a threshold effect: i.e., that a certain level of accumulation must be achieved before discharge can take place, and hence stimulation will be sought in the service of ultimate tension reduction. One can also argue that a stimulus is sought in order to modify a *structure* which is tension-generating. In other words, we must think not in terms of a single impulse being discharged in a single moment, but rather of a complex system of interrelated drives which is incapable of simultaneous total discharge so long as the organism lives, and for which it is problematic whether a given stimulus will increase or decrease the overall tension level (i.e., act as a kind of unlocking mechanism). Similarly, a specific discharge of tension may raise the level of the system as a whole, as in the case of impulse gratification being followed by guilt.

One could make a case, then, that the desire for pleasurable stimulation is purely derivative—that initially it is linked to reduction of more basic tensions (e.g., hunger), and retains this association throughout life. This is a little difficult to reconcile, however, with the licking of newborn mammals by the mother, which is independent of the feeding process, and which is not followed by stimulus-avoidance but by an awakening interest in living. Hence it is a stimulus which seems to be both independent and pleasurable in its effect. Even more conclusive are the above-mentioned studies of Olds (e.g., 24), which should put an end to this question once and for all. This suggests, then, that 1) two forces are operating with respect to the tension structure of the organism, and 2) that these forces are in the short run orthogonal to one another, but are in the long run inversely related, i.e., the drive toward pleasurable stimulation may in the short run either raise or lower the tension level of the organism, combatting the drive toward tension-reduction or being harnessed in its service; but in the long run they stand in basic opposition, the drive toward pleasurable stimulation holding the organism's search for quiescence in temporary abeyance (cf. 36, pp. 191-221).

The problem of boundary
maintenance
Thus far we have approached our problem as if the integrity of the organism were non-problematic. Yet the maintenance of boundaries is an energy-consuming, tension-generating task for any organism. Boundary-maintenance is, in fact, one of the major sources of tension, as we can observe in the fact that the subjective experience of unresisted boundary-dissolution is always accompanied by an intense sensation of tension release. (Bertram Lewin's statement that regression to a simpler structural level (22, p. 29) always releases surplus energy is also relevant, since such regression will in many cases involve boundary dissolution for the more advanced or inclusive structure). Thus the description of nirvana-like states always includes the notion of complete destruction of the boundaries separating the individual from the rest of the world.

This relationship between boundary-maintenance and tension guarantees a certain delicacy in the organism's handling of stimulation. An overloading of stimuli may lead to boundary-destruction in an effort to discharge the accumulation, and indeed, peaks of stimulation and tension are often experienced subjectively as ego-shattering (cf. 21). One wonders, in fact, if certain systemic somatic failures, such as heart attacks, are not examples of this process.

On the other hand, the very structures themselves are highly dependent upon erotic stimulation for their maintenance. Ferenczi and Alexander have both described vividly the way in which body functions are first exercised for the erotic pleasure they provide, and are only later organized into a complex interdependent system in which the erotic goal of each individual organ is relinquished in favor of a utilitarian one which benefits the structure as a whole. At this point, according to Ferenczi, the system develops a specialized organ, the genital, to discharge libidinal tension and thus free the other organs for these utilitarian functions. "If there were no such separation of pleasure activities, the eye would be absorbed in erotic looking, the mouth would be exclusively employed as an oral-erotic instrument, instead of being employed in necessary self-preservative activities. . . ." (4, pp. 16, 97-8; cf. also 1; 7, p. 86).

Hence a cessation of stimulation, particularly of an erotic kind, would be equally devastating to the equilibrium of the system. We may remind ourselves that both overstimulation and understimulation produce loss of consciousness, and may speculate that disruption of some degree of constancy in stimulus input may also produce more permanent boundary-loss.*

Libido, aging, and death

Let us now attempt to organize these observations, and the various dimensions we have isolated, into a moderately coherent whole before making a final assault on the problem of aging and death. We have discussed four different, but not always independent, dimensions thus far, and these are grouped together in a two-dimensional diagram in Figure 1. We must admit at the outset that this is a very weak and preliminary effort, and vastly too simple for the material it seeks to represent, but one must, after all, begin somewhere.†

These four dimensions have been sufficiently described above so that further definition is unnecessary. All that Figure 1 tells us is the way in which they are related to one another. Since a 90° angle represents independence and a 45° angle a positive correlation, we are saying that each dimension is a function of those immediately adjacent to it—in other words, that tension binding is a function of libidinal diffusion plus boundary maintaining, while boundary maintaining is in turn a function of tension binding and a steep priority hierarchy and so forth.

---

* One cannot escape a peculiar metaphorical image of eroticism (in the psychoanalytic sense) as a kind of Ariel-like, catalytic messenger in the service of biological development, appearing at every point at which growth and evolution are problematic. Although purely poetic, we may carry the metaphor to the point of wondering whether in the process of aging, utilitarianism wins the day altogether, and no organic function is any longer an end in itself, the spritely messenger having taken himself off to where he was more strongly needed.

† Readers familiar with factor analytic studies of the MMPI may notice a resemblance between this diagram and one conceptualization of the personality domain (see 18, 31, 32). I cannot at this point decide whether the resemblance is meaningful, or simply expresses conceptual rigidity on the part of the author. Indeed, I have no confidence whatever that the four variables in Figure 1 can really be compressed into two orthogonal dimensions instead of three or four, much less determine how they relate to an only partially over-lapping domain.

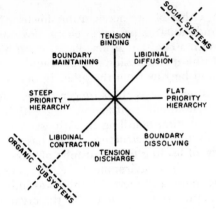

Figure 1. The way the four dimensions are related to one another.

Two further characteristics of the diagram may be briefly noted. The first is the fact that the principal diagonal, dealing with boundaries, pertains to the individual organism, while the secondary diagonal (diffusion-contraction) is transindividual in nature. It is for this reason that it is extended in both directions, to show that the same relationships will hold at the social system level and at the organ system, cellular, and even lower levels.

The second characteristic is that the tension dimension has been vertically-oriented for the deliberate purpose of capitalizing on the natural tendency to equate verticality with opposition to gravity. The reader is encouraged to view any given system as having a natural tendency to move toward the bottom of the page.

This tendency is countered, as noted before, by the input of pleasurable stimulation from the environment, which "motivates" the organism both to attach itself to other organisms and to integrate itself as a means of increasing its gratification-processing efficiency.

We may now turn to the processes of aging and death in an effort to determine what might alter this balance. The following observations come to mind:

1. Time is inherently particularizing. Each experience that an individual undergoes automatically differentiates his life further from all other men, i.e., his *combination* of experiences is increasingly unique. This uniqueness creates barriers to the diffusion of libidinal attachments, a tendency which is continually exacerbated by the accelerating frequency with which he experiences losses of love objects, as mentioned above (cf. 16, p. 268).

2. More important, perhaps, is the general wear and tear of continual stimulation on the ability of the system to maintain its boundaries. Constant assimilation and organization of new data can have a gradual but erosive effect, in the manner suggested by Selye (28).

Now at some point either of two accelerating downward spirals may be activated as the individual experiences energy loss and decreasing adaptive capacity. With a constant strain placed upon his energies by the demands both of libidinal diffusion and of boundary maintenance, he may opt for one and borrow from the other in one of two ways:

1. If boundary maintenance is the stronger concern he may "borrow" energy through libidinal contraction. By withdrawing libido from the objects around him, hoarding it, as it were, he can concentrate his efforts on his internal structure. This has the unfortunate consequence, however, of leading to the atrophy of those organs which maintain his contact with his environment, i.e., the sense organs. As these decay it becomes more and more difficult to assimilate and order new stimuli. Most frequently the structure of the organism gradually disintegrates through under-stimulation—one by one the boundary-maintaining mechanisms deteriorate through atrophy, i.e., lack of any material to process. This may either continue until decrepitude makes it impossible for life to be maintained or, at some point along the way, a sudden excessive stimulus may shatter the decadent structure and bring about death. One might even consider cerebral vascular accidents to be occurrences of this nature.

2. If libidinal diffusion receives the stronger emphasis, the organism may borrow energy from boundary maintenance, dissolving the structure in order to keep the libido diffused. In its most benign form this will express itself in terms of excursions into mysticism or other expressions of one-with-the-worldness. The loosening of the organic structure, however, with consequent decrease in the unity of the organism and, once again, increased inability to process stimuli, will lead to further decay, further borrowing, further incapacitation, and so on, until more serious symptoms of mental and physical disorganization will arise, such as confusion, incontinence, incoherence, tremor, and the whole series of symptoms usually attached to the term senility. Once again death may be sudden, resulting from overstimulation, or gradual, resulting from under-stimulation, but just as the gradual form is the more typical outcome of libidinal contraction, so the sudden is more typical of boundary dissolution.*

It goes without saying that this is a most primitive and preliminary formulation, containing many ambiguities and even contradictions. One could imagine, and might even hope, that an ultimate explanation of these processes will leave no part of it unchanged. Yet one can at the same time hope that it will contribute in a positive way to its own destruction.

---

* For a more thorough discussion of these processes see Gerard (16, esp. p. 272). Cf. also Kastenbaum's discussions (19, pp. 9-12; 20, pp. 6 ff.).

References

1. Alexander, F. Unexplored areas in psychoanalytic theory and treatment. *Behavioral Science*, 1958, *3*, October.
2. Eysenck, H. J. *The Structure of Human Personality*. New York: Wiley, 1953.
3. Fenichel, O. *The Psychoanalytic Theory of Neurosis*. New York: Norton, 1945.
4. Ferenczi, S. *Thalassa*. New York: Psychoanalytic Quarterly, 1938.
5. Flugel, J. C. *The Psychoanalytic Study of The Family*. London: Hogarth, 1957.
6. Freud, S. Analysis terminable and interminable. In *Collected Papers*, Vol. V. London: Hogarth, 1953, 316-357.
7. Freud, S. *Beyond the Pleasure Principle*. New York: Liveright, 1950.
8. Freud, S. Contributions to the psychology of love. In *Collected Papers*, Vol. IV. London: Hogarth, 1953, 192-216.
9. Freud, S. *The Ego and the Id*. London: Hogarth, 1949.
10. Freud, S. Mourning and melancholia. In *Collected Papers*, Vol. IV. London: Hogarth, 1953, 152-170.
11. Freud, S. On narcissism: an introduction. In *Collected Papers*, Vol. IV. London: Hogarth, 1953, 30-59.
12. Freud, S. *An Outline of Psychoanalysis*. New York: Norton, 1949.
13. Freud, S. The theme of the three caskets. In *Collected Papers*, Vol. IV. London: Hogarth, 1953, 244-256.
14. Freud, S. Two encyclopedia articles. In *Collected Papers*, Vol. V. London: Hogarth, 1953, 107-135.
15. Freud, S. Types of neurotic nosogenesis. In *Collected Papers*, Vol. XI. London: Hogarth, 1955, 113-121.
16. Gerard, R. W. Aging and Organization. In J. E. Birren (ed.), *Handbook of Aging and the Individual*. Chicago: University of Chicago Press, 1959, 264-275.
17. Jung, C. G. *Psychological Types*. New York: Harcourt, Brace, 1924.
18. Kassebaum, G. G., Couch, A. S., and Slater, P. E. The factorial dimensions of the MMPI. *J. Consult. Psychol.*, 1959, *23*, 226-236.
19. Kastenbaum, R. The crisis of explanation. In this volume.
20. Kastenbaum, R. Longevity and life patterns. In this volume.
21. Keiser, S. Body ego during orgasm. *Psychoanalytic Quart.*, 1952, *21*, 153-166.
22. Lewin, B. *The Psychoanalysis of Elation*. New York: Norton, 1950.
23. Lindemann, E. Symptomatology and management of acute grief. *Amer. J. Psychiat.*, 1944, *101*, 141-148.
24. Olds, J. Self-stimulation of the brain. *Science*, 1958, *127*, 315-324.
25. Parsons, T. Some reflections on the problem of psychosomatic relationships in health and illness. Unpublished manuscript.
26. Pollock, K., and Kastenbaum, R. Delay of gratification in later life: an experiment analog. In this volume.
27. Schaffner, B. (ed.), *Group Processes*, 1954. New York: Macy Foundation, 1955.
28. Selye, H. *The Stress of Life*. New York: McGraw-Hill, 1956.

29. Slater, P. E. Microcosm: Myth and Social Structure in the Evolution of Small Groups. Unpublished manuscript.

30. Slater, P. E. On social regression. *Amer. Soc. Rev.*, 1963, *28*, 339-364.

31. Slater, P. E. Parental behavior and the personality of the child. *J. Genetic Psychol.*, 1962, *101*, 53-68.

32. Slater, P. E., and Scarr, H. A. Personality in old age. *Genet. Psychol. Monogr.* In press.

33. Spitz, R. A. Hospitalism: an inquiry into the genesis of psychiatric conditions in early childhood. *The Psychoanalytic Study of the Child,* Vol. I. New York: International Universities Press, 1945, 53-74.

34. Spitz, R. A. Hospitalism: a follow-up report. *The Psychoanalytic Study of the Child,* Vol. II. New York: International Universities Press, 1946, 113-117.

35. Stuart, G. *Narcissus.* London: Allen and Unwin, 1956.

36. Szasz, T. S. *Pain and Pleasure.* London: Tavistock, 1957.

37. Taylor, G. R. The age of the androids. *Encounter,* 1963, *21*, November, 36-46.

Geriatric behavioral prosthetics

3

Ogden R. Lindsley

Human behavior is a functional relationship between a person and a specific social or mechanical environment. If the behavior is deficient, we can alter either the individual or the environment in order to produce effective behavior. Most previous attempts to restore behavioral efficiency by retraining, punishment, or physiological treatment have focused on only one side of this relation, the deficient individual. This approach implies that normal individuals can function in all currently existing social environments, that deficient individuals can be normalized, and that there are ordinarily no deficient environments. Scientists have only recently directly focused on the environmental side of deficient behavior functions and on the design of specialized or *prosthetic environments* to restore competent performance.

Prosthetic environments are not new, however. For centuries specialized environments have supported or reinforced the behavior of infants and children. Special foods, feeding devices, bedding, furniture and clothing for infants are commonplace. Special entertainments—toys, primary colors, simple books, music, games—have been less clearly recognized in their behavioral role of reinforcers designed particularly for children. All of these are provided by society in expectation of the services the child will provide as an adult.

Read at Second Annual Symposium on Old Age, Cushing Hospital, Framingham, Mass., May 21, 1963, and dedicated to my grandmother, Mrs. James Ogden Lindsley, who lived well beyond her environment and died in an institution at age 89.

Research was conducted in the Behavior Research Laboratory, Department of Psychiatry, Harvard Medical School, located at Metropolitan State Hospital, Waltham, Mass., and was supported by research grant MH-05054 from the Psychopharmacology Service Center, National Institute of Mental Health, U.S. Public Health Service.

The cooperation of the Department of Psychiatry (Jack R. Ewalt, M.D., Chairman) and the staff of Metropolitan State Hospital (William F. McLaughlin, M.D., Superintendent), the able assistance of our laboratory staff, and, most especially, the participation of our patients has greatly facilitated our research.

More recently, prosthetic environments have been extended to the physically handicapped. Blind persons use Braille books, noise-making canes, seeing-eye dogs, and specially designed houses. Paraplegic veterans of war have specially designed homes provided by a grateful public for relatively brief service to society.

But what of the aged, veterans of an entire lifetime of social service? Are they provided with special environments designed to support their behavior at its maximum? Are we using their behavior most efficiently?

To prolong health, physicians offer aging persons a wide range of physiological prosthetics, from vitamins and hormones to increased oxygen utilization, for their internal environment (8,10,17). Beyond providing eyeglasses, hearing aids, dentures, cribs, and crutches, however, science has done little to modify the external mechanical and social environments of the aged. The skills of current behavioral science, and free-operant conditioning in particular, can provide more than compound lenses, audio amplifiers, and mechanical restraint and support. Behavioral engineers can design prosthetic environments to support the behavior of the aged as crutches support their weight.

In this chapter, I will offer suggestions, developed from the methods and discoveries of free-operant conditioning, for developing geriatric prosthetic environments.*

In *free-operant conditioning* the frequency of performance of an act is altered by locating and arranging suitable consequences (reinforcement). The person being conditioned is at all times free to make the response and receive the arranged consequences, or to make other responses. By isolating the individual within an appropriate enclosure, the behavior specialist can empirically—rather than merely statistically —control all environmental events which can affect the behavior he is studying. The behavioral response and any environmental manipulations whose effects on the response are being studied can be automatically and continuously recorded. This environmental control and automatic, continuous recording mark the method as a laboratory natural science, comparable to modern chemistry, physics and biology.

Free-operant methods are suited to behavioral geriatrics for several reasons.† Concentrating on *motivational aspects,* or consequences, of behavior, free-operant conditioning alters the *immediate environment* to generate and maintain behavior. The sensitivity of the methods to subtle changes in such aspects of the person's performance as response

---

* Suggestions for designing prosthetic environments for the behavior of retarded persons have also been made recently (29).

† These reasons also make free-operant methods especially appropriate to a wide range of clinical behavioral problems. For a discussion of applications of the method to psychotherapy see Lindsley (30).

rate, efficiency and perseverance makes these methods appropriate to the study of *single individuals*. Because the sensitivity does not decrease with very long periods of application with the same individual, reliable *longitudinal studies* are possible. Free-operant conditioning methods for the analysis of functional and dynamic relationships between individuals and both their *social and nonsocial environments* can produce separate measures of mechanical dexterity, intellectual functioning, and social adjustment.

Free-operant principles and techniques may provide behavioral geriatrics with 1) a fresh theoretical approach; 2) laboratory description, prognosis, and evaluation; 3) design of prosthetic environments; and 4) individualized prosthetic prescriptions. Although I know of no free-operant experiments on the aged, and research in our laboratory with senile psychotics has not been extensive, preliminary suggestions can be well supported by the results of extensive experiments on the behavior of psychotic, neurotic, and mentally retarded individuals, whose behavioral deficits are usually as debilitating and challenging as those of aged persons.*

A fresh theoretical approach

Free-operant conditioning principles can provide a highly relevant approach for increasing the efficiency of ward management and patient care routines. In this new approach, ward attendants do not perform custodial tasks. They are instead trained to act as behavioral engineers in arranging appropriate behavioral programs and reinforcements, so that the patients themselves maintain their ward and their persons.† Most important in this application of free-operant methods are 1) precise behavioral description; 2) functional definition of stimulus, response, and reinforcement; and 3) attention to behavioral processes.

Precise behavioral description facilitates communication between behavioral engineer and ward supervisor. It not only focuses attention on the actual behavioral movement which is occurring at either too high or too low a rate, but also permits observing and counting the response and directly reinforcing it with suitable consequences.

---

* For an excellent review of these experiments see Rachman, S. (34).

† Research scientists suggesting new approaches for managing patients often overlook the crucial administrative problem of recruiting and training personnel. It is a good idea, but if it works who will put it into practice? An excellent source of behavioral engineers who could train and supervise attendants and nurses in these new prosthetic procedures would be Special Educators. Their current training, motivation, and philosophy are ideal for operant prosthetic methods. A few graduate courses and some ward experience under the supervision of an expert should make Special Educators into excellent Prosthetic Behavioral Engineers.

Functional definition of stimulus, response, and reinforcement focuses the attention of the nurse or attendant on the relationship between the behavior she is attempting to manage and her management procedures. When she realizes that an event may be a stimulus for one patient but not for another, and that a second event may be reinforcing to one patient but punishing to still another, then she recognizes the full complexity of human behavior, and in behavioral management no longer makes errors based upon misplaced empathy and generalization. For example, the socially deprived patients found in large hospitals may be rewarded by any attention from the nurse, even scolding for misbehavior. Consequently, a patient will continue to do the thing for which he was scolded in attempts to obtain the social contacts from the nurse, even though the nurse designed the topography of these contacts as punishment for what the patient was doing.

Attention to the behavioral processes of positive reinforcement, extinction, satiation, and mild punishment has proven extremely useful in engineering a ward for maximal behavioral accomplishment. Ayllon and Michael successfully trained ward nurses to increase patients' self-feeding by talking to patients only when they fed themselves (3). Ayllon also trained nurses to satiate a towel hoarder by filling her room with towels, and to punish the wearing of extra clothing by letting a patient eat only when she was below a certain weight with her clothes on (2).

Important for generating maximal behavior on a geriatric ward is the early establishment of a conditioned general reinforcer, or token, which must be used to purchase all items and opportunities of importance and reinforcing value to the patients. The ward tokens are used by the attendants and the nurses to reinforce appropriate behavior. The patients can then use the tokens to purchase personal articles, cigarettes, afternoon naps, television and record playing time, talks with chaplains and volunteers, and all other events of value and importance to them. The patients will readily perform custodial duties on their ward in order to earn the tokens. Ayllon has successfully used tokens in this way in managing a ward of chronic psychotic patients.*

High on the list of types of behavior that it is desirable to generate in a geriatric patient are very mild physical exercise and sun-bathing. The patient is immediately reinforced with a token for each exercise period and for small daily gains in his exercise achievement. Such exercise, shaped very gradually and watched carefully by the ward physician, can do much to restore physical health and well-being to a geriatric patient.

---

* Personal communication from T. Ayllon, State Hospital, Anna, Ill., 1963.

Laboratory description, prognosis, and evaluation

Free-operant conditioning methods can be used to develop a behavior research laboratory for the accurate measurement and description of behavior deficits found in the aged. Inglis has found that psychometric tests are almost useless in these applications and recommends that experimental methods be applied to geriatric problems (19).

Over the past 10 years, we have clearly demonstrated that a free-operant conditioning laboratory is useful in describing, prognosticating and evaluating psychoses (24,28). In brief, our laboratory consists of several small experimental rooms which provide controlled environments for automatically recording behavioral deficits. Patients are brought to the rooms by a technician and permitted to behave freely in them for a period of time long enough to determine accurately the presence and degree of certain behavioral deficits.

The rooms differ from one another only in the equipment necessary for measuring different behavioral deficits. One room, for example, may have a chair and a wall panel with a single knob on it. Pulling the knob is reinforced by the illumination of a television screen mounted in the panel. The rate at which a patient pulls the knob indicates the reinforcing power of the narrative material presented to him via the television system. The material televised can be standard commercial broadcasts, specialized programs recorded on audio-visual tape, or a family visitor seated in front of a closed-circuit television camera in another part of the laboratory. In this room, the differential reinforcing value of audio-visual narrative reinforcers can be objectively determined by the continuous, automatic, cumulative records of knob-pulling. Similar rooms have been developed for recording behaviors as disparate as hallucinating and pacing in chronic psychotics, social deficits, and a patient's interest in his psychotherapist or visitor (11,26, 27,28).

Fully automatic programming of stimuli and recording of responses insures completely objective measurement. Technicians who do not differentially involve themselves with the data handle the patients and equipment and therefore do not introduce complicating observer bias. Furthermore, longitudinal studies are not disrupted when technicians are changed. Because there is no observer bias, cross-hospital and cross-cultural comparisons can be made. Because a fully controlled environment and automatic recording dispense with observer ratings, longitudinal studies can be conducted without the loss of observer sensitivity which occurs with repeated measurement (21). With automatic programming and recording, verbal instructions can be used or not. This opportunity to dispense with verbal instructions permits analysis of their effects and consequently more specific behavioral analysis, as well as the study of nonverbal patients. Free-operant methods thus provide prognostic data and reliable, valid behavioral measures which can be included in case histories even more confidently than blood pressure and blood cell count, which usually involve observer bias.

Long-term laboratory measures of the type and degree of behavioral deficits of individual patients permit exact evaluation of the effects of therapeutic variables on each patient's behavior. The behavioral effects of medications, as well as the effects of such social variables as ward reassignments, home visits and deaths in the family, can be readily determined.

Since records are available on each patient, objective, high quality behavioral research can be conducted by physicians in charge of medication by occasionally referring a patient to the behavior laboratory for a current evaluation. Therapeutic dosage can be accurately adjusted to the deficit and drug-response of each patient. Individualized behavioral treatment can then be conducted with the same precision with which individualized physiological treatment is now conducted in well-staffed general hospitals.

Design of prosthetic environments

There is little hope of retarding the aging process at this time, but we can reduce its behavioral debilitation by designing environments which compensate for or support the specific behavioral deficits of each aged person.* Because we will not actually alter the deficits, but merely provide an environment in which the deficits are less debilitating, these environments cannot be considered purely therapeutic. Therapeutic environments generate some behavior which is maintained when the patient is returned to the normal or general social environment. Therapeutic environments are essentially training or retraining centers for the generation of behavioral skills which maintain themselves once the patient has left the therapeutic environment. Prosthetic environments, however, must operate continually in order to decrease the debilitation resulting from the behavioral deficit. Eyeglasses are prosthetic devices for deficient vision, hearing aids for deficient hearing, and crutches and wheel chairs for deficient locomotion.

---

* The American Psychiatric Association (1959) conducted a survey on the care of patients over 65 in public mental hospitals and gleaned the following suggestions for improving the design of geriatric facilities: tilted bathroom mirrors for wheelchair patients; better lighting with no glare; ramps and short stair risers; guardrails, hold-bars, and non-skid floors; draft-free radiant heat; higher chairs to eliminate stooping to sit; facilities for daytime naps; and work, recreational, and social activities geared to the physical abilities of the patients.

To describe suggestions for geriatric prosthetic environments as accurately as possible, I will use the analytical categories of the laboratory behavioral scientist: 1) discriminative stimuli; 2) response devices; 3) reinforcers; and 4) reinforcement schedules. The number of different types of special stimuli and devices required for prosthesis in each of these categories must be determined by the analysis of each aged individual. The types of environmental alteration required to support aged behavior cannot be determined until the number, degree, and range of behavioral deficits are determined. It may be that a given prosthetic device can be used to prosthetize more than one type of behavioral deficit. Adequately detailed analysis may also show that a single behavioral deficit can be prosthetized by more than one device. In these cases, the most economic and most general devices would be selected first.

My suggestions for the design of specific prosthetic environments for aged individuals are certainly not exhaustive. They are only suggestions for the direction of future research, examples of the kinds of things we should try in searching for new prosthetic devices. The range of prosthetic devices is limited only by the creativity and ingenuity of the investigator and the time and funds at his disposal. His time and funds are, in turn, limited only by society's interest in providing devices for restoring effective behavior to its older citizens.

Geriatric discriminative stimuli

The environmental events which signal when a response is appropriate and when it should not be made are extremely important in controlling behavior. Traffic lights are a familiar example. These colored lights are useful discriminative stimuli to a person with normal color vision, much less useful to a color-blind person, and of no use to a totally blind person. The geriatric patient may well have behavioral deficits which, like blindness, limit the range of discriminative stimuli in the normal environment which can control his behavior. The full and exact nature of geriatric behavioral deficits has not yet been determined.

The *intensity and size of discriminative stimuli* for the aged has received some prosthetic attention. Eyeglasses have been developed for amplifying and correcting visual responses. Hearing aids have been developed for amplifying sounds to serve as discriminative stimuli for people whose hearing is deficient. Touch, smell, and taste amplifiers have not yet been developed, probably because our basic knowledge of these senses is more limited.

Simple and dramatic patterns, long durations and higher intensities of stimulation should be investigated, for we can increase the intensity of the environmental stimulus when prosthetic amplifiers are not available.* It is amazing, for example, that although we give children books with large type, we force elderly people with deficient vision to use heavy eyeglasses or hand magnifying lenses to read normal-size type. We might find that even with large type, certain aged persons with deficient vision develop headaches or become nervous while reading. If we provided Braille or "talking books" for these individuals, we might find an increase in their usefulness to us and to themselves.

Multiple sense displays should be investigated in attempts to design geriatric discriminative stimuli. While an older person might not respond appropriately to a loud sound alone or to a bright light alone, he might respond appropriately to a simultaneous combination of loud sound and bright light. A normal person under the high control of a small portion of his environment is much more likely to respond to a multiple sense display than to a single sense display in the rest of his environment. Similarly, an aged person with generally weakened attention might respond more appropriately to a multiple sense display.

Expanded auditory and visual narrative stimuli should also be investigated. Melrose has found that many aged persons who cannot hear normal speech can hear expanded speech (32). Expanded speech does not differ in intensity or tone from normal speech. It is just spread out more in time, being truly slower. Melrose's finding suggests that old people cannot integrate rapidly presented information. It is the frequency of the *words,* not the frequency of the sounds, which they cannot integrate. This suggests that the visual discriminative response to a pictorial drama might also be deficient when the drama is presented at the normal rate. By using video-tape recording systems to expand visual materials, we might restore understanding of and interest in visual narration to many aged people. The possibility of using expanded auditory and visual materials as reinforcing stimuli is discussed below.

Response-controlled discriminative stimulation should be tried as a prosthetic device for geriatric patients who appear to have intermittent attention. If a patient is periodically unresponsive to stimulation, the stimuli which occur during these "dead" periods in his attention may as well not be presented. To him the world has missing portions, as if a normal person were watching a movie and periodically the projector lens was covered for brief periods of time while the narration continued. There would be many important portions of the movie narration to which he would have no opportunity to respond.

---

* I have been told that Lord Amulree of University College Hospital, London, arranged for stronger odors to be added to utility gas so that aged persons with decreased senses of smell would know when the gas heaters had blown out and would not be asphyxiated.

Response-controlled stimulation permits the narration to move along in time only when the patient is responding to it. If the patient does not respond to a given stimulus, the next stimulus is not presented. Rather, it is stored until the patient responds again. The stimulus can be stored either by stopping the tape or film or by running a small continuous loop in which the last narrative event responded to is repeated. When the patient becomes attentive again and the next response is made, the narration continues. With this technique, the "dead" portions in the patient's attention would merely increase the total presentation time without removing portions of the narration.

Response-controlled stimulation could, of course, be used for nonnarrative discriminative stimuli such as signal lights, as well as for more complicated and more socially relevant narrative forms of stimulation. Many other modifications of discriminative stimuli should be tried in attempts to prosthetize discrimination deficits in the aged. The examples given are merely suggestions of what can be done in this field.

Geriatric response devices

The design of prosthetic response devices for geriatric patients is a wide-open field. Innumerable response force amplifiers are available for normal persons. Most hand tools, for example, amplify response force. Hammers increase the force of manual pounding by extending the leverage of the arm; wrenches, the force of finger grip. In a sense, most modern machinery is designed to increase the force or accuracy of normal human action.

Response force amplifiers should be provided for old people with extremely weak motor responses. Geriatric environments should contain a much wider range of response force amplifiers than the fully automated factory or fully electrified home. Why, for example, must the aged open their own doors in hospitals when supermarket and garage doors are opened electronically?

For elderly people with feeble voices, the force of speech could be amplified by throat microphones and transistorized amplifiers. Such a simple device might greatly facilitate communication between older persons.

Wide response topographies should be provided so that palsied movements and inaccurate placement of hands and fingers would not be disabling. An individual with extreme palsy, for example, could operate a telephone with push buttons, instead of the normal dial arrangement, if the buttons were far enough apart and required enough pressure so they could not be accidentally pushed by a shaking hand. The voice-operated telephones in the Bell system design will, of course, completely prosthetize dialing deficits.

The standard electrical typewriter, sensitive to the slightest touch, is an example of a device which maximizes the efficiency of a normal person for whom accuracy and placement is no problem, but which is probably the most poorly designed typewriter for operation by an older person. The older person would make many errors of placement, and in trembling would jam the sensitive machine by depressing two keys simultaneously.

Rate switches, which operate only when repeatedly pressed above a certain rate, would be useful in maintaining high constant attention from aged persons with intermittent or weak attention. Most complicated and dangerous manufacturing machinery previously was operated by single-throw hand switches. The machine operated as long as the switch stayed in the "down" position. An inattentive operator could mash his fingers or cut off his arm. Stationary switches of this sort were found to be too dangerous even for normal individuals. They were replaced with spring-loaded switches which require continuous force in order for the machine to operate. Foot switches which must be continually depressed by the operator have greatly reduced industrial accidents, because when the operator turns away or leaves the machine, he takes his foot off the control switch and the machine stops.

An even higher degree of attention could be demanded by using a switch which had to be pressed repeatedly at a high rate in order for the machine to operate. A high rate of pressing demands closer attention than does continual depression of a switch. Impulse shorteners in the circuits of operant conditioning response levers are used for this purpose. Remember that a sleeping, dozing or even dead person could operate a spring-loaded switch and its connected machinery by the weight of his inactive body. A switch that must be continually pressed should reduce the accident hazards of machine operation for many older persons with mild attention disorders. When their attention drifted so that they failed to press the switch at the required rate, the machine would automatically stop.

Response feedback systems should be developed so that response location errors can be corrected before they actually occur. For example, if an older person could not always control his fingers, he could be prevented from pushing a wrong button or placing his finger at the edge of a saw by a loud tone which sounded whenever his finger was moving away from the appropriate response location. Such response feedback systems could greatly compensate for a reduced kinesthetic ability. In effect, they would substitute for the deficient afferent input from the aged limbs which once guided the hands so accurately.

If a little time, money, and thought were applied to the problem, I am sure that a wide range of imaginative and successful devices could be developed for helping aged persons overcome their fairly obvious response deficits.

Geriatric reinforcers

The generally low interest or motivation of the aged is very familiar. The elderly person appears capable of behaving but has lost his "will to live." We assume that he is able to respond, because on occasional brief instants he "lights up" and behaves appropriately. Rather than interpreting brief periods of appropriate behavior as normal episodes or phases in the aging process, we usually attribute them to special circumstances which temporarily increase motivation.

In precise behavioral terms, this means either that the reinforcers currently programmed in his immediate environment are no longer adequate or that the old person has simply lost the ability to be reinforced. The difference is of great importance and should be tested experimentally by attempting to reinforce his behavior with a wide range of events.

Individualized historical reinforcers. We should look closely at a geriatric patient's rare moments of high behavioral rate. Is some unusual, more appropriate reinforcer operating—something from the past—an old song, an old food, an old friend? If parts of such individualized historical reinforcers were recorded and presented on audio tape or closed-circuit television, an old person might perform regularly at high rates to hear and see them.

Expanded narrative reinforcers. Melrose's recent research suggests another possibility (32). If an aged person can comprehend expanded speech but not speech presented at a normal rate, he might be reinforced by expanded music and narrative themes, when the same themes presented at the normal rates would not be reinforcing. In seeking more adequate reinforcers for aged persons, we should explore music, movies, and video tapes expanded in both the audio and visual dimensions; for example, video tapes could be used to expand visits from family and friends.

Casual observation of music preferences of different generations supports this notion. Today's oldster, who prefers the waltz, did the turkey trot as a youth. Today's middle-ager prefers ballads and ballroom tempos, but did the Charleston or big-apple in high school and college. Today's teenage twister may also be waltzing a few decades from now. The perennial reinforcing value of the waltz to older persons may be due to their need for a slower, more expanded auditory reinforcer. Conversely, the high interest of youngsters in the chipmunk-singing, sound-effects records suggests that very young children might be more reinforced by compressed music presented at extremely high rates.

If appropriate historical or expanded reinforcers could be located for each aged individual, newer and more generally available events might even be conditioned to the idiosyncratic reinforcers—that is, the adequate but idiosyncratic reinforcers might be used to develop or restore value to the general conditioned reinforcers currently used in society. By gradual shaping and conditioning, an old person could be given a new interest in contemporary life.

Long-range personal reinforcers, such as education, development of a skill, or the building of a reputation, would have little value for an old person. Each step in the development of skill or reputation would have little conditioned reinforcement value, since it would merely be a step on a stairway which an old person could hardly hope to scale completely. He might reasonably ask, "Build a skill for what? To die tomorrow?"

A child is almost completely under the control of the immediate environment because he has not yet acquired long-range personal reinforcers. An old person may be solely at the mercy of the immediate environment, not only because of severe recent memory loss, but because long-range personal reinforcers are made impotent by brief and uncertain life expectancy. This dependence of both old people and children on immediate personal reinforcers may be why aged persons are often described as "childish."

Long-range social reinforcers which would be of value to society no matter when the older person died might be more useful with the aged. The conditioned reinforcement would be the contribution to the next generation. However, the development of this type of reinforcer would be extremely complicated, would require the participation of the members of society at large, and would still have to be conditioned to immediate personal reinforcers.

Extremely powerful, immediate personal reinforcers might be located. We should try highly compelling expanded musical and visual narrations, exciting foods, costly and beautiful clothing, and so forth. Reinforcers of this nature are costly, but they might generate such high rates of behavior in aged persons that their high dollar cost would be compensated by savings in medical care and ward management.

Geriatric reinforcement schedules

In most social situations, reinforcement occurs intermittently (14). Not all responses are immediately reinforced; only a small portion are followed by a reinforcing episode. Nevertheless, in normal individuals, responding continues at high, predictable rates which are presumably maintained by conditioned reinforcement from the occasionally reinforced responses. In our long-term experiments with psychotic children and adults, however, we have found many patients who are unable to maintain high rates of responding on intermittent schedules of reinforcement, even when adequate reinforcers are used (24). These deficits in responding for intermittent reinforcement are probably attributable to deficits in recent memory and in formation of conditioned reinforcement.

It is very possible that many geriatric patients will also prove unable to maintain high rates of responding on intermittent schedules and will have to be kept on regular reinforcement contingencies in which every response is immediately followed with a reinforcing episode. Other patients may have to be reinforced on conjugate programs in which the intensity of a continuously available reinforcer is a direct function of the response rate. Conjugate reinforcement permits the use of narrative social reinforcers and appears to go deeper into sleep, anesthesia, infancy and psychosis than does episodic reinforcement (22,25,31). Conjugate reinforcement may also go deeper into aging and generate behavior in geriatric patients who would not behave on any episodic schedule of reinforcement.

Individualized prosthetic prescriptions

If a geriatric hospital were equipped with a behavior laboratory, each aged patient could visit the laboratory upon admission. His specific behavioral deficits would be measured, and prosthetic stimuli, responses, reinforcers and reinforcement schedules prescribed. The laboratory would determine the patient's current learning ability and assess the extent to which his current behavioral repertoire could be used in place of newly acquired responses.*

In our own laboratory, we found that 90% of our involutional psychotics, 85% of our chronic psychotics, and only 65% of our retarded children had deficits in acquiring new discriminations and differentiations (6,23) †. The severe deficits in current learning ability in involutional and chronic psychotic patients were surprising, since many of these patients had large repertoires of complex behavior which they could emit at a moment's notice. Laboratory measurements proved, however, that their current learning abilities in a novel situation were extremely deficient. These patients had apparently acquired their complicated behavioral repertoires prior to developing their severe learning deficits.

---

* Barrett has recently stressed the need for individualized prosthetic prescriptions based upon laboratory behavioral measurement for use in designing and selecting different programs of instruction for retarded children (5).

† For a conclusive review of the experimental literature on learning deficits in elderly patients, see Inglis (18).

Clearly, the fact that a complicated response can be emitted appropriately is no indication that a new response of equal complexity can be acquired. Retarded children with learning deficits since birth have had no opportunity to acquire complicated repertoires. Therefore, since they never exhibit complex behaviors, casual observation of their behavior is not as misleading in predicting current learning ability as it is with psychotics or the aged. Furthermore, some involutional psychotics are very skillful at "covering up" their severe current learning deficits. In brain damaged patients, less skillful attempts at "covering up" are well known.

These data suggest that we may find severe current learning deficits more frequent among older people than in retarded individuals. These data also suggest that current learning deficits will be very difficult to ascertain by sampling current behavioral repertoires or by ward observations. Moreover, with geriatric patients we should expect general reinforcers to be less adequate because of the historical aging of appropriate reinforcers and because of the need for reinforcer expansion.

There is little doubt that each aged individual can and should have his current behavioral abilities and deficits measured in the laboratory so that an individualized prosthetic environment could be prescribed to support his particular behavioral deficits. Possibly, the patient could be assigned to a ward specializing in patients with similar, but not necessarily the same, patterns of behavioral deficits. On the other hand, we may find wards that are more efficiently designed to cover a wide range of deficits. On these vertically organized wards, the more skillful patients could act as leaders and programmers for their more deficient peers. In hospitals with a vertical ward design, patients with similar deficits could be assigned similar roles about the hospital, but on different wards.

Theories of aging

It is my opinion that theories of behavioral deviation in the grand or inclusive sense are academic luxuries unless they help us prevent or reduce the behavior pathology, or make it less debilitating. Nevertheless, there are people who insist that theories are not only useful but necessary. To validate their own position, they attribute theories to those researchers who actively state that they have none. The important points seem to be how inclusive and general theories are, how strongly they are held, and whether they are descriptive or explanatory.

The developmental theory of aging presented by Kastenbaum is an explanatory theory (20). It attempts to explain how and why aging develops as a small part of a larger general process in the behavior of man. This general developmental process is assumed to be found in both the ontogenetic development of the infant and in perception.

The same process is found reversed or in regression in the delusions of the psychotic and in the deterioration of the aged. In this sense, the inclusive property of this explanatory theory is historically related to the schools of philosophy which attempted to describe all things by the simplest possible set of laws or statements.

In contrast, I find the disengagement theory presented by Cumming more descriptive than explanatory (12). She describes the process of aging as disengagement with society and the dilemma of the aged whose behavior is no longer supported by society. In my terms, disengagement means mostly the abrupt cessation of reinforcement, or extinction.

My own approach to aging is even more finely descriptive than Cumming's disengagement theory and might be described as a descriptive multiple cause-deficit-repair theory of aging. In other words, the aged person has an accumulation of behavioral deficits in all areas, each patient with his own pattern of multiple deficits. In physiological deterioration of the aged, there is rarely a single cause of organic debility, although one specific debility may be more outstanding at a given moment in time than the others. Similarly, we may locate syndromes or patterns of specific behavioral deficits which later will be related to deterioration of specific behavioral function, and most older people have suffered so many traumas, periods of disease, abuse and poor environments, that most will have several measurable deficits in differing degrees, and each specific deficit will undoubtedly have multiple causes.

Also, as with organic illness, there undoubtedly is more than one way of treating a specific behavioral deficit. Therefore, we face not only multiple causation and multiple deficit, but multiple treatment, in both organic and behavioral medicine. In general, we now use the term *old age* whenever performance becomes less efficient without any known disruptive factor other than time and practice.

When specific geriatric behavioral deficits have been accurately measured and prosthetized, a fuller experimental analysis may permit the development of explanatory theories of specific deficit syndromes. Involved in the development of these explanatory or etiologic theories will be the experimental induction or catalysis of geriatric deficits and symptoms. I know of only one experiment of this sort which has been conducted to date. Cameron placed senile patients in dark rooms and was able to catalyze or induce senile nocturnal delirium (9). This experiment showed that senile nocturnal delirium was not due to fatigue at the end of the day as had been previously supposed, but was due to the darkness which also came at the end of the day. Further research in which the environmental variables which precipitate and control geriatric behavioral deficits are isolated will do much to produce useful explanatory sub-theories of aging.

Continuity of aging

Even though the severe deficits characteristic of aging do not show up until very late in life, the process of aging might develop much earlier. The behavioral debilities produced by this continuous process of aging may not appear because there are ample devices available for middle-aged persons to use in prosthetizing their milder behavioral deficits. For example, our recent memory may become poorer either because our ability to remember simply decreases with age or because our storage system becomes filled or overloaded. The older we become, however, the more we use prosthetic devices such as notebooks, address books, the telephone information operator and mnemonic devices. The young executive relies on his accurate recent memory, but the older and still highly productive executive relies heavily on his young secretary. It may be that it is only when he loses his secretary that he loses his "recent memory."

In other words, the age at which we see marked, severe behavioral deficits in older persons may only be the point at which appropriate prosthetic devices are no longer available. In this sense, forced retirement or "disengagement" may not only deprive a man of necessary reinforcement, but rob him of his prosthetic devices at the time they are most needed. A justification of retirement by comparing his productive efficiency before and after retirement would therefore erroneously self-validate itself unless reinforcement and prosthetic devices were equated in each condition.

Social neglect of the aged

The problem of the aged has only recently become a major one. This is not only because more people are living to an older age because of the marked success of organic medicine, but because our more urban and complicated society provides situations in which the deficits of the aged are more debilitating. The increased complexity of the behavioral tasks required of modern society members is displacing not only the less skillful aged, but also the less skillful middle-aged person.

Since our aged citizens are less able to produce in this more complicated society, they have fewer reinforcers for the rest of society and will suffer greater social neglect. They have nothing with which to reinforce social attention from either their peers or the rest of society.

Even patients with organic illnesses may have social responses with which to reinforce their attendants, nurses, physicians and family visitors. The plucky words and weak smile of the organically ill patient are extremely strong reinforcement to a nurse or visitor.

An infant has little behavior with which to acquire reinforcing objects to distribute among his family, but people are so constituted that the gurgle, smile and primitive movements of an infant are strong social reinforcers for adults. The infant also promises genetic and cultural immortality to the adults who contribute to his genetic constitution or cultural education and training. These genetic and cultural immortality factors are also strong social reinforcers.

The retarded individual, although he has little future and does not promise much genetic or cultural immortality, has much behavior which is very similar to the infant's and therefore provides society with social reinforcers to satisfy what might be called "maternal instinct." The smile or caress of a retarded child is a strong social reinforcer for those who attend him or visit him. This is probably why the retarded have always been fairly well treated by society and considered the "children of God" or the "holy innocents."

The psychotic, of course, has fared less well. And this may be because his behavior is not only less rewarding to normal adults, but in many cases is socially aversive. It is a strong attendant who can withstand the verbal onslaught of a sensitive paranoid who criticizes and verbally attacks the attendant's weakest spot. This aversive behavior of the psychotic, coupled with his inability to be a productive member of society, may be why the psychotic has been for centuries maligned, rejected, and considered "possessed by the devil." Family visits to chronic psychotics are much less frequent than visits to the mentally retarded. It is much more difficult to maintain volunteer groups to assist in the care of psychotics than it is to maintain those to care for the retarded. And again, among a group of chronic psychotics it is the laughing, joking, pleasant patient—the classic hebephrenic—who receives the most attention on the ward and is the most welcome at hospital parties and home visits.

And so with the aged, the patient with laugh wrinkles, a full head of white hair, and clean white dentures receives more attention and is more reinforcing to attendants and family than the tragic oldster with a scowl, vertical worry wrinkles, a toothless smile and skin lesions. The aged person whose countenance and behavior present aversive stimuli to other individuals is bound to be avoided and neglected. When he also has behavioral deficiencies, so that he no longer can produce in society or reinforce us with pleasant conversation, he becomes extremely aversive and subject to severe social neglect.

A realistic approach to the social neglect of the psychotic and the aged would accept the fact that they are just too aversive for us to expect highly motivated social response to them from normal middle-aged individuals. Rather than spend a great deal of time and money trying to talk people into overcoming this aversion in charitable attempts to help the psychotic and aged, it may be more economical to remove the source of aversion.

Psychotic and aged patients could be made much less aversive by cosmetic attention. Also, if prosthetic devices were developed which would permit them to communicate with normal people and produce positive, though limited, products for the use of society, they would become much more reinforcing to normal individuals and suffer much less neglect. By permanently removing the aversive causes of social neglect, this approach would be more lasting than the current attempts to reduce social neglect by repeated compensatory verbal appeals and the generation of guilt in others.

Conclusion

Since 1953, more than 100 applications of free-operant methods to human behavioral pathology have been published. Continuing, systematic investigations are being conducted in psychoses (15,21,24,28), mental retardation (6,13,33,35), neurological disorders (4), and neurosis (7,16). These experiments have demonstrated that free-operant principles and methods have wide applicability in social and behavioral research.

The method shows promise for analyzing and prosthetizing geriatric behavioral deficits. The time and money spent in developing behavioral prosthetics should be more than compensated by reduced management costs as more aged patients are made capable of caring for themselves and their peers. A properly engineered geriatric hospital, maximally utilizing the behavior of the patients, should require little more than supervisory non-geriatric labor.

At this time, no systematic applications of operant methods to geriatric behavior have been made. However, the method is ready and the hour is late. Organic medicine has shown great progress in keeping our bodies alive well past the point where behavioral medicine is able to keep our bodies behaving appropriately.

Until we can halt the process of aging, we owe our grandparents, our parents, and eventually ourselves, the right not only to live, but to behave happily and maximally. Until behavioral medicine catches up with organic medicine, terminal boredom will fall to those unfortunates who live beyond their environment.

References

1. American Psychiatric Association. Report on patients over 65 in public mental hospitals. 1959.
2. Ayllon, T. Intensive treatment of psychotic behavior by stimulus satiation and food reinforcement. To be published.

3. Ayllon, T., and Michael, J. The psychiatric nurse as a behavioral engineer. *J. Exp. Anal. Behav.*, 1959, *2*, 323-334.
4. Barrett, B. H. Reduction in rate of multiple tics by free operant conditioning methods. *J. Nerv. Ment. Dis.*, 1962, *135*, 187-195.
5. Barrett, B. H. Programmed instruction and retarded behavior. Paper read at Amer. Ass. Ment. Defic., Portland, Ore., May, 1963.
6. Barrett, B. H., and Lindsley, O. R. Deficits in acquisition of operant discrimination and differentiation shown by institutionalized retarded children. *Amer. J. Ment. Defic.*, 1962, *67*, 424-426.
7. Brady, J. P., and Lind, D. L. Experimental analysis of hysterical blindness. *Arch. Gen. Psychiat.*, 1961, *4*, 331-339.
8. Caldwell, B. McD. An evaluation of psychological effects of sex hormone administration in aged women. 2. Results of therapy after eighteen months. *J. Gerontol.*, 1954, *9*, 168-174.
9. Cameron, D. E. Studies in senile nocturnal delirium. *Psychiat. Quart.*, 1941, *15*, 47-53.
10. Cameron, D. E. Impairment of the retention phase of remembering. *Psychiat. Quart.*, 1943, *17*, 395-404.
11. Cohen, D. J. Justin and his peers: An experimental analysis of a child's social world. *Child Develpm.*, 1962, *33*, 697-717.
12. Cumming, E. Further thoughts on the theory of disengagement. In this volume.
13. Ellis, N. R., Barnett, C. D., and Pryer, M. W. Operant behavior in mental defectives: Exploratory studies. *J. Exp. Anal. Behav.*, 1960, *3*, 63-69.
14. Ferster, C. B. Reinforcement and punishment in the control of human behavior by social agencies. *Psychiat. Res. Rep.*, 1958, *10*, 101-118.
15. Ferster, C. B., and DeMyer, M. K. The development of performances in autistic children in an automatically controlled environment. *J. Chron. Dis.*, 1961, *13*, 312-345.
16. Flanagan, B., Goldiamond, I., and Azrin, N. Operant stuttering: The control of stuttering behavior through response-contingent consequences. *J. Exp. Anal. Behav.*, 1958, *1*, 173-177.
17. Garnett, R. W., and Klingman, W. O. Cytochrome C: Effects of intravenous administration on presenile, senile and arteriosclerotic cerebral states. *Amer. J. Psychiat.*, 1949, *106*, 697-702.
18. Inglis, J. Psychological investigations of cognitive deficit in elderly psychiatric patients. *Psychol. Bull.*, 1958, *54:* 197-214.
19. Inglis, J. Psychological practice in geriatric problems. *J. Ment. Sci.*, 1962, *108*, 669-674.
20. Kastenbaum, R. Is old age the end of development? In this volume.
21. Lindsley, O. R. Operant conditioning methods applied to research in chronic schizophrenia. *Psychiat. Res. Rep.*, 1956, *5*, 118-139.
22. Lindsley, O. R. Operant behavior during sleep: A measure of depth of sleep. *Science*, 1957, *126*, 1290-1291.
23. Lindsley, O. R. Analysis of operant discrimination and differentiation in chronic psychotics. Paper read at Eastern Psychol. Assoc., Atlantic City, April, 1958.

24. Lindsley, O. R. Characteristics of the behavior of chronic psychotics as revealed by free-operant conditioning methods. *Dis. Nerv. Sys.*, Monogr. Suppl., 1960, *21*, 66-78.

25. Lindsley, O. R. Conjugate reinforcement. Paper read at Amer. Psychol. Assoc., New York, September, 1961.

26. Lindsley, O. R. Experimental analysis of cooperation and competition. Paper read at Eastern Psychol. Assoc., Philadelphia, April, 1961.

27. Lindsley, O. R. Direct behavioral analysis of psychotherapy sessions by conjugately programed closed-circuit television. Paper read at Amer. Psychol. Assoc., St. Louis, September, 1962.

28. Lindsley, O. R. Operant conditioning methods in diagnosis. In J. H. Nodine and J. H. Moyer (eds.), *Psychosomatic Medicine: The First Hahnemann Symposium*. Philadelphia: Lea & Febiger, 1962, 41-54.

29. Lindsley, O. R. Direct measurement and prosthesis of retarded behavior. Paper read at Boston University, Dept. of Spec. Educ., March, 1963.

30. Lindsley, O. R. Free-operant conditioning and psychotherapy. In J. H. Masserman (ed.), *Current Psychiatric Therapies*, Vol III. New York: Grune & Stratton, 1963, 47-56.

31. Lindsley, O. R., Hobika, J. H., and Etsten, B. E. Operant behavior during anesthesia recovery: A continuous and objective method. *Anesthesiology*, 1961, *22*, 937-946.

32. Melrose, J. Research in the hearing of the aged. Paper read at Natl. Ass. Music Ther., Cambridge, Mass., October, 1962.

33. Orlando, R., and Bijou, S. W. Single and multiple schedules of reinforcement in developmentally retarded children. *J. Exp. Anal. Behav.*, 1960, *3*, 339-348.

34. Rachman, S. Learning theory and child psychology: Therapeutic possibilities. *J. Child Psychol. Psychiat.*, 1962, *3*, 149-163.

35. Spradlin, J. E. Effects of reinforcement schedules on extinction in severely mentally retarded children. *Amer. J. Ment. Defic.*, 1962, *66*, 634-640.

Is old age the end of development?

4

Robert Kastenbaum

Explicit, systematic theoretical orientations toward the later years of life—where are they? Such established schools of thought as psychoanalysis, learning theory, and developmental theory have had relatively little to say concerning the phenomena of aging, and only one new approach, disengagement theory, has come forth as a fairly broad and coherent framework (4). The social sciences cannot be said to have contributed much in the way of theoretical guide-posts to the ever-accelerating and complex field of geriatrics. Conversely, the later years of life could disappear without requiring major changes in most theoretical positions.

This chapter will not try to explain the social sciences' apparent indifference to theories of aging. Rather, an attempt will be made to explore the potential of one orientation—developmental theory—for contributing to an improved understanding of later life. We have raised the question: Is old age the end of development? This central issue provides an opportunity to examine some basic features of developmental theory in its potential application to later life while maintaining a necessarily limited scope of discussion.

The developmental point of view

The concept of development is broader than any single field of inquiry. In a volume dealing with developmental approaches to human behavior, Harris compiled contributions from biology, genetics, psychology, philosophy, anthropology, history, education and social work (8). To this list could be added the physical sciences and the arts (notably music). The developmental approach is a mode of thinking that concerns itself with the principles and processes by which one event unfolds from another. This general mode of thinking can be applied to any subject matter, but appears to be of particular significance to the life sciences.

This paper is based upon a presentation at the Second Annual Symposium on Old Age, Cushing Hospital, Framingham, Mass., May 21, 1963.

As Nagel observes, in many of its current uses the term "development" conveys ". . . the suggestion that developmental processes make
progressively manifest something latent or hidden, a suggestion that is
reinforced if we recall the original meaning of the word as connoting
an unfolding or unwrapping. We still speak of the development of
a fertilized egg, or of the development of a human personality, understanding in each case a sequence of continuous changes eventuating in
some outcome, however vaguely specified, which is somehow potentially
present in the earlier stages of the process." (29, p. 15).

In psychology, the terms "developmental" and "child" are sometimes
used as virtual synonyms. This usage reflects the significance of the
earlier years of life for existing theoretical positions and practical concerns, implying that psychological development either terminates after
childhood or becomes of little interest. More in keeping with the
general concept of development is the orientation of writers such as
Pressey and Kuhlen who were among the first to present an overview
of human development throughout the entire life span (21).

The term "developmental theory," however, presupposes an explicit,
systematic attempt to comprehend a large range of human behavior
within a carefully-organized logical framework. The developmental
viewpoint is an important aspect of the psychoanalytic tradition, well
represented currently by Erikson (5). "Pure" developmental theory
has perhaps its most significant spokesmen in Piaget and Werner (20,
27), some of whose ideas were prefigured by Jackson, Smuts, and Goldstein (9,23,7). For the present purposes we take the developmental
psychology of Heinz Werner as our starting point.

Werner postulates ". . . one regulative principle of development; it is
an orthogenetic principle which states that wherever development
occurs it proceeds from a state of relative globability and lack of differentiation to a state of increasing differentiation, articulation, and
hierarchic integration. This principle has the status of an heuristic
definition. Though itself not subject to empirical test, it is valuable
to developmental psychologists in leading to a determination of the
actual range of applicability of developmental concepts to the behavior
of organisms." (29).

The orthogenetic principle has demonstrated its relevance in numerous studies of perception. It is often said that "seeing is believing,"
and there is the tendency to believe that "seeing" is a simple photographic process of registering what is "really there." However, experimental examination of the act of seeing indicates that it consists of an
active process which must pass through several stages before the final
perception is created (25,27). The first stage of perception is global:
the situation is interpreted in terms of its "whole-qualities." The
second stage is analytic—a selective discrimination or differentiation of

parts. Finally, there is the synthetic stage; here, an integrated perception is created in which the parts are seen in relation to the whole.

Concerned primarily with the formal characteristics rather than the content of behavior, developmental psychology is applicable to cognitive, motoric, and affective-motivational aspects of organismic functioning as well as the perceptual. Adults in so-called primitive societies, and children and schizophrenic adults in our own society, can all be compared with respect to the same formal characteristics of thought, employing theoretical approaches that derive from the orthogenetic principle. An authoritative explication of developmental theory and a survey of many of its applications is available in Werner's classic *Comparative Psychology of Mental Development* (28).

One of the most imaginative features of developmental theory is the parallel between ontogenesis and microgenesis. This guiding hypothesis states, in essence, that the same developmental sequence occurs whether we are considering the formation of psychological structures over a period of years (as, for example, from infancy to adolescence), or over a period of hours, minutes, or milliseconds (as, for example, in making a rapid perceptual and sensorimotor adjustment upon entering a dimly-lit room). This powerful notion provides the opportunity to capture a wide range of phenomena within the confines of a relatively few theoretical constructs.

Another key concept is that of developmental regression. A psychological structure can crumple back into itself, repeating in reverse order the stages it had previously traversed. To cite a well-known example, Barker, Dembo, and Wright (1) placed a transparent screen between a young child at play and a set of desirable objects. This experimentally-induced frustration had the effect of "regressing" the quality of the child's play to a genetically lower stage, as evaluated on a "constructiveness" scale.

Several general types of condition are thought to favor the reversal of psychological development whether at the level of ontogenesis or microgenesis. It has been hypothesized that certain kinds of pathology are characterized by a developmental regression, and schizophrenia may be cited as a prime example (24). Certain drugs may induce transient states of regression, and here LSD has been among the most effective agents studied (18). Finally, there is the notion that the developmental process reverses itself in the later years of life (23).

This quick tour has completely neglected a number of important aspects of developmental psychology, but perhaps enough has been said to prepare the way for a discussion of the main question.

Four answers

From a logical standpoint there are at least four possible answers to the question: Is old age the end of development?

1. It is possible that development terminates at a certain point, but life goes on.

2. It is possible that development continues, and that there is no such phase as "old age."

3. It is possible that development continues through the phase known as "old age."

4. It is possible that development continues, but may or may not reach "old age," and may or may not be "development" when it does.

The first view implies a process that surges along until it has achieved its psychological purpose, and then stops. That this process ends rather early in life is suggested by several bodies of psychological research, notably studies which indicate that intellectual development, as measured by conventional tests of mental ability, reaches its peak in late adolescence or very soon thereafter, and then declines (11,12).

The period of life that is left over could be interpreted in various ways and, in fact, might be designated as either "maturity" or "old age." The "left-over life" could be regarded as years of maturity because the individual is in possession of his fully-developed resources, or as old age because these resources are on the decline and the basic psychobiological purposes have already run their course. (Admittedly, it does not seem quite appropriate to apply the term "old age" to that period of life which begins about the time one graduates from college.)

It is possible to use both terms meaningfully—"maturity" and "old age"—without compromising the viewpoint under consideration. Development ends, and a period of relative stability ensues during which time the individual has at his disposal the fruits of the developmental process. To account for subsequent changes while denying the continuation of a developmental process, we might introduce a conception of old age that emphasizes the aspect of enfeeblement, that of being "worn down" and "worn out." This view is an alternative both to denying the existence of "old age" as a genuine phenomenon, and to interpreting "old age" as a qualitatively different stage.

If this alternative is accepted, then it could be said that the end of development is *maturity,* and that "old age" is primarily a quantitative weakening of the psychological resources enjoyed in the prime of life.

This viewpoint, however, runs into some difficulties. The facts which seem to support the early termination of psychological development are based upon measures that have no clear relationship to the developmental process. Many test scores reveal little about *how* the person operates, about the developmental processes involved in what comes forth as the scorable response. It is evident by now that the same score can be achieved by qualitatively different processes, and that the developmental level at which the individual is functioning and the "accuracy" or "success" of his performance are not necessarily identical. Furthermore, the main line of psychological measurement has tended to ignore some of the most important features of human functioning because these are difficult to conceptualize and reduce to simple measurements. The experimental spirit has grown more adventuresome in recent years, as witness the revival of interest in high level cognitive processes. Until the full range of psychological processes has been investigated by appropriate methods over the total life span, it does not seem proper to conclude that development terminates in late adolescence or any other particular point.

Moreover, if development terminated at an earlier period, it would be very difficult to account for the microgenetic process in later life. It is not easy to have done with development when we recall that the same basic principles apply to the continuous formation of perceptions, thoughts, and actions as apply to psychological development over the span of years.

If it is granted, for example, that an octogenarian does perceive, then we must either grant that the microgenetic process of development continues, or that he creates his perceptions in some rather exotic way. When entering a dimly-lit room an octogenarian must instantly form his perception without going through the preliminary stages, because these stages involve a developmental process whose existence has been denied. This phenomenon would be remarkable; it would also be at variance with the plethora of investigations which have indicated that, with increasing adult age, there is a gradual slowing of sensory and cognitive processes, not the quickening implied by an hypothesis that the developmental process is by-passed in later life (26).

To sharpen this point, it will be suggested here that the process of development in the microgenetic sense is most easily observed when the individual is confronting a novel or unstructured situation—here, the process is likely to require more time and give more evident signs of its activity. We would then have to expect that in those situations which are particularly novel and challenging, the aged person instantly attains a perception, a thought, an integrated action which the younger person, supposedly in the prime of his functioning, could attain only after laboring through several preliminary stages. This phenomenon seems unlikely, but would afford an interesting avenue of research. The best assumption at present is that the microgenetic process of development does continue through the later years of life.

The second alternative is that development continues, and that there is no such thing as "old age." In favor of this viewpoint it could be said that "old age" is really just a phrase, not a phase. It is a cultural invention that need not coerce the scientist. Even the definition of the term is quite difficult unless one settles for an administrative expedient. The "old man" in a bomber crew or an athletic team may be 35 years of age, suggesting that this term refers primarily to a certain role in the social structure rather than to a psychobiological entity.

Vimala Sarma recently conducted what was perhaps the first comparative study of the life adjustment of young and old adults in India— and membership in the gerontological group began at age 40.* Examples could be multiplied to suggest that the term "old age" has been applied with such diverse criteria in mind that it has little meaning for the developmental psychologist.

From this viewpoint then, the various notions that have been denoted loosely by the phrase "old age" would be of great interest to the student of social attitudes and dynamics, but not particularly relevant for understanding the course of human development. Accordingly, the student of human behavior would proceed to study what he anticipates to be the lifelong course of development without assuming that he is dealing with a fundamentally different condition when he works with people who have reached the retirement age, or some other arbitrary station.

The third alternative is that "old age" does refer to something that is real, and that this "something" is fully a part of the total developmental schemata. It could be argued that the fuzzy, unsatisfactory use of this term which currently prevails should not be permitted to obscure the underlying reality of old age as a distinct developmental stage. Of course people change as they grow older, and this change can be understood as part of the developmental process when we have sufficiently advanced our general understanding of psychological development.

But the psychologist who affirms continued development throughout the life span, with or without "old age," must accept the challenge of specifying what are, in fact, the new psychological structures that come forth during the later years of life—a challenge that has had few "takers" so far. Another possibility for demonstrating the continuity of development is available in the phenomena of "developmental regression" previously mentioned. Three recent experiments conducted by Werner and his colleagues indicate that in later life there is a perceptual regression characterized by processes of "de-differentiation and de-hierarchization," i.e., the aged person has lost some of the higher-level functions that had gradually emerged during the course of development (2,3,25).

Sooner or later it should be decided whether the term "development" is best limited to the forward-going process that eventuates in new, higher-order psychological structures, or whether the suggested process of reversal should also be interpreted as a kind of development. If it is decided that two processes moving in opposite directions cannot meaningfully be considered the same process, then it will have been decided that development does end before "old age," and that it is

---

* Private communication.

replaced by a new process; something is going on, then, but it is not development.

The fourth alternative states that development continues, but may or may not reach old age, and may or may not be "development" when it does. There are two distinct approaches in terms of which both development and old age might be "real" and yet not necessarily make contact with each other.

One approach would fasten upon the observation that much of what is denoted by "old age" is of an undesirable nature: loss of short-term memory and other cognitive malfunctions, repetitiousness and other handicaps in social interaction, a decline in physical vigor and well-being, and so forth. These changes could be interpreted as demonstrating that what is called "old age" is a disease. If old age is essentially a disagreeable state, really a disease syndrome, then it will be the case that some people die of other causes before they have the opportunity to sicken and die of old age. It will also be the case that some people live to an advanced age in apparent immunity to this disease, as others are to mumps. This viewpoint accords with the common observation that certain people appear psychobiologically young although old in years, while others seem to have caught this disease of old age rather early in life.

Growing old, then, would be a sort of accident, a disease that afflicts some and not others. Those persons not so afflicted will either continue to develop, or will reach a plateau in which life holds its own, but does not advance. One implication of this viewpoint is that the phenomena of "old age" need not be tolerated as inevitable accompaniments of the later years of life but, rather, can be attacked as one would attack any disease that is composed of complex psychological and organic elements.

The second sense in which development and old age might miss contact is what Jung seemed to have in mind when he stated that: "Being old is highly unpopular. Nobody seems to consider that not being *able* to grow old is precisely as absurd as not being able to outgrow child-sized shoes. A still infantile man of thirty is surely to be deplored, but a youthful septuagenarian—isn't that delightful? And yet *both* are perverse, lacking in style, psychological monstrosities" (10).

On this view, becoming old is a function of a progressive maturation, a sort of intrinsic achievement. The person who settles down permanently at what should have been one of the way stations of human development has settled for less than what is potential within him. Our society may encourage huddling around the earlier stations of maturation in its worship of youthfulness (or dread of age) but, in that event, it is the entire society that is immature, propagating and tending "psychological monstrosities." From this approach then, some people never become old for the same reason that some people never grow out of adolescence, or even childhood.

Thus, from opposite viewpoints a person might not develop "old age:" he might not develop it in the sense that one has had the good fortune not to have contracted a disease: or he might not develop it in the sense that one has placed himself in a sort of suspended animation, frozen in a relatively immature posture.

The end of development

It is suggested here that old age *is* the end of development.

Old age is the end of development because one of the major outcomes of this process is the development of individuality. The global infant adjusts to the world first on a sensorimotor level, then on a perceptual level which gains dominance over the previous style of functioning, and then again on a symbolic level which masters the preceding levels, although these remain active in subordinate roles.

The symbolic level of activity can be illustrated by one of its most significant aspects, "time perspective"—that symbolic activity by which the individual organizes his life experience with respect to temporal dimensions. Time perspective has a developmental career of its own (13,17). To condense the first fifteen or so years of this career into one generalization: in a society such as ours the "normal" adolescent will have come into possession of all or virtually all the symbolic processes that are necessary for the formation of a genuine time perspective— the elements, the ingredients, all seem to be there. In this respect, the development of time perspective parallels what has been reported about intellectual development: it builds up to some point late in adolescence, and then comes to a halt. One might thus infer that psychological development terminates long before "old age," but there is more to the story.

After one has all the formal elements on hand, there remains the task of shaping them into a genuine perspective, and there remains the possibility of transforming this initial perspective again and again, each time making one's self into a somewhat different person. The first perspective that is formed provides the framework for a consistent individuality. The adolescent or young adult who has created a time perspective has thus helped to define himself as an individual with a distinctive style of life, in contrast to the loose confederation of partial selves that characterized his long process of differentiation. Once in effect, the time perspective—a form of "hierarchic integration"—plays a significant role in determining the course of the individual's life.

It seems probable, for example, that patterns of time perspective have differential implications for longevity (14). To select a fairly obvious illustration, people who do not weld their diverse psychological operations into a cohesive framework should be less likely to survive in a society as complex as ours. Such individuals will often present a clinical picture of impulsivity, and Slater has recently found that impulsive persons do not live as long as non-impulsive persons who were closely matched with them on a number of characteristics (22). On a related topic, certain kinds of time perspective permit the individual to encompass the meaning of death into his total understanding of life or, at least, provide him with the basic equipment for arriving at such an understanding as he approaches the end of his life. During that ill-defined period known as the dying process it seems possible for some individuals to transform their perspective so as to create an integration of life experiences that could be achieved at no other time, while for many people it appears that death never truly becomes a part of life (6).

Of most direct relevance is the consideration that the extent and type of subsequent psychological development is highly structured by the kind of integration that is created fairly early in life, probably around late adolescence and the next few years. This integration will weigh heavily in determining whether or not there is to be further development, moreover, whether any subsequent development will be in the reverse or forward direction and, if forward, in what particular pathway.

It is crucial to add that it is not just the means of living but the ends or goals that are formed and transformed by the developmental process, by the kind of hierarchic integration or by the time perspective one has created. One will either have written a psychological script that deletes "old age," has no use for it, or will have constructed a framework for life that requires the unique experiences and vantage of old age for psychological completion. A set of investigations by the writer indicates that some aged people are caught in an identity crisis partially engendered by the limitations of their previous time perspective, and that others "consider that they have lived out their life plan, and thus exist on a sort of 'surplus time' that is not part of the . . . lifelong system of values." (15,16). Many adolescents and young adults appear to be preparing themselves poorly for the prospect of developing further in later life, if one takes as evidence their present, limited time perspectives (12,17). Yet one knows from the biographies of many creative people and from personal observation that significant, positive psychological developments can continue through advanced "old age." "Wisdom" in old age—when it occurs—seems to refer to a special kind of perspective on life that develops within a personality that leaves "growing places" for itself earlier in life.

Thus, for some people old age is the end of development in the sense that development has terminated, is all over with, is not part of the individual life-plan—and for other people old age is the end of development in the Aristotelian sense: the end is that goal or final state toward which the entire process has been directed.

References

1. Barker, R., Dembo, T., and Lewin, K. Frustration and regression: A study of young children. *University of Iowa Studies in Child Welfare,* 1941, *18,* 1.
2. Comalli, P. E., Wapner, S., and Werner, H. Perception of verticality in middle and old age. *J. Psychol.,* 1959, *47,* 259-266.
3. Comalli, P. E., Wapner, S., and Werner, H. Interference effects of Stroop color-word test in childhood, adulthood, and aging. *J. Genet. Psychol.,* 1962, *100,* 47-53.
4. Cumming, E., and Henry, W. E. *Growing Old.* New York: Basic Books, 1961.
5. Erikson, E. H. *Identity and the Life Cycle: Selected Papers.* New York: International Universities Press, 1959.
6. Feifel, H. (ed.). *The Meaning of Death.* New York: McGraw-Hill, 1959.
7. Goldstein, K. *The Organism.* New York: American Book, 1939.
8. Harris, D. B., (ed.). *The Concept of Development.* Minneapolis: University of Minnesota Press, 1957.
9. Jackson, J. H. *Selected Writings* (J. Taylor, ed.). London: Hodder and Stoughton, 1931.
10. Jung, C. G. The soul and death. In H. Feifel (ed.), *The Meaning of Death.* New York: McGraw-Hill, 1959, 3-15.
11. Jones, H. E., and Conrad, H. S. The growth and decline of intelligence. In R. G. Kuhlen and G. G. Thompson (ed.), *Psychological Studies of Human Development.* New York: Appleton-Century-Crofts, 1963, 320-328.
12. Kastenbaum, R. Time and death in adolescence. In H. Feifel (ed.), *The Meaning of Death.* New York: McGraw-Hill, 1959, 99-113.
13. Kastenbaum, R. The dimensions of future time perspective, an experimental analysis. *J. Gen. Psychol.,* 1961, *65,* 203-218.
14. Kastenbaum, R. Life patterns and longevity. In this volume.
15. Kastenbaum, R. Deterioration as a consequence of symptom removal. Paper presented at Sixth International Congress of Gerontology, Copenhagen, August 16, 1963.
16. Kastenbaum, R. Cognitive and personal futurity in later life. *J. Indiv. Psychol.,* 1963, *19,* 216-222.
17. Kastenbaum, R., and Durkee, N. Young people view old age. In this volume.
18. Krus, D. M., and Wapner, S. Effect of lysergic acid diethylamide (LSD-25) on perception of part-whole relationships. *J. Psychol.,* 1959, *48,* 87-95.
19. Nagel, E. Determinism and development. In D. B. Harris (ed.), *The Concept of Development.* Minneapolis: University of Minnesota Press, 1957.
20. Piaget, J. *The Psychology of Intelligence.* New York: Littlefield, 1960.
21. Pressey, S. L., and Kuhlen, R. G. *Psychological Development Through the Life Span.* New York: Harper, 1957.

22. Slater, P. E., and Scarr, H. A. The structure of personality in old age. *Genet. Psychol. Monogr.* In press.
23. Smuts, J. C. *Holism and Evolution.* New York: Viking, 1960.
24. Wapner, S., and Krus, D. M. Effects of lysergic acid diethylamide, and differences between normals and schizophrenics on the Stroop color-word test. *J. Neuropsychiat.*, 1960, *2*, 76-81.
25. Wapner, S., Werner, H., and Comalli, P. E. Perception of part-whole relations in middle and old age. *J. Geront.*, 1960, *15*, 412-416.
26. Welford, A. T. Psychomotor performance. In J. E. Birren (ed.), *Handbook of Aging and the Individual.* Chicago: University of Chicago Press, 1960, 562-613.
27. Werner, H., and Wapner, S. *Perceptual Development.* Worcester: Clark University Press, 1957.
28. Werner, H. *Comparative Psychology of Mental Development* (rev. ed.). New York: International Universities Press, 1957.
29. Werner, H. The concept of development from a comparative and organismic point of view. In D. B. Harris (ed.), *The Concept of Development.* Minneapolis: University of Minnesota Press, 1957.

SOME CHARACTERISTICS OF
LONG-LIVED PEOPLE

It has often been said that the best way to attain longevity is to be prudent in one's choice of parents. There is less agreement concerning the course one is likely to follow in the later years—deterioration, improvement, or an essentially unchanged continuation of earlier life patterns. Hopefully, we can expect to learn much more about the conditions favoring longevity and the psychosocial correlates of advanced age as sophisticated multidisciplinary research focusses on these problems.

The chapters included in this section report findings and viewpoints derived from contact with four different populations of elderly individuals: independent veterans of the Spanish-American War; men and women hospitalized for a variety of physical, psychological, and social reasons; persons diagnosed as suffering from chronic psychosis; and elderly psychologists. The avenues of investigation explored here eventually should contribute much to an improved understanding of the psychosocial factors involved in longevity. The present studies already suggest that our ideas about longevity may be in for a good deal of revision, certainly for an increase in complexity. It would seem that clear, specific hypotheses and a readiness to examine diverse sets of phenomena are more to be valued than the utterance of premature generalizations. Perhaps the story of human longevity does not begin and end with the selection of one's parents.

Social correlates
of longevity

5

Charles L. Rose

Improved medical and public health practice in this country has produced a new population group—the octogenarians (4,13). While this ever-expanding group of older persons poses new medical and social problems for society, it also provides an unique opportunity for the study of life history characteristics which may be related to longevity (1).

In 1958 the Veterans Administration Outpatient Clinic in Boston set up a research-oriented geriatric clinic for the health maintenance of veterans of the Spanish-American War. To this end, the Clinic has worked intensively, both medically and socially, with over 200 of these veterans. An opportunity was thus provided for collecting medical, social and psychological data on relatively healthy octogenarians.

In this paper, selected social and behavioral variables and their interrelationships will be assessed in 149 subjects with respect to their relevance for longevity. Findings and characteristics which seem relevant to the attainment of advanced age can generate hypotheses which may then be tested by study of subjects who vary in life span. These hypotheses, in fact, are being built into a longitudinal study of aging which was undertaken as a logical sequel to the octogenarian study.

The data were drawn from surviving octogenarian veterans only, with no control group of shorter-lived veterans of the Spanish-American War. In an effort to correct this deficiency, the sample was investigated for the presence of an internal control group of shorter-lived individuals. Those who had died from 1959 to 1962 were scrutinized. Their age at death was compared to the age of the surviving part of the sample, with the expectation that the survivors might be younger.

This report is one of a series based upon work supported by the Normative Aging Study of the Boston Outpatient Clinic, Veterans Administration, Benjamin Bell, M.D., Director. The author wishes to acknowledge Theodore Karam, chief social worker of the V.A. Clinic, for his stimulation of research into social aspects of aging. Earlier versions of this paper were presented at the Annual Scientific Meeting of the Boston Society for Gerontological Psychiatry (May 14, 1963), and the Sixth International Congress on Gerontology (Copenhagen, August 11-16, 1963).

This was done by comparing the two groups by year of birth. Surprisingly, although a greater percentage of the deceased was younger, the difference was not large enough to be statistically significant (Table 1). The deceased group, therefore, could not be used as a control group. It is generally expected that older people die before younger people, and the tendency for a reversal with this group suggestes the possibility that the older octogenarians were more durable.

The data were culled from existing records which did not contain complete information on all cases. The N therefore varies and is specified in Table 1. The use of existing records also limited the number and kind of questions that could be put to the data.

Since the data were recorded in categorical form, the chi square test was used. Variables were dichotomized whenever possible at or close to the mean, and 2 × 2 tables were run. Where the distributions did not favor dichotomization, or where finer categorization was desirable,

Table 1. Relationships of selected variables

	N	χ^2	P
Young age & 3 year survival	149	N.S.	
Fathers' & mothers' longevity	123	16.919	< .001
Intelligence & education	95	7.726	< .01
Intelligence & non-manual occupation	95	7.833	< .01
Education & non-manual occupation	149	10.449	< .005
Current income & education	106	N.S.	
Current income & non-manual occupation	105	4.86	< .05
Remarriage & with spouse status	136	5.889	< .02
Remarriage & early first marriage	117	4.437	< .05
Employment beyond 70 & current income	107	N.S.	
Employment beyond 70 & education	91	N.S.	
Employment beyond 70 & non-manual occupation	112	N.S.	
Employment beyond 70 & years in major occupation	100	4.027	< .05

multiple chi squares were run on 2 × 3, 3 × 3, and 2 × 4 tables. Relationships were considered significant at the .05 level of confidence. Statements of relationship which appear in this paper are summarized in Table 1.

Descriptive data

Age. As of 1959, the time of the interviews, the average age of the group was 82. The age range was from 72 to 92, with 57% of the cases concentrated in the modal interval of 80-84 years of age. At the time of the Spanish-American War, these men were on the average 21 years of age. By 1962 the average age had risen to 85, with 76% of the group surviving. The average of all survivors of the Spanish-American War as of 1962 was a little under 84. (As of 1960, about 35,000, or 9% of the original 392,000 volunteers of the War of 1898 survived. Of this number, about 1,000 resided in Massachusetts. As of 1962, the number had dwindled to 28,000 or 7% of the original group.)

General background factors
predisposing to longevity

1. *Nativity.* The group was predominantly New England born, and of Irish and English extraction. Because they were born roughly 35 years before the large-scale immigrations of the first and second decades of the twentieth century, the large majority, 73%, were United States born, and an additional 8% were born in Canada. Of the United States born, four-fifths were born in New England. Of those born abroad, 30% were from Ireland, 20% from England and Scotland, and 15% from the Scandinavian countries.

The composition of the sample as largely native should predispose the group to be long-lived, because of the known greater mortality of the foreign born (13). Also, most of the foreign born came from English-speaking and Scandinavian countries which had the lowest mortality rates among foreign countries (27,39). The predominantly New England nativity of the group is also consistent with its longevity, since the technologically developed northeastern states are above the average of the country as a whole with respect to longevity (13).

It is also useful to note the nativity of the subjects' forebears. Fifty-five per cent of the parents were born in the New World. Of the United States born parents, two-thirds were born in New England, and of the United States born grandparents, 80% were born in New England. With reference to Old World forebears, 40% of foreign parents were born in Ireland and 27% were born in England and Scotland, while 43% of foreign-born grandparents came from Ireland and 31% from England and Scotland. The predominant nativity of parents from English-speaking countries should also add to predisposition for longevity.

2. *Clinic attendance.* The sample was drawn from those who attended a geriatric clinic and particularly from those who attended more frequently and were therefore better known. In order to attend a clinic, a patient had to be ambulatory. Clinic attendance, therefore, tended to select out the healthier. It may be conjectured that those who were motivated to attend clinic regularly were also those who had favorable health attitudes, had an unusual desire to maintain their health, and were capable of utilizing available resources for this purpose. Clinic attendance then consummated this interest by actually maintaining health through the clinic's comprehensive medical services, which was augmented by an intensive clinic program of social casework and group therapy (29).

Longevity of parents, siblings, spouse and children

The literature contains a great deal of evidence concerning the close relationship between longevity of parents and offspring (30). The transmissibility of longevity in our sample was investigated by a study of age-at-death of parents. It is difficult to separate out the genetic effect from the effect of a more favorable environment created by long-lived parents. For example, where parents live longer, children have a more favored and protected life. The following material is, therefore, to be evaluated with this consideration in mind. It might also be kept in mind that genetic effects are inextricably combined with a wide range of environmental effects, of which the fostering effect of parental care is only one example. On the other hand, under possible future conditions of optimal social welfare, the differential effects of environment will tend to be neutralized, and the genetic effects will more clearly emerge.

1. *Parents.* Fathers' average age at death was 70, and the corresponding figure for the mother was 72 (Table 2). Although the subjects were alive at an age 12-13 years older than age-at-death of their parents, the longevity of the parents is still remarkable since it substantially exceeded the longevity of their generation. For 1900-01, the earliest years for which life tables are available, the expected longevity at birth was 48 years. Our subjects' parents were born some 40 years earlier when life expectancy was even lower (40). The more favorable longevity of the mothers is particularly noteworthy, suggesting unusually good maternal health. This is consistent with Swedish and Finnish genealogic findings where the life span of offspring was found to be more influenced by maternal than paternal longevity (18). In a seven-generation family study, Alexander Graham Bell also found a relationship between longevity of parent and offspring, but the relationship was stronger when the longevous parent was the father. Bell's

work, however, was based on far less extensive data than the Scandinavian studies (3).

Another interesting background factor in the subject's longevity was the pairing of longer-lived fathers with longer-lived mothers. This patterning of parental longevity has the net effect of lengthening the time the parents were alive together which, in turn, could have a favorable effect on the well-being and longevity of offspring. From the genetic point of view, the pairing of longer-lived fathers and mothers would augment the hereditary transmission of longevity of the offspring.

2. *Siblings.* The subjects, as we have already learned, tended to be among the older of the siblings. The subjects' siblings were therefore younger as a group. Nevertheless, as of the time of the interview, when the subjects were on the average 82 years of age, only 17% of the siblings were still alive. Their mediocre longevity is also shown by the fact that 50% died before reaching age 65. In fact, 17% died before reaching age 6. As a group, then, the siblings did not share the longevity characteristics of the subjects. One might raise the question whether this finding is at variance with the notion that *as a group* children of long-lived parents are also long-lived.

3. *Spouse and children.* As of the time of the interview, 21% of the subjects' children (excluding stillborn, step and adopted children) had died. Twelve per cent died before reaching age 6. Median age-at-death of first wife was 65, substantially less than that of subjects' mothers (age 72). The difference is made more significant by the fact that the mothers were of an earlier and less long-lived generation (13).

Table 2. Parents' age at death

Age at death	Fathers (134)		Mothers (128)	
	No.	%	No.	%
Under 40	8	6	11	9
40 - 49	17	13	12	9
50 - 59	18	13	14	11
60 - 69	23	17	19	15
70 - 79	33	25	36	28
80 & over	35	26	36	28

Siblings and sibling order

The subjects came from fairly large families. More than one-half of the families, 54%, had at least 6 children. Three per cent of the subjects were only children; 30% of the families had 8 or more children.

A large number of subjects were senior in birth order: 44% were in first or second position. The significance of this, however, cannot be appraised without considering the total number of siblings. The question was therefore posed as to whether the subjects were among older or younger siblings. This was determined by cross-tabulating birth order with number of siblings (Table 3), and separating the subjects in the older half of the sibship from those in the younger half (Table 4).

Eighty of the subjects were in the older half of the sibship and 60 were in the younger half. The difference, however, was not significant at the .05 level ($X^2 = 2.86$). In the larger families, however, (6 siblings or more), there were significantly more subjects in the older half of the sibship: 52 in the older half and only 26 in the younger half ($X^2 = 8.7$, $p < .01$). The finding here is that the octogenarians tended to be among the older children if there were 6 or more siblings. A relationship between longevity and senior sibling order was also found by Bell (3).

Table 3. Birth order of subject by number of siblings

No. of siblings	Birth order									
	1st	2nd	3rd	4th	5th	6th	7th	8th	9th	>9th
1	4									
2	4	4								
3	8	6	9							
4	5	1	4	8						
5	2	4	2	1	4					
6	3	4	4	3	3	0				
7	4	4	3	2	1	2	1			
8	3	4	3	3	1	0	3	0		
9	0	0	0	2	2	2	0	0	1	
>9	3	1	4	2	3	0	2	1	2	2
	36	28	29	21	14	4	6	1	3	2

A relationship between longevity and senior birth order in a large family may be interpreted on the basis that older siblings have an advantaged "pecking order" in a large family: the older siblings are bigger and stronger than the younger ones and in the competitive situation of a large sibship are in a better position to get more food and other physical advantages. Also, older siblings in larger families have more responsibility earlier; they therefore mature faster emotionally and receive better training in adaptive skills. In general, older siblings have the advantage of younger age and greater health of parents, and of favored status over younger siblings.

A genetic interpretation of this finding would use the following argument: older siblings are born when the mother is at a younger age. There is some evidence from studies of neonatal mortality and genealogy that maternal age at birth influences longevity of offspring

Table 4. Position of subject in older or younger half of sibship* by number of siblings (derived from Table 3)

No. of siblings		Position in sibship	
		Older half (80)	Younger half (60)
2		4	4
3	Smaller families**	11	12
4		6	12
5		7	6
		28	34
6		11	6
7	Larger families	12	5
8		13	4
9		3	4
>9		13	7
		52	26

*Cases in middle position (in families with odd number of siblings) were evenly divided between the upper and lower halves.

**The four "one sibling" cases (where subject was only child) are excluded, since they do not fit into an older half-younger half scheme.

(19,48). Therefore, the older sibling lives longer because his mother is younger when she gives birth to him. (This relationship between maternal age and longevity of offspring was, however, not confirmed in a study of mice (36).

Education, occupational status and intelligence

Fifty-five per cent of the subjects did not enter high school; 28% had some high school, while 17% completed 12 grades or more. This distribution is higher than that of the general population during the last quarter of the 19th century when our subjects were of school age. According to the 1889-90 census, 3.5% of the population were high school graduates, considerably below our subjects, 17% of whom were high school graduates (45).

According to the 1950 census, the average schooling of the population in the 70 to 74 year old group was 8 years, which corresponds to our subjects' educational attainment. The difference between the 1890 and 1950 figures suggests that, in the general population, the *more educated* survived into advanced years. Our subjects, interestingly, are similar in education to all others of this age group in the population, which is a point in favor of generalizing from the present finding (44).

The I.Q. (Wechsler Adult Intelligence Scale) was available on 95 subjects (10,47). Those of higher I.Q. also attained a higher educational level. It should be noted that the group had an unusually high I.Q., one-half having an I.Q. of 110 or more. (The I.Q. data were furnished by Dr. Andrew B. Dibner.)

The subjects were classified on an occupational status scale on the basis of the major occupation followed during their lifetimes. A four-point scale was devised to fit our sample: 1) professional, managerial and proprietary; 2) white collar (clerical and sales); 3) skilled labor and foremen; 4) semi and unskilled labor. The scale derives its ancestry from Edwards' Scale of Social Class (15). As a group, the subjects ranked high in the scale, with 68% in the skilled, white collar and higher categories. In the general male population of 1920 (this decennial census was chosen since by this time our subjects would have been in their major life occupation), only 37% were in the skilled category or higher. Our subjects were thus considerably higher in occupational status than the population norm (44).

As might be expected, those who ranked higher in occupational status also ranked higher in educational attainment and I.Q., as is the case in the general population (42). The high occupational characteristics of these long-lived males is consistent with previous findings that high socio-economic status predisposes to longer life (9,14,31,35). Lower status is associated with occupational hazard, smaller earnings and less favorable nutrition, sanitation, housing, and associated conditions (34). It has been pointed out, however, that the relationship between low socio-economic status and higher death rate has become weakened with the constriction of the socio-economic range in the progressively urbanized and industrialized contemporary American society (20).

Intelligence, education, and occupational status form a triad of statistically interrelated variables, and the nature of their interrelationship may be conceptualized as follows:

Independent variable   *Intervening variable*   *Dependent variable*

Intelligence →   (Education) →   Occupational
                                           status

Since occupational status is related to longer life, the possibility of intelligence also being related to longer life may be raised. In our sample, the high I.Q. may simply be due to the fact that 1) volunteering in the Spanish-American War may have attracted the more intelligent; 2) the attendance at a geriatric clinic may attract the more intelligent and; 3) the more intelligent selectively take greater advantage of medical benefits and therefore found their way into the study sample in greater numbers. On the other hand, if the less intelligent among the Spanish-American War veterans died before the inception of the study, then the above-average I.Q. of the survivors might well be related to their longer life.

If there were a linkage between intelligence and longevity, it would probably work in the following manner: higher intelligence would result in higher socio-economic status which is, in turn, associated with an environment favoring longevity. Another possibility is the direct association between intelligence and longevity on constitutional grounds: the same constitutional or genetic features which produce higher intelligence would also produce higher longevity. The literature contains no population studies on the relationship between intelligence and age at death, since intelligence data in the past have not been available on large population groups. The three following studies, however, are suggestive: 1) honor college graduates were found to be more long-lived than ordinary college graduates (25); 2) Terman reported that gifted children followed for 35 years showed a lower mortality rate than the general population—this was attributed to their superior physique and health in childhood as well as their generally superior intellectual and economic status and its concomitants (37); and 3) in a longitudinal study of twins, high intelligence test scores appeared to be prognostic of long survival (21,22).

The use of empirically derived age-specific norms in intelligence test construction raises a problem for the testing of the intelligence-longevity hypothesis. For example, the effect of selective survival by intelligence would be obliterated by the Wechsler Adult Intelligence Scale which uses empirical norms for age (11). One might try to get around this problem by using raw scores uncorrected for age, but another problem would remain to negate a rise in I.Q. in a cross-sectional comparison of age groups: the natural decline or deterioration in performance, especially in speed, of certain tasks which have been identified as measures of intelligence (6,10,16). This problem could be solved either by selecting intelligence measures that do not deteriorate with age, or by getting the I.Q. scores of a cohort at a given age, such as age 40, and after the members of the cohort have died, relating age-at-death to these scores. This method of testing a cohort and then waiting for its members to die admittedly presents the disadvantage that the investigators may not live to see the conclusion of their research. One can think of two other approaches that will avoid this problem: 1) tabulate the academic grades (an indicator of intelligence) of high school students in one of the older cities of the United States for the year 1900 and then determine if those who had higher grades lived longer (suggested by A. S. Dibner), and 2) relate Army Alpha scores obtained at induction of deceased World War I veterans with their age at death. (The use of Alpha scores was independently suggested by L. F. Jarvik, *et al.*, 21).

Current income
The prevailing sources of income for these octogenarians were pensions of various sorts. In addition to old age insurance and private pensions, these subjects also received a Veterans Administration pension as Spanish-American War veterans. The veterans' pension was, at the minimum, $101 per month. Almost half, 45%, had a current income of $200 per month or more. They were considerably better off than non-institutionalized males in the general population, only 27% of whom had an income of $200 per month or more in 1958 (44). This favorable record was mainly due to the veterans' pension which, on the average, comprised more than one-half of the total income. These subjects were well insulated from public assistance rolls. Further than that, the status of "Spanish-American War Veteran" afforded a special social prestige. All in all, these subjects enjoyed economic and social advantages by virtue of their membership in the oldest extant war veteran group.

In the working population, the income level varies directly with occupational status and education. In our subjects, on the basis of current income, these relationships tended to break down, presumably since reduction of employment with age has a leveling effect on income. Thus, current income and education were unrelated and, interestingly enough, there was an *inverse* relationship between current income and occupational status. A possible explanation is that the professional, managerial and proprietary group was more apt to be self-employed and, therefore, less likely to be accruing retirement pensions which were the prevailing source of the octogenarians' income.

Children

Though the subjects came from families where the average number of children was 6, they themselves had far smaller families. Twenty-seven of the 137 married subjects (20%) were childless.* The 110 married subjects with children had an average of 2.3 children who were live-born and an average of 2.0 who survived beyond age 6. The total group of 137 married subjects had an average of 1.6 children.

One would have expected a larger number of children from the generation which these octogenarians represent (17,41). One might conjecture the linkage of small number of children with advanced longevity, as follows: fathers with fewer children have less responsibility, financial obligation and strain. By the same token, the wives can devote more of their time to the care of their husbands. Consequently, the husbands are able to live longer.

In a larger context, small number of children may be related to longevity as one of the consequences of high socio-economic status (24,42).

The hypothesis of inverse relationship between parental longevity and number of children was tested on subjects' parents, since their age at death and number of children were known. Slightly more of the longer-lived fathers had a smaller number of children, but not enough to be statistically significant. The same data concerning the mothers did not show even this slight finding.

A confounding problem is the fact that if the death of the parent occurs during his reproductive years, this will cut down the number of children produced and will obscure a possible relationship between parental longevity and small number of children. In our sample, only 9% of the mothers and 6% of the fathers died before age 40, so this was not a problem. Interestingly enough, all 8 of the subjects' fathers who died before age 40 had 6 or more children, and 8 of the 10 mothers who died before age 40 had 6 or more children. Death of a parent during reproductive period is, in any case, an obvious variable to be controlled in any investigation of the relationship between longevity of parent and number of children.

"With spouse" status

There were 12 bachelors (8%) in the sample. While 92% of the sample were married, only 40% of the adult male population (1910) in

---

* The sterility rate of 20% is also characteristic of the general population, and has not changed over the past 100 years despite medical advances.

the United States were married. The sample thus had a markedly higher incidence of marriage as compared to population norms (46). Of the 137 who married, 106 married once, 30 married twice, and one married three times. Eighty-three of the married (61%) were currently living with their spouse. Fifty-eight (42%) of the subjects who married were still living with their original spouse. Of the 54 not living with a spouse, 46 were widowed, 7 were divorced, and one was separated. Thus, 92% of the group married, and 61% were still living with a spouse in their advanced years. The 92% married in the sample compares with 58% in the 1960 census of all males 75 years of age and over who married. The census does not offer data on current "with spouse" status, but the lower population figure of those who married suggests a correspondingly lower "with spouse status" than in the case with our subjects (44).

There was a relationship between marrying more than once and the current status of living with a spouse, indicating that remarriage did serve the purpose of maintaining a marital partner into old age. As will be seen later, remarriage for this purpose was necessary since the subjects outlived their first wives. The likelihood of remarriage also seemed to be related to early first marriage. According to census and vital statistics data, there is a definite relationship between longevity and living with a spouse (28,33). The rationale is that the healthier marry on the basis of a natural selection, and the marital state is associated with a more favorable biological and social environment. The "with spouse" characteristics of our sample might therefore possibly be related to their longevity.

The relationship between marital status and longevity has been challenged by Beard, who points out that since the turn of the century relatively more "never married" individuals survive to old age than those who have married (2). In a critique by Milhoj, it was suggested that Beard's finding may be explained by decreased marriage rates which, subsequently, were reflected by more single people in older groups (38). To this critique the present writer would like to add the following: basically, the married state is advantageous for longevity and the single state is disadvantageous. As a married person gets older, however, he is at a greater risk to lose his spouse by death. This not only neutralizes his advantage, it places him at a disadvantage because of the catastrophic loss of a lifelong partner. The above explanation, in addition to that of Milhoj, certainly does not exhaust all the possibilities. For example, it could be argued that a single person has an advantage because he has no family responsibility. Another possible explanation for Beard's findings is the relegation of kinship functions outside the kinship system, which facilitates adjustment outside of the marital bond. With increasing industrialization and mechanization, this effect will increase and may, in time, upset the venerable actuarial relationship between the marital bond and longevity.

Although the sample was a marrying and remarrying one, it was a somewhat *late* marrying one. Also, the subjects did marry women definitely younger than themselves: the subjects' median age at first marriage was 28, and that of their wives was 23. The national male average for age at first marriage in 1900 was 26 (4). Lateness of marriage in these longevous individuals may be related to late maturing, which appears to be characteristic of Anglo-Saxon and North European stock. Implicit here, of course, is the notion that late maturing individuals are more long-lived. Also, marrying a younger wife may have helped maintain a spouse into older age.

Education, occupational status, length of time in service, and age at entry into military service were investigated as possible correlates of lateness of marriage. No significant relationships were found except for a borderline relationship with lateness of entry into service.

Maintenance of occupational role

Our subjects did not, as a group, quit work at age 65. A goodly majority (78%) continued in at least part-time employment after this age (Table 5). The average age of complete cessation of employment was 70. Six per cent were still doing some form of remunerative employment at the time of the interview.

This evidence of a refusal to "disengage" became even more remarkable when no relationship was found between current income and age of complete cessation from work. This suggests that these elderly gentlemen kept their fingers in employment out of a desire to remain useful or creative rather than for economic gain. Busse, in his Durham,

Table 5. Age of cessation of gainful employment

	No.	%
Under 60	12	10
60 - 64	13	11
65 - 69	35	30
70 - 74	36	31
Over 74	12	11
Still working	7	6
	115	100

North Carolina sample of elderly subjects, found that those who continued to work had fewer depressive episodes than those who were retired or unemployed. This suggests the psychological-integrative value of the maintenance of the occupational role (5). The fact that our subjects worked into their elderly years may be related to their longevity through the greater maintenance of morale, adjustment and sense of belonging. In fact, a study of nonagenarians by Dunbar revealed a three-way relationship between longevity, maintenance of occupational role and absence of depression (12). It should be kept in mind that "retirement at 65" is only a recent social norm. Our subjects of an earlier generation did not subscribe to it.

The question was raised as to whether continuation of employment into the elderly years was related to such things as educational attainment or former occupational status. No such relationships were found. A relationship *was* found with number of years spent in major occupation. Presumably, those who kept on working tended to remain in their own occupations rather than turn to a different line of work, thus prolonging the years spent in their major occupation. This was verified by perusing the case histories of those who continued working. The tendency was to stay in a familiar type of work or one where the past occupational skills could be advantageously used. Our subjects, therefore, enjoyed a certain life-integration as they grew older, cushioned somewhat from the wrenching experience of loss or change in occupational role. They were helped by the fact that they were overwhelmingly in non-manual occupations and could more easily stay in the same work as they aged.

Summary

The expectation of longer life because of medical advance has whetted interest in predicting and increasing longevity, and the increased incidence of long-lived individuals facilitates study of their characteristics for the delineation of longevity hypotheses. This chapter focusses on the social correlates of longevity and attempts to expand the literature which has been largely limited to the marital and occupational areas. Subjects were veterans of the Spanish-American War, average age 82, who attended a VA geriatric clinic and participated in an interdisciplinary aging study. Relevance of selected social characteristics for longevity was suggested by statistical analysis of their interrelationships and by comparison with findings in the demographic, actuarial and longevity literature.

Although this chapter does not deal directly with the genetic and physical-environmental factors in longevity, it is clear from the analysis of *social* factors that the three classes of variables may be mutually interacting, with each variable playing an antecedent, independent, intervening or dependent role. An example is a long-lived parent who has both a genetic effect on longevity of offspring and a social effect by supplying an intact home. Another example is the better endowment from being born early in the formation of a large sibship while the mother is young, and the learning of better adaptive skills from being an older sibling.

Keeping in mind social factors as one class of elements located in a larger heterogeneous system of interacting elements, we may consider the following social factors as hypothesized correlates of longevity which have been suggested by this study: 1) *parental longevity* which maintains intactness of primary fostering environment; 2) *senior birth order in a large family* which encourages earlier formation of adaptive skills; 3) *the triad of intelligence, education and occupation* which leads to a social position more conducive to health maintenance; 4) *status group membership* which provides resources and morale; 5) *small number of children* which limits the economic and emotional burden on the parent and breadwinner; 6) *maintenance of "with spouse" status* which provides physical and emotional support; and 7) *maintenance of occupational role or its surrogate into elderly years* which bolsters self-esteem and usefulness. As an overall hypothesis, the presence of these social factors in combination augments the longevity outcome.

Because we conceive longevity as an outcome of interacting intrinsic and extrinsic factors, the hypotheses cited (as well as others) are ideally tested in a longitudinal interdisciplinary investigation with an N adequate for the control of genetic and physical-environment variables. Such a study is in progress in the Boston Veterans Administration Outpatient Clinic. Another approach, which will yield a test of the hypotheses more quickly, is the study of deceased persons of varying age at death. Such a study has also been launched in the Veterans Administration and will be based on interviews of survivors of individuals who have recently died from natural causes.

References

1. American Public Health Association. Problems of an aging population (a symposium). *Amer. J. Public Health,* 1947, *37,* 170-188.
2. Beard, B. B. Longevity and the never married. In C. Tibbits and W. Donahue (eds.), *Social and Psychological Aspects of Aging.* New York: Columbia U. Press, 1962, 36-50.
3. Bell, A. G. *The Duration of Life and Conditions Associated with Longevity—A Study of the Hyde Genealogy.* Washington, D.C.: Geneological Record Office, 1918.
4. Brogue, D. J. *The Population of the United States.* Glencoe, Ill.: The Free Press, 1959.
5. Busse, E. W. Psychoneurotic reactions and defense mechanisms in the aged. In P. H. Hock and J. Zubin (eds.), *Psychopathology of Aging.* New York: Grune and Stratton, 1961, 274-284.

6. E. J. Chesrow, *et al.* A psychometric evaluation of aged white males. *Geriatrics,* 1949, *4,* 169-177.
7. Comfort, A. *The Biology of Senescence.* New York: Rinehart, 1956.
8. Cummins, J., and Sidley, T. Patterns of aging in healthy veterans. Research proposal. Veterans Administration Outpatient Clinic, Boston, Mass., 1962.
9. Dario, J. Mortality, occupation, and socio-economic status. *Vit. Stat. Spec. Reports,* Selected Studies, 1951, *33,* 175-187 (mimeo).
10. Dibner, A. S., and Cummins, J. Intellectual functioning in a group of normal octogenarians. *J. Consult. Psychol.,* 1961, *25,* 137-141.
11. Doppelt, J., and Wallace, W. Standardization of the WAIS for older persons. *J. Abnorm. Soc. Psychol.,* 1955, *51,* 312-330.
12. Dunbar, F. The long-lived: Aging and illness. In *Old Age in the Modern World,* Proc. of the Third International Congress of Gerontology, London, 1954. Edinburgh and London: East S. Livingston, 1955, 412-420.
13. Dublin, L. I., Lotka, A. J., and Spiegleman, M. *Length of Life.* New York: Ronald Press, 1949.
14. Dublin, L. I. Longevity in retrospect and prospect. In A. I. Lansing (ed.), *Cowdry's Problems of Aging.* Baltimore: Williams and Wilkins, 1952.
15. Edwards, A. M. A social-economic grouping of the gainful workers of the United States. *J. Am. Statistical Assoc.,* 1933, *28,* 377.
16. Howell, R. J. Changes in Wechsler subtest scores with age. *J. Consult. Psychol.,* 1955, *19,* 47-50.
17. Interagency Committee for National Conference on Family Life. *The American Family: A Factual Background.* Washington, D.C.: U.S. Government Printing Office, 1948.
18. Jalavisto, E. Inheritance of longevity according to Swedish and Finnish genealogies. *Ann. Med. Intern. Fenn.,* 1951, *40,* 263-274. Cited in F. Kallman, Genetic factors in aging, in P. H. Hoch and J. Zubin (eds.), *Psychopathology of Aging.* New York: Grune and Stratton, 1961, p. 230.
19. Jalavisto, E. A study of Scandinavian genealogies. In P. Close, The genetics of longevity. *J. Geront.,* 1952, *7,* 126-128.
20. Jarvik, L. F., *et al.* Survival trends in a senescent twin population. *Am. J. Hum. Genet.,* 1960, *12,* 170-179.
21. Jarvik, L. F., *et. al.* Longitudinal study of intellectual changes in senescent twins. In C. Tibbetts and W. Donahue (eds.), *Social and Psychological Aspects of Aging.* New York: Columbia U. Press, 1962.
22. Jarvik, L. F., and Falek, A. Intellectual ability and survival in the aged. *J. Geront.,* 1963, *18,* 173-176.
23. Jones, H. B. Background paper on research in gerontology: Biological. White House Conference on Aging, Jan. 9-12, 1961.
24. Kiser, C. V., and Whelpton, P. K. Fertility planning and fertility rates by socioeconomic status. *Milb. Mem. Fund. Quart.,* 1948, *27,* 388.
25. Metropolitan Life Insurance Company. College honor men are long-lived. *Stat. Bull.,* 1933, *13,* No. 8.
26. Montiyama, I. M., and Guralnick, L. Occupational and social class differences in mortality. In D. J. Brogue, *The Population of the United States.* Glencoe, Ill.: The Free Press, 1959.

27. National Office of Vital Statistics. *Summary of International Vital Statistics, 1934-1944.* Washington, D.C.: U.S. Government Printing Office, 1947.
28. National Office of Vital Statistics. *Health and Demography.* Washington, D.C.: U.S. Govt. Printing Office, 1956.
29. Nichols, M., and Cummins, J. Social adjustment of Spanish-American War veterans. *Geriatrics,* 1961, *16,* 641-646.
30. Pearl, R., and Pearl, R. D. *The Ancestry of the Long-Lived.* Baltimore, Md.: Johns Hopkins Press, 1934.
31. Pedoe, A. Occupation, social class, and mortality. *Trans. Soc. Actuar.,* 1960, *12,* 227-257.
32. *Registrar-General's Decennial Supplement, Part I: England and Wales, 1951.* London: H. M. Stationery Office, 1954.
33. Shurtleff, D. Mortality among the married. *J. Am. Geriat. Soc.,* 1956, *4,* 654-666.
34. Stocks, P. The effects of occupation and its accompanying environment on mortality. *J. Royal Stat. Soc.,* 1938, *101.*
35. Stockwell, E. G. Socio-economic status and mortality in the United States. *Pub. Health Reports,* 1961, *76,* 1081-86.
36. Suntzeff, V. Possible maternal influence on longevity of offspring in mice. *J. Gerontol.,* 1962, *17,* 2-7.
37. Terman, L., and Oden, M. *The Gifted Group at Mid-Life. Genetic Studies of Genius,* Vol. 5. Palo Alto: Stanford U. Press, 1959.
38. Tibbitts, C., and Donahue, W. (eds.). *Social and Psychological Aspects of Aging.* New York: Columbia U. Press, 1962.
39. United Nations. *Demographic Yearbook, 1957: Mortality Statistics.* New York: United Nations, 1957.
40. United States Bureau of Census. *U.S. Life Tables, 1900-1931.* Washington, D.C.: U.S. Govt. Printing Office, 1936.
41. United States Bureau of Census. Differential fertility, 1940 and 1910. In *16th Census of the U.S.: 1940, Special Reports.* Washington, D.C.: U.S. Govt. Printing Office, 1947.
42. United States Bureau of Census. *Special Report on Education.* Washington, D.C.: U.S. Govt. Printing Office, 1950.
43. United States Bureau of Census. Income of families and persons in the United States, 1958. In *Current Population Reports: Consumer Income,* Series P-60, No. 33 and Series P-20, No. 114. Washington, D.C.: U.S. Govt. Printing Office, 1960.
44. U.S. Bureau of Census. *Historical Statistics of U.S., Colonial Times to 1957.* Washington, D.C.: U.S. Govt. Printing Office, 1960.
45. United States Department of Health, Education, and Welfare. Historical survey of public elementary and secondary school statistics, 1870-1956. In *Biennial Survey of Education in the U.S., 1954-1956.* Washington, D.C.: U.S. Govt. Printing Office, 1957, p. 24.
46. U.S. Public Health Service. Mortality from selected causes by marital status: U.S., 1949-1951. In *Vital. Stat., Spec. Reports, 39,* No. 7. Washington, D.C.: U.S. Govt. Printing Office, 1956.
47. Wechsler, D. *The Measurement of Adult Intelligence.* Baltimore, Md.: Williams and Wilkins, 1944.
48. Yerushalmy, J. Neonatal mortality by order of birth and age of parents. *Am. J. Hyg.,* 1938, *28,* 244.

6

Longevity and life patterns

Robert Kastenbaum

The social sciences have had relatively little to offer concerning the fundamental question of what keeps people alive. The more subtle operation of psychosocial variables in longevity has been pretty much ignored as a subject of systematic investigation, although suicide—in the restricted sense of an obvious instrumental process of self-destruction—has been receiving steady attention (e.g., 14,15). A number of interesting clinical observations have been made, but controlled, programmatic studies seem to be at a premium (3,8).

Against this background, the recent and continuing work of Rose is an encouraging exception (13). His findings indicate that useful information can be obtained by applying techniques already well within the repertoire of social scientists, although there are some vital questions in this area that cannot be tackled without developing new procedures. The purpose of this chapter is to highlight some of the theoretical issues implicit in the work of Rose and to suggest additional lines of approach. The availability of Rose's own report, in the preceding chapter, make it unnecessary to repeat the details here.

Life patterns and longevity

Consider one kind of frequently encountered newspaper interview of a local citizen who is celebrating his one-hundredth birthday. Invariably the reporter will ask the centenarian how he accounts for his longevity. "Young man," snaps the reply, "I've lived the good life—never allowed the Devil Tobacco or the Devil Alcohol to touch my lips, stayed away from the women, kept decent hours, and practiced moderation in all things."

The secret of life thus yielded by this centenarian is likely to be secret indeed so far as the next centenarian is concerned: "A bottle of wine, a good cigar, and women, women, ah! women—now, that's what makes life worth holding on to, young fella!"

This chapter is based upon a paper read at the annual scientific meeting of the Boston Society for Gerontological Psychiatry, May 14, 1963.

Must it be that one of these centenarians is mistaken? Is there one way and one way only to achieve longevity? Is it possible that what seem to be diametrically opposed patterns of life can result in the same effect? And, if so, then *do* living patterns have anything to do with staying alive?

These questions prompt a return to the Spanish-American War veterans studied by Rose. Among other characteristics of these octogenarians was noted an unusually high level of intelligence and of education, and a social status that appears decidedly advantageous. But it is also relevant to note that there are other octogenarians among us whose level of intelligence and education is lower than average, and whose social status appears decidedly disadvantageous. These people include aged residents of institutions for the mentally retarded, a number of geriatric patients and some individuals living in the community. A preliminary report of intellectual, educational, and occupational levels of hospitalized octogenarians supports the observation that one *can* survive into the ninth decade without a high rating on this triad (4).

Somehow, then, we must either find a process so basic that it accounts for differential longevity without significant influence by purely psychological factors, or we must advance our sensitivity to the point where we can specify *how* individual patterns of organizing life experience operate to affect longevity. It would not be enough to find that more abstainers or more indulgers, or more intellectuals or more dullards achieve a long life—the question is rather, *how* does a person of a certain kind of make-up behave in such a way as to prolong or shorten his life span? Under what conditions, for example, does the bright, high-status person survive, and under what conditions perish?

Several approaches might be considered in dealing with these questions; here, attention will be called to one of the alternatives which might otherwise be considered as too remote for application to problems of longevity.

Living: a conditional response

Classical conditioning is one of the oldest and most firmly entrenched areas of experimental psychology. Russian wolfhounds have been salivating on cue for more than half a century, and research activity in this field has come to represent psychology in one of its most "tough-minded" forms.

To recall the basic classical conditioning set-up: an organism produces what is called an "unconditional response" when cued by an experimentally presented stimulus. This stimulus is also "unconditional" as it seems to elicit the response in an automatic, reflex-like manner relatively free from previous learning. The unconditional response might be salivation, an eye-blink, accelerated pulse rate, or any of a number of phenomena that are not usually under voluntary control. From this beginning, the rat, dog, raccoon or undergraduate is progressively conditioned to come forth with his mouth-watering, blinking, or pulsing when presented with stimuli that have less and less to do with the response. So, for example, the taste of meat as a stimulus for salivation is replaced by the sight of meat, and the sight of meat by a bell that has been associated with the meat, the bell by a light, and so on. The response at this stage is termed "conditional" or "conditioned" because its appearance is contingent upon the presentation of stimuli that initially had no power to elicit the behavior. Much of classical conditioning research has been restricted to infrahuman subjects, but by now a sizeable amount of information has been accumulated concerning the investigator's own species.

In relating classical conditioning to human longevity it should be noted that Pavlov's original investigations were intended to advance the understanding of the digestive process (11). It is obvious that the conversion of ingested material to a form that will nourish the body is one of the most fundamental activities of the living organism, and is of relevance to longevity.

To add another link, it could be suggested that *all* human behavior is conditional. For behavior to occur in a certain way, certain conditions must obtain. For behavior to occur at all, certain other conditions must be fulfilled. Little, if anything, of what we recognize as behavior in an adult human being was present at birth or has come to fruition without being shaped by psychosocial processes. Human behavior, then, is conditional, that is to say, contingent upon psychologically meaningful circumstances. What we call "living" could be construed as a pattern of particular conditional responses, and the persistence or extinction of these responses could be predicted, explained or controlled by knowledge of the conditions on which they are conditional.

Let us briefly consider two closely related laws of behavior which the conditioners themselves judge to be firmly established (9).

One law is that behavior which is "reinforced" *some* of the time will be "stronger" than behavior which is "reinforced" *all* the time. This phenomenon is known as the Partial Reinforcement Effect (PRE). A second law is that reinforcement that is delayed is more effective than reinforcement that immediately follows the response. In other words, to build up the strongest possible response tendency, we would be advised to reinforce the response at irregular intervals and after a certain optimal period of delay.

To glimpse the possible relevance of these laws to human longevity, let us construct a hypothetical situation. A man is ill. He has been ill before, but this time the situation is different. Let us say that he has a different physician, and something about the way in which this physician reacts toward his illness conveys to the patient the notion that he is in a very bad way indeed. The patient obediently begins to behave the way he has learned that a dying man should. When his friends and relatives visit, they are taken aback to observe the change. The patient detects this changed attitude on the part of his visitors and interprets it as a confirmation of the severity of his illness, prompting him to a further grave-ward turn. If, at this point, we ask his physician to predict the outcome, he will tell us that it could go either way, recovery or death.

Suppose now that this man has had a lifelong pattern of expecting that some day something really wonderful was going to happen to him —a "big break" that would transfigure his life and make up for all the disappointments of a buffeted existence. To this purpose he has frequently entered contests, writing innumerable jingles in 25 words or less. A month before his illness he had entered another contest. Today he receives a telegram announcing that his jingle has been selected as one of the final entries which the judges are considering for the big prize. Will this message influence the outcome of his illness? Here we can find a clue to what is yet required to make classical conditioning a useful scientific resource in the study of longevity.

Time perspective

From classical conditioning we would expect that irregular (partial) and delayed reinforcement should strengthen behavior, in this case the totality of behavior that operationally defines human life. The catch is this: we have to determine what, in fact, constitutes "reinforcement," "irregularity" and "delay" for a given individual or, at least, for well-defined classes of individuals.

Suppose, for example, that the telegram states the final decision will be reached in three months. The three-month delay of reinforcement might be an ideal prospect for this patient—he has a way of organizing his life that accords genuine meaning to events that may arise within the next several months. The three-month delay is close enough to be meaningful to him, far enough away to require him to mobilize his resources for survival. Because the fantasy of a "big break" has been central in his view of life, it is highly reinforcing to him simply that the prospect has moved to the verge of actualization. The reinforcement is partial or irregular in a more complex sense than classical conditioning has yet been able to accommodate, but discussion of this topic would take us too far afield.

In contrast to the above situation, it might be the case that a delay of three months is much too long to mean anything to this patient. If he has lived his life on a day-by-day basis, then he might not have at his disposal the psychophysiological apparatus necessary to respond to the implications of this delay.

These contrasting responses to the same period of delay illustrate basic individual differences in the organization of experiences. One productive way to approach the organization of experience is through the study of *time perspective,* sometimes also referred to as "the temporal horizon." A succinct statement concerning this function is given by Fraisse: "In this ever-changing world, our actions at any given moment depend not only on the situation in which we find ourselves at that instant, but also on everything we have already experienced and on all our future expectations. Every one of our actions takes these into account, sometimes explicitly, always implicitly. To put it another way, we might say that each of our actions takes place in a temporal perspective; it depends on our *temporal horizon* at the precise moment of its occurrence." (5, p. 151).

This description by Fraisse emphasizes general aspects of time perspective. Individual differences, however, are pronounced, and are of particular relevance here. A gross distinction could be made between those persons whose daily life is surrounded by a psychological framework that projects extensively in both directions, past and future, and those who invariably "take things as they come." This distinction, of course, is much too simple—it does not take into account those who project in only one direction (past *or* future); it does not consider the qualities attributed to the projected time (e.g., a feared or hoped-for future), nor orientations that have developed in reaction to specific life circumstances (e.g., acute stress or bereavement) and that do not characterize the individual's usual outlook.

For the sake of brevity, however, consideration will be limited to the gross distinction between those who do and those who do not operate within a well-developed temporal framework. There is evidence that the temporal framework expands markedly during the early course of development and, in fact, constitutes one of the most significant aspects of personality growth (1,10,6,12). Apart from age-related differences in time perspective, it has been noted that delinquent adolescents, mediocre college students and schizophrenic adults have more limited outlooks than non-delinquent adolescents, academically-successful collegians and non-schizophrenic adults (2,16,17). This list of differences will probably be lengthened by subsequent research. Of particular interest is the likelihood that basic differences will be found *within* classes of people often treated as though relatively homogeneous. Not only, say, do schizophrenic and non-schizophrenic adults tend to differ with respect to time perspective, but two equally "normal" adults at age 30 might also differ radically in this respect—a psychological difference that could make a difference in survival three or four decades later.

Once it is known how a person has structured his life with respect to time, it should be possible to determine the nature of the conditions crucial to the maintenance of his particular mode of functioning. A promise dated three months in advance, for example, could be a "life-saver" for an ailing or stressed "planner," and have no reinforcing value at all for a person who attends chiefly to proximal stimuli. Thus, as we increase our understanding of how the individual organizes his own experience, there will be increasing opportunity to make specific application of general laws that are emerging from such fields of basic research as classical conditioning.

Returning to the Spanish-American War veterans, it might be ventured that the psychosocial factors which differentiated between survivors and non-survivors are *different* than the factors which selected out many Cushing Hospital patients from contemporaries with whom they might have been matched. My guess is that the typical surviving Spanish-American War veteran has had a relatively complex, extensive, elaborated time perspective, and succeeded throughout his life in obtaining relatively few and crucial reinforcements—while the typical institutionalized aged person has lived within a simpler time perspective that favored longevity by enabling him to utilize a greater variety of reinforcements that are more easily obtained. Failure to obtain a single, highly-valued reinforcement would thus be more likely to affect adversely the longevity of the former than of the latter person (although there may be something about an elaborate time perspective that converts certain kinds of failure into partial reinforcement).

This speculation is based upon indirect, circumstantial information concerning the war veteran population, i.e., inferences from the reported educational, occupational and intellectual levels rather than data on time perspective *per se*. Experience with the Cushing Hospital population suggests that day-by-day functioning has been the typical lifelong mode of organizing experience. A study involving 57 patients disclosed, as a sidelight, that only 19% had reported material that could be interpreted as indicative of a planful approach to life (7).

Longitudinal studies of time perspective provide the best alternative —perhaps "antidote" is the word—for such speculations. In the meantime, however, much can be learned by attending to individual patterns of organizing experience in cross-sectional studies, and exploring ways of relating this material to general laws of behavior being established through classical conditioning and other experimental methods.

References

1. Ames, L. The development of the sense of time in the young child. *J. Genet. Psychol.*, 1946, *68*, 97-125.
2. Barndt, R. J., and Johnson, D. M. Time orientation in delinquents. *J. Abnorm. Soc. Psychol.*, 1955, *51*, 589-592.

3. Brill, A. A. The concept of psychic suicide. *Internat. J. Psychoanal.*, 1939, *20*, 246-251.
4. Cushing Hospital. Some biographical characteristics of institutionalized octogenarians. Framingham, Mass., 1963 (mimeo).
5. Fraisse, P. *The Psychology of Time*, tr. by Jennifer Leith. New York: Harper and Row, 1963.
6. Hartmann, H. *Ego Psychology and the Problem of Adaptation*, tr. by D. Rapaport. New York: International Universities Press, 1958.
7. Kastenbaum, R., Slater, P. E., and Aisenberg, R. Toward a conceptual model of geriatric psychopharmacology: Experiments with thioridazine and dextro-amphetamine. Presented at seventeenth annual scientific meeting, Gerontological Society, Boston, Mass., Nov. 9, 1963.
8. LeShan, L. A basic psychological orientation apparently associated with malignant disease. *Psychiat. Quart.*, 1961, *35*.
9. Lewis, D. J. Partial reinforcement: A selective review of the literature since 1950. *Psychol. Bull.*, 1960, *57*, 1-28.
10. Lhamon, W. T., Goldstone, S., and Boardman, W. K. The time sense in the normal and psychopathological states. Progress report, Grant M-1121. Baylor Univ. College of Medicine, 1957.
11. Pavlov, I. P. *Conditioned Reflexes*, tr. by G. V. Anrep. New York: Dover, 1955.
12. Piaget, J. *The Growth of Logical Thinking from Childhood to Adolescence*. New York: Basic Books, 1958.
13. Rose, C. L. Social correlates of longevity. In this volume.
14. Schneidman, E. S., and Farberow, N. L. *Clues to Suicide*. New York: McGraw-Hill, 1957.
15. Henry, A. F., and Short, J. F. *Suicide and Homicide*. Glencoe, Ill.: The Free Press, 1957.
16. Teahan, J. E. Future time perspective, optimism, and academic achievement. *J. Abnorm. Soc. Psychol.*, 1958, *57*, 379-380.
17. Wallace, M. Future time perspective in schizophrenia. *J. Abnorm. Soc. Psychol.*, 1956, *52*, 240-245.

Behavioral changes of
aging chronic psychotics

7

Otto F. Ehrentheil

In spite of the enormous amount of literature about schizophrenics and an almost equal amount about aging, very few studies have been published about aging schizophrenics, least of all about changes in the behavior of these patients as they grow old. This was appropriately noted by Kant (14) in 1942: "The end stage of the disease (schizophrenia) has remained a step-child as far as research is concerned." The situation is the same today.

The findings of those authors who did report on behavior changes in aging schizophrenics are sometimes contradictory. For example, in contradiction to Arieti (2) whose findings will be discussed later, Fleck (11) emphasized in 1928 the decreased reactivity of older men, be it normal or schizophrenic. Similarly, Barucci found in most of his 80 schizophrenic patients 70 or more years old an attenuation of the violent impulses and a general improvement in behavior (3). He regarded this not as a disappearance of symptoms, but rather as an absence of reaction. "If a young schizophrenic patient while at dinner perceives of being offended he stops eating and throws his plate against 'the enemy,' the old schizophrenic, under the same conditions, continues eating." Furthermore, an apparent adaptation takes place, according to Barucci, but it is not because of a better rapport with the environment. Sociability is found very rarely, and an indifference to fellow man is most prominent. Christian Mueller found in aging schizophrenics a lessening of reactivity and reported that 55 of 101 institutionalized schizophrenic patients were socially improved in their old age, while 14 were socially worse and 32 were unchanged (21). Yet, while Fleck, Barucci and Mueller found a reduction in motor

The materials presented in this chapter derive from a project supported in part by grants from the National Institutes of Health, U.S. Public Health Service (M-1905 and M-4690A). Text and tables are a composite of papers by the author (5, 6, 7, 8, 9) which have appeared in *A.M.A. Archives of General Psychiatry, Journal of Nervous and Mental Disease,* and *Bedford Research* and which were abstracted and printed here with permission of these publications.

activity in old schizophrenics, Arieti observed a more or less sudden increase in motor activity in patients who continue to regress indefinitely (1). In addition, he reported that this increase is often lasting rather than transitory. For Arieti, this moment marks the beginning of the terminal stage of dementia praecox. He stated that the actions of patients in this stage appear sharply reactive or impulsive: the patients show voracious appetite, grabbing food and putting things into their mouths. A paper by Lanzkron and Wolfson about distortion of temporal orientation in chronic schizophrenics will be discussed later (17).

The otherwise excellent *American Handbook of Psychiatry* has no discussion whatsoever about behavioral changes of mental patients while they grow old (2). I am of the opinion, however, that a fertile field for clinical investigation lies in the observation and evaluation of the behavioral changes of mental hospital patients as they grow old, especially as the prolongation of the life span of man and the increased longevity of chronic psychotics permit these changes to be seen better now than was possible in the past. In the following pages I wish to summarize the contributions of my co-workers and myself in this field.

Motor activity of
schizophrenic patients
Authors reporting on improvement or worsening of the psychiatric status of patients are faced with the difficulty of how to measure these elusive characteristics. Rating scales such as the Multidimensional Scale for Rating Psychiatric Patients by Lorr *et al.* (18,19) or the Institute of Living Clinical Rating Scales by Reznikoff and Zeller (22), or the Kraus-Bedford Clinical Rating Scale (16) can be used to rate patients from direct observation, but it is impossible to use these scales when only the information reported in the clinical records is available. It was felt that in focussing on a single aspect—the motor activity level—one would have at least one measurable characteristic to describe and evaluate behavior and behavior changes which can be determined from the case histories of 25 to 30 years ago and from observation at the present time. Thus, my co-workers and I examined patients who were still living in the Veterans Administration Hospital, Bedford, Massachusetts in 1959-1960, and who, having been admitted during the first few years of this hospital's existence, had spent about 30 years there (7). Of course, many patients were discharged, and quite a few died during this period. Between 1949-1959, 25 patients were put on a trial visit or discharged following one year on trial visit, after they had spent at least 20 years in the hospital. We were interested in the changes in *motor activity* of mental patients when they grow old and how such changes in motor activity influence the possibility of their living outside the hospital walls.

Initial motor activity level hypothesis

The following hypothesis was formulated and examined. As a result of the aging process, the level of motor activity of many patients declines. Consequently, some patients who at the time of their admission to the hospital (30 years ago) were hyperactive now show motor activity levels within the normal range. Elderly patients with normal motor activity levels may in this way become socially acceptable and have a chance to be put on trial visit and perhaps later discharged, even though their psychotic *ideation* has not changed. Other patients when they were admitted 30 years ago showed motor activity levels which were within the normal range or underactive range. As a result of the aging process, these patients would have activity levels that are far below the normal range. Many of them have become withdrawn, seclusive, even mute. Their chances of leaving the hospital are very small. If this hypothesis is correct, then we may expect to find in the clinical records of those patients who now have ground privileges, live outside the hospital on trial visit, or have been discharged, reports of higher motor activity 20 to 30 years ago than we will find in the records of those patients who are still in the hospital without ground privileges. The main method of testing this hypothesis was to ascertain the patients' present status and the present rating of their motor activity, then to compare these data to findings obtained by the rating of clinical records concerning these patients' motor activity in the first 5 years after admission to the hospital.

Procedures and material. All the elderly patients examined in these studies were still alive when the investigation was started in fall, 1959, in the Veterans Administration Hospital, Bedford, Mass. This institution was opened in July 1928, and through the years has served chiefly as a mental hospital for chronic psychotic patients. The patients discussed in this report were mostly veterans of World War I, but a very few Spanish-American War veterans were included. One hundred and two schizophrenic patients were chosen who were still alive and hospitalized and who had been among the first cases admitted (between July 17, 1928, and January 3, 1930). Their ages at the time of admission to the hospital ranged between 22 and 42, with a mean age of 32 and a median age of 33. During this time, about 380 other patients, with various diagnoses, were also admitted.

Furthermore, the records of 31 general paretics were similarly compiled. To find a sufficient number of general paretics who were still living, we had to include patients admitted through March, 1939. Their ages on admission were slightly higher than those of the schizophrenics. It was still more difficult to find a sizable group of epileptics with psychosis who had been hospitalized for a long period, because of the relative rarity of this condition. The first patient in this group was admitted on July 17, 1928, but the fifteenth had only 6 years of continuous hospitalization. It was therefore decided not to include this group in the investigation of the influence of aging on motor activity, but it was used in the comparison of initial motor activity in the various diagnostic groups.

The Registrar Division was helpful in providing the names of all the patients who had been put on trial visit or discharged during the preceding years. The records were checked, and only those patients with uninterrupted hospitalization of 20 years were used. Twenty-five patients met this requirement. The reason that we limited this phase to the investigation of patients who had been hospitalized continuously for at least 20 years was that we wanted to have as a comparison a group of patients who were in many respects similar to those still in the hospital. The ages of the 22 schizophrenic patients in this group ranged on admission from 30 to 43 with mean and median age of 36. Because of the bulkiness of the records it was necessary to abstract them while preserving all the important material for evaluation. The senior author worked with a record secretary through several cases until she could do the work alone. One hundred and eighty records were abstracted. All of these 180 patients were alive when the study began, and most of them had been admitted about 30 years previously. One hundred and fifty-five patients were still cared for in the hospital, and 25 were on trial visit or had been discharged after at least 20 years' hospitalization.

The diagnostic categories were as follow:

128 schizophrenics (23 on trial visit or discharged)
31 general paretics (hospitalized 20 to 30 years)
15 epileptics (hospitalized 6 to 30 years)
6 miscellaneous diagnoses (2 on trial visit)

The abstracts of the clinical records were used for *rating of motor activity during the first 5 years after admission* (mostly 30 years ago). Two independent raters carried out this procedure, the details of which have been reported elsewhere (7).

The present living status of the patients was ascertained; a) living in the hospital without ground privileges; b) living in the hospital but having ground privileges; c) living outside the hospital (trial visit or discharged).

Present motor activity status. For evaluation of the present motor activity status of patients still hospitalized, a short questionnaire was used, a selection from The Multidimensional Scale for Rating Psychiatric Patients by M. Lorr (18). Only those questions were selected from this scale which are relevant for movements and speech (Table 1). The questions were answered by the ward nurse and nursing aides and recorded by the author. The following information was also obtained: Has the patient ground privileges? (yes or no). Is patient getting medication? (tranquilizer, energizer or antidepressant).

Table 1. Motor activity rating scale

Movements:

A. (Lorr No. 42) How much does he move around? Does he sit all day unless pushed to
follow routine? Or is he usually walking around or restlessly moving some part of
his body?

1	2	3	4	5
Usually motionless	Underactive	Moves about as appropriate	Restless	Almost constantly moving

B. (Lorr No. 45) When in action (walking, talking, dressing, eating), does he move
slower, faster, or at about the same rate of speed as the average person?

1	2	3	4	5
Markedly slower	A little slower	At an average rate	A little faster	Distinctly faster

C. (Lorr No. 46) Does he usually seem tired and worn out or lively and energetic as
compared to others?

1	2	3	4	5
Almost completely worn out	Tired	As lively as most	Livelier and more energetic	Extremely lively and energetic

Speech:

D. (Lorr No. 8) Compared to the average person, how taciturn or talkative is he? Judge
only the amount of speech; do not consider its relevance nor whether it was spontaneous
or elicited by questioning?

1	2	3	4	5
Mute	Less talkative than average	As talkative as average	More	Conspicuously overtalkative

E. (Lorr No. 52) Typically, how much does he talk if spoken to?

1	2	3	4	5
Does not answer	Only 3 or 4 words	As much as the ordinary person	Rather more than the ordinary person	Hard to stop

F. (Lorr No. 56) How often does he speak to others? Does he ask for things, say hello,
ask questions, make comments, or otherwise start a back and forth conversation?

1	2	3	4	5
Never	Occasionally	As often as the ordinary	Nearly always speaking to someone	Hard to stop

G. (Lorr No. 20) Compared to others, how loud or intense is his speech? Is it barely
audible or is it loud and (or) intense?

1	2	3	4	5
Almost inaudible	Less audible than average	As loud as average	Louder	Shouts or yells

At the time of this investigation none of the patients was receiving any antidepressant drugs or energizers. Since the percentile number of patients treated with tranquilizers in the group of patients who were underactive 30 years ago was almost equal to the number in the overactive group, it was decided that in this sample the use of tranquilizers did not have any marked influence on the results of this study. However, in the original publication the instances of psychotropic medication were precisely reported.

Summary of results

1. A comparison of the motor activity in the various diagnostic groups showed relatively more underactive patients in the general paretic group than in the schizophrenic group. A great majority of the epileptic group was in the middle-active group.

2. It was found that patients who were overactive in the first 5 years after admission had a better chance for trial visit or discharge after 20 years of hospitalization than did initially middle-active and underactive patients. This seemed to support the hypothesis; however, the finding failed to achieve statistical significance.

3. The initially middle-active patient group received more ground privileges 30 years later than did the over- and underactive group. This finding did show statistical significance but was not expected from the hypothesis. The overactive group seemed to fare somewhat better in this respect than the underactive.

4. A diminution of motor activity level after 30 years is suggested by comparing the ratings of activity levels during the first 5 years after admission, based on the clinical records, with the motor activity levels at present, determined by a questionnaire. The uncertainties of such a procedure are obvious, but the method employed was the only way to arrive at a comparison.

Fixation of thought content
in hospitalized mental patients

The purpose of this study was to explore the expressed and elicited thought content of chronic psychotic patients and to compare present findings with those recorded at the time of admission 30 years earlier (8). Specifically, two questions were of interest: 1) how does the present thought content of these patients compare to that at time of admission? and 2) are many psychotics still involved in the same problems which they faced at the time of the onset of their psychosis?

Fixation of thought content in relation to withdrawal

The following *hypothesis* was tested by careful scrutiny of hospital records in comparison with recent psychiatric evaluation: the main thought content (preoccupation) of completely withdrawn chronic psychotic patients remains the same throughout the years of their illness. The degree of adherence to the same thought content is directly related to the degree of withdrawal. Expressed differently, the degree of change in present thought content from that of 30 years earlier (at the time of admission) is in reciprocal relationship to the degree of withdrawal from the environment.

Procedure. The *case material* used in this study was the same as that in the previous study. The admission notes and the progress notes for the 5 years following admission were used to determine the expressed thought content 30 years ago. In a 12-month period during 1959-1960, all these patients were still alive and were given a thorough psychiatric re-evaluation, with special emphasis on eliciting present thought content and preoccupation. The entries for the first 5 years after admission to the hospital and the recent psychiatric examination protocols were compared and rated independently by two psychologists, who at that time did not know the purpose of the study. The rating marks were: 1) "inaccessible," 2) "no change," 3) "slight change" and 4) "change." The *degree of withdrawal* was evaluated by the nurses and aides who were in constant contact with the patients. In July, 1961, a questionnaire was filled out by the nurses with the help of the aides. During this series of studies, 6 patients were transferred to other hospitals, one went on a trial visit, and 13 died. The questionnaire was therefore completed for 135 patients as follows: 92 schizophrenics (42 hebephrenics, 27 paranoids, 18 catatonics, five other types); 28 general paretics; 11 epileptics; 4 miscellaneous psychoses. The 4 items of the questionnaire designed to measure withdrawal were taken from Lorr's Multidimensional Scale (8) (Table 2).

Results. Tables relating degree of fixation of thought content and diagnosis (Table 3) and degree of fixation of thought content and degree of withdrawal (Table 5) represent the findings of one of the two raters. (These data were tabulated for each of the two raters, with closely equivalent results.) Table 3 shows the accessibility of the patients and their thought content persistence or change in the various mental diagnoses. It is not surprising to find that 30 of the 47 hebephrenics (63.8%) were inaccessible, and that 18 of 23 catatonics (78.3%) were inaccessible, while among the 29 paranoids only 4 (13.8%) were inaccessible. A note of caution must be expressed here, as a diagnosis of schizophrenic reaction, paranoid type, could hardly be made with any degree of certainty in mute psychotics. (The opinion may even be ventured that if the 4 paranoid patients who were mute at the time of the follow-up had been mute or inaccessible at the time of their admission, a diagnosis of paranoid type would not have been made.) Of the general paretics, 51.6%, and of the epileptics 20% showed various degrees of inaccessibility.

Table 2. Withdrawal rating scale

A. (Lorr No. 53) Does he typically keep himself clean, or must he be reminded to wash or be washed? Does he keep himself neat and his hair combed, or are his clothes unbuttoned, disarranged, or soiled with food, dirt, or feces?

1	2	3	4
Requires special handling. Wets or soils	Distinctly sloppy and dirty	As neat and clean as most	Neater and cleaner than most

B. (Lorr No. 56) How often does he speak to others? Does he ask for things, say hello, ask questions, make comments, or otherwise start a back and forth conversation?

1	2	3	4
Never	Occasionally	As often as the ordinary person	Nearly always speaking to someone

C. (Lorr No. 57) How much interest does he show in the things going on around him? Which of the following does de do? a) listen to the radio or watch televsion; b) play ball or ping-pong; c) read newspapers or magazines; d) play cards or checkers; e) talk about ward happenings; sports or news events; f) write letters.

1	2	3	4	5
Interested in nothing. Just sits	Any one	Any 2 or 3	Any 4 or 5	All 6 or more

D. (Lorr No. 58) Does he stay by himself and avoid others, or does he like being with people?

1	2	3	4
Always stays by himself. Ignores everyone	Usually by himself. Mixes sometimes	About as much alone as with others	Usually in company with others.

Table 3. Accessibility of the patients and degree of thought content fixation in relation to psychiatric diagnoses (155 chronic mental patients)

	Inaccessible	No change	Slight change	Change	Totals
Schizophrenic, paranoid	4	11	13	1	29
Schizophrenic, hebephrenic	30	3	8	6	47
Schizophrenic, catatonic	18	1	3	1	23
Schizophrenic, other	3	0	2	1	6
General paretic	16	3	7	5	31
Epileptic	3	1	4	7	15
Miscellaneous psychotic	1	1	0	2	4
Totals	75	20	37	23	155

Table 4 shows the withdrawal ratings of patients in various diagnostic groups, made by nurses and aides. Roman numeral I indicates the highest degree of withdrawal; IV, the lowest degree of withdrawal from the environment. The table shows, as expected, the highest number of withdrawn patients in the catatonic (83.3%) and hebephrenic (78.6%) groups. The general paretic group shows that 71.4% of these patients were rated as withdrawn. Although 55.6% of the chronic paranoids were withdrawn, none were rated as belonging to the most withdrawn group. (1)

Table 5 plots the degree of adherence to the same thought content in relation to the degree of withdrawal in 70 chronic mental patients. It is apparent that only 3 of 24 non-withdrawn mental patients showed adherence to the original thought content, while of the 36 withdrawn patients, 15 (41.7%) adhered to the original thought content. These data were statistically analyzed under the assumption that withdrawal and thought content were independent. (Such an assumption is, of course, in contradiction to the original hypothesis.) The analysis rejected the statistical assumption, and supported the hypothesis that the degree of fixation of thought content is roughly proportional to the degree of withdrawal ($p < .02$, chi-square). The second rater's findings were also used, and yielded equally significant differences ($p < .02$). Examination of the group of schizophrenic patients alone yielded similar results. Mute and otherwise inaccessible patients were excluded

Table 4. Withdrawal rating for 135 chronic mental patients according to psychiatric diagnoses

	Withdrawn		Not withdrawn		
	I	II	III	IV	Totals
Schizophrenic, paranoid	0	15	7	5	27
Schizophrenic, hebephrenic	10	23	9	0	42
Schizophrenic, catatonic	6	9	3	0	18
Schizophrenic, other	1	1	1	2	5
General paretic	9	11	6	2	28
Epileptic	0	3	6	2	11
Miscellaneous psychotic	1	2	1	0	4
Totals	27	64	33	11	135

from Table 5, because obviously it was not possible to compare their thought content of 30 years ago with thought content at the present time. Furthermore, muteness is so much regarded as a part of withdrawal that the characteristics would probably be identical. On the other hand, whether there is a change of the thought content or an adherence to it is not implicit in the description of withdrawal. The data given in Table 3 supports the hypothesis underlying this study.

Summary. It was hypothesized that the degree of adherence to the same thought content in chronic psychotic patients is roughly parallel to the degree of withdrawal. Case record notes during the first 5 years after admission and reports of a psychiatric examination 30 years after admission were independently rated by two psychologists in respect to adherence to or change of thought content. Withdrawal was rated by the nursing personnel. These data were analyzed and a relationship was observed that supported the hypothesis.

Table 5. Adherence to or change of thought contents in relation to withdrawal in 70 accessible chronic mental patients

| | Withdrawn | | Not withdrawn | | Totals |
	I	II	III	IV	
No change	1	14	3	0	18
Slight change	0	12	14	7	33
Change	0	9	7	3	19
Totals	1	35	24	10	70

Does time stand still for some psychotics?

Elderly hospitalized psychotic patients were asked their age. We noticed that some patients answered by stating a much younger age than their chronological one. In checking case histories, we found that the alleged age coincided for some patients with their age at onset of psychosis. This phenomenon has been known to experienced psychiatrists for a long time. Thus, Weygandt described in 1904 some old patients whose minds still lived in the geographic, political and monetary condition of about 50 years earlier (23). Similarly, Lanzkron and Wolfson reported that many of the chronic deteriorated schizophrenic patients gave an age which coincided with the age at which they became ill or were hospitalized (17). These patients believed at the time of their more recent examination that cigarettes and cars were selling at the same price as at the time of the disease onset many years previously. Lanzkron and Wolfson found this phenomenon only in clinically dull, apathetic and regressed schizophrenics.

How old are you?

We decided to ask 50 elderly, long-institutionalized patients the simple question, "How old are you?" The patients with the longest hospital residence in 3 diagnostic groups were chosen for this study (6). One group consisted of 30 patients with the diagnosis of schizophrenic reaction; all had been hospitalized since 1928 or 1929. These 30 patients had the following subdiagnoses: hebephrenic schizophrenia, 14; catatonic, 8; paranoid, 7; and simple type, one. The two other groups consisted of 10 patients with dementia paralytica (general paresis) admitted between 1928 and 1932, and 10 epileptics with psychosis. Only 3 of these epileptics had been hospitalized for 30 years; the others had been hospitalized for 16 to 24 years. The ages of these 50 patients were between 59 and 72, and there was no age difference among the three groups.

Replies to the question "How old are you?" were as follow: Of the 30 schizophrenic patients, 9 were mute or otherwise inaccessible and gave no answer; of the 21 remaining schizophrenics, 7, or one-third, gave as their ages approximately their ages at the onset of their psychoses; one gave a younger age than the onset age; one gave an age younger than his real age but older than he was at the onset of his sickness, and 12 stated their chronological age (Table 6). Most of the patients who gave their ages as they were at the onset of their psychoses were hebephrenic, and 2 other patients who gave much younger ages than their chronological ones had the same subdiagnosis.

We may now compare the answers of these schizophrenics with those given by patients with dementia paralytica and by epileptics with psychosis. Of the 10 patients with dementia paralytica, 5 were inacessible and did not answer; 3 gave the correct answer about their age; one gave a grandiose answer ("I was born when the world began. I am 48,000 years old. You see, you people died and I did not"); one gave his age as that at the onset of his sickness. Of the 10 epileptics, 9 gave their age correctly. It seems that the apparent "standing still of time" is present more in schizophrenics than in the other groups which were examined. Among the subgroups of schizophrenia we encountered it most frequently in the hebephrenics.

These answers given by the 7 schizophrenics are of interest in view of the studies on the meaning of time in current philosophy and psychiatry. It is well known that time is experienced differently by various individuals and by the same individual differently, dependent on his age and his emotional state at that moment. Erikson discusses some psychoanalytic aspects of time in his article on the problem of ego identity (10). He describes a special crisis in the individual development at the transition from adolescence to young adulthood, which lies in the difficulties of achieving an ego identity. This development can be disturbed. Erikson states that in some instances of delayed and prolonged adolescence an extreme form of a disturbance in the experience of time appears which, in its milder form, belongs to the psychopathology of everyday adolescence. In its severe form, however, it consists of a decided disbelief in the possibility that time may bring change —and yet also of a violent fear that it may. This contradiction is often expressed in a general slowing up, which makes the patient behave within the routine of activities (and also of therapy), as though he were moving in molasses. It may be that similar processes in the transition from adolescence to young adulthood in general, as investigated by Erikson, may also explain the phenomenon of time standing still as seen in one group of our schizophrenics.

For the existential analysts time is a central concept, and they regard the future, in contrast to present or past, as the dominant mode of time for human beings. Minkowski describes a disturbance of the depressed patient in relation to time, namely, the inability to comprehend a future (20). Consequently, the depressed person is unable to

Table 6. Patients' replies to the question: How old are you?

Diagnoses	No. of patients	No answer	Chronological age	Age as of onset of psychosis	Other ages
Schizophrenic, hebephrenic	14	3	4	5	2
Schizophrenic, catatonic	8	5	2	1	0
Schizophrenic, paranoid	7	1	5	1	0
Schizophrenic, simple	1	0	1	0	0
Schizophrenic, total	30	9	12	7	2
General paretic	10	5	3	1	1
Epilepsy with psychosis	10	0	9	0	1

feel any hope or sense of continuity with the morrow. Binswanger however, points out that if the depressed patient could become entirely merged with the past without "knowing" anything further about future and present, he would no longer be depressed (4). The time of the depressed person, even though slowed down, still moves. The predominance of the past (or more correctly of the have-been), in unison with the falling apart of the comprehension of the present and future, seems to Binswanger fundamental for the understanding of what is called the psychic life of the schizophrenic.

Summary. A substantial minority of regressed schizophrenics stated their ages to be that which they were at the onset of their illness. This finding is discussed in the frameworks of various theoretical conceptions of time.

Thought contents of mute
chronic schizophrenic patients

*Interviews after injection of amobarbital sodium
(sodium amytal) with metamphetamine
hydrochloride (methedrine)*

The paucity of research papers concerned with old schizophrenics was mentioned before. Moreover, there existed almost nothing in the literature in regard to old schizophrenics who are also mute, and whose muteness has lasted for many years. This state of affairs is understandable, since the very fact that these patients are mute produces an almost unconquerable barrier to understanding and to psychotherapy. Some of the pertinent questions which await examination are: What are mute schizophrenic patients thinking about? With what are they preoccupied? Do they think at all? Schizophrenics whose muteness has lasted for many years have seldom been regarded as an appropriate subject for research. The psychiatrically mute patients are really the forgotten men, who, after a few years have passed, are no longer visited by their closest relatives.

Kant was able to appraise the state of inner organization even in completely withdrawn patients through utilization of Sodium Amytal interviews (14). He found that extreme cases of behavior disturbance are always accompanied by extreme inner disorganization. The withdrawn catatonic also exhibits marked fragmentation of thought. Kelley, *et al.* mentioned an increased number of Rorschach responses in old mute schizophrenics after injections of Sodium Amytal, but no attempt was made to describe thought contents of patients in either paper (15). Any comprehensive account of withdrawn and mute schizophrenics must eventually present a picture of the thought contents and problems that concern such patients.

In a study by the present author with Grob and Lipton, Sodium Amytal and Methedrine were used in an attempt to administer Rorschach tests to psychiatrically mute, schizophrenic patients (5). This drug combination was recommended by several workers because they found that patients did not become as sleepy as they did when injected with Sodium Amytol alone (12,13). A control group of 6 schizophrenics who were not mute and an experimental group of 13 mute chronic schizophrenics whose muteness had been present for 3 to 26 years were given Rorschach tests before and after injection of Sodium Amytal with Methedrine. The findings included the following: a) after administration of the drugs non-mute patients became more expressive without significant change in their thought contents; b) of the 13 mute patients, 7 or 54% talked for 2 to 3 hours after receiving the injections.

A further study was undertaken to discover the *main thought content and interests* of schizophrenic men who had not spoken for many years and who had spent their lives sitting in hospital dayrooms day after day. Injections of Sodium Amytal, followed by Methedrine, were used to temporarily overcome the muteness (19). Those 3 mute patients who had talked best during the experiments mentioned above were used in the present investigation. No psychotherapeutic aims were projected for this study. The interviewing of these patients was regarded as a pilot study, and the method used changed from patient to patient. No rigid or stereotyped sequence of questions was asked. When patients spoke freely, they were not interrupted by questions which would disturb the free flow of speech and association. When they hesitated, questions were asked which in most cases referred to their last remarks; at times questions were asked to clarify, if possible, remarks not clearly understood by the examiner.

The sentences spoken by these 3 patients were often rambling and disconnected. I have, however, arranged the most significant statements of each patient according to topics and in this way it is much easier to appraise their thought content and the range of their interests. *The apparent similarity of the 3 mute patients disappeared as soon as they spoke.* The different educational levels and backgrounds, the different aims in life and the different frustrations became evident. The impression gained from these patients was that *they were all concerned with problems which occurred before or at the time of onset of their illness,* but that they were not concerned with their present environment.*

I should like to add here that one must be cautious not to equate muteness and withdrawal. It is granted that in most of the cases of chronic psychiatrically mute schizophrenics an extreme degree of withdrawal is also present, but this is not always so, as was seen in a fourth

---

* For the actual protocol the reader is referred to the original publication (9).

patient, Mr. D. After many years of being completely mute and keeping his eyes rigidly closed, Mr. D.'s behavior changed in 1955, perhaps
owing to medication (at that time he received reserpine). He became
smiling and friendly, helping on the ward with cleaning. Because of
his friendly and helpful behavior and his winning smile, he soon became the pet of all the personnel. Nevertheless, he remained completely mute, not even saying "aah" when his throat was examined.
Various tranquilizers and energizers were given. In April, 1960 he was
transferred to another ward. Finally, in June, 1960, while on Stelazine
10 mg. twice daily, a renewed effort was made to motivate the patient
to talk. He was given ground privileges, and later was promised a pass
to visit his family if he would ask for it. After two hours of apparent
internal struggle, the patient came sweating to his therapist. With
great effort and in a very low whisper he asked for the permission to
visit his parents. Permission was given, but with the remark that the
next time he would have to speak louder to have his request granted.
In the following days the patient spoke with slowly increasing loud-
ness, and he was highly commended for it. After a few more days, he
visited his previous therapist and other personnel, and it became evident that this patient knew very well the names of the nurses, aides,
and doctors who had been treating him at the time that he was still
completely mute but the friendly, smiling pet of all the personnel.
Thus, this patient was in good contact with his surroundings during
the last years of muteness but apparently had been afraid to talk, probably because he was afraid to disclose some secret thoughts. It may be
of interest to mention in this connection that Mr. D. was also one of
the patients who had received in 1952 a Sodium Amytal and Methedrine injection but I had not been able to overcome his muteness at
that time.

Summary

1) It was possible to elicit the thought contents of three chronic psychiatrically mute schizophrenic patients with the aid of Sodium Amytal
and Methedrine. 2) The previously apparent similarity of these patients disappeared as soon as they spoke. The different educational
level and background, the different aims in life and frustrations became
evident. 3) Withdrawn, mute patients are thinking about events which
occurred before or at the time of their psychotic break. 4) Although
muteness is often a manifestation of withdrawal, this is not always the
case, as illustrated by the report of a mute but not withdrawn patient,
who later improved, talked and showed that he had observed the
events around him during the time of his muteness.

Many questions remain for investigation in this area of research.
Perhaps of greatest significance is what factors in the environment and

what factors in the behavior of the aging psychotic himself affect his chances of returning to life in the community. Certainly, the fact that not much work has been done in describing, evaluating and explaining the behavioral changes of psychotics when they grow old makes this field an untapped reservoir for interested researchers.

References

1. Arieti, S. Primitive habits and perceptual alterations in the terminal stage of schizophrenic. *Arch. Neurol. Psychiat.*, 1945, *53*, 378-384.
2. Arieti, S. *American Handbook of Psychiatry.* New York: Basic Books, 1959.
3. Barucci, M. La vacchiaia degli schizofrenici. *Riv. Pat. Nerv. Ment.*, 1955, *76*, 257-284.
4. Binswanger, L. The case of Ellen West. In R. May, E. Angel, and H. F. Ellenberger (eds.), *Existence: A new dimension in psychiatry and psychology.* New York: Basic Books, 1958.
5. Ehrentheil, O. F., Grob, S., and Lipton, M. The use of Sodium Amytal and Methedrine for psychological testing of mute schizophrenic patients. *Bedford Research,* 1953, *2*, No. 3, 1-17.
6. Ehrentheil, O. F., and Jenney, P. B.: Does time stand still for some psychotics? *A.M.A. Arch. Gen. Psychiat.,* 1960, *3*, 1-3.
7. Ehrentheil, O. F., *et al.* Motor activity of schizophrenic patients observed over thirty years. *A.M.A. Arch. Gen. Psychiat.,* 1962, *7*, 266-276.
8. Ehrentheil, O. F., and Davis, E. T. Degree of fixation of thought content in relation to withdrawal versus non-withdrawal in hospitalized mental patients observed over 30 years. *J. Nerv. and Ment. Dis.,* 1962, *135*, 455-549.
9. Ehrentheil, O. F. Thought content of mute schizophrenic patients: Interviews after injection of amobarbital sodium (Sodium Amytal) and methamphetamine hydrochloride (Methedrine). *J. Nerv. & Ment. Dis.,* 1963, *137*, 187-197.
10. Erikson, E. H. The problem of ego-identity. *J. Am. Psychoanalyt. Assoc.,* 1956, *4*, 56-121.
11. Fleck, U. Über Beobachtungen bei alten Fällen von Schizophrenia. *Arch. Psychiat. Nervenkr.,* 1928, *85*, 705-760.
12. Gottlieb, J. S., and Coburn, F. E. Psychopharmacologic study of schizophrenia and depression. Intravenous administration of Sodium Amytal and Amphetamine. *Arch. Neurol. & Psychiat.,* 1944, *51*, 260-263.
13. Huston, P. E., and Singer, M. M. Effect of Sodium Amytal and Amphetamine Sulfate on mental set in schizophrenia. *Arch. Neurol. & Psychiat.,* 1945, *53*, 365-369.
14. Kant, O. Clinical analysis of schizophrenic deterioration: An investigation aided by Sodium Amytal interviews. *Psychiat. Quart.,* 1943, *17*, 426-445.
15. Kelley, D. M., *et al.* Intravenous Sodium Amytal medication as an aid to the Rorschach method. *Psychiat. Quart.,* 1941, *15*, 68-73.

16. Kraus, P. S. Theoretical consideration for a proposed rating scale to measure clinical change in psychotic patients. *Bedford Research,* 1957, *4,* 4.

17. Lanzkron, J., and Wolfson, W. Prognostic value of perceptual distortion of temporal orientation in chronic schizophrenics. *Amer. J. Psychiat.,* 1958, *114,* 744-746.

18. Lorr, M. Multidimensional scale for rating psychiatric patients. Hospital form. Veterans Administration Technical Bulletin, 10-507. Washington, D.C., November, 1953.

19. Lorr, M. Rating scales and check lists on the evaluation of psychopathology. *Psychol. Bull.,* 1954, *51,* 119-127.

20. Minkowski, E. Finding in a case of schizophrenic depression. In R. May, E. Angel, and H. F. Ellenberger (eds.), *Existence: A New Dimension in Psychiatry and Psychology.* New York: Basic Books, 1958.

21. Mueller, C. *Über des Senium der Schizophrenen.* Basel: S. Karger, 1959.

22. Reznikoff, M., and Zeller, W. W. A procedure for evaluating the status of schizophrenic patients. *J. Clin. Exp. Psychopath.* 1957, *18,* 367-371.

23. Weygandt, W. Über alte dementia praecox. *Zbl. Nervenheilk.,* 1904, *15,* 469-470.

8

What happens to old psychologists? A preliminary report

Ruth Aisenberg

Introduction

Increasing attention has recently been focussed on the later years of life—their special characteristics, problems and rewards. Experience with the scientific literature leads one to conclude that very little is known about the psychological aspects of growing older. Indeed, except for those who present pressing social problems or are ill, there is precious little data available on what life after middle age is really like. It seemed logical to approach for information those who not only have reached the so-called retirement years but also have had the psychological background to enable them to provide personal insights while maintaining some degree of objectivity. It was for these reasons that the investigation to be described was undertaken.

For purposes of clarity, this chapter has been divided into three sections. The first describes the survey procedures and subjects. The second presents the results, together with explanatory notes and remarks. The third contains a brief commentary.

The sample

Survey procedures

The 500 subjects for this study were selected at random from the 797 members of the American Psychological Association who were at least 65 years of age by December 31, 1963. Four of these no longer lived in the United States and were excluded from the study. A questionnaire together with an explanatory letter and stamped return envelope was sent to each of the 496 remaining subjects. The questionnaire, coded to assure the respondent's anonymity, consisted of 7 pages of questions. The first section, requesting primarily normative data, and the second, labeled "Personal Experience," were intended for all re-

Valuable help in the statistical analysis of data reported here was provided by Dr. Sol Aisenberg.

spondents. The third section, "Employment," requested information from those who considered themselves employed, whether or not they worked full time or received pay. The fourth and final section, "Retirement," contained questions for those who considered themselves retired, even though they may do some work as a hobby or pastime. At the end of the questionnaire space was provided for remarks, ideas and suggestions.

At this writing, the status of the 496 questionnaires is as follows:

Returned, completed	174
Returned, address unknown	11
Returned, subject deceased	7
Returned, "not applicable to me"	2
Returned, too ill to answer	2
Returned too late for use	2
Returned without explanation	1
Not returned	296*

The subjects

The first efforts in data analysis were directed toward discovering the general characteristics of the respondents.

1. *Age and sex distribution.* The group of 174 respondents consisted of 106 men, or 37% of the original total male sample to which questionnaires were sent, and 68 women, or 36% of the original female sample. Their age distribution is summarized in Table 1.

It can be seen from Table 1 that there is little difference between the ages of the male and female respondents. Although well into the so-called retirement years, the subjects as a group would not be considered extremely old.

2. *Marital status.* The data on subjects' marital status is more thought-provoking (Table 2).

The sex differences in present and past marital status are striking. Almost all of the men in the sample have been married at some time in their lives; but only a little more than half of the women. Thus, the marriage rate for the female subjects is not only lower than that for the males but appreciably lower than that for women in the population as a whole. The divorce rate among women subjects, by contrast, is significantly higher than that for the men; the re-marriage rate is just about the same. Further, a much larger proportion of the female than male subjects has been widowed. This finding, however, is not unexpected.

3. *Types of dwellings.* It was discovered that 83% of the men and 68% of the women live in houses which, in the main, they own rather

---

* Since questionnaires were sent 4th class, the post office was not required to return those which were undeliverable. A few were returned despite this. However, we have no way of estimating how many others never reached the addressees.

than rent. One per cent of the men and 2% of the women have both a house and an apartment. The remaining subjects live in apartments. That the majority of subjects live in houses seems surprising in view of the fact that very few still have children living at home, and many actually live alone.

4. *Number of children.* As a group the respondents have relatively few children (Table 3). This is true of the males as well as the females, although to a lesser extent. Calculations were based on the number of subjects who reported having been married at some time in their lives; hence, the low percentage of children for women subjects cannot be attributed to their low marriage rate.

5. *Religion.* With regard to religion, the group of subjects both as a whole and when separated by sex is remarkably homogeneous. Of the total sample, 72% is Protestant, 4% is Catholic and 3% is Jewish; 10% stated they have no religion. The remainder gave miscellaneous responses.

Table 1. Subjects' age and sex distribution

	Male	Female	Total
Mode	66	65	66
Mean	70.9	70.4	70.8
Median	70	69.5	69.5
Range	65-89	65-92	65-92

Table 2. Marital status of male and female subjects in per cent

	Married	Widowed	Divorced	Single
Male	88.8%	7.5%	.9%	1.9%
Female	33.8%	16.2%	5.9%	44.2%

	Married more than once	Remarried*	Ever married
Male	24.3%	27.4%	98.1%
Female	8.8%	26.1%	55.8%

*Indicates married now; but married to someone else previously.

Table 3. Per cent of married or previously married subjects who have number of children indicated

Number of Children						
	0	1	2	3	4	5
Male	22.2%	22.2%	27.9%	18.2%	5.8%	3.9%
Female	42.1%	21.1%	31.6%	2.6%	2.6%	—

These then are the respondents. To speak of a "typical" subject does violence to what individual differences the data reveal. However, it may be helpful to summarize the average respondent to provide a first frame of reference in considering the results which follow. Our typical respondent is Protestant, about 70 years of age, and lives in a house. If male, he is married and the father of two, one or none. If female, she is likely to be single; if married she is the mother of no children or of two.

It is obvious on the basis of even this scanty data that the group studied is hardly representative of older Americans generally. However, no professional group would be; and, it will be remembered that some of the unique attributes of this particular professional group were the very reason for its selection.

Results

Results presented in this report are in no way complete. Some of the questionnaire items are not considered; the data for those discussed have not yet been completely analyzed statistically. However, the number and variety of areas surveyed seem to warrant their presentation in different forms at different stages of analysis. Topics included in this report were selected on the basis of their general interest and possible implications. To facilitate later reference to the results, they will be summarized under descriptive headings. None except the last two of these appeared in the original questionnaire. Neither is the order of the questions considered necessarily that found in the questionnaire. The wording and numbers, however, have not been altered.

Several of the items included in the questionnaire and analyzed below were drawn from procedures developed for an investigation of elderly institutionalized patients, but considered to be of more general significance.* Some comparison of the present findings with data

---

* Partial report presented by Robert Kastenbaum, Philip E. Slater and Ruth Aisenberg, "Toward a conceptual model of geriatric psychopharmacology: Experiments with thioridazine and dextro-amphetamine." Paper read at 16th annual scientific meeting, Gerontological Society, November 9, 1963 (Boston, Mass.).

obtained from elderly patients can be found in Chapter 19 of this volume.

A. Self-perception

To what extent do subjects who would generally be considered "old" see themselves this way?

Q. 23. *Do you think of yourself as being old?*

98% of the subjects answered this question. Of these, fully 70% said "no." Only 18% said "yes." The only apparently significant sex difference was that a greater proportion (22%) of men than women replied "yes."

It is readily apparent that the self-perception of the majority of the respondents is at variance with the generally held conception of when old age begins. The comments of many subjects reveal an awareness of the discrepancy between their own image of themselves and that generally held by others: "I know my age but can laugh at it;" ". . . but I think about ten years younger."

The group that did feel old was questioned further:

Q. 23a. *If so, when and under what circumstances did you first begin to think so?*

More than half of the women and somewhat less than a third of the men began to feel old after the onset of illness or physical handicaps. 16% said that they started feeling old at retirement. None of the women in the sample felt that simply reaching a particular age (e.g., 65) made them feel old; but 22% of the men did. Also approximately 6% of the men but no women thought that the attitude or behavior of others made them feel old. That illness and retirement affect self-perception is not surprising; but that age *per se* or the behavior of others affects males in this respect and not females certainly is.

B. Past and present compared: ideas, capacities,
time's apparent flow and its use

Subjects were asked to compare the past with the present along several different dimensions and to specify the changes they believe to have occurred:

Q. 41. *Are your present ideas about "old age" different from those you had when you were 35?*

Over half of the subjects (52%) believe that their present ideas about old age are different now. 22% do not believe that their ideas have undergone any changes. Only 12% of the sample stated that they never thought about old age when they were 35; and 5% were uncertain. (Remaining responses were distributed among miscellaneous categories.)

The men as a group reported somewhat less attitude change than did the women. One cannot help but speculate about the relationship, if any, between this finding and the results cited under Q. 23a above. Do more men than women feel old when they reach age 65 because they retain their earlier, more negative attitudes toward the elderly to a greater extent than women do?

Subjects were asked to specify changes:

Q. 41a. *How? (do present ideas differ)*

The variety of responses and percentages and subjects giving them are summarized in Table 4.

It can be seen that many of the changes specified could be considered "positive" or "desirable" (e.g., "feel better than expected," "its pleasanter," "occurs later"). More than half of the subjects mentioned these. A few of the changes seem more or less neutral ("have more experience," "more realistic"). Only one change is definitely negative in feeling tone: "feel worse than expected." Thus, on the whole, to these subjects, old age once experienced is apparently somewhat less unpleasant or upsetting than anticipated. Answers to Q. 33 are relevant and partially corroborative.

Table 4. Changes in ideas of "old age" and per cent of subjects mentioning each*

Idea changed	Male	Female	Total
It occurs later than anticipated	23%	28%	25%
Different attitude, generally Different life philosophy	21%	7%	14%
Enjoy it more than expected; pleasanter	8%	7%	8%
Feel better psychologically or physically than expected	6%	12%	9%
Think about old age more now	8%	0	4%
Elderly more able, interesting than expected	6%	14%	10%
More realistic now	4%	0	2%
Have more experience	2%	2%	2%
Feel worse than expected	2%	7%	4%
Miscellaneous	6%	6%	6%

*Since not all subjects changed their attitudes and some mentioned more than one change, figures do not add up to 100%.

Q. 33. *Are there some ways in which you feel yourself to have improved or become more capable as compared with when you were younger?*

85% of the subjects who responded answered "Yes;" 8% said "No" and 3% were uncertain. Quite obviously there is again a marked difference between this sample's responses and the notions about old age held by the general population. Perhaps these responses stem from wishful thinking. Needs influence perception, after all. Everyone knows that cheese and wine may improve with age; but after 40, people certainly don't—or do they? In what way could all of these people have "improved?"

Q. 33a. *Please specify:*

A great many different responses were given. Relatively few were repeated. The only answers given by 10% or more of the sample were:

"More capable professionally"	12%
"More tolerant"	10%
"Better judgment"	10%

The following responses were made by between 5 and 10% of the sample group: "more understanding," "better emotional control," "improved socially," "more at ease or less anxious," "wiser" or "more mature," and "think," "plan" or "organize" better. A few individuals state that they now have broader interests, better perspective, are better informed, and have more insight than formerly. There were other miscellaneous replies.

Negative changes were also surveyed:

Q. 34. *Are there some things you do not do as well as you used to do?*

Results here are unequivocal. "Yes" was the answer of 90% of the total sample. The remaining responses were divided between "no," "uncertain" and "no answer."

Q. 34a. *Please specify:*

There was a high degree of agreement on negative changes experienced. 59% of the respondents mentioned being less capable of acts requiring physical endurance, coordination, strength, etc.: "tennis," "walk," "jump," "climb," "fornicate." 22% felt that memory was less reliable. 9% reported various sensory problems. Other difficulties have been encountered by small numbers of subjects: a great many more women than men feel that they now move more slowly.

The physical depletion and memory loss reported support the general experience of laymen and observations of gerontologists. This self-report together with the high total proportion of subjects admitting to decreasing capabilities testifies to the relative objectivity of the respondents and tends to lend greater credence to the validity of their responses in less explored areas.

In addition to comparing past and present ideas and capabilities, the psychologists were asked:

Q. 28. *Do you find that time seems to pass more slowly, more swiftly, or at about the same rate as it did when you were younger?* Responses were straightforward and about as expected:

"Faster"	64%
"Slower"	4%
"Same rate"	26%
"Misc., no answer"	6%

Whether or not subjects who replied "same rate" differ in any consistent way from the majority which answered "faster" has not yet been determined. It is possible that members of the smaller group simply use their time differently; but a further investigation of their personality and normative characteristics seems warranted.

Q. 30. *Concerning the following general areas of interest, would you say that you now spend more, less, or the same amount of time as you did when you were younger?*

The areas surveyed were: home and family; profession; local politics; social causes; personal financial status; sports; sex; social life; travel; art; literature; music and other hobbies.

Group trends emerged. Compared with earlier years, subjects now spend more time on travel, hobbies and home and family; less time on profession, sports, and sex, and about the same amount of time on local politics, social causes, financial status, social life, art, literature and music. An unusually large proportion of subjects did not answer some parts of the question. 20% said nothing about "other hobbies." Whether they had none or didn't wish to specify is unknown. 17% gave no response to "sex." (Obviously the possible explanations advanced for omission of "other hobbies" cannot apply.) It must be assumed that the subject who wrote "very personal—why answer?" speaks for the group. 16% did not respond to "financial status."

80% of the subjects said that they do have hobbies. Pastimes mentioned revealed a wide diversity of interests ranging in physical activity level from "tennis" to "thinking about psychology . . ." and, in relationship to their profession, from actual voluntary research in the field to snorkeling and raising dogs. The two hobbies mentioned most frequently were writing and gardening.

C. *"Remembrance of things past" and second thoughts on past decisions*

We have already seen (Q. 34a. above) that 22% of the survey respondents believe that memory is less efficient now than formerly.

Whether in those subjects affected this impairment is an all-pervasive or a partial one, applies only to remote or recent events, or is equally characteristic of both men and women, remains to be determined.

Q. 40. *How vividly can you remember when you were the following ages: 12, 21, 30 and 45 years?*

A five-point scale ranging from "not at all" to "very clearly" was provided. Intermediate points were not labeled.

Of the total sample, 96% answered this question. Their replies indicated a fairly consistent tendency for increasingly remote ages to be remembered less well. The data indicate no tendency whatever for early years to be recalled clearly and later ones forgotten. These findings were characteristic of both men and women. There was one consistent sex difference. The women as a group tended to recall every age more clearly than did the men. The differences between the two groups in recall of age 12 were especially great and will most likely prove to be statistically significant. Differences for age 45, though less, may also be significant.

The real meaning of these results is still in doubt. We do not know how clearly people younger than the subjects recall their earlier years; or, at what point, if indeed it can be pinpointed, memory begins to deteriorate. We do not know to what extent memory loss in later years is a universal phenomenon, or if it is inevitable. Obviously, many older people are organically impaired and literally cannot remember. But what about the apparently healthy, still independent older people who show some memory loss? Are repression and denial at work here? How much of the memory problem common among old people is that they *prefer* not to recall certain things?

Subjects were asked to look back and re-evaluate their decisions. Only 16% were unwilling or unable to do this.

Q. 35. *If you had your life to live over, in what areas would you make a different major decision? (Please be as specific as possible.)*

28% of the total sample would change no major decision. Whether this reflects real satisfaction with past or present life or merely a belief that changes would have been impossible or useless is unknown.

It was possible to isolate several areas in which respondents would like to have made different decisions: emphasis in work; personal life; education; choice of profession; use of leisure; self-confidence and use of money. The two broad areas of work emphasis and personal life command the greatest attention. More major decisions would be altered in these than in other areas (24%). It is interesting to note that many more men than women would change decisions about emphasis in work. More women would change decisions in personal life. A typical male response was, "I'd teach fewer hours and publish more." A not infrequent female response was ". . . add a husband and children."

12% of the subjects indicated changes in decisions about education. These generally involved taking different courses (not a different major); finishing school earlier or taking another degree.

9% of the psychologists would prefer to have entered a different profession. The one most frequently specified was "M.D." or "psychiatrist;" but "artist," "musician" and academic fields were also mentioned. One apparently battle-weary respondent indicated an interest in continuing to teach, but "a less controversial subject than psychology."

The answers in the miscellaneous category were interesting. They include among others: "be listed in 'Who's Who!' "; "have wife take care of the budget;" have "regular physical exams" to avoid later surgery; and "be less rash in sexual matters. . . ." One male respondent stated that this whole question was just plain "silly."

In looking back to the period when they were receiving their professional training, a large number of the psychologists surveyed felt that the newest, most important trends or "schools" of psychology at the time, were behaviorism, Gestalt psychology and tests and measurements. (Fewer mentioned Freudianism and miscellaneous areas.) The subjects were also asked:

Q. 20. *In what general area of psychology did you specialize? Why?*

Q. 21. *If you were just starting out in psychology today, what general field of specialization would you select? Why?*

Initially the overall response trends to both of these questions were deceptively simple. However, closer inspection of the data revealed that, in some instances, responses could not legitimately be reported for the group as a whole because of the wide sex differences: some of the apparent changes in the choice of the whole sample really reflected answers given solely or primarily by members of one sex. Also, in some cases in which seemingly no change had taken place, men and women subjects had actually altered their choices—but in reverse directions so that the changes canceled each other out. Hence, for some fields of specialization the responses of men and women are considered separately. The major findings were:

1. Compared with their previous, actual choices a larger proportion of both men and women said that they would today specialize in clinical psychology (31% vs. 28% formerly); physiological psychology (8% vs. 3.5%) and industrial and personnel work (5% vs. 2%). It should be noted that although both men and women would select clinical psychology in greater numbers today, the sex differences in preference for this specialty are unusually great: 19% of the men and 41% of the women were actually trained in clinical psychology. If they were choosing today the figures would be 21% for the men and 44% for the women.

2. Compared with their past, real choice, a smaller number of both men and women would today specialize in experimental psychology (10% vs. 14% formerly) and tests and measurements (3% vs. 7%). (Only one of the people who would leave experimental psychology was a woman; only 7 had selected it originally.)

3. Today fewer men would choose applied psychology (2% vs. 6% formerly). Very slightly fewer men would selected learning (4% vs. 5%) and general psychology (2% vs. 3%). No women had selected applied psychology originally and none would now. Learning and general psychology had each been the fields of specialization of only one woman. Each would be chosen by two women today.

4. Fewer women today would choose child and developmental psychology (9% vs. 16% formerly). One more man would than formerly (5% vs. 4%).

5. There were minor changes in the field of vocational guidance: More men (10% vs. 8%) would choose it today. One less woman would select this area now than in the past (7% vs. 6% formerly).

6. Only one man specialized in theoretical psychology in the past. Three say they would today. In addition two men stated that they would select history and systems now. No women either actually in the past or today chose these fields.

7. There was almost no change in the proportion of psychologists mentioning personality and individual differences as past or present choices: 4.2% formerly vs. 4.6% now (one more male today).

8. 4% did and 6% would today select miscellaneous specialties (aesthetics, mental hygiene, statistics, the influence of heredity, etc.).

9. Less than 3% of the subjects gave no response to either question.

10. Less than 2% of the subjects answered Q. 21. with a field other than psychology.

Insofar as answers to the question "Why?" are concerned, there was very little difference between the reasons given for actual choice of specialty in the past and hypothetical choice today. The main difference was that several psychologists mentioned the influence of former professors upon past decision (Thorndike, T. Kelley and Lashley, for example).

Otherwise, responses were generally of three kinds: 1) The most numerous were those in which personal themes predominate: "it fits my personality;" "it's fun for me;" "enjoy it;" "interesting to me," etc. 2) Others gave what might be called "external" or seemingly objective reasons: "it's a livelihood," "job opportunities;" "need for more information" in that area; "a neglected" but important field; "useful;" community need; etc. 3) Some answers were combinations of the first two categories: "reconciliation of self interest and altruism;" "interesting and useful;" "fun and needed;" etc. Often the same reason was given for a number of different choices. For example, several people said that they had chosen experimental, general or clinical psychology because it provided "the best general background" for all fields of psychology. One clinician spoke for many who were well satisfied with their original choice, "Therapy still thrills me." The most unusual reason for selecting a field of specialization was given by the man who wished to study the "biochemical determinants of behavior to kill off the psychoanalytic school."

Analyses are still incomplete; but it seems quite clear that there is no particular reason or group of reasons associated with the choice of specialty either actually in the past or hypothetically at present. When one considers the multiplicity of factors affecting vocational choice, people's insight into their own motivation and their willingness to share it, this is not particularly surprising. In light of the sophistication of the sample group, the response of one 72-year-old subject is certainly germane: "You should know better than to ask 'Why?' "

Q. 53. *Do you feel that being a psychologist has been of help to you personally in making adjustments and/or meeting problems in your own life?*

A large majority of the sample, 79%, felt that being a psychologist had been of help to them personally in meeting life's problems. An additional 3% thought that it had helped "some" or "a little." 4% of the sample group was uncertain. Only 4% answered "no" or its equivalent. 9% of the sample gave no response.

It is interesting to note that despite the relatively large proportion of respondents trained in clinical psychology only one of those who answered "no" was so trained. Apparently being a clinician is especially helpful to the individual personally (or the subjects felt that they should say it is). The largest number of people from any one field who thought that being a psychologist had not helped them personally were originally trained in physiological or experimental psychology (3 each). Others who also said "no" had studied industrial and applied psychology, education, personality and miscellaneous combinations of fields other than clinical psychology.

A few of the subjects who answered "yes" volunteered additional comments. Two stated that being a psychologist had been of personal value to them because it led to their undergoing psychoanalysis. Two others believed that it increased their understanding of people's behavior. Another remarked, "I always try to take the medicine I prescribe."

Whether or not there is a relationship between the answer to this question and general job satisfaction remains to be determined. However, we do know that not all of those who found no personal help in psychology are dissatisfied with it: One subject responded to Q. 53: "Not a bit; but it's been a lot of fun."

D. Life expectancy, religion and life after death

Q. 31. *If you had a choice, how old would you live to be?*

Only 5% of the total sample refused to deal with this question. This supports the notion that older people are not nearly so reluctant to talk about death as younger people are to ask about it.

Answers were of two types—specific age or a descriptive statement. The two largest response groups consisted of those who wished to live "as long as healthy and independent" (27%) and those who wished to live "81-90 years" (20%). A larger number of men than women chose either relatively "early" death (between 70 and 80 years) or relative immortality (101 years or more). Also, the men as a group were less able to decide on an answer.

Q. 32. *To what age do you expect to live?*

The subjects' estimates of actual life expectancy, when compared with length of life desired, are somewhat more modest and realistic. 12% had said that they would like to live to be 101 or more. Only 2% thought that they might actually live this long. However, 37% of the subjects expect to live to be between 81 and 90 years old.

Q. 13. *Importance of religion to you: great, moderate or little*

Replies can only be described as "unremarkable." 37% answered "moderate." An equal number of subjects (26%) said "great" and "little."

Q. 43. *Do you believe in life after death?*

The distribution of responses to this question was unusually even: "yes" 35%; "no" 33%; "uncertain" 26%. There appears to be no significant sex difference. An attempt was made to determine to what extent belief in life after death has remained constant through the years:

Q. 44. *Have you always felt this way?*

For the group as a whole, the proportion of subjects who believe in life after death has apparently diminished with the passage of time: of those who replied that they do not now believe in life after death, almost two-thirds say that this was not always so. By contrast, among those who do now believe in life after death, 79% have always felt this way. In addition, of the 32% who are now uncertain, 23% state that they believed more firmly previously. Hence, the net change over the years has been in the direction of less rather than greater faith in an after-life.

E. Smoking, drinking and health

    Q. 36. *How much do you smoke cigarettes, cigars, pipes?*

If the smoking habits of our elderly psychologists were representative of the American population as a whole, the cigarette manufacturers would surely go bankrupt. In the sample studied, 76% of the men and 83% of the women do not smoke cigarettes at all. Only 6 people (3.5%) could be considered heavy smokers of cigarettes (one pack a day or more); 7% smoke moderately (½-1 pack daily). The other respondents were divided equally between those who smoked "little" and those who smoked "very little."

Cigar smoking was even less common. All but one of the females and 84% of the males never smoked cigars. Only 5 men (4.7% of the sample) smoked two or more cigars daily. An additional 4% smoked up to one cigar daily. The remainder smoked much less—many almost never.

None of the women smoke pipes. However, 18% of the men do smoke them—and some rather heavily at that: "20 lbs. of tobacco a year," "6 hrs. a day," "pretty heavy." No comparison with figures for the population as a whole have yet been made; but 18% seems rather high.

Thus, the elderly psychologists as a group cannot really be considered "smokers" save for a minority who are pipe devotees.

    Q. 37. *How much do you drink beer, wine, liquor?*

Although a considerably larger proportion of our subjects drink than smoke, they could hardly be considered "drinkers."

55% of the men and 69% of the women never drink beer. 21% of the whole group (significantly more men than women) report that they drink "very little," "almost none," "one glass a month," etc. Only one subject, a man, reports that he is a "heavy" drinker of beer—"twelve glasses daily."

Wine seems to be our sample's favorite alcoholic beverage. Even so, 34% of the men and 28% of the women drink none whatever. Of those who stated that they drink it regularly, the amounts used ranged from one glass a month to two or (in a few cases) more glasses daily. On the whole, men consume larger amounts. Of those who did not mention the amount of wine used, the largest groups, 19% and 18% respectively, answered "rarely" or "occasionally."

With regard to liquor, the situation is only a little different. The proportion of non-drinkers is larger: 43% for the men and 37% for the women. Of the 12% of the respondents who use liquor regularly, amounts mentioned range from one drink a month to three daily. Of those who used descriptive phrases, rather than stating amounts, only 2% replied "often" or "very often." 16% said "occasionally;" and 13% said "rarely" or an equivalent response.

Q. 38. *Do you have any health problems? (Please specify, if possible.)*

30% of the sample, significantly more men than women, replied "none." The findings, in general, hold few surprises: between 10% and 15% of the total group mentioned arthritis, other musculo-skeletal problems, cardiovascular ills other than heart attacks, gastrointestinal illness and sensory problems. Responses given by between 5% and 10% of the subjects included: respiratory ills, allergies, high and low blood pressure, genitourinary problems, cancer and past heart attacks. There was a wide variety of miscellaneous answers.

There was some obvious sex difference: 36% of the men but only 21% of the women listed no health problems. Why this is so, remains to be explained. It is possible, of course, that the men simply did not regard with equal gravity problems which the women listed. It is also possible that we have an unusually healthy group of men or an atypically sickly group of women. There were other sex differences which were not unexpected: more arthritis, other musculo-skeletal problems and allergies were reported by the women. More past heart attacks and genitourinary problems were reported by the men.

F. Employment

The data of the entire survey revealed few results so unexpected as those concerning employment. Seventy-five men and 49 women, or 71% of the total group studied, consider themselves employed. This includes some who work part time, with or without pay; but the majority of those who do even voluntary work have remained in their chosen field.

The mean age of the employed psychologists is very slightly younger than that of the sample as a whole: men, 70 years; women 69 years. The proportion of the sample employed full or part time is summarized in Table 5.

Subjects were asked for their "job titles." Space does not permit a complete account. However, these titles were listed more than once:

Job Title	No. Subjects
Professor	40
Psychologist (clinical, counseling, school, etc.)	37
Director (clinic, hospital, research foundation, business)	27
Chairman (committee, board of directors, psychology department)	5
M.D. (also psychologists)	2

The above seems to indicate that a large proportion of the sample is made up of unusually competent, active people. It would also appear that a relatively broad spectrum of work opportunities is available to psychologists in their later years. This certainly does not correspond to the employment situation in most fields. Further investigation is in order; but it is possible that this freedom of job choice is more apparent than real.

Table 5. Per cent of total sample employed full time, part time or both (2 jobs)

	Full time	Part time	Both
Male	45%	25%	2%
Female	44%	25%	1%

Q. 65. *Do you feel that you have ever been discriminated against in employment because of your age?*

Responses again were rather surprising: 87% of the men and 63% of the women said "no." Subjects were quite explicit: "Hell, no. I can't seem to avoid jobs;" "no, I could get more work if I wanted it;" "never." 12% of the total group (more women than men) have had difficulties: compulsory retirement age; "in business and industry;" "was hard to get training;" less pay or prestige; etc. Most of the people who complained of compulsory retirement age had been working in a college or university.

6% of the women felt they had been discriminated against because of their sex. Surprisingly, these results tend overall to confirm the implication noted above that the older psychologist who wants a position can usually find it—and often a rather good one at that. (We do not know, of course, about the characteristics of the nonresponding subjects. It is still possible that most of those in the original sample (496) are unemployed.)

Q. 66. *Has your age proved to be an advantage in any way in your work? If so, please explain.*

More than half of the subjects replied, "yes." About one-fifth said, "no." The remaining responses were divided among "uncertain," "not age but experience" and "no answer." There were no significant sex differences. There was also very close agreement between men and women on just what advantages age confers. Arranged in order from most to least frequently mentioned (those under the same numbers were mentioned equally), they are: 1) more experience and/or wisdom; 2) more prestige and/or respect; people have more confidence in older psychologists; 3) can speak with more authority and less fear; 4) accepted better by children; have better judgment and perspective; accepted better by adults; "in work with the aged;" have "maturity;" and 5) more influence, more insight; seniority. There were other miscellaneous replies.

G. Retirement

Eighty-nine or 51% of the total sample consider themselves to be retired. Since some work in retirement, there is some overlap between the retirement and employment groups. The percentages of those fully and partially retired are:

	Fully Retired	Partially Retired
Male	26%	27%
Female	29%	26%

The mean age of retired men is 72.9, of retired women 72.4 years.

It can be seen by referring to Table V, that more of the older psychologists studied are fully employed than fully retired. Not unexpectedly, the mean age of retired subjects is greater than that of employed subjects, although only by 3 years. However, there is a great deal of overlap in age of subjects in the two groups.

Following the pattern set by the employed, the group of retired psychologists gave some unexpected responses.

Q. 70. *Has your standard of living changed appreciably since retirement? If so, how?*

Surprisingly, 80% of the sample replied, "no." Only 16%, and more women than men, said, "yes." Of those who did answer "yes," 67% of the men and 31% of the women believed that their standard of living is now *higher*. 17% of the men and 37% of the women (who answered "yes") thought it is now lower. A few additional subjects said that their living standards had changed "a little," but did not indicate the direction of change. Since a total of only 14 felt there had been any change at all, the results for this group can hardly be considered reliable. Nevertheless, responses support the overall impression that relatively few people in the group have serious financial problems—possibly fewer even than before retirement.

Q. 73. *What things about being retired do you like the most?*

There was a great deal of agreement on the advantages of retirement:

	Answer	% of Subjects Who Gave It
1.	More time	30%
2.	More freedom	26%
3.	No set schedule	16%
4.	Less pressure	12%
5.	Independence	12%
6.	Varied activity	3%
7.	Less responsibility	3%
8.	Can work also	3%

The majority of the responses given, including the miscellaneous ones not mentioned here, are so closely related that many can be seen as different aspects of the same factors, for example: 1, 2 and 5; 3, 4 and 7; 3 and 5; 6 and 8.

Q. 74. *What things about being retired do you like the least?*

12% of the subjects simply said "nothing" or "like it just as is." Several of the remaining subjects agreed on the following negative features:

Answer	% of Subjects Who Gave It
1. Fewer contacts with others, especially students	20%
2. Fewer contacts with professional people	11%
3. Less income or too little money	11%
4. Less physical competence or vigor	8%
5. Boring	5%
6. Non-productive or useless	5%

Very small percentages answered "lack of order or routine," "no work," "don't feel part of life," "feel life's ending," "people feel sorry for me," etc.

Q. 75. *What would you consider to be an ideal retirement life for yourself?*

20% of the sample did not answer this question and 46% felt the life they already had was ideal. Of those remaining 14% stated that their present life would be ideal, if only they could find some work: "part time work;" ". . . to be able to do humanitarian work 2-3 hours a day;" "a chance to do some research."

The next largest single group (10%) wanted a chance to travel. A limiting factor was the money travel requires. (This may partially explain "3" above.) 7% (more women than men) wished for improved health. Two people hoped for a sudden death so that they would never have to be dependent.

Q. 69. *How do you usually spend your time since retirement?*

Only 5% did not answer this question and those who did were quite specific:

Answer	% of Subjects Who Gave It
Read	37%
Employment	33%
Household chores, improvement or maintenance	28%
Write and/or edit ·	25%
Travel	25%
Garden and/or yard work	18%
Community service	17%
Social life	9%
TV, movies, radio	9%
Play cards	8%
The arts (theatre, music, etc.)	8%
Hunt, fish, boat	5%

Almost every other educational or recreational activity conceivable was mentioned at least once. Most subjects listed more than one activity and a great many listed several. The overall impression created was of an active, integrated group of people. There was a small minority who did little and seemed depressed. Most of these proved to have relatively serious health problems.

Commentary

Space does not permit a detailed discussion of, or speculation about each area of the survey reported. Suffice it to say that many of the preliminary findings do not conform very closely to the generally accepted, rather negative picture of life in old age: the proportion of subjects employed, the positions they hold, their reported standard of living, general life satisfaction and their broad range of interest and activities were surprising. To be sure, the group studied is atypical, although its subjects undoubtedly have much in common with members of other professional groups. Nevertheless, its responses raise questions of general interest to gerontologists:

1. Of 174 people, a sizeable group is active, independent and very much involved with life—and all of this despite the fact that they give evidence of many of the degenerative ills associated with old age. What is it about the background, personality, or way of life of these people which has facilitated their adjustment to the later years, and enabled them to continue to live creatively? What is there—or what is lacking—in the smaller group of subjects which prevents a similar achievement? What compensatory qualities, if any, have the better adjusted developed? What can be done to aid others to adopt or develop equally successful techniques?

2. The whole problem of social attitudes toward the elderly not tapped directly in the questionnaire is obviously an important determinant of much of the subjects' everyday behavior and many of their responses: subjects reported that they do not think or feel like old people, although they know they are, that the attitudes and behavior of others made them feel old, that they began feeling old as soon as they reached the 60's despite the fact no other appreciable change had recently occurred, and so on. It would be interesting to discover what mannerisms, behavior patterns and self-attitudes generally associated with old age are obediently adopted by some elderly people simply because they seem to be expected. It may well be that due to medical advances which enable the conquest or control of many diseases or physical problems, our ideas about what ages are "old" need to be revised. This may be the reason why our relatively "young" sample of "old" psychologists (mean age—70 years) appears so different from what the stereotypes about old age lead us to expect. Perhaps real "old age" with severe physical or mental handicaps, marked restriction of activi-

ties, dependence, etc., can no longer be considered to begin in the mid-sixties, but must be thought more characteristic of age 70 or more. Certainly there are great individual differences among old people. A "they're-all-alike" attitude is the hallmark of prejudice. Yet all of the older people of today must live with the attitudes developed generations ago. We may not be able to turn back the clock with medical progress and modern gadgetry, but I harbor a strong suspicion that social attitudes toward the elderly may be responsible for advancing it at an unreasonable rate. Society has a sense of what is "proper" for the elderly—and that sense is very easily offended: "there's no fool like an old fool;" "you can't teach an old dog new tricks." It is natural that some misconceptions should exist. The respondents themselves indicate that there has been quite a change in their attitudes over the years. However, part of the problem stems from the fact that there is so little contact between people of different generations. With the continued flow of younger people to the suburbs, while the old tend to remain in more convenient urban areas, the problem is aggravated. Since the proportions of the very young and very old people in the general population are both increasing, it may be necessary to make special efforts to foster contact between the generations and, hopefully, increase understanding so that further problems can be avoided.

3. Many theoretical papers have been written about old age and countless investigations of the ills afflicting the elderly are now in progress. Such papers and studies are, of course, valuable. However, it would appear that the time is long past due for more widescale investigations of the elderly themselves—and perhaps most especially those who have been able to maintain their independence.

CLINICAL EXPLORATIONS

Some elderly people require clinical services. But how many people? Who are they? What services do they require? Answers to these questions are highly dependent upon the observer's frame of reference. Estimates are influenced not only by the type of elderly person with whom the observer happens to be most familiar, but also with the particular combination of sensitivities and blind spots that have been "trained into" or developed by the observer. Thus, for example, large-scale surveys, conducted and interpreted by persons trained in polling techniques and limited to respondents who are willing and able to answer questions in the appropriate manner, seem likely to generate an overly sanguine view of the status of elderly persons. By contrast, clinical psychologists, psychiatrists and others who are oriented to probing beyond appearances and to establishing contact with confused, withdrawn and handicapped individuals are likely to give a higher estimate of both the number of elderly persons requiring therapeutic services and the variety of services required. This picture also can be misleading if the clinicians lack sufficient experience with elderly persons who are in excellent psychosocial and physical condition.

The chapters in this section derive from clinical experiences with aged individuals and are concerned with the identification of problems and the application of diverse therapeutic approaches. Have the contributors explored more approaches than are necessary for more problems than really exist—or have they just begun to break through stereotyped perceptions to uncover some of the factors which undermine life satisfaction in the later years?

The reluctant therapist

9

Robert Kastenbaum

As the title implies, psychotherapists, in general, tend to avoid rather than seek contact with the aged. This reluctance both derives from and contributes to barriers against understanding old age.

Is it true that psychotherapists are reluctant to work with the aged? One place to look for an answer to this question would be in the statistical information available from mental health surveys and records of professional practice. The information presently available is neither so accurate nor so comprehensive that one could arrive at a firm conclusion from statistical considerations alone. But these considerations do at least hint that with increasing age there are diminishing opportunities for psychotherapy, even when the desirability of this form of treatment is fairly evident.

There is, however, a more instructive source of information. I am referring to the routine observation that many clinicians register surprise and puzzlement when they learn that a colleague has been devoting time to psychotherapy with people who are old. Such a practice is still regarded as a curiosity. The puzzled clinician often will state that he has no inclination toward working with the aged; he thinks it is "interesting" or even "noble" that his colleague should be doing so, but frankly wonders why.

This honest question deserves serious consideration, although it is seldom raised when clinicians are discussing psychotherapy that is conducted with children, adolescents or younger adults.

Why is there a reluctance to conduct psychotherapy with the aged? Let us first consider some realistic factors. Few clinicians have received adequate preparation for gerontologic or geriatric practice. General training programs do not typically offer the necessary informed experience, nor have many programs yet been developed with the specific intent of preparing psychotherapists to meet the needs of the aged.

Furthermore, there is a corresponding deficiency in the intellectual resources from which the psychotherapist ordinarily hopes to obtain guidance and insight. It is not just the case that clinical training has been relatively neglected in gerontology, but research and systematic theory also have lagged behind. Virtually all major approaches to the understanding of personality were developed with little consideration of "old age." Consequently, such "classical" approaches as learning theory and psychoanalysis do not presently offer a solid background for the clinician who insists that his psychotherapeutic efforts be related to a large body of relevant and organized knowledge; when dealing with the aged, the psychotherapist is much more on his own.

So it would seem that the conscientious psychotherapist might reasonably be expected to hesitate a moment before offering his services to an aged person. He feels the realistic need for more experience and systematic knowledge.

But it is not possible to attribute all the observed reluctance to the factors just mentioned, nor is it necessary to assume that the neglect of adequate training and research in old age has itself been the outcome of realistic factors. Indeed, this neglect is difficult to understand if one considers realistic factors only.

We are now going to examine some of the unexamined attitudes which psychotherapists frequently hold in respect to the aged. It is these attitudes which tend to block efforts at psychotherapy. They are derived not from scientific or professional considerations, but from the clinician's failure to disentangle himself from biases and misunderstandings prevalent in our society at large. These attitudes have been rather arbitrarily divided into three sets.

The first set of attitudes centers around the problem of status. Hollingshead and Redlich and others have shown that the patient's status has much to do with his prospects of receiving psychotherapy (2). People with relatively higher status are more likely to be recommended and accepted for psychotherapy. Higher status here refers primarily to the individual's socio-economic background. But there is another significant status dimension in our culture that is based upon age. As we become old, other things being equal, we enter a lower status group. The aged neither produce nor consume enough to retain the status they enjoyed when younger. Our culture tends to find much value in youth but little value in age. The old person, having suffered a loss in status, might for that very reason be a good candidate for psychotherapy aimed at helping him come to grips with this loss. However, the potential therapist is likely to recoil. Association with a low-status patient may be felt as contamination—lowering the clinician's status in his own eyes. Besides this magical contamination, the clinician may recognize that psychotherapy with the aged frequently takes the form of support. Conventionally, supportive therapy is sometimes regarded as a second-rate procedure. It is perhaps not real therapy at all. Thus, to conduct psychotherapy with an aged person is to enter a relationship with a low-status individual and to employ a technic that carries a low-status connotation with respect to its challenges to professional skill.

As soon as these implications have been made conscious, most clinicians can be expected to immediately disavow them. The experienced clinician has learned that meaningful support in the psychotherapeutic relationship often requires the utmost skill and sensitivity; he will reject the notion that supportive psychotherapy is of necessity a low-status technic. He will probably also reject the notion that growing old is a sufficient basis for the status of the individual to be lowered.

The second set of attitudes centers around the satisfactions and anxieties of the clinician. Some day we may have machines programmed to perform psychotherapy. But until the Freudiac arrives, patients must accept help from fellow human beings whose own needs and personal feelings will complicate the proceedings. The good therapist is skillful in using his own feelings and needs to promote rather than interfere with the patient's benefit from psychotherapy.

But the prospects of even a reasonable balance between personal pain and pleasure may seem rather bleak to the therapist when he regards the aged patient. Consider one of the threats of pain. In working with an aged person, the clinician may be deprived of the insulating distance that sometimes serves him well in other circumstances. To form and maintain an intimate psychotherapeutic relationship with a severely psychotic person, for example, can make great demands upon the clinician. But generally he is able to gain some assurance from the fact that he, himself, is unlikely ever to become psychotic; this particular anguish will never become personal. But the old patient's anguish may well be a forecast and foretaste of the clinician's own future dilemma. The psychotherapist himself will face death one day and, as that time approaches, may also experience the painful loss of relationships and abilities. It may seem "too much" that a person should be forced to run the gauntlet more than once. To share over and over gain the anguish that old age can bring is not a prospect that most therapists are likely to find appealing.

Detachment may suggest itself as an obvious alternative by means of which the clinician can offer psychotherapy to the aged patient without emotional strain to himself. But seldom does such detachment serve its therapeutic purposes. LeShan and LeShan (3), two of the few psychologists to write from experience on this topic, state:

"The psychotherapist . . . cannot protect himself by the defense maneuver that necessity sometimes dictates to the purely medical specialist whose patients often die—the surgeon, for example, or the oncologist. This defense—brusque, armoured manner, the uninvolved relationship, the viewing of the patient's disease as of primary interest and the concentration on its technical details to the exclusion of as much else of the person as possible—may save the physician a great deal of heartache, but it is a defense which is impossible to assume for one who is in a psychotherapeutic role."

In addition to the threat of pain there is also the bleak outlook for satisfaction. As Levin has suggested, more old people are suffering from depressive states than is commonly recognized (4). We do, however, react to our sensing of the apathy, withdrawal and apparent loss of the capacity for pleasure. And the manner in which we react is sometimes with apathy, withdrawal and the anticipation that no pleasurable interaction will be forthcoming. The psychotherapist does not always escape from the implication of the presented symptoms, namely, that he personally is in for a grim time, and he can look forward to none of the moments of inner satisfaction and pleasure he has experienced with younger patients.

It may seem that the threat of pain and the dim prospect of pleasure which confront the psychotherapist are based solidly upon realistic factors. I suggest, however, that reality here provides a plastic situation that has been cast unnecessarily into a mold by the clinician's own unexamined attitudes. If the clinician is a "normal" person in our culture, he probably has given relatively little serious consideration to the meaning of death. Limited to shallow, contradictory or defensive attitudes toward death—in any event, to unexamined attitudes toward death—the clinician may be unable to manage the prospect of death even as well as his prospective patient does. It is the individual clinician's failure to transcend his culture's superficiality on the subject of death that limits him in this aspect of his relationship with the aged patient.

The anticipation of a joyless relationship with an aged patient often represents again the clinician's uncritical acceptance of cultural stereotypes. Love and pleasure are emotions associated with young people; the same therapist who would regard a depressed expression on the face of a young person as an unnatural phenomenon to be alleviated with the help of his professional skills may regard a similar expression on the face of an old person as a reinforcement of his unexamined belief that joy naturally evaporates with age.

The third set of attitudes and, really, the most perplexing is concerned with a basic conflict in established values. The arguments advanced so far derive from the general body of scientific and clinical knowledge. Eventually these points could be settled in a more convincing manner by additional clinical and experimental research; none of the problems are essentially intractable to empirical study. But we confront a fundamentally different situation when we ask, "Why do psychotherapy with the aged?"

When a person who offers this question has been drawn out, frequently he responds, "Old people do not have much time left to live.

Psychotherapy is an arduous procedure that demands a major invest-ment of time and effort on the part of both participants. Therefore, psychotherapy should be reserved for those people who have the pros-pect of a long life ahead. It is just not worthwhile to put in so much effort for so little return."

Behind this reasoning we can discern more than the rather sensible outlook of an individual who happens to be a psychotherapist. We can discern a massive tradition in thought and values that has been known to the world for centuries. In its present manifestation, this tradition expresses itself most readily in terms of the market place. It is really not good business to invest in such a transient and doomed enterprise. "This man will be dead, you know, and all your science and craft will have been wasted."

"Time is money" is what this approach says. Even when money is not at issue, the time-is-money paradigm underlies the logic. Thus, there is a quantitative transformation at work in the "why help them" question. Qualities of human experience are replaced by convention-alized, external units.

I do not for a moment deny that this approach makes a kind of sense and exerts a kind of natural, persuasive power over our minds. This cannot be a surprising phenomenon when we consider that our minds have been conditioned by the same society that has transformed human life into time and time into money and money back into time, over and over again in the apparently endless iteration of a magical formula.

This approach places great value on duration, showing its kinship with the hedonic calculus: a pleasure that endures for a longer period of time is to be preferred over a pleasure that endures for a shorter period of time. And this, too, makes sense and seems to support the reluctance to invest time and effort in psychotherapy with people who will not live "long enough" to make it worthwhile.

I suggest that it is precisely the value orientation just described that is mainly responsible for the reluctant therapist. Let us look then at an alternative tradition.

This tradition reminds us that the present moment is the only lived-in time that any of us ever enjoys, although the present moment can be said to change or replace itself from moment to moment. On this view, it makes both bad logic and bad psychology to over-evalu-ate duration in time. It is bad logic because when the future comes—the future for which the psychotherapist has dutifully been preparing his younger patient—this future will be merely another unvalued mo-ment of present time. To deny therapy to the aged because they do not have a "long-enough future" would be self-deceit. Either a person is worth helping now or he is not worth helping. It is bad psychology, because an emphasis on futurity and long duration is effective training to produce an emphasis on futurity and long duration; it is not an effective way to foster the ability to use time when it is actually here to be experienced.

And just what is meant by a "long-enough future?" What quantitative indices ought one establish to guide the psychotherapist? Should he treat a person who can expect to live twenty years, but not one who can expect to live only ten years? Or, perhaps, we should make that: ten years, yes! Five years, no! Or, perhaps, a more refined measure could be developed: so many hours of psychotherapeutic time conducted at such-and-such a quantitative level of effort will be provided for persons whose life expectancy has been estimated at such-and-such a figure. The more seriously we take the quantitative transformation of human life, the more absurd we feel. All human beings have a limited life span. How can a therapist accept one patient in treatment and then ever again deny treatment on the implicit or explicit basis of "not enough time to make it worth-while?"

Let us move from absurdity to paradox. While long duration has been taken as a favorable dimension of values, precisely the same is true in certain instances of short duration. We even value certain things because they last for a long time, yet the value of other things seems to be enhanced by the fact that they have such a brief life. Now, which standard are we to apply to human life itself? Are we to "write off" the aged person as an unprofitable enterprise because he does not have long to live, or are we to regard his life as even more precious and worth-enhancing because there is so little time left to it?

This brief analysis has suggested that the psychotherapist's reluctance to work with elderly persons is based largely upon attitudes and values that have been uncritically absorbed from views prevalent in our society. These stereotyped conceptions include unwillingness to enter into what is perceived as a low-status relationship, the anticipation of threatening and unhedonic interactions, and the calculation that an aged person will not live "long enough" to "pay back" the therapist's "investment."

A number of once-reluctant therapists have reported considerable accomplishment and unexpected personal satisfaction from working with aged patients—after having been "trapped" into offering their services by circumstances. Observations of this nature, as well as the experiences of long-time practitioners with the aged, lead one to hope that these barriers to initial contact with elderly patients eventually will be surmounted by critical examination and the favorable results of reality-testing (1,5).

References

1. Goldfarb, A. I. Psychiatric problems of old age. *New York J. Med.,* 1955, *55,* 494-500.
2. Hollingshead, A. B., and Redlich, F. C. Social class and mental illness. New York: John Wiley, 1958.
3. LeShan, L., and LeShan, E. Psychotherapy and the patient with a limited life span. *Psychiatry,* 1961, *24,* 318-323.
4. Levin, S. Depression in the aged: the importance of external factors. In this volume.
5. Meerloo, J. A. Geriatric psychotherapy. *Acta Psychother.,* 1961, *9,* 169-182.

10

Group therapy
with the very old

Eugenia S. Shere

Why do psychotherapy with the aged? This question, commonly raised by clinicians, was analyzed by Kastenbaum, who suggested that the "reluctance to work with elderly persons is based largely upon attitudes and values that have been uncritically absorbed from views prevalent in our society." (3). The present chapter takes this inquiry another step further: why do *group* psychotherapy with geriatric patients?

Among psychotherapists who work with elderly people, the opinion seems to prevail that group methods are not appropriate. Accordingly, one finds few published accounts of the use of group psychotherapy techniques with the aged. Moreover, in the few reports on hand the participants were between 60 and 75 years of age, i.e., among the "younger generation" of the aged (1,2). The question then arises: are people aged 75 and older considered as not being in need of group therapy, are they "not worth the trouble," or what?

Lowy's positive attitude toward using the group as a means of helping older people is based on the view that ". . . older adults in our society have become a subculture, and therefore have certain common needs." (6). Are octogenarians and nonagenarians perceived as not even belonging to this "subcultural class"? Are they people of a different class, of a class without any common needs? Whatever might be the reasons for the neglect of group psychotherapy with the very old, it seems that they deserve more opportunities for such experience.*

To my knowledge, it is Linden who should be credited as the first to report and encourage the initiation of group psychotherapy with octogenarians (4). These considerations prompted a "reluctant therapist" to experiment in group therapy with residents of the most ad-

---

* The writer recently participated in a workshop on old age at a conference for group psychotherapy. When she reported the advanced age of the participants in the Cushing Hospital group therapy, this shared experience was met with expressions of great surprise, laughter, and comments such as, "That's something I've never heard before!"

vanced age at Cushing Hospital. The venture became more challenging upon noticing that the extent of "disengagement" symptoms—isolated and aloof behavior—was not different among the younger (65-75 age range) than that observed in the older (80-98 age range) patients. Since the establishment of group therapy for the very old patients at Cushing Hospital was a pioneering endeavor, I shall hereinafter refer to this service as a clinical experiment.

Goals and procedure

In choosing the oldest patients for group therapy, I limited myself to two major goals: 1) to re-vitalize social drives which still appeared to exist in latent form, and 2) to induce group formation and re-socialization among the hospital residents at large through providing an example in the persons of the most aged patients.

Criteria for patient selection. The primary criterion was advanced age. Originally, it was planned to organize a group of patients aged 85 and over. However, not enough suitable patients could be secured in this age span at the time the group was formed, thus the patients obtained ranged from 82 to 98 years of age. Mental fitness was a second criterion. Each candidate was interviewed at least twice to evaluate his or her ability to follow group discussions. Heterogeneity with regard to sex was also considered as useful. Physical difficulties such as dependence for help in mobility (because of amputations, fractures, severe arteriosclerosis, etc.) were disregarded. The initial group consisted of 6 women and 3 men. Membership was left open, as it was foreseen that dropouts would occur. They did occur, and changes in the group constellation took place. A few younger patients were included at their own request, others were selected by the therapist. In a few months the membership had increased to 15, with a low age of 72 and a high of 96. Since the dropouts occurred only among the females with the initially selected males remaining faithful and new ones added, eventually the total number of the males exceeded that of the females.

Willingness to participate. Many of the patients contacted flatly refused to participate. They gave reasons such as: "I like it this way." "I am not lonely." "What good will come of it." "You only get in trouble when you *talk!*" Those who consented to come to the first meeting emphasized that they would do so only on a trial basis. Although the goals were explained to the prospective participants, it seemed that they were set for a classroom-type experience exclusively.

Location and attendance. A room in the area of the patients' library was the meeting place for the first five sessions. The subsequent sessions took place in the reading room (same library area), where there was more space. With the change of location there was also an improvement in the seating arrangement. In the first room the patients were seated at a rectangular table, with the therapist choosing the center (avoiding the head) of the table, while in the second room it was possible to make more flexible arrangements, including semicircular and circular groupings.

The weekly sessions were held in the morning, each lasting an hour to an hour and a half. Attendance varied from 6 to 11 members per session, with average attendance of 8; 4 members were particularly regular. Absences occurred because of two major factors: 1) reasons stemming from "without," such as having been assigned for a conflicting appointment with the dentist, chiropodist, optometrist, beautician etc.; not having been notified by the nurse about the meeting (on the day prior to the meeting each nurse was sent a memo indicating the place, date, and names of participants from her ward); and 2) reasons from "within," such as "not feeling like talking," "forgetfulness," physical illness, not "wanting to be wheeled," and so forth. (Resistance toward dependence in locomotion was particularly strong in Mr. B., a 96-year-old man whose functioning will be discussed later.)

The group in operation

At the time of this writing, a total of 47 sessions have been carried out. Except for the first meeting, sessions 14, 25, and 34 were randomly selected for illustrative purposes. This presentation will be followed by four brief case histories of patients of varying ages.

Session 1

Of the 9 patients who originally consented to be "guinea pigs," only 7 (4 women and 3 men) attended. Mrs. B., a 98-year-old patient, later said that she had been interrupted by an unexpected visitor from the outside, while Mrs. T., an 82-year-old wheel chair patient, reported she had not been ready because her routine injection was not given on time. (Mrs. B. remained resistant and did not attend any of the subsequent meetings.) The average age of the participants in this first session was 89.7 years; three were wheel chair patients.

Everyone engaged in active discussion except Mr. Q., a 92-year-old man who had been reluctant to join the group. At the outset of the meeting he declared he would participate only by being a "listener." The most active participants were the three oldest patients (96, 92, and 92).

Four main issues were raised:

1. "Why do they ('they' implied the children, and society at large) take our pride away from us?" This question was raised and reiterated by Mr. B.

2. "This group is not different from that on the ward . . . so much suffering in here, too." This feeling was expressed by Mr. J., a

92-year-old wheel chair patient, and supported by all the group members.

3. "Why are we being commanded, ordered about so much in here, and deprived of the freedom we had at home?" This objection was introduced by Mr. B. and supported by the other members.

4. Conflict of opinion was voiced between expressing and suppressing feelings of resentment toward children or other relatives for the institutionalization.

Discussion of this latter topic aroused a great deal of anxiety. The strong negative feelings initially expressed by the two animated male patients were later regretfully taken back "in order to avoid trouble." The female participants became quite defensive and tried to justify the children for having arranged for the parents' institutionalization. Moreover, at this point several patients requested the use of the bathroom. The "silent" Mr. Q. commented emphatically, "I don't like such meetings. I don't like to talk about my family and blame them . . . you only get into trouble!"

Session 14

Eleven members were present, 3 females and 8 males. The average age was 82.9 years.

At the outset, Mrs. H. said, "Let's talk about the exciting news"— referring to President Kennedy's announcement of the establishment of a quarantine around Cuba. This suggestion was quickly picked up by Mr. M., who engaged in polemics about current events. Questioning with regard to their "first thought" upon hearing the quarantine news elicited a variety of responses, the majority feeling "what a horrible thing it would be if war would come," while Mr. P., a 93-year-old, expressed the readiness to "put myself in that blockade."

One's personal future in case of war was seen by a number of the participants in terms of "I'm not leading a useful life anyway," so "why bother to think of oneself?"

Session 25

There were 10 participants, 5 females and 5 males, with an average age of 83.2. The discussion was opened by a new 84-year-old female member who related her experiences of "fighting" her "crippling condition." A discussion centering on "the will to live" developed. Warding off the loss in "pride" was seen as an important factor in overcoming illness. Mr. N., a recently admitted 82-year-old patient who had shown marked deterioration in functioning upon his institutionalization remarked, "With your help (addressing the therapist) I was able to change my attitude toward life. . . . Now I can love other people . . . enjoy other people in the hospital . . . don't think I can only love my daughter and must live with her. . . ."

Other topics brought up during this session concerned the difference between criticism and advice, as well as the positive versus the negative consequences of "arguments."

Session 34

Attendance consisted of 4 males and 3 females, with average age of 81.7. Discussion was initiated by a new female member, Mrs. W., who, up to this time, had been seen individually. Previously, the therapist's frequent invitations for her to join the group were met with great resistance: "They are too old . . . they are all mental." Mrs. W., aged 75, presented complaints about her lot: she "envies" the people who live on the outside; life in the hospital is equivalent to being "robots;" moreover, "watching the old people being sick and miserable" creates a pessimistic outlook on life, and she prefers death to life under such circumstances.

Except for Mr. M., the other participants disagreed with Mrs. W. and stated they "care to live longer."

The topic shifted to the pros and cons of medicating old patients. The majority expressed the feeling that the application of drugs to very sick old people should be abandoned. Mr. Q. insisted, *"No one can prolong life; man lives as long as God wants him to live!"* The concept of death was then touched upon. However, the discussion remained limited to formal definitions.

Therapeutic effects

The 4 cases that follow were chosen to represent septuagenarians, octogenarians, and nonagenarians. Each case will serve to illustrate individual changes that occurred within the group treatment period. The nonagenarians will be represented by 2 cases in order to illustrate variations within this age level.

Case 1, Mrs. T.

This patient is a short, round-faced, large-featured, and hunchbacked woman of 82 years. She is a widow, mother of two married daughters, one of whom also is widowed. Mrs. T. had been admitted 2 years previously and diagnosed as being afflicted with 5 conditions: hypertensive cardiovascular disease, generalized arteriosclerosis, osteoarthritis of the spine and hip joint, history of acute gastric hemorrhages, and postoperative status for colectomy and appendectomy.

Although neat and clean, her appearance was, to say the least, not appealing. She spoke in a harsh tone of voice, and her stern looks reflected intense feelings of anger. Mrs. T. was confined to a special wheel chair in which she crouched from the time of rising to bedtime. Except for periods of eating, bathing and toileting, she was very faithful to her "living quarters," consisting of a surface near the front side of her bed. On the little table nearby, in addition to a clock and some personal items, she usually kept a *Reader's Digest* open; however, this apparently was more for looks than for use, as she was never seen reading it. Mrs. T. was generally observed to be "snoozing," to use the patients' lingo.

This woman's emotional state in the initial contacts can probably be most accurately described by quoting her self-evaluation when asked how she felt: "Ugly." There was never a smile on her face, nor any expression denoting contentment. She appeared alert intellectually, had adequate contact with reality, and her participation in group discussions was felt to be promising. The patient expressed a preference for individual sessions, but consented to the group experiment, "I would like to try." When the group constellation was explained to her, Mrs. T. reacted negatively to the mixture of men and women: "I am not particularly fond of men . . . they are not interesting."

She failed to come to the first session for which she had been scheduled, saying that her morning injection had not been given to her on time. She came to the next session, however, and, on the whole, except when she had a cold, or felt "miserable," or had not been attended with injections, baths, etc. on time, her participation was quite regular. Her activity in the first two sessions was limited. Although she seemed to follow the discussions, she said little, and left before the closing, giving bladder incontinence as the reason.

Therapeutic effects began to be evident as early as the third session: Mrs. T. talked more, and "bladder incontinence" no longer interfered with remaining for the full session. The disappearance of the latter symptom seemed to have come as a surprise to the patient herself, as after the session she commented, "I was a good girl today, wasn't I?" The "good girl" quality remained in the patient's possession throughout the group therapy period.

As the sessions continued, the therapist (instead of the patient!) began to be surprised by more positive changes. Instead of continuing to defend children's rejection of their aged parents (by intellectualizing that "the modern homes don't have enough rooms," or, "I don't want to be bothered with younger people"), she seemed to have developed the freedom to express criticism against children. They did not "care enough for the parents." Furthermore, instead of denying dissatisfaction with her given lot, especially regarding her mobility handicap, Mrs. T. was able to say in front of the group, "I *envy* people who can walk!" (Session 38). The initial fears and resentments she expressed toward the opposite sex evolved into a friendly interest in men, as manifested in a positive attitude toward remarriage "regardless of age" (Session 33), and as observed in friendlier behavior and more tasteful and decorative dress.

Case 2, Mr. B.

Mr. B., a slender, medium-sized, blue-eyed widower, had been a machinist (an "experimental man," he described himself). He had completed 3 years of high school. On his transfer from a nursing home 4 years previously he was diagnosed as suffering from general arteriosclerosis, and admitted to the hospital for custodial care. He had two living married daughters, and had lost two married sons during his stay in the hospital. Mr. B. was 96 years old when the group began.

The patient kept himself neat and meticulously clean. His private room was orderly and cheerful, the walls decorated with newspaper clippings, photographs and greeting cards. On the table there were always one or more little plants.

When he was first contacted in his room, Mr. B. greeted the therapist with much friendliness and showed a great need to talk. Conversation centered on his past life. With great pride he spoke about having "only one marriage for 49 years," of having been professionally "a top man," entrusted with a great many responsibilities and that, because of this role, he might be called a "trouble shooter." As to joining group therapy, he liked "the idea of helping *others,*" and, after being given reassurance as to his expressed concern about "confidentiality," he consented by saying, *"If this will help you."* Until recently, his attendance has been regular unless he was physically ill or not notified about the meeting by the ward nurse. He was one of the early arrivers, and would be the last one to leave.

As early as the first session it became apparent that Mr. B. still needed to be "the top man." He captured the group by his incessant talking, and persistently reached out for recognition of his knowledge and acceptance of his views. Interruptions or disagreements were met with overt and covert resentment. The topics he persevered with centered on the following: a) "Why do they take our pride away from us?"; b) "Why do they order us around so much?"; c) "We are only existing. . . . We should have sympathy and not congratulations on our birthdays"; and d) "There is no cooperation here."

Mr. B. was not only a faithful follower of the "good, old times," but criticized "the modern ways," and vehemently disagreed with anyone who expressed favoritism for any kind of "progress" that had been made in the last few decades (including equal rights for women). Although he acted in an especially polite manner toward the women (if an occasion arose, he did not fail to say, "Ladies first," would compliment them, or wonder if he "could be of any help"), he forcefully spoke up against women smoking because, "It is not ladylike!"

After a few months of consistent attendance he became ill and was transferred to the acute ward. When I visited him there (on the day after the group therapy session) he appeared very touched, broke out in tears, and put his arms around my shoulders. "I looked at my watch this morning and wished I could be there (therapy room implied) . . . I wished they (attendants implied) would appreciate and show more cooperation. . . ."

He resumed his participation the following week by being wheeled up to the group therapy location. He was rather passive, and appeared worried throughout the session, without offering an explanation for his behavior. Mr. B.'s usual enthusiasm also was not present the following week. However, he was able to give vent to his feelings of resentment by stating that if he would not be allowed to walk, he would not come to another session (there is a long walk through a hall on highly polished floors from his room to the therapy area). He added that he always enjoyed walking very much, and still felt capable of doing so by himself. Moreover, he rationalized that he "should not impose upon the nurses, who should give their time to those who need them more." Indeed, he kept his "promise," and failed to come to subsequent sessions until permission to walk eventually was granted. Upon that, he resumed his attendance. At times he would walk by himself, without using any support. At other times *he would wheel the empty chair* (instead of consenting to wheel himself!). It was clear that the effort of walking was no longer easy for this man, as on his arrival he would show great fatigue and shortness of breath. But walking seemed to provide great satisfaction and fill him with pride, as reflected in his beaming face and his acting like "the old self."

As time went on, Mr. B. became weaker physically, showed more frequent memory lapses, and tended toward perseverative thinking. His need to be the leader became more pressing. This need, in turn, was less tolerated by the other group members, especially those who, in the process of therapy, had themselves become more active. Mr. B. quickly sensed the lessening of his acceptance. His fear of losing more "pride"—in addition to threats of losing independence in mobility—became very apparent. He verbalized his feelings by saying, "I don't think I am needed any longer . . . I don't think I am of any help. . . ." Facial expressions and gestures also evidenced his sense of frustration and uneasiness. Subsequently, his attendance again became irregular, this time with lengthier periods of absence. He explained his absences on two grounds: "I think I should keep myself closer to my room" (implicit fear of admitting dependence in locomotion), and "I don't think I am of any help" (implicit fear of losing his "top man" role).

While uttering these statements, Mr. B. spoke in a moving tone of voice and with tears in his eyes. One had the feeling that he really wanted to say, "I am lonesome. I'd like to be a member of the group, but how can I admit it? The price is too high for such a luxury!"

Indeed, how can a man of 96 years do away with his last possessions, his only treasures in life—the last straw of pride and the last aspect of independent living? That Mr. B. actually was longing for the group is seen in the fact that quite recently (after weeks of absence) he returned. How did he make it? He gleefully pushed the empty wheel chair to the meeting place and proudly assumed the "top man" role again.

Case 3, Mr. Q.

Mr. Q. is a reddish-faced, tall, broad-shouldered, and somewhat pot-bellied 92-year-old widower of Scotch-Canadian extraction. His erect posture, neat, clean and healthy appearance make him look younger than his age. He was admitted from his home at the age of 87 for custodial care. His wife was admitted at the same time, and died 3 years later. Mr. Q.'s formal education ended with grammar school. He had been a carpenter. During his "64 years and 9 months" of marriage he had raised 2 sons who provided him with 4 grandchildren and 16 great-grandchildren. The diagnostic impression on admission was arteriosclerotic and hypertensive heart disease, and long standing varicose veins of the right leg with indurated edema.

I first noticed this man sitting alone in the social hall (known as "Times Square") while on my way to the wards to scout for group therapy candidates. I watched him for several days and was struck by the stereotypy of his behavior: day in and day out this man sat alone, silently looking at the walls of the long hall. Although in physical proximity to other patients, he was never observed talking to his neighbors, or even facing them. Neither was he seen in contact with objects. His characteristic behavior: sitting and looking into space.

When I first interrupted his "activity" by waving at him, I was pleasantly surprised by getting a smile in response. He showed surprise, blushed and stuttered when I approached him on a later occasion. In response to my efforts to start a conversation he said that he was "Oh, just thinking . . . my thinking is just as good as it was 50 years ago . . . but there's no one to talk to." After a few more contacts he appeared much more comfortable, and reacted to my "intrusion" by stating, "I thought I'd be alone, and now you come here." After *I* became more comfortable, and invited him to join group therapy, he did not hesitate to declare, "Absolutely not. I don't want to have responsibilities . . . I want to be in the old rags (implying a wish not to get 'dressed up') . . . I like your company," adding, "I have no pains in my body, not even a corn on my toes." In later contacts he expanded on his reason for a negative decision: "They are all invalids . . . I don't want to be associated with that class. . . . They are done, their work is done. . . ." Still later he added, "They talk about what their parents have done to them . . . What is the aim of it? . . . I don't want to hear it . . . I am just happy to sit by myself." Finally, he consented to join on a trial basis, although still wondering "why couldn't we talk here?" (in the hall).

He came early for the first session, and has remained a faithful participant. Mr. Q. has missed only one session, and that was because of a cold. In the first few sessions he showed his determination to be "happy to sit by myself." He would arrive promptly, choose an outside seat (rather than one at the table), and leave the session as quickly and as quietly as he entered. When attempts were made to draw him out he would comment, "Better to say nothing," or, "I don't know."

It was not until the fourth session that Mr. Q. allowed himself to take part verbally. "At 65 they don't want us any longer!" he said with anger during a discussion on fitness for work in old age. Verbal interaction increased from that point. Moreover, he began to show a gradual development of empathy, a widening of interests and a change in values. Not only did he abandon his previous rejection of the other patients, but Mr. Q. began to show warm feelings for them. Instead of leaving hastily, for example, he volunteered to wheel a female patient to her ward (Session 7), a task he spontaneously selected for himself, and continued to help whoever was in need on that particular day.

Mr. Q.'s initial attitude that "I don't want to be associated with that class" has changed into behavior which implies an equal partnership and a membership in "that class." He not only listens readily to what "I don't want to hear . . .," but freely relates his own experiences and colors his contributions with appropriate sayings and witticisms. Furthermore, instead of being content to sit by himself, he shows a liking for people, an interest in reading, and a need to share his satisfactions with others, e.g., bringing in a copy of Bernard Baruch's book, *The Public Years,* to read aloud a passage he had enjoyed. A change in values was suggested by his admission that he had become ambitious and now desired pleasurable situations. A liking for "red colors . . . they are cheerful and bright . . . (Session 16), a wish "to be a captain on a ship" (Session 17), and a desire to be visited by "a couple of friends, go out for dinner, for a lobster dinner with them" (Session 37) are all now part of the mental outlook of this 92-year-old man.

Case 4, Mr. M.

A tall, well-built, youthfully-dressed and good-looking 75-year-old married man, Mr. M. is a college graduate and World War I veteran. His work history was spotty—employed here and there as a salesman, and as a clerk in a law office. Most of the time he had lived on a comfortable income from his father. He described his wife, who is 13 years his junior, as self-supporting and "not able to take the cold New England weather" and who, therefore, spent her winters in Bermuda. Mr. M. has had periodic states of depression and admission to mental hospitals. He was transferred to Cushing from a mental hospital (diagnosis: "manic-depressive type") at the age of 70 for medical care.

On admission his diagnosis was "cerebral arteriosclerosis and chronic depression."

In the course of individual interviews, Mr. M. explained his institutionalization in terms of not having anyone to care for him at home. During the summers his wife would return to New England and they would get together "quite often." His interests in the hospital included reading, helping the patients' librarian, and "doing research in genealogy." He said he did not have many friends on the outside, nor had he made friends here. The latter fact he ascribed to the failure on the part of other patients to respond to his initial attempts to socialize, and he "just gave up."

The invitation to join group therapy was resisted. He did not think that group meetings were of any value, doubting that he, in particular, could benefit. Moreover, he kept himself "busy, and I am not lonesome." Nevertheless, he consented to try.

At the outset, Mr. M. had a chip-on-the-shoulder attitude. He would make sure to enter the room after everyone else was seated, take a chair in the back, and leave just before the end of the session, after consulting his wrist-watch. Such social amenities as "hello" and "good-by" were absent. His typical behavior during the discussions was argumentative and belligerent. Contradictory opinions were met with defiance, and often with turning for support to his only friend—the dictionary. When he felt defeated, Mr. M. would react either by saying, "Now I have to leave," or that his main interest was "in research" (genealogy implied). Nevertheless, his attendance was regular, and on the few occasions of absence he would notify the therapist prior to the session.

Identification with the therapist was shown as early as the third session. When a 93-year-old female patient was ill at ease about the sex heterogeneity of the group and wondered if the intent of the sessions was "match-making," he responded emphatically, "This is *not* a marriage bureau!" Signs of identification with other group members became apparent in the ninth session, at which time he also offered to wheel a patient to her ward, an activity he continued.

Gradually, Mr. M. not only lessened his aloofness, rigidity and need to display superior knowledge, but appeared to have become a friendlier and happier person. Instead of maintaining the role of an indoctrinator and limiting the content and purpose of group therapy to didactics, he was able, in the nineteenth session, to express his wish to discuss "something pleasant." Moreover, he broadened his activities, developed empathy and showed a growth in interpersonal relationships. While his participation began with avoidance of people and lack of minimal social amenities, he now engaged in group interactions, and also interactions outside of the group. He consented, for example, to become a member of a proposed patient-government committee—a move he had previously strongly opposed. He also showed concern over the discomfort and illness of other members, and participated actively in a number of social activities at the hospital.

It was Mr. M.'s thirty-fifth session when he announced that he had decided to leave the hospital and return to live in the community by himself (his wife, he added, would be traveling from Bermuda to Spain). He accounted for this decision on the grounds of feeling well, being able to take care of himself, and looking forward to a more active and pleasurable life.

The patient was, in fact, discharged. In an individual session prior to his departure, his self-evaluation could be summed up as follows: he had always felt well physically, but was "mentally depressed." Group therapy had helped him to become more active, to find out that he "could think clearly," and "to give up arguing with people, just for the sake of saying the opposite." Moreover, it had helped him to see that he "could make friends and not feel so alone." When asked about his genealogy research, he stated that during the past few months he "did other things instead."

Thus, it appeared that group therapy enabled this patient to achieve some insight into his authoritarian-dependency difficulty, and into his control mechanisms of isolation and intellectualization. Instead of quasi-relationships with people, as reflected in his genealogical research, he seemed to have become ready for genuine contacts with people, and for an active life.

Reflections on the experiment

What has been learned from this endeavor? A conclusive answer to this question cannot be given. The following discussion, however, is aimed toward sharing the therapist's experiences regarding methods and therapeutic effects.

Methods

Linden's observation as to the necessity of "a new therapeutic approach . . . applicable to groups, practical to administer, and harmonious with a philosophy and scientific concept of aging" (5, p. 137) deserves ample consideration. The necessity for a new approach was felt with special urgency while engaged in group therapy with the very old.

As indicated previously, enhanced socialization was the main objective of the experiment. It was also noted that the patients were rather reluctant to enter group therapy, moreover, that they consented to participate on a trial basis only, and expected an educational setting. Therefore, it seemed most practical to assume a cautious, "let's see" attitude as to the choice of method, in preference to a doctrinaire plan.

The therapist was guided by the premise that the patients constituted a group of very old people with special needs, needs that had arisen from a status "imposed" on them by "old age." Thus, the participants were regarded simply as citizens who had enjoyed a long life, and not as psychiatric patients. With such an approach, the primary therapeutic question was how to meet best the very old person's current needs. It was felt that any method harmonious with the fulfillment of their needs was justified. For example, if Mr. B., in his 96 years of age, showed the strong need to retain the status of a giving father—and this could be exercised by his viewing the therapist as his child—then an appropriate opportunity for the fulfillment of this need was granted. Again, if calling on the participants to express their views (rotating method) yielded better results than did the encouragement of free association, then the latter method was abandoned in favor of the former.

At the outset of therapy, the patients shared a sense of discouragement and depression that had strong grounding in their reality situation. It proved necessary for the therapist to assume a rather active role to provide the group with leadership and a source of continuing stimulation. A great deal of patience and perseverance was also required of her to enable the patients to overcome their fears associated with revealing their true feelings. Moreover, sustaining such a group over a period of time also required considerable flexibility with regard to the topics and level of discussion.

In sum, while it was useful to apply diverse techniques at various times, the main approach focused upon meeting the particular needs of very old people who lived in an institutional setting.

Therapeutic Effects

Linden's observation that "improvement among the geriatric group is more a measure of comparison between a patient's behavior before and after group therapy than an estimate of approach to 'community normality'" (5, p. 150) is particularly applicable to our group of very old citizens who (with varying degrees of willingness) accepted Cushing Hospital as their "home." Nevertheless, the improvement of group members did include the restoration of one man to full "community normality" (Mr. M.). Here I will summarize self-report statements made by the patients that pertain to therapeutic results, and also behavioral changes noted by others (therapist and other staff members).

"Subjective" or self-report signs of improvement can be illustrated by the following verbatim statements, each of which represents a separate patient:

1. "We learned to stand up for ourselves today."
2. "I enjoyed getting together . . . I like to be of benefit to people."
3. "I learned to be contented . . . not to be grumpy . . . not to be picky on everyone . . . Everyone has faults."
4. "You (directed at the therapist) are the girl who kept me from sorrow . . . You gave me courage."
5. "You think you lost it all . . . but then I enjoyed this . . . this did a lot."

The outstanding therapeutic effects, as observed by the therapist, included:

1. Feelings of loneliness and depression were diminished.
2. Self-respect was reinstated.
3. Old pleasures were revived.
4. Social drives were re-activated.
5. Intellectual interests were re-awakened.
6. Readiness and ability for resuming community life were developed.

The effects at large may be described in terms of a main product and a number of by-products. The main product consisted of a rise in morale and esteem: the group had initially been labeled derisively as "mental" (by the participants themselves, other patients, staff members and visitors). This stigma was lost, and it became known instead as *the* group, also as "the Tuesday group," or "Dr. Shere's group." This change in attitude led to the following by-products: 1) favorable regard from visitors and relatives for "this kind of activity;" 2) contagion to the occupational therapy department as reflected, e.g., in arranging a special party for nonagenarians only.

On the whole, group therapy with the very old was experienced as a worthwhile endeavor. This experience may serve to stimulate the "reluctant therapist" to engage in therapeutic work with very old people as well as the researcher to clarify the hypothesis that mental development does not cease with old age. In conclusion, I would like to express my credo in group psychotherapy with the very old in the words of one of the pioneer group therapists, L. Cody Marsh: "By the crowd have they been broken; by the crowd shall they be healed" (7).

References

1. Allen, R. E. A study of subjects discussed by elderly patients in group counseling. *Social Casework*, 1962, *43*, 360-366.
2. Apake, T. K., and Sanges, K. B. The group approach in a general hospital. *Social Work*, 1962, *7*, 59-65.

3. Kastenbaum, R. The reluctant therapist. In this volume.
4. Linden, M. E. Group psychotherapy with institutional senile women. *Internat. J. Group Psychotherapy,* 1953, *3,* 150-170.
5. Linden, M. E. Geriatrics. In S. R. Slavson (ed.), *The Fields of Group Psychotherapy.* New York: International Universities Press, 1956, 137-150.
6. Lowy, L. The group in social work with the aged. *Social Work,* 1962, *7,* 43-50.
7. Marsh, L. C. Group psychotherapy and the psychiatric clinic. *J. Nerv. Ment. Disease,* 1953, *81,* 381-393.

Margaret Wallace

Introduction

The classical literature on aphasia states that prognosis for speech rehabilitation is less favorable with increased age of the patient and with
increased length of time between etiological trauma and initiation of
therapy. With research and clinical experience to support this thesis,
it might be assumed that a consideration of speech therapy in an institutionalized population of geriatric aphasic patients might be less than
productive.* We find little evidence in the literature to prove or to
disprove the worth of such a consideration. The literature of gerontology and communicative disorders has few references to speech therapy in the general rehabilitation program of the aged. If anything, the
literature tends to suggest (by way of omission) that although post-CVA
patients of 65 or older may regain some degree of self-sufficiency in
walking and self-care while hospitalized, aphasia is a handicap one
should simply accept unless speech returns spontaneously.

We are not concerned here with those isolated cases in which families seek assistance in the large medical and rehabilitation centers or
in the speech and hearing clinics of universities and welfare agencies.
We *are* concerned with those patients who because of physical debilities, mental confusion and generally handicapped condition are placed
in private nursing homes or state institutions for custodial or rehabili-
tational care when the family no longer feels equipped to care for
them—the chronic institutionalized patients without speech.

In the recent burst of attention to the physical, social and vocational
rehabilitation of the aged, there are few specific references to the need
for retraining in speech. Institutions provide facilities for medical,
dental and optical care, for psychotherapy and psychological research,
for physical and occupational therapy, for handicrafts, sewing and
reading, and for entertainment and local excursions. Why then not

---

* Because of the preponderence and severity of speech debilitation attributed to
aphasia in the population to be discussed, the program's primary emphasis has been
in working with post-CVA hemiplegics who have aphasia.

speech and language? Has speech therapy merely been overlooked? Is it considered a waste of time? Is the medical profession *familiar* with speech therapy as an aid to rehabilitation—more important, is it convinced of its usefulness?

Only within very recent times has any serious attempt been made to approach this area of inquiry in geriatrics. Work by Rusk (19, 29, 30, 31, 32) offers some interesting theories and hopeful inferences for geriatric speech therapy; at the November 1963 convention of the American Speech and Hearing Association a section was devoted to the "Communication Problems of the Aging," where reports from the University of Chicago (25) and the Veterans Administration Outpatient Clinic in Boston (20) were presented, as well as a significant study by D. E. Morley of the University of Michigan (21). Another paper by Morley in 1962 points out research needs in communication problems of the aging and provides important data and a listing of pertinent references (22).

The author was asked to present a personal reaction to the problem of geriatric communication disorders on the basis of her rather brief experience in a rehabilitation setting with the geriatric population of Cushing Hospital. The request and the months which followed it led to a siege of anxiety in this therapist who by far prefers doing speech therapy to writing about it. Then, too, like many who find themselves working among the aged, she had had little training or experience in gerontology and felt hesitant in presenting ideas which did not have the benefit of a background of inquiry and experimentation. Lastly, during the brief existence of the one-man speech therapy program there was little time to collect quantitative data with which to document observations and impressions.

The following, then, is a narrative description of the germination, organization and development of a speech therapy program among the rehabilitation disciplines already present in a geriatric hospital, and includes representative case histories and therapy observations. Here will be found ideas, attempts, successes and failures, the surmised reasons for each, and an attempted evaluation of the existing program on the basis of patient response, personnel reaction and research potential. An effort has been made to avoid "how-to-do" speech therapy. Theory and techniques are available to the reader in quantity and quality in the works of experts in the field, and these are found in the bibliography of the chapter.

We begin with an emphatic nod to the affirmative: yes, there are benefits which justify a geriatric speech therapy program. We find it possible to show examples of re-learning, improved emotional adjustment and increased environmental contact which to all indications are, at least in part, direct consequences of a therapeutic attempt to re-build, re-organize or merely "polish up" the communicative skills which have for one reason or another deteriorated with age. We propose that speech and language rehabilitation fits very well into the stated goals, theory and practical application of general geriatric rehabilitation. In fact, we suggest that it is *necessary* for a *comprehensive* rehabilitation approach.

Many negative factors must be considered: relatively high frequency of recurrent cerebrovascular accidents (CVA's), the increased mortality rate, the tendency toward generalized physical and mental deterioration, and the isolation from an integrated life among family and friends, without the motivations of vocation and activity. Also, there are the pertinent questions of learning, retention and general motivation of the aged.

Let us first look at the general problems of age and time lapse. McCoy and Rusk conclude from their study at the Bellevue Medical Center that age and time lapse did not "appear to be *strong* factors" in success of rehabilitation. In this study, 39 (8.2%) of the 476 patients examined were aged 65-74 and, of these, 16 had suffered CVA's; 5 (1.1%) of the total were 75 years and older, 3 of these status post-CVA. A number of these aged patients were accepted for, and to some degree successful in, a program of rehabilitation (19). In another article Rusk states, "Many of the successes (in aphasia therapy) . . . have been brought to patients who had been unable to communicate at all for years . . . some of them . . . bedridden . . . in hospitals." (29).

Among the patients responding to speech rehabilitation in the Cushing program, some had been without rehabilitation efforts for 5-8 years since the time of the trauma. Of 32 patients referred to the program for evaluation, therapy was initiated with 19 aphasics. The age range was 65 to 86. Of twelve patients under 75, 5 showed measurable and distinct progress in acquisition of speech, 5 demonstrated little or no gain, and 2 have just begun therapy with results yet to be evaluated. Of 6 patients between the ages of 75 to 84, 5 showed considerable gain with one patient just beginning in therapy. Thus, in this sample of patients beyond the age of 65 we can show 10 of 19 who have made progress and who are demonstrating the ability to regain speech within the framework of organized speech therapy. The range of time between trauma and initiation of therapy varied from one month to 8 years. In considering the extremes, we find that 5 of the 19 patients in therapy were seen within 6 months after cerebral insult, and of these, 4 showed visible gains, with the 5th not yet ready to be evaluated; 8 of the 19 were seen from 2 to 8 years after trauma, with 4 demonstrating notable progress. The statistical breakdown of speech evaluation referrals and their outcome is given in Table 1. Admittedly, the *better* results are obtained when therapy can begin immediately after the cerebral insult, but potential for *improvement* is not lost just because therapy is not begun promptly.

As therapists we know that youth and immediate therapy provide good prognostic signs. Yet even with these on our side we sometimes fail. Likewise, some aged patients are not going to respond—as therapists we will fail with them—but *some* have rehabilitation potential. We cannot allow these people to lie on geriatric wards by the hundreds in inactivity and silence while they passively accept old age and deformity without hope. And, if we are going to teach them to walk and to wash themselves, we must also teach them to talk again, to rejoin the language community.

Other factors limiting rehabilitation are the amount of brain damage sustained by the patient, type of trauma, and judged ability to learn. All these factors must be evaluated, and therapy designed around them.

Another consideration of immeasurable importance in reaching the rehabilitation potential of our patients is their emotional and motivational status. This is an area in which speech and language therapy can serve a vital function. Rusk states that "in about 50% of adults with physical disability [emotional factors] determine the success or failure of rehabilitation." (30). This point is well developed in an article by Hulicka on the psychological problems of geriatric patients in which she states, "An unhappy, apathetic, poorly motivated patient resigned to his present fate because he perceives neither reason for, nor hope of improving, manages to negate the best rehabilitative efforts of the staff." (12). She adds, "Hospitals designed primarily for physical care tend by their very nature to treat patients on a biologic basis and to center the patient's activities around bodily functioning. . . . This biologic segmental orientation makes it much more difficult to reach the patient as a living, thinking human being, and naturally impedes utilization of unique opportunities to help him gratify his emotional needs. . . . Thus, one of the major sources of fuel for rehabilitation—the patient's own aspirations—becomes less available."

How do we reach patients at this level? Through communication. And what if the patient is non-verbal? We attempt through speech therapy to give him some way in which to express his fears, his emotional needs, and in the case of receptive disturbances to open a way for offering emotional support through language. It is our opinion that these two goals alone (and these are not the only goals) can stand as adequate justification for geriatric speech therapy.

The problems the aged face are real, intense and threatening: physical decline, approaching death, family rejection, lack of independence, separation from job and community. Add to these the needs which all people seek to fulfill—affection, belonging, hope, achievement, recognition and self-esteem—and the adjustment problem becomes increasingly complex. The accepted means of working out these types of problems in all age groups is verbalization—"talking out" the feelings and the questions. If general rehabilitation is largely dependent on emotional adjustment and emotional adjustment is to be accomplished most easily through verbal communication, then again we state that speech therapy must be an integral and complementary (not supplementary) discipline in the rehabilitation setting for the geriatric population.

And for those to whom an emotional plea is less than convincing, we point to the difficulty in caring for a patient who is unable to say that he wants to go to the bathroom, that his stomach aches, that he feels as if he's going to vomit.

Let us look at a program of geriatric communicative rehabilitation.

A speech rehabilitation program

Within the Cushing Hospital setting there exists a newly-organized rehabilitation ward, housing 44 of the 650-patient population. Of these 44, approximately 15 actively participate in a full program of physical therapy and occupational therapy. This number is determined in part by evaluated rehabilitation potential and, equally as important, by the availability of trained ward personnel. Other patients participate only in varying degrees in these two programs but may be involved in other activity areas such as recreation, handicrafts or psychological studies. Patients living on other wards who are interested and physically able are also included in as broad an activity program as is feasible.

Speech therapy was added to this program, first as a part-time discipline, later on a full-time basis, and was housed in a small office on the rehabilitation wing. The administration and staff who generally were unfamiliar with speech therapy supported a trial program with the following objectives in mind: 1) to determine its effectiveness with the type of patient at Cushing Hospital, 2) to assist in evaluating patients being considered by staff physicians for rehabilitation, 3) to familiarize the staff at large with the nature of speech problems and the approaches of the speech therapist and 4) to determine by patient-survey whether there was a need for a permanent speech therapy program in the institution. The first objective was the initiation of a small program to test therapy results against age, type of problem, physical health and time lapse since trauma.

In the first 4 months of the 6 hour per week program, 16 patients were referred for evaluation and recommendation. At the end of that 4-month period, 6 patients were being seen in regular bi-weekly therapy sessions; 3 were being seen periodically for less intensive work on minor residual dysarthrias or for supportive guidance in the use of re-learned speech skills; 3 were still being tested or observed; and 4 were yet to be interviewed. In the succeeding 6 months, therapist time was increased to 25 hours and an additional 16 patients were referred to the program. Classification and treatment of these patients is reported in Table 1.

To date we have interviewed, and in most instances evaluated, a total of 32 patients, 9 of whom are now actively participating in therapy. Three of these patients have died since the program began.

Three case histories will illustrate the work being done in the program. In this way the reader may see the patients on a more personal level, trace their progress or regression, evaluate the therapy goals or

Table I. Speech evaluation referrals and their outcome

	Age 65-74			Age 75 +			Grand total
	Male	Female	Total	Male	Female	Total	
Number of referrals	8	9	17	5	10	15	32
Evaluated with Eisenson examination	6	8	14	3	7	10	24
Interviewed: impossible to test	2	1	3	1	1	2	5
not necessary to test	0	0	0	2	2	4	4
History of cerebral insult	8	9	17	3	8	11	28
Judged aphasic or dysphasic	7	6	13	2	6	8	21
Excluded from therapy: speech judged adequate	1	2	3	3	3	6	9
severe C.B.S.* or emotional disturbance	1	1	2	0	1	1	3
Taken into therapy	6	6	12	2	5	7	19
significant progress	3	2	5	1	4	5	10
too soon to rate progress**	2	0	2	1	0	1	3

*C.B.S.: Chronic brain syndrome.

**Therapy has already terminated in 9 cases: 6 cases with no progress (one since deceased), one with progress adequate for dismissal and 2 cases in which treatment was terminated by by death; of these latter cases, both had shown significant progress.

procedures, sense the feelings and motivations expressed by the patients, and judge, to some degree, effectiveness of therapy in individual cases.

Case histories

Miss D.L. is a sprightly and alert 83 year old aphasic patient who holds a Master's Degree from a teachers college and was for many years an elementary school teacher. She is a ward resident, semiambulant, and rather seriously handicapped in expressive language after suffering a CVA approximately 8 years ago. There has been some mental and emotional deterioration; nevertheless Miss L. retains a superior intelligence, an intellectual curiosity, a need to associate actively with her environment, and the oft-thwarted desire to be challenged and stimulated. One of Miss L.'s greatest irritations is that she is living among many people whose age and health hinder their interests, their abilities and the continuation of a rich inner life. She seeks stimulation. The major problem seemed to be that the patient was frustrated by her inability to express herself after years of high level expression and an authoritarian role in society. She was depressed and apparently ready to give up. Rehabilitation measures seem to assist this woman toward fulfillment of these needs.

Miss L. was transferred 3 years ago from a nearby nursing home where she had resided for several years following the CVA. On admission to Cushing the patient was seen as status post CVA, "with emotional and a certain amount of mental deterioration, arteriosclerotic disease of the brain, and right-sided hemiplegia."

She was admitted to a custodial care ward, where she apparently received no physical therapy. Occupational therapy provided her with a brace for her right leg and involved her in activity programs in which she learned to write and to paint with her left hand. Her art work showed potential and was framed and displayed in the hospital activity center. She took limited advantage of the hospital library facilities and recently has participated in its bi-weekly talking-book activity. She had not initiated social contact with the other patients but had been friendly with hospital personnel and maintained close friendships with two lifelong friends who continue to make regular weekly or bi-weekly visits with her. Though not given supervised assistance in walking or exercising, she continued her own exercise program, walking around the ward pushing her wheel chair for support, even walking unaided for short distances, and doing range-of-motion exercises with her paralyzed right arm. The ward nurse judged Miss L. to be among the most clear and lucid patients on the ward but rather demanding in her bid for attention and care.

The patient was seen by the speech therapist whose testing and clinical observation indicated that receptive language ability was relatively unimpaired. In the expressive sphere Miss L. could imitate and identify auditory stimuli and speech sounds, was able to give one or two word answers to simple questions, to imitate almost all speech stimuli and to solve simple arithmetic computations. The more obvious symptomatic characteristics were an inability to recall words needed to express a thought, the tendency to become completely unintelligible and disorganized under stress, impatience with her inabilities, refusal to expend the necessary time and energy toward more self-control in communication, and perseverative responses to both visual and auditory stimuli. It was the therapist's impression that Miss L. had more potential ability than she was utilizing and that therapy should be initiated.

The estalishment of rapport and an increase of motivation were the immediate goals. They were achieved through appealing to the woman's pride in her past accomplishments, an acknowledgement of her present abilities and surmised potential for relearning, and a direct appeal from one "teacher" to another, later to be supported by the therapist's genuine appreciation for the patient's keen mind and quick sense of humor. Therapy was always very direct and to the point (disguises would have been an insult to the patient's abilities and perception); procedures were explained, goals outlined, and evaluations asked of the patient herself.

Therapy has continued over a period of 8 to 9 months and has been designed toward vocabulary building, word-finding associations, self-controls for speed and clarity of utterance and thought, activities directed toward helping the patient to think and act within a structured, organized, symbolic framework. Miss L. is now speaking in complete sentences a good deal of the time; reading skills are improved; and communicative behavior is generally more organized and more functional. The patient is keeping herself busy with oral and written homework for several hours each day and is showing more interest in reading the daily news and library selections.

A problem which has appeared throughout the therapy process has been Miss L"s dissatisfaction with her limited achievement in light of her former abilities. She has a tendency to belittle her rehabilitation accomplishments. Hulicka (12) confronts this as a common problem in geriatric rehabilitation when she says ". . . what they do achieve . . . is likely to be judged by them (the patients) in terms of 'what used to be.' Hence what is a real achievement in terms of present limitations may be perceived by the patient as being less good than it ought to be." Thus, it is necessary to keep Miss L. aware of the increasingly difficult goals and to encourage an objective appraisal of present over past (hospital) performance.

The nursing staff has indicated a recent interest in moving the patient to a ward where patients might provide a more stimulating environment in which she can participate. At this point it is important for the patient to begin using patients for satisfaction of her intellectual and social needs, thereby reducing her dependence upon staff for this function.

The most severe enemy of any geriatric rehailitation endeavor is the high mortality rate. In working with hemiplegic patients there is the high probability of recurrent cerebral accident with resultant regression or death. If death does not come with repeated CVA it may threaten as the result of circulatory diseases, diminishing physical strength or any of the numerous debilities of advancing age. In research reported by Adams and Merrett (1) they state that "although age (65-70 years) made relatively little difference on recovery, it had considerable importance on the question of survival." Obvious though such a statement is, it points out a drawback in work with the aged in terms of continuity of case study, control of research studies and, most important, staff and patient motivation. It is difficult for the staff not to become discouraged at the sudden death of a patient who has progressed nicely through a carefully planned and encouraging process of physical, mental and emotional re-growth. And it is difficult for the patient to maintain hope and optimism in the face of sudden debilitation and the realistic threat of approaching death.

Mrs. L.V., 82 years old, had been admitted to Cushing Hospital for re-ambulation following a hip fracture. Patient reportedly completed a grammar school education and had spent her working years as a cook at a well-known college. Admission diagnostic impressions: "post hip fracture, chronic arthritis, obesity, fully oriented, cooperative, good memory, intact cranial nerves, no evident sensory anormalities." Following a nine month hospital stay for nursing care and beginning rehabilitation, Mrs. V. suffered a CVA with right-sided hemiplegia and aphasia, and was placed on the danger list. Post-traumas days witnessed a "return of slurred speech and some improvement in strength of right-sided extremities but the patient remained completely disoriented." Within a few days there was a second CVA leaving the patient with an additional left hemiparesis and a more total loss of speech. Rehabilitation was begun a second time. Patient's status was as a bed-chair patient with no recognizable speech.

Mrs. V. was then seen for an initial speech and language evaluation at which time selected items were administered from the Eisenson Examination for Aphasia (7) in relation to the patient's observed level of abilities and evident tolerance for a testing situation. The patient's success on the visual agnosia items suggested little deficiency in visual recognition. Auditory recognition also appeared to be intact. Because of the patient's inability to give verbal responses, no tests for receptive or expressive aphasias (as contrasted to agnosias) were administered. Gross motor reactions were slow, unsteady, and labored. Verbal motor responses were, for all practical purposes, non-existent. Little, if any, intelligible speech was observed and the only vocal utterance was a vowel-like groan with some attempt to use the tongue and lips. Comprehension and orientation were good.

Receptive language abilities were apparently intact for simple stimuli, but the patient seemed unable to respond to more complex language stimulation.

Retraining procedures centered around the re-teaching of actual speech movements and word production. The intial approach to the teaching was made through reading, since this seemed most effective with the patient.

Initial progress was rapid and retention was good. Work was begun by giving her ten cards on each of which was printed a word important for expressing an immediate need. In the first session it was found that with a good example to follow the patient was able to imitate all of these words with a fair degree of accuracy. Her husband, himself a resident of the hospital, and the ward attendants agreed to practice the use of these words with her each day. Within less than one month (speech sessions were held twice per week) these and additional words were being used with increased clarity in propositional speaking situations, and short phrases and sentences began to appear. As this progress was being observed, specific drill work was being done to elicit voluntary verbal and non-verbal lip and tongue movements and differentiated vowel approximation. This proved to be much more difficult for her, and progress in this area was slow.

In a month's time Mr. V. reported that his wife had begun using occasional phrases and sentences in visiting with her friends. At about the same time the therapist had observed that the patient was trying more often to put words together, and although these attempts were for the most part unintelligible, there were distinct articulatory movements to indicate the presence of separate syllables and words.

Throughout the next month there were three basic areas of speech activity involved in the work with Mrs. V.: vocabulary building (using printed words and picture cards); increased use of utilitarian language in her environment (directed question and answer encounters in which the questions were phrased to elicit a newly acquired word, and constant language stimulation by the patient's husband and all ward personnel); and voluntary control over the isolated movements of the speech mechanism.

Speech behavior steadily improved for several weeks, then performance seemed to become heavily dependent upon the patient's daily emotional status. After a tiring session with the occupational therapist she was unable to maintain consistent control in speech and adequate motivation to work. On these days our sessions were cancelled or changed to short, social visits. A failure in a session with the physical therapist would upset her and break down her communicative attempts. This pattern reached a peak a month later. A therapy progress entry at this time stated: "Recently patient has seemed very tired and discouraged; speech work is slowing down considerably. Physically she appears weaker; her attention span is shorter; motivation is poor. A plateau or possibly even a period of regression has been reached. Speech therapy temporarily discontinued." Social contact was maintained with the patient on the ward.

Two months later therapy was begun again. A few days later the physician's report stated: "Patient began complaining of loss of vision (most likely a thrombosis); also suspected urinary tract infection." Mrs. V. was transferred to an acute illness ward and given intensive nursing and medical care. Rehabilitation procedures were necessarily halted. Then a progressive decline in physical condition was observed, terminating in the patient's death, five days later.

Here was a patient who, at the age of 82, had survived a hip fracture and two relatively severe CVA's. She was alert, clear, cooperative, highly motivated and receptive to therapy. She was fully engaged in programs of physical and occupational therapy, and although she had not yet begun to walk or could not be judged "self-care," she was learning to pull herself onto her feet and to feed and wash herself. Speech therapy was meeting with success. As with many motor or expressive aphasics, progress was seemingly rapid, retention was good, and communication was slowly being re-established.

The rapid decline and death of this woman was a setback to the entire staff associated with her rehabilitation program. But the time and effort must not be considered lost. Her last months were productive and optimistic.

Cushing Hospital's rehabilitation program utilizes a "team approach." The "team" is coordinated by a staff physician and composed of consultant medical specialists, social service staff members, occupational therapists, a physical therapist, speech therapist and psychologists. A nucleus group representing these various disciplines meets every week in conference or on rounds to evaluate new patients and/or to reevaluate and to discuss continuing patients who may be presenting various types of rehabilitation problems. This group contact provides, among other things, an opportunity to share knowledge of one another's specialties, to educate and to encourage carry-over of one type of skill onto other rehabilitation goals, to request guidance in problems the solution of which exceeds therapist experience or training, and to refer from one therapy to another when the original therapy no longer seems to be providing maximum gains.

The case of N.B. may be used to illustrate (among other things) the thread of coordination among the various staff members in dealing with a patient's entire symptomatology.

Miss N.B., a 75 year old retired shoe worker, was admitted to Cushing Hospital two months after suffering a CVA. She was diagnosed "cerebral hemorrhage with right hemiplegia and residual aphasia, deafness, and moderate hypertension." At admission she was a bed-chair care patient unable to walk, and incontinent. Mental status could not be evaluated well "because of her incapacity of speech." She appeared to be depressed but seemed to be in some contact. She liked to talk at length, but mumbled to herself most of the time, and could not be understood at all. To compensate for a hearing loss of ten years the patient was wearing a hearing aid.

Ten months after admission the physical medicine consultant examined the patient for inclusion into the rehabilitation program and reported that she should eventually be able to walk with a brace, had shown definite improvement during her stay, was more mentally clear and was showing some awareness of the use of her extremities, but that her speech was still "restricted." A program of daily exercise, activities-for-daily-living and occupational therapy was initiated. Since there was no speech therapist on the staff at that time, the occupational therapist began working in the area of vocabulary building and handwriting training.

One year after admission, Miss B. had told a psychologist that she cried when she "can't say it right," and complained that she could not remember names. The psychologist concluded that the patient's "primary difficulty lies in fearing to pronounce the words rather than not remembering them," and that a "therapeutic relationship promises to be beneficial." Such a psychotherapeutic relationship was established between the patient and the psychologist, reportedly with a resultant increase in the use of speech and language.

During the initial stages of rehabilitation, lack of self-confidence and emotional problems interferred with the progress in physical rehabilitation more than any other factor. At the time of a rehabilitation conference regarding the patient, one and one-half years after admission, the occupational therapist stated that the patient had improved remarkably in her speech and in activities for daily living. The head nurse stated that the patient was still easily upset and when in an emotional state was hindered in her usual performance abilities. The director of the occupational therapy program reinforced the above observations in stating that the patient was able to adapt to new circumstances, though rather slowly, but that any emotional upset would slow her progress significantly.

The consistent observation throughout this patient's recovery process to the time of the conference was the effect of her "emotional upsets" on the course of rehabilitation measures. These emotional upsets seemed to involve impatience with her own inabilities, frustration at being unable to express her needs, anger at any inefficiency in the ward's schedule which affected her functioning, and anger at individual members of the staff who might be involved in her failures or upsets. This impatience and frustration is easily understood when one considers the patient's pre-morbid personality tendencies. According to a nephew, Miss B. had always been an active and social person who had many friends; she had lived in and cared for a four room apartment alone; she like to cook, clean, read, watch TV, and to spend time with her nephew and his children. This social, self-sufficient woman had become a noncommunicative invalid living in an institutional setting with rigid schedules, few personal belongings, no privacy, and considerable loss of contact with family and friends. The frustration and emotionality is easily understood, but nevertheless, the behavior had to be dealt with since it was inhibiting her progress in rehabilitation. The conference staff re-set Miss B.'s rehabilitation goal as "self-sufficiency within the hospital environment."

This therapist first saw the patient at the time of the rehabilitation conference and was immediately impressed with the amount of speech and language displayed, some a result of natural recovery processes, much a result of personal communicative relationships with the clinical psychologist and the occupational therapist. Language stimulation and supportive counseling had been an early and important part of her physical and emotional convalescence and the results were striking. Rather than moving in and assuming the responsibility for speech and language retraining for this patient, thus taking away some of the responsibility from other disciplines who had been integrating it into their own approach, the therapist offered assistance to the other staff members and worked along in a complementary, supportive role with this patient. A few specific language techniques seemed to be needed, and this was accomplished in short, bi-weekly speech therapy sessions.

Administration of the Eisenson examination indicated that basic receptive language abilities were relatively intact. The major receptive disturbance to be found was in the area of auditory or visual retention in dealing with more complex stimuli. In speech this deficiency manifested itself in sound and word reversals, telegraphic speech, incomplete words, phrases and sentences, and difficulty in orally completing thoughts. Receptively the patient had difficulty in following directions given in complicated or lengthy sequence. Expressive language was more severely affected. The patient demonstrated severe dysarthria, with sound substitutions and distortions, apparently due to lack of muscular control of the speech mechanism, undue speed of attempt, all of which was complicated by her impatience. Another major area of expressive deficiency was in word finding—or anomia. The word-finding process seemed to be complicated by the patient's inability to retain an auditory symbol long enough to use it as a search clue and by her difficulty in producing motorically the symbols which she finally *was* able to find.

It seemed evident that besides the usual goals of lengthening retention span, clarifying sound production and rebuilding word-finding ability the most important goal was to assist the patient in accepting her imperfect attempts and in increasing her tolerance and frustration levels. The speech therapist could agree in part with the psychologist's earlier emphasis on fear as an inhibiting factor in Miss B.'s expressive ability. However, on the basis of test results and indications of organic involvement, she refused to say that the fear and emotional involvement constituted the "primary difficulty."

The early months of speech therapy were devoted to vocabulary building and ease of usage, articulatory drill for improving clarity of sound production, attention to reading, writing and spelling activities in order to integrate the ability to deal with various forms of verbal symbolization, activities designed to facilitate word-finding associations, and experiences in slow, easy, unpressured conversation. Progress was evident in most areas but Miss B. remained perfectionistic, impatient, emotional, and in need of constant reassurance.

Then, six months after the initiation of therapy, the psychologist asked the therapist to serve in her two-month absence as a supportive listener to the patient's need for emotional expression. The therapist had already been serving this need in part but agreed to assume the psychologist's role as a primary one during this period. The experience was not a beneficial one either to patient or speech therapist. In the past the patient had come to expect a certain amount of structure and guidance from the therapist within the usual speech training procedures. When the therapist became a more passive listener the patient became more emotional and self-effacing, crying that she talked too much about her complaints and fears and asking for definite work to do. When given more work and less time to express herself freely, she wanted more freedom. It became difficult to establish a mid-line between the two roles, and the relationship suffered a serious setback with the patient unhappy and the therapist somewhat irritable. It became apparent that the patient needed both the psychologist and the speech therapist.

For the two months Miss B. worried about everything—being ignored, misunderstood, disliked, regimented or bored. She seemed to be extremely insecure, needing constant reinforcement from the staff that they liked her and that she was doing well. When they were too busy to satisfy her constant demands for reassurance and listening to her problems, she cried and complained, then reproached herself for complaining—saying that the staff would turn against her for talking and crying too much. The psychologist's support had been removed temporarily; the speech therapist's approach had become ambiguous; and the patient seemed to be searching everywhere for the security and structure to be replaced.

At the end of the two month period the speech therapist reestablished a directive, structured, and disciplined approach with Miss B. The patient did not react favorably to this immediately, but her speech improved almost at once and she seemed less upset and fearful. Work was begun on abstract language forms and syntactical language structure. Time was also given to the development of auditory retention span and ability to handle memory sequences.

After one and one-half months the speech therapist decided that the patient's speech and language ability had progressed to the point at which environmental self correction was now more beneficial than formal speech therapy sessions. However, she felt it imperative that some type of psychological contact be re-established with the patient in order that she might make an adequate adjustment to her increased skills, verbal and physical, but also to come to accept the obvious limitations of her rehabilitation and of her environment.

In the absence of speech therapy other disciplines had assumed the responsibility for giving this woman some language with which to deal with her post-traumatic condition and with the strange new hospital environment. These disciplines *might* have failed in their attempts at language re-training, but so might speech therapy. In this case remarkable gains were made. Language stimulation had existed from the very beginning. To quote Rusk again, " . . . the psychological effect of knowing that someone is interested in his condition and understands the nature of his difficulty will build up the patient's morale immeasurably." (29).

At the age of 75, Miss B. had begun re-learning how to express herself. The speech therapist then was able to add a degree of speech and language structure within which the edges of intelligibility could be "polished up." After several months it became apparent that the patient had attained the basic skills with which to continue improving on her own, but that she needed again a more intensive psychotherapeutic setting. Now that she had become verbal, she needed someone to listen to her problems, to help her become more accepting of her present physical condition and the threats of her old age, and to assist in rebuilding perspective regarding herself and the changing world around her.

Recently there was a re-evaluation of this patient by the physician who originally devised the rehabilitation format for her care. He reminded the staff that at her admission two years earlier she had been unable to walk, to care for herself, or to talk. As one of the first patients on the rehabilitation ward she was given care and attention by an early rehabilitation team who crossed inter-disciplinary lines in meeting her obvious needs, regardless of individual responsibilities or duties. Progress was observed in all areas as the joint program was administered. At this recent conference Miss B. was judged to be ready to walk with a cane, was considered capable of self-care with only minimal assistance, was talkative and sociable. She jested with the doctor, commented on her progress, and demonstrated her abilities. The physician pointed with pride to this woman as an example of the rehabilitation that is possible in a team-care geriatric program.

**Staff participation and
in-service training**
Although to date the more formal therapy has been done by this therapist, much intra-staff participation has guided and complemented the therapy. The goal of the administration—and some of the medical staff—with regard to speech therapy is to generate among the nursing personnel such an awareness of and interest in the speech and language abilities of the patients that, in a generalized sense, speech therapy becomes part of the daily care given the patients on the ward by the nurses and attendants. The staff speech therapist would then serve chiefly as a consultant, evaluating patients, planning therapy, guiding the attendants in developing therapy attitudes and skills, and coordinating the efforts at speech rehabilitation with the goals of the other rehabilitation disciplines.

In modified form this is beginning to take place on the one ward devoted solely to rehabilitation patients. Since the therapist's office has been on this ward she has been able to maintain daily contact with the nurses and attendants in informal discussions and visits. There has been no teaching as such, but there has been a subtle growth of interest in speech therapy and a gradual dissemination of indirect therapy methods.

The therapist has been able to wander informally among the patients, watching the exercising, participating in family visits, and assisting with a troublesome wheel chair or piece of apparel, with the result that she is receiving an education in nurses' aiding while the attendants are becoming increasingly aware of how to lead the patients into more productive language exchanges. The process is painless and productive. Often the therapist has sat at her desk and overheard an attendant patiently helping with a difficult word while lacing a shoe or giving a bath. And, just as frequently, there are interruptions at the door from an attendant who wants to report the appearance of a new word or phrase or even to share the news that a patient has just pulled himself out of his chair for the first time.

In a more direct manner the educational process of developing an integrated speech therapy program is taking place in planned in-service programs. As this is being written, the therapist is participating in the training programs for attendants and practical nurses and making occasional visits to the registered nurse staff meetings for purposes of sharing information and coordinating the efforts. At this early date the primary goal is to develop an awareness of speech problems and an elementary knowledge of what speech therapy is and what it aims to accomplish. Later on, it is hoped that there can be some training in basic therapy procedures applicable to environmental functioning.

The attendants participate in weekly sectional meetings conducted by a nursing supervisor. Pertinent to our interests here, a month is being devoted to a study of CVA's, with the first week given to a consideration of the anatomy, physiology, and symptomatology, the second week to nursing care and patient observation and interviews, the third week to aphasia and speech therapy demonstrations, and the fourth week to educational films and summary. Time is limited and the instruction brief, but it is a rewarding endeavor which is producing a more informed and more interested staff. Concurrently with the attendant sessions on hemiplegia and aphasia, the speech therapist presents supplementary information to the nurses and the licensed practical nurses.

It is not surprising to note that when the information is presented at the level of individual cases and daily contacts and problems which the therapist has observed on the wards, interest is heightened and personnel responses are more immediate. Thus a concerted attempt is made to maintain a meaningful balance between general theory and application to specific and familiar patients.

Plans for the future include a survey to determine the frequency and type of speech problems existing within the entire hospital population. The results of this survey might lead to more extensive speech therapy here and perhaps at other institutions as well by bringing the need to the attention of state officials. It is also planned that speech therapy and psychology will share test findings and interview impressions on a more consistent basis to obtain a better over-all view of each patient.

References

1. Adams, G., and Merrett, J. Prognosis and survival in the aftermath of hemiplegia. *British Medical J.*, 1961, *5222*, 309-314.

2. Aronson, M., Shatin, L., and Cook, J. Social-psychotherapeutic approach to the treatment of aphasic patients. *J. of Speech and Hearing Disorders,* 1956, *21,* 3, 352-364.
3. Berry, M., and Eisenson, J. *Speech Disorders.* New York: Appleton-Century-Crofts, 1956.
4. Birren, J. (ed.). *Handbook of Aging and the Individual.* Chicago,: The University of Chicago Press, 1959.
5. Cooper, E., Ipsen, J., and Brown, H. Determining factors in the prognosis of stroke. *Geriatrics,* 1963, *18,* 1, 3-9.
6. Costello, Jr., J., Tanaka, G., and Toro, J. The long-term rehabilitation service of the St. Louis Chronic Hospital program for the aged. *J. of the Amer. Geriatric Society,* 1960, *8,* 3, 210-216.
7. Eisenson, J. *Examining for Aphasia.* New York: Psychological Corporation, 1954.
8. Feldman, L. A positive approach to management of cerebrovascular accident. *Geriatrics,* 1951, *6,* 4, 214-220.
9. Filer, R., and O'Connell, D. A useful contribution climate for the aging. *J. of Gerontology,* 1962, *17,* 1, 51-57.
10. Hoerner, E., and Horwitz, B. Diagnosis, prognosis and rehabilitation in patients with aphasia. *J. of the Amer. Medical Association,* 1958, *166,* 1573-76.
11. Hudson, A. Communication problems of the geriatric patient. *J. of Speech and Hearing Disorders,* 1960, *25,* 3, 238-248.
12. Hulicka, I. Psychologic problems of geriatric patients. *J. of the Amer. Geriatric Society,* 1961, *9,* 9, 797-803.
13. Kaplan, O. (ed). *Mental Disorders in Later Life,* 2nd edition. Stanford, Calif.: Stanford U. Press, 1956.
14. Longerich, M. *Manual for the Aphasic Patient.* New York: MacMillan, 1958.
15. Longerich, M., and Bordeaux, J. *Aphasia Therapeutics.* New York: Macmillan, 1959.
16. Lorenze, E., Cancro, R., and Sokoloff, M. Psychologic studies in geriatric hemiplegia. *J. of the Amer. Geriatric Society,* 1961, *9,* 1, 39-47.
17. Manson, M. Study of a geriatric psychiatric population: Significant characteristics affecting hospital discharge. *Geriatrics,* 1961, *16,* 11, 612-618.
18. McClellan, W. *Physical Medicine and Rehabilitation for the Aged.* Springfield, Ill.: C. C Thomas, 1951.
19. McCoy, G., and Rusk, H. An evaluation of rehabilitation. *Rehabilitation Monograph,* 1. New York: University-Bellevue Medical Center, 1953.
20. Melrose, J., Welsh, O., and Luterman, D. Responses of aged males to time-altered speech stimuli. Paper delivered at the 39th annual convention of the American Speech and Hearing Association, Chicago, Ill., November 3-6, 1963.
21. Morley, D., Curriculum planning and professional training for communication disorders of later maturity and old age. Paper delivered at the 39th annual convention of the American Speech and Hearing Association, Chicago, Ill., November 3-6, 1963.
22. Morley, D. Research needs in communication problems of the aging. *J. of the Amer. Speech and Hearing Assoc.* (ASHA), 1962, *4,* 10, 345-347.

23. Nielson, J. *Agnosia, Apraxia, Aphasia,* 2nd edition. New York: Prentice-Hall, 1947.
24. Nielsen, J. Speech defects of middle life. *Geriatics,* 1963, *18,* 11, 827-836.
25. Neugarten, B. Personality changes in the aged. Paper delivered at the 39th annual convention of the American Speech and Hearing Association, Chicago, Ill., November 3-6, 1963.
26. Penfield, W., and Roberts, L. *Speech and Brain Mechanisms.* Princeton, N.J.: Princeton U. Press, 1959.
27. Rae, J., Smith, E., and Lenzer, A. Results of a rehabilitation program for geriatric patients in county hospitals. *J. of the Amer. Med. Assoc.,* 1962, *180,* 6, 463-468.
28. Raven, J. Changes in productive and reproductive intellectual activity between 60 and 90 years of age. *J. of Gerontology,* 1960, *8,* 8, 760-67.
29. Rusk, H. in I. Page, *et al. Strokes—How They Occur and What Can Be Done About Them.* Collier Books (1st edition). 1963, ch. 8.
30. Rusk, H. *Rehabilitation Medicine.* St. Louis: C. V. Mosby, 1958.
31. Rusk, H. Geriatrics and rehabilitation. *Geriatrics,* 1951, *6,* 143-50.
32. Rusk, H., *et al.* Survey of ninety-five custodial patients in a municipal hospital. *Rehabilitation Monograph,* 7. New York: Goldwater Memorial Hospital, 1954.
33. Schuell, H. Auditory impairment in aphasia: Significance and retraining techniques. *J. of Speech and Hearing Disorders,* 1953, *18,* 14-21.
34. Schuell, H. Diagnosis and prognosis in aphasia. *Archives of Neurology and Psychiatry,* 1955, *74,* 308-315.
35. Schuell, H., and Jenkins, J. The nature of language deficit in aphasia. *Psychological Review,* 1959, *66,* 45-67.
36. Schuell, H., Carroll, V., and Street, B. Clinical treatment of aphasia. *J. Speech and Hearing Disorders,* 1955, *20,* March 43-53.
37. Sett, R. Simplified tests for evaluation of patients with chronic illness (cerebro-vascular accidents). *J. of Amer. Geriatrics Soc.,* 1963, *11,* 11, 1095-1103.
38. Steinmann, B. Rehabilitation in geriatrics (German text). *Geriatrics and Gerontology Abstracts,* 1962, *5,* 8, abstract #1182.
39. Travis, L. (ed.). *Handbook of Speech Pathology.* New York: Appleton-Century-Crofts, 1957.
40. Van Riper, C. *Speech Correction, Principles and Methods,* 4th edition. New York: Prentice-Hall, 1963.
41. Wepman, J. *Recovery from Aphasia.* New York: Ronald Press, 1951.
42. Wepman, J. The relationship between self-correction and recovery from aphasia. *J. of Speech and Hearing Disorders,* 1958, *23,* 3, 302-305.
43. West, R., Ansberry, M., and Carr, A. *The Rehabilitation of Speech,* 3rd edition. New York: Harper, 1957.
The author wishes to call attention to three additional references which were overlooked in the original review of the literature but which should be of considerable interest to the reader:
Lefevre, M. Speech therapy for the geriatric patient. *Geriatrics,* 1957, *12,* 12, 691-695.
Mitchell, J. Speech and language impairment in the older patient. *Geriatrics,* 1958, *13,* 7, 467-476.
Pichot, P. Language disturbances in cerebral disease: Concept of latent aphasia. *Arch of Neurol. and Psychiatry,* 1955, *74,* 1, 92-95.

Depression in the aged: The importance of external factors

12

Sidney Levin

For many professional workers the term "depression" denotes a psychotic state such as involutional melancholia or manic depressive illness. In the present chapter the term "depression" will be used in a broad sense to refer to the entire range of depressive reactions, most of which fall short of the severe forms of disorder which we refer to as "depressive illness." Since patients with psychotic depressions comprise only a small percentage of cases in which significant depressive feelings occur, it seems reasonable to broaden the use of the term "depression" so as to include the more frequent non-psychotic disturbances. Therefore, if depression is defined as "a painful degree of dejection," one has a more comprehensive definition. One can then think quantitatively, in terms of degrees of depression, as well as qualitatively, in terms of various types of depression.

The existence of a state of depression often goes unrecognized. This is true not only for patients with mild depression but also for patients with severe depressive illness. It is not uncommon for relatives or friends of a severely depressed person who has committed or attempted suicide to remark, "I didn't even know he was depressed." In other words, people as a rule do not exhibit their depressive feelings. Furthermore, they may not only hide these feeling from others; they often hide them from themselves. For the psychiatrist in training, considerable experience is often required before he is able to recognize and to evaluate quantitatively the underlying depressive feelings of his patients. Until he is able to do so, he is apt to deny the existence of these feelings in certain patients. Furthermore, he may become annoyed at those psychiatrists who talk about particular patients as being depressed when he cannot perceive the depressive feelings to which they refer. Similar reactions of annoyance are seen in medical students, social workers, psychologists and other professional workers who collaborate with psychiatrists.

It is well known that the incidence of depressive illness tends to increase with age, and that suicide becomes a progressively more frequent occurrence with advancing age (1). It is less well recognized that the milder forms of depression are also more common in the aged. This lack of recognition is a barrier to understanding old age. One of the main reasons for this lack of recognition is the fact that depression in the aged tends to take a form which is somewhat different from that usually found in younger individuals. The form of depression to which I refer is characterized by a state of "apathy." I do not mean to imply that apathetic features are not present in the depressions of younger individuals. But I do mean to imply that apathy is less characteristic of depressions in earlier years and more characteristic of depressions in the aged. Elderly depressed patients often appear to be disinterested in their surroundings and to lack drive. They are apt to sit idly with a somewhat vacant stare on their faces, appearing preoccupied. These apathetic states are often not diagnosed as depression and are usually attributed solely to some underlying senile or arteriosclerotic changes. This error in diagnosis may arise not only from lack of recognition of the state of depression itself, but also from the fact that some underlying organic changes are usually present and may contribute to the development of the apathetic features.

A similar error in diagnosis may arise when an elderly depressed patient shows mental confusion. When a patient has some underlying organic brain disease or a reduced cerebral reserve, the development of a state of depression may accentuate the organic manifestations and lead to symptoms such as mental confusion. When this occurs one may incorrectly attribute the patient's mental state entirely to organic causes and ignore the psychogenic precipitating factors and the state of depression itself. As a consequence, a basic diagnosis of organic brain disease may be made and lead to a degree of therapeutic nihilism. On the other hand, if one does not ignore the depression and is able to take steps to counteract it, the symptoms of mental confusion may diminish or disappear.

In *Growing Old,* by Cumming and Henry, the phenomenon of "disengagement" on the part of the aged is well documented (2). Disenagagement is defined as a "decreased interaction between the aging person and others." These authors also maintain that when disengagement is successful an elderly individual usually lives a reasonably happy life. For example, in referring to the very old, they state: "Given an adequate income, the very old enjoy their disengaged existence. They have reduced their ties to life, have shed their cares and responsibilities, and turn to concern with themselves. They lead static, tranquil, somewhat self-centered lives which suit them very well and appear to provide smooth passage from a long life through an inevitable death." Is it true that such individuals are usually as happy as they appear? I do not believe so, and I would like to suggest that the self-centeredness to which these authors refer is frequently a manifestation of narcissistic regression occurring in an apathetic type of depression. Furthermore, I believe that such depressions are often reversible. Although it is clear that older patients do become disengaged, it is reasonable to raise the question in any particular case as to how much of the disengagement is a product of the normal process of giving up certain activities because of diminished physical and mental capacity and how much of the disengagement is a product of depression itself. Since young people tend to become disengaged when they become depressed, is it not to be expected that the aged will show similar effects of depression?

In considering the factors which may precipitate depression, much of the psychiatric literature of today focusses upon the stress concept of "loss." It is well established that loss of a love object or loss of anything in which narcissistic libido is invested, such as a talent or a part of the body, typically leads to a depressive reaction. Since the aging process usually involves progressive loss of love objects and of highly valued functions, such as sight and hearing, many of the problems of the aged can be thought of in terms of this single stress concept of "loss." However, it is my contention that too much is attributed to "loss" and too little to other types of psychological stress, which I choose to classify in terms of three additional concepts, namely "attack," "restraint," and "threats."

As I use it, the concept "loss" refers to a "deficiency" of those external supplies which are necessary at any particular time to satisfy the libido. A loss can vary in intensity from a minor loss, such as a brief separation from a love object, to a major loss, such as the death of a love object. The permanent loss of an object is of great significance to the aged and it is not uncommon for an older person to begin to slip both mentally and physically after the death of a spouse.

The concept "attack" refers to any external force which produces discomfort, pain or injury. On a physical level, an attack can vary in intensity from a mild pain to extreme physical violence. On a psychological level, an attack can vary in intensity from a mild criticism to severe hostility. Older people are subjected not only to numerous forms of physical attack derived from physical illness, but also to numerous forms of subtle psychological attack, much of which is derived from the common prejudices toward the aged, a topic to which I intend to return shortly.

The concept "restraint" refers to any external force which restricts those actions which are necessary for the satisfaction of one's basic drives. Any major restriction of activity may contribute to the development of a depression since it can interfere with the gratification of basic drives, especially those of a sexual nature. For example, a patient with a coronary attack may become depressed not only because of the attack itself, but also because of being restricted to his bed for a prolonged period of time. When such a patient is given greater freedom to move about, his depression may lift considerably. In other words, freedom from restraint implies the opportunity to find satisfactory outlets for one's drives, and therefore implies freedom to be active when one has a need to be active.

The concept "threat" refers to any event which warns of possible future "loss," "attack," or "restraint." It is apparent that the threatening significance of any particular event is determined not only by the external reality but also by the individual interpretation of that reality. Some of the major threatening events in the aged are those which warn of desertion, disability, suffering, or death. As one gets older the realistic threat of death increases progressively. However, clinical observation indicates that the degree to which an individual fears death is based not only upon the degree to which a realistic threat of death exists but also upon the degree to which a state of depression exists, whatever the source of the depression may be. One finds that when patients who are young and physically healthy become depressed, they, too, may develop strong fears of death even though no realistic threat of death is present.

The concepts "loss," "attack," "restraint" and "threat" are clinically useful in classifying external factors which contribute to the development of depressive reactions. I would like to illustrate the use of these concepts by considering some cultural factors which play a part in the development of depression in the aged. There are many cultural forces which subject the elderly to excessive loss, attack, restraint and threats, and which lead to disturbances in libido equilibrium with consequent depressive reactions. Take, for example, the attitude that elderly people do not need any sexual gratification. This cultural attitude can lead to a major restriction of sexual activity since it contains a threat of criticism or ridicule if sexual restraint is not exerted. The net result is that the elderly members of our society are less free to find the types of sexual outlet which are available to younger members of our society.

There are many other forms of cultural restriction of the aged. Even psychotherapy is restricted by cultural attitudes. Individuals may be considered "too old" to undergo psychotherapy, especially with a "young doctor."

The presence of psychological "attack" in the form of rejection is ever present for the aged population. No matter how much effort younger people make to conceal their feelings, they cannot help but transmit in some way their attitudes that old people are weak and inferior. The very fact that our society is geared so much to the young and middle-aged population implies a prejudice against the aged. In our culture, we value highly those who are able to "do things" and since the aged are limited in their ability to perform they are destined to fall low on our value scale. Furthermore the lack of earning capacity of the aged may lead younger individuals to consider them an economic burden. The aged are apt to perceive unconsciously that the younger members of society not only expect them to die soon, but either consciously or unconsciously wish them to die. In Cummings and Henry's (2) book this attitude is illustrated by the following footnote: " A newspaper reporter tells us that, as a cub writing obituaries, he could guess the age of the deceased from the telephone conversations. When young people die, even when there has been some warning, there is devastation; old people leave a composed sadness. It was not, he felt, because they were less loved, but because there is 'a time for living and a time for dying.' " Would it not be more correct to state that, in many instances, when old people die the grief of those who remain is diminished in part because their libidinal attachments have already been severed to some degree? Is it not also true that long before an old person dies he intuitively feels the withdrawal of libido on the part of others and that, furthermore, he intuitively perceives that others are not only waiting for his death but also wishing for it?

Erikson (3) has used the term "crisis" to refer to any state of development in which the individual undergoes "a decisive encounter with his environment." Difficulty in achieving successful adaptation at a time of crisis leads to emotional disturbances which often take the form of depressive reactions. Since old age usually requires major new adjustments, one can also think of this period as one of crisis. Retirement would be an example of the type of event which may require major new adjustments. I recently saw a 65 year old man who retired to Florida under the pressure of his wife's repeated urging. As soon as he had made the move he became depressed and wanted to return to Boston. He made several trips back to see his former business associates, and on these trips he felt much better. It took many months before he was able to develop new relationships in Florida which could replace those he had lost. In this instance, the patient had not been aware of the strength of his attachments to his business associates and was therefore not prepared for the intensity of his reaction to separation from them.

It is common for an individual to be oblivious to the strength of his attachments and therefore to be unconscious of the cause of his depressive reaction when a loss is experienced. For example, a 50 year old secretary who had worked for the same boss for 20 years became depressed when this man died. However, she did not attribute her depression to his death but to the fact that she had to change her job and to learn new ways of doing things. She was not conscious of the intensity of her attachment to her boss and, therefore, did not realize that she was having a severe and prolonged grief reaction.

The aged members of our population experience many losses due to death and separation without being aware of the significance of these losses to their libido equilibrium. Such losses often occur, for example, when a redevelopment program is instituted and members of a community have to disperse.

Many relationships in a community may be considered minor when in actuality they are of considerable importance. For example, relationships with the druggist, the mailman, the bus driver, the owner of the corner store or the delivery man may be more important than one realizes. In many instances what appears to be a cursory relationship can be of major sustaining value for a particular individual. One may raise the question as to why people are so oblivious to the strength of these attachments. One might answer that, in general, individuals are strongly motivated to repress or suppress their awareness of those attachments which are not culturally accepted as major relationships. In other words, there are many sexual taboos above and beyond that of incest. However, the libido does not respect these taboos, even though the ego may show its respect by eradicating from the field of consciousness the nature of the libidinal attachment. In order to understand problems of depression one must recognize the hiding places of the libido. This includes recognizing the objects in which the libido is unconsciously invested. I recently had the opportunity of observing a 75 year old woman who, following the death of her husband, had to give up her home and move into a small apartment. I expected her to be depressed but was pleasantly surprised to find that she was in as good a mental state as she had ever been. When I sought the explanation for this paradox, I found it in the fact that she had developed a close relationship with a young woman who had several children. She had acquired a daughter and grandchildren through her move and had become well integrated into this new family life. It is worth noting that the old woman had no children of her own and had considered her lack of success in having a family as a major disappointment.

In this chapter I have paid little attention to internal factors in the development of depression. Since they are obviously of major significance, I will comment about them briefly. The most significant internal factors which protect against the development of depression are those which help to maintain the individual's self-esteem. Of considerable importance in this regard are the individual's attitudes toward his level of performance, not only in the present but also in the past and in the future. For many older people their success in the past plays a major role in maintaining self-esteem. For others, performance in the present or anticipated performance in the future plays such a role. Since the activities of one's love objects can become built into one's concept of self, the successes of others, such as off-spring and grandchildren, may also be of major significance.

To summarize: in evaluating problems of depression, I believe that it is useful to focus one's attention not only upon internal factors but also upon external factors, which I have classified into four main categories: 1) loss, 2) attack, 3) restraint, and 4) threat of loss, attack or restraint.

Factors which fall into these four categories occur in various combinations and are present to some degree at all ages. However, these factors tend to occur more commonly in old age. Since their impact is often unconscious, they frequently remain unrecognized not only by the patient but also by others, including those who are committed to his care and treatment.

References

1. Batchelor, I. R. C. Suicide in Old Age. In E. S. Schneidman and N. D. Farberow, *Clues to Suicide*. New York: McGraw-Hill, 1957.
2. Cumming, E., and Henry, W. E. *Growing Old*. New York: Basic Books, 1961.
3. Erikson, E. H. Identity and the life cycle. In *Psychological Issues*. New York: International Universities Press, 1959.

13

The nurse and the elderly patient

Sally O'Neill

The nurse-patient relationship is important in every hospital, but becomes even more vital in a specialized institution. Nursing in an institution dedicated to treatment and research in geriatrics requires special skills in interpersonal relations. Here, the nurse's role as mediator and interpreter between the physician and members of other disciplines and the patient is intensified. To manage the patient with understanding becomes essential.

Unless the nurse can communicate effectively with the patient, he may develop undue anxiety, antagonism and resistance to treatment and research methods that often bewilder and frighten him. It is imperative that the nurse not only be aware of the scientific process, but that she also be alert to the patient's emotional needs and skillful in coping with them. Problems have a way of increasing tremendously when a fearful elderly patient is in the care of a nurse or attendant who is not sensitive to emotional needs. The following incident is typical, although not all such incidents have a favorable outcome.

An attending nurse made an appointment with the writer to register a complaint. She reported, with great resentment, that a certain patient had been asking for the bedpan time and time again during the night and then did not use it. These repeated requests, sometimes 12 a night, tired and annoyed the attendant. Instead of receiving sympathy, the attendant was asked: "Why might the patient have engaged in this demanding behavior? Could there be some underlying reason that would make sense out of this peculiar behavior?"

At first, the attendant drew a blank. The writer asked if anything had happened that might have caused the patient to become fearful. Then the attendant remembered—less than two weeks previously, a patient had died on that unit, and died during the night. After a few minutes of further discussion, a working hypothesis was developed: perhaps the patient was afraid of dying in her sleep and had been seeking reassurance that somebody was available that she could depend upon. If this were the case, then the attendant might try bringing a chair up close to the patient's bed and taking some time to reassuring her, letting the patient know that she was not alone and could call for attention whenever she felt she needed it. This little experiment was carried out, and quite successfully. The patient's fears subsided, and she soon was peacefully asleep. Subsequently, the attendant and the patient were able to speak frankly about fears of being abandoned or dying during the night. These conversations lowered the patient's anxiety level and gave the attendant a better insight into the feelings that sometimes underlie a patient's "troublesome" behavior.

Fears of death and abandonment in elderly patients are more common than one might think, particularly during the night. These fears are more often felt than expressed. The patient is more likely to engage in peculiar or even bizarre behavior at night, and this, in turn, can serve to increase his discomfort by alienating the nurse who sees only the "troublesome" behavior and not the underlying fear.

At the present time, there is much greater emphasis on human relations skills in the nursing-school curriculum than was formerly found. But what of the graduate nurse who completed her formal education before the relevance of these skills was so extensively recognized? How can she be helped to acquire concepts and techniques of interpersonal relations in an on-the-job situation? Can this be accomplished through in-service training?

In an attempt to answer these questions, a series of seminars was scheduled for all head nurses at Cushing Hospital; a clinical psychologist acted as group leader. The meetings were designed to help the nurse use her psychological knowledge more effectively in providing adequate care of the whole person. Meetings were scheduled for one hour each week for a period of 16 weeks.

An introductory meeting was devoted to a general consideration of the interests and goals of the group. From this discussion evolved the framework for procedure and content of the course. The needs of the group crystallized in three definite categories:

1. A review of psychological theories of human behavior, for the purpose of formulating a background of knowledge and terminology with the group.

2. A discussion of specific patients who presented problems in management. This would afford an excellent opportunity for the nurses to apply their knowledge.

3. An investigation of nurse-patient relationships to provide more comprehensive insights into patients' behavior and, perhaps, to make a contribution to general knowledge in this area.

The first regular session was devoted to a basic problem in any interpersonal relationship: mental health. A working definition of mental health was developed, focussing on the way a person feels about himself, the way he feels about others, and the way in which he meets the problems of living.

A scale was developed by which each person might develop his own and others' accomplishments in each of these areas. This scale embodied a hierarchy of mental health skills, starting with knowing, accepting, and feeling comfortable with one's self, progressing through acceptance of differences in others, and culminating in the ability to take concrete and constructive action about situations that demand it.

The nurses rated themselves on the scale. They were surprisingly frank and often could identify basic blocks in their own personality functioning. They agreed that "mental health is more often caught than taught." This agreement led them to talk about their responsibility, as professional people and leaders, for setting the emotional climate on the ward.

The second session was designed to lead—from the insights gained in the review of mental health—to an understanding of the patient's behavior through an interpretation of the expectations of a patient coming to a hospital for the first time. Discussion developed along three interrelated lines: 1) what the patient presenting himself for treatment and hospitalization expects; 2) what the nurse caring for him expects; and 3) what frustrations may arise when the expectations are not complementary or compatible, and how they may be dissolved.

Again, the group's consideration was fruitful in promoting insight and interest. Histories of several patients known to the group were presented in order to highlight background experiences which might explain specific behavior on the ward. The group agreed that responsibility for adjusting to the situation and correcting erroneous expectations lay chiefly with the nurse.

This topic led to the third topic, human behavior. It was pointed out that all human behavior is influenced by the goals that are being sought, and that the nurse's task is to discover the particular goal or reward which is being sought by the patient whose actions create a problem. Specific cases were then discussed and the possible reasons for the patient's and nurse's behavior were analyzed.

This discussion brought into focus basic human needs which, in turn, became the subject for the next sessions. The nurses analyzed several common nursing situations by pointing out how needs within themselves had interacted with needs within the patients to produce management problems. Again, the consensus was that it was the responsibility of the nurse to accept leadership, and to prepare herself in the skills of effective interpersonal relations. The two final sessions analyzed the psychological background of nurse-patient relationships, emphasizing problems associated with carrying out the various phases of the nurse's role.

This in-service training program was felt to be of value by the participating head nurses. It had alerted them to the emotional needs of their patients and helped them in guiding new personnel toward sensitive patient care. It is obvious that in-service training should be extended to all personnel whose services affect the well-being of the patients. Because institutional life involves communication between patients and all staff members, it is necessary that everyone maintain a consistently therapeutic approach. A disgruntled kitchen worker, for example, can be a detriment to the best-planned program. It is often observed that patients tend to gravitate toward those staff members from whom they feel they get gratification from either a satisfying *or* irritating relationship. Interpersonal gratification should be available to the patient from many sources, including, but not limited to, the nursing service.

When the nurse has formed a good interpersonal relationship with her elderly patient she can use this relationship to promote his well-being in many ways. Nutrition is a significant example. It is very difficult to alter basic eating habits by appeals to reason alone. The nurse should recognize this in dealing with the aged either in the home, the clinic or the hospital. If she makes use of her understanding of the patient's need for companionship and approval and shows genuine interest in him, she may achieve success in persuading him to eat adequate meals since her thoughtfulness may develop confidence in her suggestions. The nurse must be a good listener, since food idosyncrasies become of less importance in the mind of the patient when he has found a sympathetic audience.

Before the nurse makes suggestions about diet, she should study the patient's eating habits. She must remember, it is not important in what form or at what hour the patient gets certain foods, but it *is* important that at some time during each day he receive all the basic nutriments. Some people may follow a monotonous diet day after day, yet analysis of the food intake may prove to be near to meeting their nutritional needs.

Often, in an effort to "stay young," the aging person will become a victim of food cultists who offer miracles through diet. He may spend his money on mineral water and "tissue juices," while not being able to purchase essential items of food. Other old persons decide upon a list of foods that cause gas, create an acid condition, produce constipation, give them headaches and in many other ways do not agree with them. The remedy probably lies in economic and social rehabilitation in which the nurse can play a useful role.

Every effort must be made to stimulate the appetite of the older person suffering from malnutrition. Appropriate exercise in the fresh air often improves appetite. Well-seasoned broths and various seasoned appetizers such as strong cheeses may also stimulate appetite. Unless specifically contraindicated, tea and coffee, as well as moderate amounts of wine, beer, and other alcoholic beverages should be permitted if they are desired, since they, too, often stimulate appetite.

The nurse can be instrumental in seeing that the aging person enjoys his meals in a quiet and pleasant atmosphere. In the home, the elderly person should eat with the rest of the family. Special provision may be necessary for his needs, but this should be as inconspicuous as possible. The elderly person should never be made to feel helpless by having attention drawn to his need for ground or chopped meat, the use of an extra napkin, or to his shaky hand.

In any illness, perhaps the greatest single stimulant to the patient's appetite is the serving of attractive meals with special consideration for individual taste and preference. The patient will likely relish a dish that caters to personal food customs, or a special sauce seasoned at his own direction. Aged people are inordinately grateful for any small favor done them. An old lady will cherish a single flower on her tray or a special dainty salad. A pleasant, unhurried environment and cheerful conversation are most important in insuring a good appetite during illness. The thoughtful nurse will not tell the patient that he should eat certain foods "because they are good for you." The patient may already be struggling to preserve his identity as an individual, and thus will resent, consciously or unconsciously, the implication that he no longer knows what is good for him. Best results will follow if he has small servings of attractive food that he likes with no mention of the specific constituents of his meal.

It is clear that an alert, well-trained nurse can promote the health of the elderly patient through her relationship with him, using the relationship both directly (e.g., to calm his fears) and indirectly (e.g., to gain acceptance for a program of good nutrition).

Staff members frequently differ among themselves as to the type of patient that should be admitted to or excluded from a geriatric hospital. It is the composition of the professional staff and the physical facilities available that largely determine what comes to be known as the "justified admission" policy of the hospital. Generally speaking, when a hospital has a staff that is well trained in the care of patients with a particular type of disease, it will readily admit patients requiring treatment for such disease.

One of the most recent admissions to Cushing Hospital was an 86 year old woman who 1) is paraplegic, 2) has an indwelling catheter, 3) has extensive decubitus ulcers, and 4) has a fractured hip. A few years ago her admission would have dismayed the staff. Now there is a sense of willingness and competence to cope with such cases. The patient who would have been regarded as unsuitable for admission or, at best, a tremendous burden for attending personnel, now is welcomed as an appropriate challenge to the technical and interpersonal skills of the nursing staff.

Effects of wine on the interpersonal behavior of geriatric patients: An exploratory study

14

Robert Kastenbaum and
Philip E. Slater

There is a popular notion that institutionalized aged people enjoy each other's company, enjoy swapping nostalgic stories and philosophizing upon the state of the world. Unfortunately, the more typical situation is that of social impoverishment. The virtual absence of interpersonal behavior among peers has been observed repeatedly in geriatric wards and other settings in which aged people are institutionalized. The dearth of peer interaction is sometimes tantamount to no human interaction at all, as such forgotten places often lack a staff that is adequate in size, training and relevant motivation, hence, in useful accessibility to the elderly residents they serve.

It will be the operating assumption here that the atrophy of social interaction among many institutionalized aged persons is neither a desirable nor a necessary phenomenon. Some theoretical implications of this problem will be considered in the discussion at the end of this chapter. At this point, however, it may be sufficient to note that there is a widespread need for new knowledge and new methods that might help transform the dismal asocial atmosphere in geriatric units around the nation.

Approach

Previous clinical and research experience at Cushing Hospital, in particular a project in psychopharmacology, led to new ideas concerning possible additions to the therapeutic program. One of these ideas pointed in the direction of a "different kind" of psychotropic agent. It had been found that response to widely-used "tranquilizers" and "stimulants" was quite complex in this geriatric population, including a number of paradoxical reactions. There was reason to believe that

This study was supported in part by a grant from the Wine Advisory Board, State of California.

Significant contributors to this study were made by William J. Dowling, M.D., Nancy Durkee, Deborah Green, Brian Langdon, and Marion Purington. The study was under the general supervision of J. Sanbourne Bockoven, M.D.

attitudinal factors frequently modified, negated or counteracted the putative influence of the medication (2,3).

While currently available psychotropic drugs seemed to deserve further investigation, it also appeared advisable to consider what might be the properties of a more effective agent with this type of population. The following characteristics seemed to be indicated: 1) the agent should possess psychotropic properties of a socially-facilitating nature; 2) it should be perceived by the patient as something that he himself values and desires to receive; and 3) it should function as an appropriate symbolic representation of the relationship one would hope the geriatric patient and his environment could establish with each other.

The second and third points are based upon the consideration that "drug effects" take place in a highly complex inter- and intra-personal milieu. In general, "the pill" is not in itself a valued object, although sometimes it is gratefully received as "a something" that the world cares to provide. Frequently "the pill" is rejected outright (openly or surreptitiously) by patients jealous of their independence, or it is accepted in a grudging manner. The familiar phrase, "I guess I have to take my medicine," indicates the meaning some patients attach to "the pill"—feeling, in effect, that "I am old, not much good, a burden to others—I will just have to accept my punishment for being a burden, take my medicine."

A more satisfactory agent would be one that conveys a heartening psychosocial message to the patient in addition to its specific biochemical effects. An appropriate message would be: "You are a responsible adult, still capable of enjoying life on an adult level and moving in a mature sphere of interaction." Moreover, it would be a further advantage if the agent possessed connotative meanings suggesting vigor, heartiness and so forth.

These considerations eventuated in the selection of red port wine. As Lucia has documented in his book, *The History of Wine as Therapy* (4), wine might well be considered "the oldest of medicines." Lucia declares that "There is already clear evidence that specific wines are useful as therapeutic aids in uncomplicated cases of diabetes, in simple anemias, in such digestive disturbances as the mal-absorption syndrome, in the initial treatment of alcoholic cirrhosis, in minimizing acidosis in certain kidney conditions, in the treatment of anorexia, in relieving the infirmities and suffering which accompany old age, and in combating many of the diseases in which anxiety and tension are among the underlying factors . . " (4, p. 208).

Wine has had an equally ancient and distinguished career as a component of religious ceremonies and social occasions. Although chiefly concerned with the physiological effects of wine, Lucia notes that this beverage is of value to the physician ". . . not only as a nutrient and a medicine, but also for its psychopharmacodynamic effects." (4, p. 13). It is presumed here that these psychopharmacodynamic effects are closely linked to the rich connotative meanings that have accrued to wine by virtue of its religious and social history.

It was hypothesized that wine might contribute to the well-being of the geriatric patient by its double action—through both physiological and psychological routes. The connotations of wine as an accompaniment of social conviviality and, more remotely, as "the blood of the grape" that imparts vigor and new life, were recommendations for its use. Red wine appeared to be a particularly good symbol through which "society" (the hospital staff) could communicate its sanguine wishes to the patient. Red port wine was the final choice, taking into account its likelihood of being reasonably familiar to most of the participating patients, its reputed value as an appetite stimulant and the fact that it could be served appropriately without refrigeration.

The effort, then, was to evaluate red port wine as an agent that might possibly promote the social interaction of geriatric patients. Enhanced social interaction would be expected to have a favorable influence on self-esteem, mood, independence and other aspects of the patient's general psychological functioning. The value of wine as an appetite stimulant could also be studied as a side issue.

In formulating the research design, a variety of possibilities were considered. The final decision was to conduct the study in a "real-life" setting instead of an isolated experimental situation. It was felt that more would be learned by permitting the study to be permeated by the flow of daily life, that patients would more willingly participate, and that the experimental program, if leading to positive results, could more easily be incorporated into the hospital program as a permanent feature. Additionally, it was important to determine what reception a wine program would receive in the general hospital milieu. (Wine and brandy had been prescribed for individual patients from time to time, but the practice was infrequent.)

In consultation with the director of professional services, it was decided to present the study to the patients chiefly in its aspect of an attempt to stimulate appetite.* This purpose was worthy in itself, would provide a positive medical reason for inclusion, and would not direct attention self-consciously to the primary purpose.

Method

Subjects

Twenty male patients were selected as participants in the experimental program. These men ranged in age from 68 to 86 years, with a median age of 76 and a mean age of 76.6. The sample was drawn

---

* Effects of wine upon appetite will be reported elsewhere.

from the patient population of "Ward I," following medical evaluation performed by the director of professional services. Another sample of 20 male patients was selected from "Ward II" to serve as a
control panel. The men in this set ranged in age from 68 to 91, with
a median age of 73 and a mean age of 75.4.

Wards I and II both enjoyed the reputation of being "good wards,"
i.e., the patients were among the most alert and independent in the
hospital. Nevertheless, social interaction was minimal on both wards.
Solitary "sitting around" and "walking around" were prevalent activities. That social interaction was so limited in quantity, variety and
quality was particularly conspicuous on these wards, as many of the
patients appeared capable of a higher level of functioning.

Basic design

The framework of this study included the following phases:
1. A period of gathering base-line information.
2. Division of the experimental subjects into two equal groups,
   Group A beginning with the wine treatment, Group B beginning with the control beverage, grape juice.
3. A cross-over period of equal length in which the beverages are
   reversed for Groups A and B.
4. A critical free-choice period.
5. An extended free-choice period.

Phase one was identical for the included patients on both wards.
Thereafter, periodic samplings of patient behavior were made on the
control ward through sociometric techniques, but with no other inter-
ventions introduced.

Procedures

1. *Baseline.* During the initial medical examination each participating patient was given information to the following effect (worded
for comprehension by the patient): "This study is designed to test two
appetite stimulants, each of which is contained in a different liquid
vehicle with a different taste. Every patient who participates in the
study will get one stimulant for 3 weeks and then switch to the other
for 3 weeks. Upon completion of the 6-week trial, each patient participating in the study can elect to continue on whichever stimulant
he prefers for as long as he wishes. Each patient will be interviewed
once before and once after the 6-week stimulant period, and there will
be regular checks on appetite and sleep, but the results of the study
will *not* influence what stimulant the patient receives after the study.
This will be left entirely to the personal preference of the patient."

The next procedure consisted of psychological interviews with each
experimental patient. These interviews were intended to elicit additional factual information, provide the basis for judgments concerning

the mental and emotional status of the patients and encourage attendance at the experimental sessions.

Interviewers who were not otherwise associated with the study then initiated the first in a series of regular sociometric interviews with personnel on both wards. The first interview included the gathering of background information concerning the nurse or attendant serving as rater, and the oral administration of an open-ended sociometric questionnaire. This sociometric form did not present the names of any patient, whether or not included in the study; rather, it was the respondent's task to determine which patients on the ward could be classified appropriately in terms of the various items. Another and briefer form was presented in a separate interview; this form requested a three-alternative, forced-choice rating of the peer status of each patient on the ward who had been included in the study.

An observer was assigned to check food consumption (and mealtime interaction) of the experimental patients at lunch and dinner in the hospital cafeteria. Observers also made spot checks of activity on both wards, with particular attention to the mid-afternoon whereabouts and activities of the patients who had been selected as subjects.

The base-line phase was conducted over a 4-week period.

2. *First run.* The two solaria on opposite ends of the ward were set aside for purposes of the experiment at 3 P.M. every weekday. Those patients who would constitute the membership of Group A were asked to report to the northside room, members of Group B to the southside. A participant observer was assigned to each group. These observers had as their major responsibilities: administering the beverage to the participating patients; preparing quantitative and qualitative reports of each session; serving as host and intermediary between the patients and the hospital staff; and being a "good companion" without stepping into the role of a group psychotherapist or any similar role. The assignments of participant observers to their respective groups was permanent for the period of time covered by this report, and for several subsequent weeks.

Group A received port wine for the first 3-week period while Group B received grape juice. Both beverages were served in small, attractive glasses (distinct from the plastic "glasses" used for other administrations in the hospital), and trays of simple crackers were provided. Each patient was offered a one-and-a-half ($1\frac{1}{2}$) ounce serving of his beverage, with one refill available upon request. The patients were free to do whatever they wished from the moment they accepted the glass of wine or juice in each session (e.g., could drink it or not, stay in the solarium, return to their beds, leave the ward, etc.).

The sociometric interviewing continued during the first run, as did daily appetite checks.

3. *Second run (cross-over).* Group B now received wine for the next 3 weeks, while Group A received grape juice. Other procedures continued as during the initial run.

4. *Critical free-choice period.* At the completion of phase three, each group had met 30 times, half of these sessions involving wine, half grape juice. The next session was structured as a free-choice period—all participating patients had their choice of either, both, or none of the beverages. After this session the follow-up series of clinical interviews was conducted.

5. *Extended free-choice period.* After the single session which constituted phase four, patients were informed that any further continuation of the meetings was up to them. Attendance would be in no way "required" (during the previous phases patients could decline or forget to attend, of course, but an effort was made to hold them to their "contract" of participating in the study). From this point forward, all participating patients had the completely free option to attend or not, and to select either, both or none of the beverages on any given day. The beverages and the participant observers were thus available to the patients, but would be provided only in so far as the patients "prescribed" this treatment to themselves. Sociometric interviewing continued through this phase. Appetite checks were continued on a daily basis for 2 weeks, then reduced to 2 cafeteria observations per week.

Results

General considerations

This first attempt to study systematically the interpersonal effects of wine on geriatric patients seemed to be well accepted by the various staff members upon whose co-operation the investigation was dependent, e.g., nurses, physicians, pharmacist, social workers, occupational therapists, dieticians. From some of these colleagues direct services were required; from all of them we needed an attitude of acceptance and willingness to schedule their own services so as to avoid interference with the wine study. Apart from the specific results of the study *per se,* then, we learned that the hospital staff in general welcomed the experimental introduction of wine as a potentially useful addition to the therapeutic program.

The beverage-administration sessions were held as scheduled, with no exceptions, from the first meeting to the date of preparing this report.

Patient preference: wine vs. grape juice

Quantitative findings and qualitative impressions are in complete accord with respect to which beverage the patients preferred.

Critical free-choice period. Fifteen patients selected wine, 3 selected grape juice, and 2 were not having either. The frequency of preference for wine over grape juice is significant beyond the .05 level of confidence, employing the chi square test.

Extended free-choice period. Relative popularity of the two beverages over the subsequent free-choice period can easily be gauged by comparing the number of servings consumed. Data have been tabulated for the first 6 weeks of the free-choice period. As seen in Table 1, there is a continuing preference for wine that is statistically significant well beyond the .001 level of confidence. Both experimental groups manifested this preference at the same level.

Verbal expressions of preference for the port wine were frequent.

Table 1. Beverage consumption during six-week extended free-choice period (in number of servings)

Week	Group A		Group B		Total	
	Wine	Juice	Wine	Juice	Wine	Juice
1	39	18	57	16	96	34
2	43	8	54	10	97	18
3	59	10	58	10	117	20
4	55	7	55	10	110	17
5	58	5	64	10	122	15
6	61	15	67	10	128	25
Total	315	63	355	66	670	129

Duration of sessions: wine vs. grape juice

Assessment of social interaction is a complex task which is further complicated by the necessity to differentiate effects that might be specific to one particular variable (e.g., wine or grape juice). The duration of group sessions can be used as a crude index of how much appeal the patients found in the opportunity to be with each other in a social setting. Comparison of duration for wine and juice sessions would provide a rough indication of possible differences between these beverages as socializing influences for geriatric patients.

A comparison was made between the duration of wine and juice sessions by means of the Wilcoxon matched-pairs signed-ranks test. If accepted practice were followed and one "strange-looking" juice-section were discarded for this analysis. then the result would be $z = 2.52$, significant at the .02 level of confidence. In taking a more conservative approach and retaining the "sore thumb" session, one obtains a z value of 1.91, significant between the .06 and .05 levels of confidence.

The observed difference was in the direction of more time spent (by both A and B groups) when the wine condition prevailed in comparison with the juice condition.

Observed interaction

During the time span included in this report the interpersonal behavior of the participating patients was directly observed in 60 sessions for each group, in regular cafeteria checks, and in encounters that developed preceding and following the group sessions. This paper will consider chiefly those observations made during the experimental sessions *per se*.

General effects. There appeared to be an overall increase in the amount of interpersonal behavior exhibited by the experimental subjects as a function of their participation in the study. This statement is independent of analyses which attempt to relate the observed change to the type of beverage served.

Perhaps the simplest way to indicate the increase in social interaction is to note that the bare beverage-administration situation became elaborated into club-like meeting-times, and that these meetings have persisted on a completely voluntary basis (6 weeks of extended free-choice period covered in this report, and an additional 10 weeks at the time of this writing). It will be recalled that patients never were required to remain in the room after receiving their first drink of the session, and that the meetings would have been terminated by positive decision or general apathy at any time following the critical free-choice session (31st meeting).

Relative to the very low level of social interaction previously observed on this ward—during the base-line period and earlier—this interest in forming and maintaining a social group represented a notable change. No precedent for this kind of behavior can be recalled by hospital personnel.

The daily notes compiled by the participant observers document the growing importance of the experimental situation for the patients. The early sessions were marked by aloofness toward peers and occasional efforts to form a private, "special" relationship with the participant observer (PO). Gradually, patients began talking about each other through the PO and, still later, direct discussions were carried out from patient to patient. As a point of interest regarding small group dynamics, it should be noted that many patients sought an occasion to "solo"—to engage thoroughly the ear of the PO and, peripherally, that of the group—and following that performance became more involved in the proceedings of the entire group. The follow-up clinical interviews also indicated that many patients had found the group experience quite rewarding.

Differential effects. The general effects of the experimental program were plainly visible. To evaluate possible differential effects of wine and grape juice, however, required a more detailed analysis. Accordingly, an assessment of Group Involvement was undertaken. Group Involvement is a molar construct that includes several more specific indices as its components: regularity of attendance at the experimental sessions (including tardiness, "playing hard to get," etc.); verbal participation (quantity and quality); nonverbal participation (e.g., volunteering to rearrange the chairs); expressive behavior (e.g., joining in a group expression of merriment or anger); and forming new relationships with peers.

Data for this analysis were drawn from the detailed daily accounts of experimental sessions recorded by the POs and from weekly summaries and biographies of each patient's behavior over the course of the study, which were also prepared by the POs. Two raters (not the POs) evaluated the observed behavior of each experimental patient during initial and cross-over phases, in accordance with the criteria for Group Involvement outlined above. Inter-judge reliability was .936 (Pearson product-moment correlation). Discrepancies between the raters were resolved jointly.

Difference scores on Group Involvement, wine as compared with juice sessions, revealed that 8 patients had shown no change, one had become more involved while on grape juice, and 11 had shown more involvement while the wine condition was in effect. The direction and extent of change was significant at the .01 level of confidence, employing the Wilcoxon matched-pairs signed-ranks test (*see* Table 2).

Table 2. Summary of statistical tests

Problem	Test	Probability level	Direction
Choice of beverage (critical free-choice)	x^2	.05	Wine preferred
Consumption of beverage (extended free-choice)	x^2	.001	Wine preferred
Duration of sessions	Wilcoxon	.06	Wine sessions more lengthy
Group Involvement	Wilcoxon	.01	More involvement during wine sessions

Reported interaction (sociometric)

Raters. An attempt was made to obtain a series of sociometric ratings from all the personnel on both the experimental and control wards. The number of personnel on these wards varied during the course of the study (summer vacations take their toll, along with illness, and necessary reassignments). The number of raters available for each set of interviews also varied, ranging from a low of 2 raters per ward to a high of 5 raters. It must be noted that the rating task was a disagreeable one for a number of the ward personnel—in particular, they expressed a great reluctance to report anything that might be interpreted as a negative statement (e.g., that one patient is less popular than another).

Variables. Data from the forced-choice form were analyzed in terms of a Social Interaction variable, defined at its extremes by "popular" and "isolated." The open-ended form yielded data on several other dimensions. The total number of mentions for each rating period served as a general measure of the patient's "visibility" in the eyes of the staff. The algebraic summation of favorable and unfavorable mentions was treated as a separate variable, providing a "good patient" score. Other items provided information concerning the independent-dependent dimension, the score being an algebraic summation in this case as well. Still other items constituted a demanding-not-demanding scale. Finally, perceptions of improvement or deterioration in the patient's general condition were expressed in an "up-down" score. These various scales did not overlap with each other in respect to the items incorporated.

Findings. Both general and differential effects may be discussed together, as no significant differences—or even substantial trends—could be discerned. This negative conclusion applies to reported behavior on both wards and for all phases of the experiment (initial, cross-over, and free-choice).

Reported social interaction for the selected patients on both wards was quite low throughout the course of the study. This statement is based upon the obtained mean and median values in comparison with the range of possible values. Thus, for the control ward the grand mean of interaction for seven samplings was .75, with a "median median" of .67. For the comparable number of samplings, the experimental patients had a grand mean of .76, and a "median median" of .75. A mean of 1.0 would have located the obtained social interaction at the midpoint of the theoretical scale. Thus, this finding seems to support the general impression that interaction among geriatric patients is meager.

The raters frequently omitted those items which pertained most directly to the patients' sociometric status, preferring to report only upon the amount of nursing care required.

Discussion

Within the limits of the scope of the present study and of the analyses thus far performed, certain findings emerged with clarity:

1. Wine was preferred to the control beverage, grape juice, both at the time a critical free-choice selection was required, and over a more extensive free-choice period that followed.

2. The simple beverage-administration situation developed into well-attended group meetings with something of the character of a social club. These meetings persisted on a voluntary basis beyond the time limit set for participation in the study.

3. Sessions in which the wine condition prevailed tended to be more lengthy than sessions in which the juice condition prevailed.

4. Working from the detailed observational notes of participant observers in the experimental groups, it was determined that Group Involvement was significantly greater under wine than under juice conditions.

5. Sociometric reports of social interaction and other aspects of patient behavior made at regular intervals by ward personnel failed to reveal any substantial trends toward change, whether as a function of the general experimental program or any of its specific phases.

To these findings could be added a rich account of the comments, skirmishes, discoveries, exuberations, and slow proliferation of painful efforts toward social engagement that characterized the progress of the experimental sessions. Material of this kind will be reported later in connection with other studies now in progress.

At present it appears that the promise of wine has been partially fulfilled. Daily servings of port wine were accepted by the patients, and stimulated a heightened level of involvement with each other during the group sessions. Direct observations by project staff members also indicated that several friendships formed during the course of the study were not limited to behavior in the group meetings, but became core social relationships for the patients involved. It was also noted that the phenomenon of "group-within-a-group" had occurred, and that this development seemed to provide the included patients with a greater sense of security and belongingness—a differentiation of self from the generalized perception of "a mass of helpless, useless old codgers." Those patients excluded from the inner group (and those not originally participating in the study at all) seemed to become more socially sensitive, some trying to earn a "promotion" to full acceptance, others preferring to offer a "loyal opposition." The general effect seemed to be in the direction of heightening sensitivity to the possibilities of a social life within the institution, with individual patients reacting in various ways to these perceived possibilities.

It was noted by Silverman* that "With only 1½ or 3 ounces of port as the dosage, the blood alcohol levels would be far below those which are known to produce any physiological inefficiency." This comment suggests that social interaction can be stimulated by rather small quantities of wine, a point worth considering in view of the dangers inherent in over-medication of aged individuals.

The negative finding with respect to sociometric ratings introduces a note of ambiguity into the interpretation. It is not clear whether patients' behavior on the ward did remain unchanged throughout this period, or whether changes occurred but were not reported. Both alternatives are challenging.

If there was in fact no alteration of behavior on the ward, then it might be the case that the patients had come to use the group as an "alternative world," a masculine meeting-place which had its own rules and privileges, offering a welcome change from daily existence in a female-dominated, passivity-inducing institutional setting. To preserve this "secret society," one would insulate it from the rest of the environment—retain one's habitual defenses and noncommital behavior until he is safely within his inner circle, perhaps within the innermost circle. Such a possibility would make sense within the framework of developmental theory—the meeting-and-drinking place would be serving an exceedingly useful psychological function by permitting the patient to have two distinct reference points from which to interpret his experience (general ward life and the "club"). It is essential to possess at least two reference points in order to develop a genuine perspective, hence one should expect that patients participating in the drinking club should over a period of time maintain a higher level of intellectual functioning than those not so favorably advantaged.

There is some basis for speculation that behavior change did occur on the ward but was not reported.† The busy nurses and attendants might simply not have observed enough behavior to make sensitive judgments, or they might have blocked at reporting some aspects of what they did observe. Results from ward ratings made in a previous study were rather similar—not a great deal was reported, with some interesting omissions (3).

---

* Private communication.

† A spontaneous report came to the research staff from the physician who had been in charge of the ward before the study began and, after a change in assignment, returned to Ward I when the investigation was in an advanced stage. She declared that the ward was "a different place! You wouldn't believe it!" She cited fewer complaints and improved morale and contentment.

Still another possibility is that the heightened social interaction directly observed during the study may require a longer period of time to become apparent in ward behavior. Because the sociometric interviews are being continued, data will be available to test this prospect.

Should subsequent analyses of the present data, or further investigations indicate that ward personnel fail to respond to behavior change, one would then like to explore the possibility that there is a pervasive staff-attitude factor which plays a significant role in the maintenance of a socially drab atmosphere.

Whatever might be the complete story concerning the origin and perpetuation of social apathy among institutionalized aged persons, it is the viewpoint here that this situation should be regarded as pathological—not as a natural, benevolent form of "disengagement." The concept that the aging person *normally* tends to disengage himself from society is a fruitful idea (1). However, this viewpoint would be warped out of shape if it were applied to the typical asocial situation of the institutionalized aged. There is danger that such a mis-application will be made as people seek to rationalize away some grim facts. From our experience in this investigation we would agree with Levin who believes that aged people are frequently depressed when others believe them to be contentedly stoical, and that they respond most profoundly to a sincere effort on the part of the environment to understand them and offer them appropriate reinforcements—and demands (5).

Further studies of wine effects are in progress. It is hoped these studies will clarify areas of ambiguity remaining in the present investigation and extend our knowledge of wine effects to dimensions not included here. While the present study does not permit a comparison between the effects of wine and other psychotropic agents, the results seem to justify further clinical explorations.

Summary

Twenty aged male patients of Cushing Hospital participated in a controlled, cross-over investigation of the effects of wine upon interpersonal behavior. Two groups of equal size met 5 afternoons a week for 3 weeks, one group receiving grape juice, the other wine. This procedure was then reversed for another 3-week period. Next, a single free-choice session was held in which the patients were requested to select the beverage they preferred. Finally, a prolonged series of free-choice sessions was instituted on a completely voluntary basis, a series that continues to the date of this report. Basic observations are derived from detailed accounts of the group meetings by participant observers, clinical interviews, and sociometric ratings obtained regularly from ward personnel. A panel of 20 patients on a matched ward served as a control for the general effect of the experimental activity.

The major findings:

1. Wine was preferred to the control beverage both at the time a critical free-choice selection was required, and over the subsequent extended period of free-choice.

2. The simple beverage-administration situation developed into well-attended, long-lived group meetings, indicating that sessions involving either of the beverages contributed to heightened social interaction.

3. Sessions in which the wine condition prevailed tended to be more lengthy than sessions in which the juice condition prevailed.

4. Group Involvement, a measure of social interaction during the experimental sessions, was greater under wine than under juice conditions.

5. Sociometric reports failed to reveal any substantial trends toward change in on-the-ward behavior during the period of time covered in this report.

Theoretical interpretations were offered, centering on the idea that wine possesses a distinctive advantage as a therapeutic agent for the aged. The advantage of wine is seen in terms of its contrast to the mixed action thought to occur frequently in the administration of psychotropic drugs to the aged.

References

1. Cumming, E. Further thoughts on disengagement theory. In this volume.
2. Kastenbaum, R., and Slater, P. E. Drug effects on behavior and cognition in geriatric patients. Progress Report, USPHS grant MHO-4818, Cushing Hospital, Framingham, Mass., July, 1962.
3. Kastenbaum, R., Slater, P. E., Aisenberg, R., Rosenfelt, R. H., and Kempler, B. Behavioral, methodological, and ethical dimensions in geriatric psychopharmacology. Set of three papers presented at sixteenth annual scientific meeting, Gerontological Society, Boston, Mass., November 9, 1963.
4. Lucia, S. P. A History of Wine as Medicine. Philadelphia: Lippincott, 1963.
5. Levin, S. Depression in the aged: A study of the salient external factors. In this volume.

| Social services for the aged: A reconsideration | 15 |

Isabel Banay

The methods by which we have dealt with the so-called "problems of the aging" over the past 20 years are in response to attitudes that do not have the best interests of the individual older American at heart. The artificial division of the total life span into chronologically determined segments, each being accorded special treatment, often results in a *de facto* segregation that ignores the bio-philosophical concept of a continuous filament threading through the life cycle of sentient beings, and vitiates patterns of natural intergenerational family life.

The setting apart of older people also fails to utilize the advances that have recently been made in all fields of scientific endeavor and to weld these contributions into a holistic approach for the treatment of individual and social problems. Program planning in which certain age groups have more provisions that are peculiar to themselves than provisions that are common to all has the effect of sanctioning the policy of "separateness." This policy seems to run counter to the philosophy of interdependence and social responsibility inherent in our democratic system.

As stated in *The Older American,* published by the President's Council for the Aging (1963), "The problems of the Older American have come dangerously close to making him a second-class citizen." (3). Not least of the injustices he has suffered has been his separation from normal community and family life, and consequent traumatic break in the life sequence caused by his deportation to special facilities for the aged.

Trial and error
During and immediately following World War II, the "baby boom" was identified and its implications in the field of education fully recognized and explored. Simultaneously, there emerged the shadow of a problem affecting another special-needs group, the aged. The years between 1945 and 1965 may come to be regarded as a period of trial and error in the planning, care and treatment of elderly people. The

population boom among the 70 to 100 year olds burst upon most industrialized, "advanced" societies, and found them largely unprepared
to meet the presence in their population of such large numbers of
people who had reached the last quarter of the life span.

Between 1950 and 1960, investigations by legislative committees,
reports, statistics and data of many kinds rolled off the presses of
municipal, state, federal and private organizations. In essence, they
all reported the fact that there were *millions* of people of advanced
years in our population, a large number of whom required special
facilities and care of one kind or another—care that was not available
in the right place at a price they could afford.

While it is true that sporadic attempts have been made to meet the
urgent demands for space in hospitals, nursing homes, rest homes,
private homes and other congregate living facilities, such efforts have
remained expedients. They could never really catch up with the problems that changed as fast as one could improvise means of meeting
them. In other words, the United States and many other nations have
failed to provide adequate plans for elderly people whose increasing
numbers derive from medical advances of the past few decades.

Planning to catch up with the lag and to implement new programs
has proceeded at varying rates and with varying success all over the
United States. *Most of the programs have been based on the belief
that not only are special services needed, but modifications or radical
changes in the environment of elderly people are essential.* To move
a person out of his setting became a *sine qua non* in dealing with the
problems of the sick elderly. The programs instituted, however, still
might be considered as token measures only and as an earnest of things
to come.

Programs of total care and the provision of a variety of living units
to meet individual differences of elderly people have in some degree
relieved the acute situation of 10 years ago (although these programs
are still lagging behind many European countries, notably the Scandinavian). Awareness of the critical situation was accelerated by the
White House Conference on Aging, held in 1961.

The immense cost of good care in suitable homes, and the realization
that even the best care and optimum environment in communal facilities still leaves emotional and social needs largely neglected, lead one
to take a more critical look at the way we are attempting to overcome
the lag. We might ask whether it is either practical or desirable to
pursue the policy of moving large numbers of people from their homes
into special care units, developed specifically for geriatric patients, or
whether we should spend our substance by re-deploying all available
trained personnel so as to enlarge our already existing home-care treatment teams as well as to develop a new service corps or vastly expanded
home-care service units. The latter might be comprised of psychia-

trists, psychologists, physicians, nurses, social workers, occupational therapists, home-makers and volunteer auxiliary helpers.

Senator McNamara, chairman of the Senate Sub-Committee on Problems of the Aged and Aging, heard expert testimony and views from some of the best informed people in the nation. He then stated, in 1959, that the financial burden to this country of a growing number of institutions for the aged will be "too fantastic to conceive. We just cannot continue to build more and more state institutions". (1). Although this committee emphasized the practical economics of providing institutional care, other surveys have included the emotional and social deprivation of uprooted elderly people within their frames of reference.

There are some elderly people who find in institutional living a way of life acceptable and even rewarding to them, but these are greatly in the minority. It has become an accepted practice to remove people from a home situation to provide special medical and nursing care that cannot be provided in their homes. The practice of easy, almost automatic removal of elderly people to alleviate the home situation needs to be scrutinized closely—particularly as the working population receives full sanction and unquestioned approval from society for its ambitions to improve its standards and increase production, even though the individual rights of an elderly dependent relative may be seriously violated in the process.

The tendency of people to identify with the problems of adult children and give moral support to any action that bestows freedom of movement and increased earning potential on the young and middle-aged is a culturally-determined fact that militates against the elderly. Its goals and objectives are materialistic. Opportunities for retaining or advancing family life as a stabilizing factor, with its educational, social, and cultural functions, are thereby still further weakened, and social life impoverished.

The institution has traditionally provided a group living experience for those who are no longer able to manage in the community. Recent years have seen the increase of elderly people in the isolated, sick, dependent portions of our institutional population, with a corresponding decrease in the younger age groups. This gradual concentration and consequent segregation seems to offer the best means of providing comprehensive care and a substitute social life at the same time. Nevertheless, the proficient, professional services thus made available lack the personal quality of family-style living. Because institutional living is not the typical living arrangement for people in our society, the impact on the individual who enters an institution or other congregate facility can be traumatic in the extreme.

The loss of significant people and familiar objects can be devastating, producing a feeling of defeat and uselessness. The security of well-learned patterns of daily living and environmental clues is suddenly swept away. The newly-institutionalized elderly person becomes anchorless, often rejected and unloved; rudderless, without family or familiar guide lines. In a milieu quite foreign to his experiences he frequently adapts by bizarre defensive behavior that further isolates him from his fellows. It is doubly unfortunate that those elderly people who have had the fewest opportunities in their youth to engage in educational, cultural or recreational pursuits seem to have a lessened tolerance for adaptation in the later years and little reserve of experience to help in their adjustment to the massive change inherent in group living.

Adaptive patterns of elderly people and their "caretakers" in homes for the aged were discussed in a recent paper by Ruth Bennett (2). Dr. Bennett summarized studies which indicated a relationship between "the growing trend toward institutionalization of the aged and their enforced isolation in the community. . . . At this point, approximately 6% of the aged population of the United States resides in homes for the aged and mental institutions."

Commenting on the meaning of institutional life for administrators and members of the professional staff, the author reported that a "social worker was asked to list the criteria she was using of a well-adjusted resident. They were: 1) one who isn't afraid of authority; 2) one who maintains outside contacts; 3) one who participates in activities in the Home; 4) one who can face the frustration of regulations, e.g., by obeying the doctor and taking his medicine or by not going out in the snow; 5) one who accepts a roommate even if he has grounds for complaints."

The administrative point of view, however, was somewhat different. One administrator is quoted as declaring that "residents are expected to behave as ladies or gentlemen. They are expected to be courteous and say 'hello' to all, including staff members. They should be clean and dress nicely. . . ." Complaining is discouraged, as illustrated by an anecdote about remarks made at the funeral of a deceased Home resident, "She's been very happy here; she never complained."

Dr. Bennett notes that "some of the psychiatrists approve of neither the social work nor the administrative point of view. According to their observations, adaptive patterns which are best suited to the Home fall into the category of passive integration. They believe that everything in the Home reinforces regression or immature behavior. . . . Aggressive residents are negatively sanctioned by not becoming staff favorites."*

---

* Quoted with permission of the author and *The Gerontologist*.

On the intake service of an institution, the social worker is made acutely aware of ambivalence in attempting to rationalize difficulties and in maintaining a professional role and an objective viewpoint. The moral aspect of what amounts to discrimination against a certain group is inescapable when attempting to do case work with a family that includes an elderly person. The generally accepted practice of removing elderly people to relieve the burden on wage-earning young and middle-aged adults produces conflicts which further confuse the social worker. The resultant conflicts often lead to relinquishment of her role as professional case worker for the geriatric patient, and its replacement with an administrative, functional role. The social worker becomes, in short, an accessory after the fact, and is an unwitting aid to the abandonment of the old person on grounds of "expediency."

A new departure

Perhaps it would be more realistic and fruitful to plan along different lines for people now entering their later years, i.e., those becoming 60 and 70 within the next two decades, rather than spend our efforts and substance in patching up past errors. There appears to be a turn of the tide in thinking about elderly people, as reflected in more sophisticated public education programs. There are definite signs, too, of a rebellious attitude among older people themselves. Instead of the depressed, subservient, vulnerable and resigned attitudes prevalent a few years ago, we see the beginnings of an organized, aggressive, self-expressive group, fighting for the right to continue living in an accustomed and preferred manner. Unquestionably, this reassessment of themselves and their position has come about partly as a result of public education, fact-finding, and soul-searching during the last several years. Also, federal utterances and legislation for the economic relief of the underprivileged have given elderly people more confidence to make themselves heard and voice their expectations of the society in which they live.

After considering the most advanced European patterns of congregate living and hospital-building for the elderly, one might be convinced that we should make haste and catch up to their standards. But this course might lead to a situation similar to that which presently exists with respect to mental illness, i.e., after building facilities and filling them up, we might well find ourselves with new concepts of aging and have the embarrassing and costly task of emptying the buildings we have so zealously constructed. If dislocation of the elderly became generally recognized as an unsatisfactory expedient, we would be forced to go through the wasteful and disturbing revolution of relocating elderly people back into the community.

The geriatric institution
as a resource

When the social service department of an institution caring for the elderly has an active intake service and intensive pre-admission services, it is in an advantageous position to obtain an overview of the problems affecting many families in which an older person is involved. The problems uncovered by such a department might be considered as representative of a semi-urban, industrialized community in the United States.

Requests for custodial care are ostensibly precipitated by a health problem, but the total problem is of a much more complex nature, including such factors as personality traits, economic status, cultural patterns of living, degree of urbanization, propinquity of children, availability of hospital facilities and even climate. All aspects of the situation must be considered.

Except in the case of acute illness which requires the services of a general hospital, the modification of any single factor among those mentioned above often can alter the picture completely. A pressing, critical situation that appears to call for radical intervention and removal to a hospital can be transformed into a family matter that can be solved with combined effort and consultation. This approach would result in fewer deportations of elderly persons from their home setting.

At Cushing Hospital there have been approximately one thousand inquiries for admission per year; of this number, only 25% eventuate in the elderly person entering the institution. Allowing for the fact that a certain number of inquiries are based on inaccurate information concerning the hospital, fully 50% of those making inquiries find solutions that do *not* include removing the older person from his home at the time. The alternative solutions are worked out through consulting and referral services of the social service department. That such efforts can succeed is an indication that one need not automatically rely upon institutionalization as the answer.

An intake social worker in a geriatric hospital finds herself torn between the broad social problem of millions of elderly people in greater or lesser need, and the problems of the individual elderly persons whom she comes to know well. The overall social problem of "the elderly" as a concept generally is easier to deal with, and perhaps prevents the social worker from thinking through the question of possible ways in which she can be of optimum help in the role of caseworker or therapist to an elderly individual. It is easier to accept the theory of "disengagement" as an inevitable part of the aging process.

The question as to who constitutes "the elderly" has been discussed and debated to little effect. There seems to be no advantage in defining any particular group within our population as "elderly," except for the express purpose of providing suitable medical care and of meeting the economic needs peculiar to the retired person.

The sheer numbers and economics involved in the social problem have tended to cloud the personal problems that accompany aging. It is the aging process and the ways of meeting it with which the social worker is and should be most concerned. Case work offers a method of helping elderly people and their families. With professional help, families can work through many crises that might otherwise be catastrophic. It is evident, however, that the number of people in need are too great and the number of social workers too small to make a dent in the case load of people with emotional problems concerned with aging. Case work with the aging needs no justification. The success of it has been proven but the methods are time-consuming, laborious, and vulnerable to the social, economic and psychological attitudes surrounding the aged person.

From the experience of three years in an institution that serves the elderly, and seeing the dilemmas of families that included some three thousand elderly people, it is clear that not only are we *not* adequately meeting their immediate medical and nursing needs, but we also are *not* meeting the psychological needs of many elderly people who find themselves displaced, dislocated and distressed. Whether they are distressed chiefly at finding themselves uprooted in an alien environment, or whether they are distressed chiefly by the process of aging itself is a matter of concern to the intake worker.

Much can be done to relieve physical discomfort, but we have done very little to meet the underlying distress that may accompany the aging process. New planning might well begin with the recognition that we have already failed those who are now between 75 and 90 years of age—we were so ill-prepared for them. We might then devise ways and means of keeping our future older people as contributory members of the social scene as long as possible. We should harness the medical knowledge we have gained and combine *all* the social services available in every community to *carry care to the people where they live.* This approach represents a radical departure from the predominant current practice.

Perhaps a recognition of the lag between medical advance and planning and innovation in the social realm is the greatest lesson to be learned from the present situation. All advances for the care of the elderly must be on a broad front with coordinated efforts which include all of the social sciences and medicine. It is only in this way— and with the support of the church and all the helping professions— that society can withstand the mores that spring from the pressures of an industrialized, mobile and expanding economy. Society can and must carry the responsibility and guilt for its treatment and attitude toward the elderly casualties of our unpreparedness. Elderly persons should be allowed to remain in their own homes or places of their choosing.

Perhaps the mature adults of the present day who are now entering the second half of their life span will benefit by personal participation in planning for persons who are now elderly. Retirement and later life could be anticipated with pleasure instead of dread if prior attention were given to the importance of maintaining social usefulness and emotional satisfaction.

References

1. The Aged and Aging in the United States; Summary of Expert Views before the Subcommittee on Problems of the Aged and Aging of the Committee on Labor and Public Welfare; United States Senate; June 16-18, 1959; Washington, D.C.
2. Bennett, Ruth. The meaning of institutional life. *Gerontologist,* 1963, *3,* 117-125.
3. *The Older American.* Pub. by the President's Council for the Aging, 1963.

Aspects of geriatric care and treatment: Moral, amoral, and immoral

16

J. Sanbourne Bockoven

Since the writer is practically non-conversant with the literature of the social sciences he regards himself as singularly unhampered and free to make judgments of our society. It also spares him the tedious work of preparing a bibliography.

It is fair to assume that anyone would grant that more people of all ages are "better off" in affluent America today than at any other time or place in the history of mankind. Americans have arrived at this desirable state of affairs through a generally haphazard, undirected and unorganized output of human energy and inventiveness of rather enormous magnitude. Direction and consequences of energy output have been and still are given little thought beyond achieving immediate objectives. Each endeavor is basically an amoral and irresponsible enterprise. The most significant outcome is that the socially damaging immoral components of these enterprises tend to cancel each other out. Furthermore, enterprises tend to survive and grow which actually bring the greatest good to the greatest number, irrespective of whether or not their authors are, in fact, anti-social schemers with the worst possible intentions or idealistic do-gooders. It is even likely that the best results can be traced back to those with the worst intentions. For example: as repulsive as one may feel vultures to be, they are preferable to accumulations of stinking carcasses.

**Public problem number one:
our delinquent society**
For several years now there has been intense preoccupation with the matter of juvenile delinquency. Of late a giant stride of insight was disseminated in the phrase, "there are no juvenile delinquents, only delinquent parents!" The next stride may place the origin of the problem in the laps of our grandparents. But for the present, at least, citizens in the productive years of life must consider themselves the generation culpable for selfish neglect of both the generation preceding and the one following them, and hence doubly delinquent.

Of those in the productive years of life, members of the medical profession occupy the brightest spot in the limelight of public criticism for not living up to public expectations based on heart-warming hearsay from the past. The several decades during which such criticism of the physician has had its greatest growth also delimit the period during which society has adopted what might be portrayed as medical mores in place of religious mores. The ancient Hippocratic ethic that the physician must give freely of his healing powers to princes and paupers, innocents and sinners alike was for many centuries limited to physicians. During the past half-century or so, tacit adoption of this ethic in the United States has led to social legislation and social welfare administration practices which, in effect, require application of this ethic by agencies other than physicians. In other words, American society has chosen to deal with its members along the same lines that physicians, nurses and medical social workers deal with their patients.

The rapid growth in influence of psychological, psychiatric and psychoanalytic perspectives in medicine, in education and in criminology has very nearly brought the dominant philosophy behind our social policies to a point where it is a clinical, i.e., bedside, philosophy of society's relation to the individual. It would appear that society and the individual have been pursuing a course of mutual seduction, one of the other, into a one-way donor-recipient relationship somewhat akin to the tender loving care that doctors, nurses and social workers are expected to give sick people. Do Americans have such a yearning for "TLC" that they willingly call themselves sick to get it? An affirmative answer helps explain why the American physician is the object of criticism at a time when he is actually giving much better service than when he was the subject of praise several decades ago. The explanation may be a simple one: the physician does not accept society's self-diagnosis that it is any sicker or any more vulnerable to becoming sick than it ever was. Indeed, the fact of a disproportionately high incidence of coronary deaths among physicians in their prime years has not led them to adopt any special measures to protect their own health.

In a way somewhat similar to the American farmer, the physician cherishes the image of himself as being a self-employed individualist. He retains, furthermore, a degree of belief that he possesses in his person intuitive diagnostic and therapeutic powers which generations of physicians have handed down from medicine men of prehistoric, primitive times. His basic faith still resides in the healing powers of nature, and his basic role is that of a servant of nature who secures for her the conditions necessary for her to do her work and who serves as the medium between her and the afflicted one. In some respects, the heritage of the physician carries him in a direction dramatically opposite that of modern science which has as its avowed aim the winning of *mastery* over nature. Even today, there are not a few physician-servants of nature who have formal religious convictions as well. Most of them tend to refuse to accept the scientistic attempts of modern psychology to account for the physician's intuitive therapeutic powers in terms of non-mystical dynamics.

There are physicians of quite a different bent, however, whose voices have begun to find larger audiences in recent years. They are most frequently trained in either psychiatry or public health, and occasionally both. In some respects they deserve the appellation of philosopher-physicians, for they are often gifted with fertile imagination and high motivation which are invested in systematizing medical knowledge and practice. Historically speaking, there has been a strong tendency among philosophically-minded physicians to observe the social scene of their country in search for analogues in society of pathological processes in the human body. Their counterparts in the field of social philosophy and in present-day social science have, on the other hand, given close scrutiny to the health of various segments of the population in relation to medical customs and practices. In the very recent past these two groups have joined forces in conducting research studies. Between them, i.e., the social-science-minded physician and the medically minded social scientist, they have contributed to the emergence of a new perspective on the role of medicine in modern society. By and large, this perspective reflects an image of the rank and file of American physicians as deporting themselves in a manner which is reactionary, archaic, obsolete and seriously in need of reform. This perspective is based on a conviction that the American physician, especially as represented by his strongest national organization, is failing to recognize the true medical needs of society. Most of the rank and file of American physicians, however, have no such abstract idea of meeting the needs of society for they are fully occupied taking care of the complaints of individuals.

There is a third party in this picture which may well have more influence than either the physician or the social scientist. This crucially important third party is the communications industry with its enormous productivity and great speed of disseminating messages. It is almost entirely through its channels that *informed public opinion* comes into existence. Of even more critical importance: it is also the source of *misinformed public opinion* and political action. Herein lies a problem of major proportions, for in this rapidly changing world of scientific advance in which truth is often stranger than fiction, who can separate fiction from truth?

The recent emergence of the professional science writer and editor appears to be a beginning in coping with the problem and may well be a development of historical importance. The trained medical science writer of the future could also find himself wielding more influence over public opinion than either physician or social scientist. He would likewise carry a proportionately greater burden of responsibility for any new patterns of medical care which will likely come into existence in the future. At present, however, it appears largely a matter of chance whether the mass media will foster or counteract disease phobias, hypochondriasis, or appetites for brand-name pharmaceutical products.

The magnitude and efficiency of our communications industry is not simply a matter of quantitative importance from the point of view of the number of people it influences. It has also brought about a qualitative change in the form of an occurrence in the social conscience. This occurrence bears signs of being as vital an event in human history as the Biblical account of Adam's discovery of individual knowledge of individual good and evil. The communications industry has, for some time, accomplished the feat of arresting the simultaneous attention of the entire membership of a society. As the instrument of mass psychology, it has contributed to a new phenomenon of collective knowledge of collective good and evil. The result, as with the individual, is a new collective self-consciousness and collective self-censorship. It is not difficult to identify strong tendencies to collective self-accusation, collective confession, collective atonement and collective good works. We have collectively brought about a system of taxation and public service whereby we collectively meet human needs varying from feeding the poor to psychiatric treatment of juvenile criminals.

Once again the topic of delinquency presents itself, this time entering from another door. It would appear that we are in the processes of reaching a solution which has been present all the time. It is plain that our society has already passed judgment on itself even if it has not put it in the form of a public announcement. It judges itself to be delinquent on the straightforward grounds that juvenile delinquents are the blameless products of their delinquent parents who are in turn the blameless products of a delinquent society. But what has society done about the self-judgment, this confession of being at fault? It has made collective retribution by directing its representatives in the legislatures of the land to pass laws which provide funds from tax money to build and staff *treatment* centers for young delinquents. So here is the gimmick. Delinquency is regarded as a sickness in the first place. Society does not regard anybody to be at fault individually or collectively. It takes the handiest "out" and diagnoses itself as a sick society and pays for treatment of the presenting symptom in the form of the juvenile delinquent. By paying for treatment of its sick products, society also gains a sense of having made retribution even if there is some blame involved. But like any similar hypocrite of Biblical times, society salves its conscience with a token payment of retribution which is nowhere nearly enough for even palliative treatment.

Juvenile delinquency is, of course, but a selected example of one of the relatively minor pieces in the jigsaw puzzle of problems with which the collective consciousness and conscience of American society is confronted. Statistical reports from the data-gathering establishments of the federal and state governments and of private agencies appear at weekly, monthly and yearly intervals to provide a score card for almost every conceivable undesired event ranging from a count of illnesses and injuries to all manner of accidents and criminal acts. As the collective conscience and self-consciousness grows in intensity, it experiences one awakening after another to distressing facts of life, many of which have been present all along. This rapid growth in collective sensitivity to human suffering naturally results in many hasty endeavors to run to the rescue the moment the deplorable discoveries are reported by those charged with the task of searching for them. This appears to be a picture of a conscience-stricken society running in high alarm to mend the error of its ways. But, as noted in connection with juvenile delinquency, the "mending" is often only a token gesture which salves the collective conscience for a time and then aborts itself.

One of the most recent awakenings our society has experienced is that which pointed to the fact that there are a rather large number of old folks in modern society. Apparently there has been a widespread notion that since our times are ultra modern they must be populated by ultra late model people! At any rate the knowledge that there are appreciable numbers of people in our midst who are 75 and 80 years of age has come as a sort of shock. Perhaps the middle generations of today actually lost a decade or so in the fast moving events of World War II and are truly surprised to find their parents and grandparents so far along in years.

In any event there is an abundance of conscience-stricken collective action going on which is making haste to do many things to better conditions for our elder citizens. Once again, it is worthy of note that it is the collective conscience which is involved and collective action which is being mobilized. Also, once again, the solution is sought by turning the problem over to medical management and putting the problem people away in medical institutions.

Cushing Hospital
founded on a myth

The rebuilding and establishment of Cushing Hospital as a geriatric inpatient facility is an example of an action resulting from hasty mobilization of the collective conscience. This action was based on a belief held by the lay public, by physicians in private practice, and by the psychiatrist directors of mental hospitals that a considerable number of harmless elderly people with no ailment other than simple senility were being inappropriately held as insane patients under commitment in the state hospitals of Massachusetts. It was not until many months after Cushing Hospital began admitting patients in the fall of 1957 that the facts of the case came to light—namely, that the state hospitals had practically no patients with simple senility to transfer to Cushing. The patients who ultimately were transferred were those with long-standing chronic psychoses since youth and middle life who had passed the age of 65 in the course of their mental hospital stay.

During these same months, awareness spread among the public that Cushing Hospital was open for admissions at a cost of one-half to one-third of most nursing homes. This resulted in a great demand for admission not of elderly folk with simple senility but of severely ill bedridden patients in their eighties. The hospital was at that time not yet equipped or staffed to receive such large numbers of cases requiring round-the-clock bedside care. Admissions were, therefore, held to a very small monthly quota; this resulted in considerable vexation not only among those families who desired early admission of the elderly patients for whom they were responsible, but also among a number of administrative officers and legislators of the Commonwealth as well.

The hospital recently completed its fifth full official (fiscal) year of operation. During the last three of these years the hospital administration has sought to apply a rule of "ambulatory patients only" as a prerequisite for consideration of applicants for admission. This rule was necessary for the hospital to fulfill its assignment of caring for the less severe cases of senility and thus spare them commitment to a state mental hospital. The desirability of sparing persons afflicted with simple senility was based on a sentiment shared by the public, the state legislature and the Department of Mental Health that the stigma of the mental institution was a source of distress which senile patients and their families should not be forced to endure. Furthermore, the distressing condition of deprivation generally acknowledged to exist in state mental hospitals was regarded as an even more damaging hardship to be circumvented.

The course of events of the five-year period Cushing has been in operation has confronted the hospital administration with the necessity of providing services to a much broader spectrum of need than were included in its initial assignment. The greatest pressure from the public is its demands for admission of bedfast patients in their eighties who require round-the-clock nursing care and daily medical attention for advanced stages of physical infirmity.

Moral Treatment in
gerontologic medicine

"Moral Treatment" as a medical term in its own right (in reference to a philosophy and a practice of physicians) is all but unknown to readers of modern medical literature. Briefly, Moral Treatment (which was developed in the early 19th century in France, England and the United States) is a method for applying comprehensive treatment for the purpose of restoring soundness of mind and body to those afflicted with mental ills.

Without going into the details of Moral Treatment as applied in the care of the mentally ill,* suffice it to say that the concept it embraces has cogency to hospital practice in modern medicine. Its value derives from its assigning priority to planning a therapeutic program for the patient's person rather than for his ailment. Specific measures for treatment of particular disease processes were, from the Moral Treatment standpoint, so arranged and timed as to fit into the personal regimen of the patient in a manner which contributed most to his total well-being.

The use of the term Moral Treatment today, in reference to the personal considerations necessary to provide adequate care of patients, admittedly has an apparent drawback—its connotation of moralistic medical practice. The term as used by its inventor, however, did not refer to either, but to emotional and psychological considerations as in the term "moral philosophy" which was current in the same period.

There may be, nevertheless, some value in using the term Moral Treatment today *because* it has accompanying overtones which suggest a moral issue. It is not too farfetched to wonder whether or not completely mechanistic impersonal treatment of patients in hospitals treads on the threshhold of the amoral if not the immoral. Certainly no one can miss the point in extreme examples such as the rescue of a patient from death from coronary occlusion only to be exposed an hour later to an angry verbal battle between an orderly and a housekeeper. A hospital whose physicians give guidance in planning a Moral Treatment regimen for its patients is in a position to eliminate adverse experiences as the very least of the contributions to its patients' welfare and recovery.

The elimination of adverse experiences from the patients' life in the hospital is not a small matter. Safeguarding the patients' sensibilities from flagrant insults would appear to require little more than ordinary intelligence and common sense. Yet even in this most obvious and

---

* Editor's note: The author will not be permitted to escape entirely the weight of a "tedious bibliography." The bibliography should contain at least one entry, germane to the present point: Bockoven, J. S. *Moral Treatment in American Psychiatry.* N.Y.: Springer, 1963.

simple-minded matter of protecting patients from noxious stimuli, appearances are deceiving. The ever-present problem remains: that people of even extraordinary intelligence and common sense can and do conduct themselves in a manner which further adds to the strain that disease has already imposed on the patients' adaptive capacities and healing powers.

Knowledge that living in a hospital is accompanied by misadventures which counteract the gain made by specific treatments for the diseases suffered by patients carries with it an obligation of serious proportions for those who control the destinies of the hospital as an institution and as an habitat for people whose lives are in jeopardy. The achievement of modern medicine is that it has acquired rather extensive ability to alter the course of physicochemical and anatomical disease processes by physicochemical and mechanical means. The irony of modern medicine is that so often, when the human factor enters the picture, ground is lost which was gained by victories of the physical sciences.

A therapeutic regimen which is tailored to a disease and not to the needs of a person forces the person to arrange his life around the disease or the diseased organ. The almost complete absence of any acknowledgment that the patient might have some purpose in life of more importance to him than nursing a diseased organ is some indication that physicians do not accept the role of counselor or general health advisor to their own patients. Abdication of the physician from the role of health authority and advisor has created a hiatus in modern society which cannot be filled by the psychiatrist or others. The choice of the physician to be a technical specialist rather than a guide to lifetime health has its counterpart in the prevalence of hypochondriasis and specific organ neuroses in the population at large.

Certainly medicine must consider what the future will bring in this era of mass management of human beings by governmental and private agencies. The downgrading and disregard of human individuality which inevitably takes place in the interest of organization efficiency in any system of mass management is, unwittingly perhaps, being reenforced by the modern medical man. There is evaporation of regard for the individuality of the individual as citizen, as employee, as patient. He is a nonentity among nonentities in practically all of his life settings. The experience that the physician has respect only for a component part of his bodily machine, and not for *him*, would surely confirm in the patient's mind that he stands in the same relation to his physician as to his employer who also has respect for one of his physical attributes but not for him. The point I wish to make is that for medicine also the individual's individuality or personality has little worthwhileness even as an object of interest, let alone as an object of respect and crucial concern. Medicine is contributing to, rather than counteracting, a growing tendency to regard human individuality and personality as superfluous, obsolete and expendable. Medicine, thus, is not fulfilling its purpose. On the contrary, it is contributing to the undoing of its own efforts to the extent that it participates in demoralizing its patients and undermining their will to live.

Mankind would have destroyed itself long ago were it not for the fact that man's inhumanity to man and powers of destruction of his own kind have not quite been a match for the resiliency and functional reserve of human individualities, human bodies and human organs and tissues. We must also give credit to man's versatility, adroitness and serendipity as a social animal skilled in getting himself out of trouble as well as into it. With this thought in mind, it does not appear unlikely that human individualities will be able to withstand even more highly organized and impersonal society.

There comes a point, however, when one must consider those whose resiliency and functional reserve is on the decline.

Moral Treatment is not a synonym for maid service or catering to the patient's whims in any sense. Quite to the contrary, it aims at strengthening independence, autonomy, self-reliance and self-care. It rests on a foundation of thorough evaluation of the patient's capacities and capabilities, reveals them to the patient, and arouses and assists him in learning to use them.

Geriatrics

Because of the frequency with which elderly patients who are referred for hospital care are found to be fragile and vulnerable, both physically and psychologically, programs of treatment must be based on determination of the total needs of the patient. In other words, treatment programs must be regimens which include all aspects of daily living. The patient's regimen must be reviewed at suitable intervals and revised and added to as indicated. The goal with each patient is to press forward toward completeness in meeting needs which must be met to restore maximum health, morale and self-determination.

Because elderly patients are those who have been exposed to wear and tear and stresses and strains for the greatest length of time, they are more vulnerable than others. The accumulation of impairments, both to organ systems and to psychological functions, render older persons particularly vulnerable to the reciprocal damaging effects of the mind upon the body and of the body upon the mind. These considerations point up the need of elderly patients for medical care which is programmed to meet their mental health and physical health needs simultaneously.

Elderly individuals are in varying degrees *displaced persons*, i.e., strangers in their own families and communities largely as a result of rapid socio-economic changes which took place during the latter half of their lives and for which many had little opportunity to prepare. A number of these persons live in desolation. They are the casualties of the social forces which have dislocated their habitual way of life. Many of them may not be in need of medical attention. They do, however, have a need for counselors who have a broad knowledge of community life and can help them find more satisfactory modes of living. Collectively, they are in need of corrective measures in the community aimed at making the community more livable.

Varieties of disorders in senescence. Senescent persons may be classified roughly into six types:

1. Those with long-standing chronic physical disorders many of which began in pre-senescent years
2. Those with chronic mental disease many of which began in pre-senescent years
3. Those who have had chronic mental disorders which lasted through a great portion of the patients' adult lives but became inactive in the senescent years
4. Those who undergo acute physical disorders for the first time in association with senescence
5. Those who undergo acute mental disorders for the first time in association with senescence
6. Those whose senescence is not complicated with any well-defined physical or mental disorder but who are demoralized by having no role in life and who become invalids due to sociogenic and iatrogenic forces.

Theoretically, Cushing Hospital is designed for groups 3 and 5. In practice, however, patients in all six categories are admitted because of the considerable overlap of emotional and behavioral disorders with physical disorders of all types. There are but few exceptions: terminal cases of cancer are referred to special chronic disease hospitals as are certain cases of advanced neurological disorders.

Senescence, like adolescence, has its own characteristic stressful problems which are independent of disease processes *per se.* The problems of individuals who bring already existing chronic diseases with them into their senescent years constitute a class of problems wholly separate from the problems of senescence uncomplicated by chronic disease. The person who enters senescence with an already existing, long-standing chronic disease has already become deeply intrenched in the sick-role. He has become habituated, so to speak, in the hobby of being a semi-invalid or he may have become a professional at playing the role of the total invalid.

The individual who enters his senescent years without the complications of already existing chronic disease may nevertheless gravitate to the sick-role *because* our society offers to those in their post-retirement years readier access to this role than any other.

The invitation to enter the sick-role is extended by physicians who are ready to diagnose organic brain disease on the basis of poorly evaluated superficial evidence of disturbances of orientation in one or all three spheres of the sensorium.

Hints as to the nature of deteriorative aging

A helpful though generally speculative formulation of the psychophysiopathology of deteriorative aging, as opposed to developmental aging, is that deteriorative aging is a form of functional psychosis beginning with depressive reactions and progressing to schizophrenic reactions in which psychophysiologic energy is introverted and expended on somatic cellular structures in a manner favoring catabolism and cell destruction.

Early senescence has a number of physiologic components in common with psychotic depressions: for example, elevated blood pressure; constipation; dehydration; psychomotor retardation; muscle weakness and increased fatigability; mental weakness and increased fatigability; sleep disorders; loss of appetite; increased incidence of suicide.

Later senescence has a number of physiologic components in common with schizophrenic reaction, e.g.: surrender and apathy; withdrawal and isolation; low blood pressure; silky texture to fingers; automatic obedience or negativism; loss of control of bowel and bladder.

By and large, the more submerged the behavioral components of functional psychosis, the more there is of cell destruction and physical deterioration.

The fact that a perceptible gradiant of physical or mental deterioration, or both, is a universal accompaniment of increasing age, after the child-bearing and child-rearing phase of life is completed, strongly suggests that the habits and customs of human society—which so thoroughly inculcates its individual members with belief in their uselessness when child-rearing is over—may be the source of the demoralizing force which sets the submerged psychotic process in motion. This possibility bears exploration for there is little doubt that every individual *is* thoroughly inculcated with the belief that his inevitable deterioration will take place soon after he reaches the years of grand-parenthood. Certainly the unanimous belief of all mankind is a psychological force of sufficient magnitude to produce extensive psychologic and psychosomatic effects in a lone, psychologically dependent individual. The most damaging component of this belief is the message it contains of personal uselessness and worthlessness on reaching a particular point in life. As the individual approaches this point he is confronted with the painfully preposterous indignity of the problem presented by growing awareness of dependence on the affection and good will of others in order to have a role in human society.

He already feels partially rejected by way of a belief he shares with the human society with respect to his approaching phase in life. Feelings of partial rejection are inescapably followed by terror of impending full rejection and rage toward those from whom it is expected, including himself. Feelings of terror and rage are withheld from expression at all cost, however, and are buried deep within the privacy of the self, for this expression would evoke the very rejection the anticipation of which gave rise to them. The greater the amount of alienation the individual already feels because of loss of co-workers following retirement or loss of proximity to children because of marriage, the greater will be his strivings to win back his rightful place in the hearts of his children or other younger people with whom he has been associated. Failure in these strivings may be followed by irascible aggressive attempts in the exercise of moral suasion or in the use of punishment and reward. Failure in this approach may be followed by self-denunciation and depressed behavior and physical illness or by a complete schizophrenic surrender with apathy and withdrawal. Regression to childish behavior may occur out of identification with children by way of reaction formation to infanticidal phantasies and impulses.

It would appear that, for the majority of people, emotions of these magnitudes cannot reach outward expression or awareness but are absorbed entirely by the tissues of the body. In some, damage to brain tissue results in a breakthrough of strong emotion and disturbed behavior.

General comment
A re-reading of this rather disconnected essay creates the impression of diving at a target and hitting its hard outer edge only to glance off and hit the edges of other somewhat unanticipated targets. This is the tangential thinking of a mind on the run when smitten with the overwhelming task of trying to make sense of the terminal years of human life and at the same time trying to avoid getting lost in contemplating the meaning of human life *in toto*. That this is in some measure the case perhaps also with others explains, in a hazy sort of way to be sure, why both medical and social gerontology tend to be rather unimaginative superficial disciplines. The "why" of this, I suspect, is a consequence of our unfamiliarity and discomfort with the philosophical and mystical heritage of our own and other cultures. This is relevant, in some degree at least, for those of us who are professional specialists reared in the scientific tradition. It appears to me that we are fast approaching a time when we could profit from taking into consideration both the newer knowledge now emerging from physics and chemistry and the ancient mystical knowledge of mankind. Per-

haps in so doing we could discover common ground for building solidarity among the various disciplines desiring to serve the elderly
better. Similarly, common ground might be discovered for greater
social solidarity between the generation of elders who feel burdened
by longevity itself and their descendents who feel perplexed by un-
happiness produced by progress.

VIEWS OF OLD AGE

How is old age to be viewed? Sage counsel is not lacking; for example:

"Think young," but "Act your age!"

"Grow old gracefully," but "Do not go gentle into that good night!"

"You are as old as you feel," but "You're washed up at 65!"

Contradictory elements in contemporary attitudes toward old age are examined from an historical and cross-cultural perspective by sociologist Philip E. Slater. He relates "the peculiar ambivalence in our own attitudes toward old age" to our double heritage: "the classical Greek view that aging is an unmitigated misfortune" and "the Middle Eastern view that old age is the summit of life." Dr. Slater's analysis does not shy away from certain considerations that one might prefer to wish out of existence, but through these considerations it may be possible "to reduce some of the guilt . . . (which) is a great generator of good intentions destructively executed."

Attitudes of young and elderly adults toward old age are explored in a pair of chapters by psychologists Robert Kastenbaum and Nancy Durkee. New findings and results reported by other investigators are combined to provide an evaluation of what has thus far been learned and what remains to be learned about attitudes toward old age. Particular attention is given to points of accord and discord between the outlooks of young and elderly adults.

Philip E. Slater

If we concentrate our attention on that segment of our culture which derives from the written word, we are forced to acknowledge the fact that our ideas about the aged are inherited from two contradictory traditions.

On the one hand, we have the classical Greek view that aging is an unmitigated misfortune. As Guthrie points out, this is found as early as Homer and persists in the upper, or at least literary, strata of Greek society until the late Roman period (2). The attitude is best expressed by the seventh century Ionian poet, Mimnermos of Kolophon, who said: "Brief is the fruit of youth, no longer than the daily spread of the sunlight over the earth; but when that spring-time of life is passed, then verily to die is better than life, for many are the ills that invade the heart."

On the other hand, we find the Middle Eastern view that old age is the summit of life. This view permeates the Old Testament and, as Raphael Patai has noted, characterizes the Middle East to this day. Age brings status and prestige to a man, not only in his family but also in the community, where it almost automatically confers political influence. The well-known title "sheik" originally meant simply "old man," and thus the fact that Arab patriarchs have always been prone to exaggerate their age is no surprise. Great age is also viewed as a sign of innate virtue and divine blessing, and it is undoubtedly for this reason that such extravagant ages were assigned to the early Biblical patriarchs. The ancient Hebrews believed that the wicked die young, while the Greeks not only said, "Whom the gods love die young" but invented two or three myths to prove it (3).

One could plausibly attribute to this contrast the peculiar ambivalence in our own attitudes toward old age, although on the surface it might appear that our orientation is entirely derived from the Greek. We value youth and fear old age, which in our society confers no dignity but only losses. We even try to deny the existence of old age in the words that we use, such as the term "aging," which is as if to say, "Old age is such a depressing state that we must never admit that anyone has finally entered it—even a man in his 80s is only moving toward it."

The more strongly we hold this view, however, the more strongly we feel that we should not. The individual who reacts to every sign of his own aging with horror and who treats his own elderly parent with condescension, contempt or sadistic motherliness may show profound deference and respect to an aged stranger. We are uncomfortable with our worship of youth and our distaste for old age.

This conflict in attitude tends to introduce a sharp tone of artificiality into our relations with the elderly. We are ashamed of our negative feelings and try to mask them or at least put them in such a form as will enable us to hide them from ourselves. We assume a pose of respect and interest which we often do not feel. Our position is somewhat like that of a hypochondriacal, obsessive man who greets an old and dear friend who has contracted a loathsome, highly contagious disease. He finds it impossible to behave honestly because he can bear neither his friend's condition nor his own reaction to it.

An artificiality of this kind always multiplies interpersonal distance between people. I suggest that this dishonesty—this unwillingness to accept the existence inside us of these negative attitudes toward the elderly—does far more to make an old person feel isolated and alienated than do the attitudes themselves. In many societies the aged are valued far less than in ours; indeed, they are assigned the lowest possible status. Yet interaction between the young and the old is free and comfortable within that context. The loss of status causes suffering, discontent and a sense of loss, but everyone at least knows what the problem is and can talk about it. The young can commiserate with the old and the old with each other; they can extract those benefits which derive from their loss, for high status is always a mixed blessing.

But how can the young commiserate with the old when we dare not admit to ourselves that old age is a misfortune—when it is taboo even to speak of decline and deterioration and approaching death to those experiencing it? Would it not, perhaps, be better to engage in frank condolences than to pretend, as the young often do, that nothing is happening or changing, that no misfortune has taken place, and that retirement, failing health, and compulsorily abandoned activities and relationships are occasion for bland and superficial cheerfulness?

I need hardly point out that this is not the usual method of approaching this problem. It is more customary to castigate the Greek view unmercifully and give inspirational talks enumerating the manifold benefits of old age and the superiority of cultures, such as that of the Chinese, in which the elderly are respected.

But rather than attempt to manufacture these attitudes, would it not be wiser to examine some of their causes? Positive or negative attitudes toward old age and the aged do not occur randomly but are based on the social, economic and political characteristics of the society in which the attitudes prevail. If we are to resolve our ambivalence in this area, we must first get a clearer notion of the factors that determine the meaning of old age and the position of the elderly in a given society.

It seems obvious, for example, that the aged will be valued and deferred to in a society in which they perform some important function. In a primitive society in which there is no written language but rather a fixed body of knowledge which must be transmitted orally, the older a man is, the more of an expert he will be on this knowledge, and the more dependent upon him the other members of the tribe will be. In our society the knowledge acquired by an old man is largely obsolete. He may be wise and experienced, but much of his wisdom and experience is irrelevant. The younger man knows less, but his selection may be more useful. Children in the eighth and ninth grades know more physics and chemistry than most adults, and the techniques and skills we have spent our lives acquiring will be of purely historical interest in a decade or two. How many of us will be willing to reorient ourselves as these changes occur—to abandon modes of operation into which we have poured so much energy and devotion?

In his cross-cultural study of the aged in 71 societies, Leo Simmons compiled an extensive list of traits, some pertaining to the general social and environmental characteristics of these societies and some to the specific treatment accorded to the aged in each (4). Simmons analyzed many of the relationships between the two, while others can be analyzed with the raw data he makes available in his book. There is great variation among these societies in the treatment of the aged—ranging from the most profound respect and reverence to callous rejection, abandonment and deprivation. In some societies the aged are even killed, rather than allowed to die of starvation and exposure.

One crude generalization that emerges from these data is that the prestige of the aged is highest in those societies falling in the middle range of cultural development. It is among the most primitive societies, in which the barest subsistence is problematic, that killing or abandonment of the aged is most often found. Yet those societies which approach or achieve a level which we traditionally call "civilized," particularly when characterized by a fairly advanced technology, also show, in many cases, an attitude of disregard for the aged, although tempered by a sense of obligation with respect to their maintenance and care.

But leaving aside now the question of degree of cultural achievement, is it true, as has been suggested, that the prestige of the aged in a given society is dependent upon the number of important functions they perform in that society? Simmons' data provide an unquali-

his question so far as men are concerned. For women,
nplicated by other factors relating to variation in the
nen in general, but the same relationship seems to hold
into account.

This, then, is the first reality we must face: we cannot expect the
prestige of the aged to be high in a society in which, as a group, they
perform few important functions.

Some might wish to offer an alloplastic solution to this dilemma,
such as outlawing compulsory retirement plans. But even if such a
proposal were feasible, it seems unlikely that we would be prepared
to make the sacrifices that it would entail. Many people assume that
retirement plans represent nothing but prejudice against the aged.
But certainly an important factor in their prevalence in our society is
change—changing technologies, methodologies, and occupational ide-
ologies—and the fact that people are reluctant to discard the knowledge and skills they have spent their lives acquiring and become neo-
phytes once again. Are we willing, then, to retard this process of
development? But even more, are we willing to bring about the widespread unemployment that would follow such an attempt to keep the
elderly in the work force? It is important to recognize the fact that at
one level, compulsory retirement has nothing whatever to do with the
aged, as such, but is simply one of many adjustments to becoming a
leisure society. At a time when automation is spreading throughout
all segments of the economy, when full employment is a chronic head-
ache, and when agitation increases for a shorter and shorter work week,
it seems rather foolish to talk of raising the retirement age. If anything, retirement will occur earlier in the future than it does today.

The second reality we must face, then, is the fact that, since all
Americans must adjust more and more to an existence characterized
by a surplus of leisure and since the work which remains will be distributed preferentially among the young and uncommitted, the func-
tionlessness of the aged is a permanent fact of our society. This does
not mean, of course, that individual old persons will not have vital
and prestigious roles to play: we are talking about the aged as a group
and in comparison with the young, assuming comparable knowledge
and talents.

However, there is even a third reality, which is, perhaps, the most
unpleasant of all. If we examine Simmons' data, we find that those
societies in which the elderly have a high degree of prestige are characterized by a number of traits which not only do not appear to any
extent in our society but also are in basic opposition to some of our
most cherished values. Leaving aside the fact that respect for elderly
persons is correlated cross-culturally with such irrelevancies as can-
nibalism and human sacrifice, we cannot avoid the awkward fact that
societies in which the elderly have high prestige are generally authori-

tarian, totalitarian, collectivistic, and static. They are typically governed by monarchs, chiefs, or restricted councils of oligarchs. They usually have hereditary castes or classes. The important decisions of life, such as the choice of a mate, are made by the society or the extended family—not by the individual.

In societies in which the aged have low prestige, on the other hand, government is by general assembly or some other democratic system. Individualism is prevalent and highly valued. Able people can improve their social and economic position. Geographical mobility is also high, with people changing residence frequently. I think few would disagree that the latter comes closest to being a description of our own society, as it is, or as most people would like it to be.

Now it may be objected that these relationships have been torn from the social context in which they belong and do not demonstrate that a free, dynamic and democratic society must depreciate the aged. To an extent, this argument is well taken. Understanding, tolerance and respect for the individual are also democratic values, and a correlation is not a compulsion. Hopefully, all of us feel an obligation to fight bitterly against the denial of human dignity which often characterizes behavior toward the aged. But in this respect, the aged fall into the same category as any other group experiencing such denials.

The point I wish to stress here is that a positive orientation toward the aged cannot be based upon some artificial attempt to reverse the prestige structure of our society. A society which values change and freedom and is suspicious of authority and tradition, impatient of restriction, and hungry for new ideas and ways of doing things is never going to welcome old age or accord high prestige to the elderly—no matter how much we talk to it.

The third reality, then, is that a high value on youth, or overestimation of youth, is inherent in a democratic society such as ours, and if we wish to improve the welfare of the aged in this society we can only do so in the context of a frank recognition that, for an American, old age is a misfortune. The aged American does not, on the average, have an important role to play in our society.

Before concluding I would like to present one or two further thoughts which can be extracted from the anthropologic literature and which may help a little toward the understanding of these problems.

First, it might be useful to reduce some of the guilt that is typically aroused by these comparisons with real or imagined societies in which the elderly are revered and admired, for guilt is a great generator of good intentions destructively executed.

In fact, if we examine the data more closely we find that attitudinal differences between "age-oriented" and "youth-oriented" societies are often exaggerated. In many societies which are traditionally believed to show great deference to the elderly, only the intelligent and able

ones are respected (just as they are in our own society) , while the less
capable are shown no respect at all. In others, the aged are valued and
admired only until they begin to show signs of weakness, incapacity,
illness or senility, at which point an abrupt change takes place and
they are treated harshly and rejected. Only continuing usefulness, or
continuing power through the control of property, will enable them to
maintain their position.

Still other societies have achieved the reputation of age-deference
solely by virtue of written records containing admonitions to the young
to defer to their elders—data which we might just as well interpret as
revealing a lack rather than a prevalence of respect. Such admonitions
may be found in all societies, including our own.

Finally, in many societies the notion of the "golden years" is a universal ideal and myth which, however, reveals itself as such to those
who enter this period. The elderly then complain bitterly that in
their youth they respected the aged and looked forward to the time
when they would be old but now find it a difficult and unpleasant
condition. As one old Hopi woman said, "See how we suffer. It is
foolish to look forward to such a time." (4, pp. 50-81 and 234) .

A more detailed examination of the anthropologic literature may
also help us understand some of the rather strange behavior which we
can observe in both the aged and their relatives during the process of
institutionalization.

The aged have always been closely associated with sorcery in the
minds of men (witches and wizards are almost always old), partly because of the association between age and knowledge of all kinds and
partly because old age is a period of life which the young have never
experienced and which, therefore, seems strange and uncanny to them.

But a part of this association undoubtedly comes from the increasing
passivity, weakness and helplessness of the aged, which makes them
seem more vulnerable to the accumulated hostile impulses of their
offspring. As a student in a training group once remarked, "Old people are inactive, so we attribute magical powers to them." Similar
attitudes are often evoked by therapists and group leaders who play
passive and nondirective roles, and even the silent members in therapy
or training groups are often provided with impressive attributes ("the
silent ones," "the evil ones," or "they sit like slumbering volcanoes").
One function of this attitude is to counteract the increasing frustration
of dependency needs: if they are not old, impotent and passive, but
actually old, omnipotent and active, then one need not fear having to
face life alone and unprotected.

A second function is facilitation of projection. Other things being
equal, the fewer stimuli emitted by an object the easier it is to project
upon that object. In practice, this seems to be particularly true of hos-

tile, malevolent impulses, which are most typically attributed to passive, silent persons.

With aging parents, these processes may become integrated in a rather simple way. The increasingly obvious powerlessness of the aged parent weakens the remaining vestiges of awe which have survived in a semiconscious way from the early infancy of the child. Repressed or suppressed hostile feelings of a rather archaic nature threaten to emerge. At the same time, somewhat more contemporaneous angers at the ultimate annihilation of the child role, the extinction of dependent status, the necessity—on the contrary—of meeting the dependency needs of the parent, and the anticipation of final desertion by the parent through death begin to make themselves felt. But all these feelings seem inappropriate to a normal, middle-aged adult and cannot find direct expression.

A solution to most of these difficulties is provided by the conviction that it is not oneself but the old person who is malevolent—that it is not oneself who has suddenly acquired an unwonted power over not only one's own but one's parent's destiny, but rather the old person who has acquired mysterious and magical powers.

Although in modern urban societies the belief in sorcery has somewhat declined, to the extent that few people would openly admit to such feelings, much of the attitude of both parent and child toward hospitalization is surprisingly reminiscent of the responses of people in primitive cultures to sorcery (1). Thus, the fear of magical contagion may often be observed underlying the intense need to isolate and insulate the aging parent in a hospital; there is a sense of self-protection which is inappropriate to the realities of the situation. The malevolence of the relatives during hospitalization often bears the quality of an attempt at counter-sorcery, and the mysterious collapses of patients following hospitalization resemble nothing so much as the equally mysterious collapses and deaths of sorcery victims in primitive societies, where there seems to be something fatal in knowing that one is virulently hated and plotted against. All this may seem far removed from the everyday world of families and hospitals, but magical thinking and responses did not disappear with the practice of magic, and all of us at times act on primitive assumptions of which we are totally unaware. The notion that a problem will disappear if you put someone in a hospital is an excellent example of magical thinking—one of the most pervasive in our society.

References

1. Bockoven, J. S.: Observations.
2. Guthrie, W. K. C. *Orpheus and Greek Religion.* London: Methuen, 1952, 148-150.
3. Patai, R. *Sex and Family in the Bible and the Middle East.* New York: Doubleday Dolphin Books, 1959, 229-233.
4. Simmons, L. *The Role of the Aged in Primitive Society.* New Haven: Yale U. Press, 1945.

Young people view old age

18

Robert Kastenbaum and
Nancy Durkee

How young people view old age is of interest because these attitudes are likely to influence their interactions with persons who are elderly, and likely also to influence the individual's own adjustment as he joins the ranks of the aged. This chapter examines views of the aged that have been expressed by young and middle-aged adults, including findings reported by other investigators and data presented here for the first time. Attention will be given first to views of elderly people and then to views of one's own later life. Attitudes of elderly people toward old age are considered in the following chapter.

Procedure

Six samples of young adults participated in the new studies to be summarized here. For ease of later reference, these samples and the data-gathering procedures will be presented below.

The subjects. The groups will be identified alphabetically, proceeding from youngest to oldest. Basic characteristics of the subjects are given in Table 1. Group A, the youngest, was comprised of 123 junior and senior high school students (68 females, 55 males) in Worcester, Massachusetts. Group B consists of 102 adolescent boys from a near-by industrial school for the rehabilitation of juvenile offenders. Group C consisted of 108 junior college students (24 females, 84 males), and Group D included 126 trainees enrolled in a professional school of embalming (4 females, 122 males). Group E was comprised of 53 graduate nurses (all females) pursuing additional studies at Boston University. Group F consisted of 85 residents of New York City interviewed on the streets in downtown Manhattan (46 females, 39 males); this group includes 12 persons over the age of 55 whose responses are given separate consideration. The basic sample reported here consists of 585 persons ranging in age from 13 to 55.

The authors wish to express their appreciation to Douglas Borlund, David Calverly, Pamela Frasier, Richard Kiely, Barbara Makin, and Isabel Patterson for their cooperation in gathering some of the data reported here.

The techniques. Most of the findings reported here were obtained through the use of two procedures, "Important Years" (IY), and the "Age-Appropriate Attitudes Technique, Part 1: Six Futures" (AAAT).

The IY procedure requests the subject to select from the total lifespan—past, present, and future—the three years which he considers most important. Respondents are encouraged to use their own lifespan as the frame of reference. It is entirely up to each subject to determine what constitutes an especially "important" year. The subject is also asked to indicate the reason for each choice. The most significant quantitative aspects of the IY are as follow: *range* of the life span between first and last important years, inclusive (e.g., a person who selects "5" as the earliest important year and "21" as the oldest important year has a range of 17 years); *future extension,* the number of years, if any, by which the oldest year given exceeds the chronological age of the subject; *past extension,* the number of years, if any, by which the earliest important year antedates the chronologic age of the subject; *absolute ages* selected for first and last important years (this analysis does not consider the subject's own chronologic age). The reasons for selecting each of the important years are analyzed on a qualitative basis. Particular attention is given to affective tone (positive or negative) and to temporal directionality (e.g., specifying a past year for the influence it has upon the future).

The AAAT presents a set of six brief character sketches (Table 2). Each of the fictitious individuals described has a different outlook on futurity. The characters and the outlooks represented are: Harry, the Null Future; Phil, the Uncertain Future; Charlie, the Exuberant Future; Grant, the Satiated Present; Ted, the Beloved Past; and Sam, the Despised Past. The subject's task consists of 1) estimating the most

Table 1. Experimental sample

		Male	Female	Total	Age range	Mean age
Group A	High school students	55	68	123	13-18	15.3
B	Juvenile offenders	102	0	102	14-18	16.4
C	Junior college students	84	24	108	18-28	20.9
D	Professional trainees	122	4	126	17-53	22.4
E	Graduate nurses	0	53	53	21-47	27.8
F	New Yorkers	39	46	85	13-77	42.0

likely age of each character, 2) explaining the basis for the answer, and 3) reporting what the subject would say to each character after becoming familiar with his outlook. At the conclusion of the task the subject is requested to state which of the characters' point of view is closest to his own outlook. The AAAT lends itself both to quantitative and qualitative analyses. Taking the age named as "best guess" for each personality sketch, for example, it is possible to rank-order the six futures sequentially. With this arrangement one can approach the question: what is regarded as the normal succession of outlooks as the person proceeds along his life line? The possibility that certain attitudes are considered appropriate to certain age-ranges can be explored, and the respondent's own chronologic age related to his assignment or age-appropriate attitudes. Qualitative points of analysis include the subject's choice of a character with whom to identify, and interpretation of the comments he would make to each character—with special attention to what he would, in effect, be saying to himself.

Space limitations have required a selective rather than a comprehensive report of the findings yielded by these procedures. Other procedures were also employed, and other samples studied. Subsequent reports will consider the material neglected here.

Table 2. AAAT — Part 1: Six futures

Sketch	Outlook
Harry is feeling very blue. He has decided that the future holds nothing for him.	The Null Future
Phil wonders if he is really getting any place. He does not know whether he should be hopeful or pessimistic about his future.	The Uncertain Future
Charlie is feeling great. He feels his life is just beginning, that nothing can stop him.	The Exuberant Future
Grant feels that he has everything he wants. He is completely satisfied with his life, and desires nothing more.	The Satiated Present
Ted does not like new things. He prefers the old way of doing things, feeling that things are not as good as they used to be.	The Beloved Past
Sam has no use for the old way of doing things. He prefers everything new, believing that things are getting to be much better than they used to be.	The Despised Past

Attitudes toward elderly people
Much of the empirical work conducted in this problem area points toward two general conclusions: 1) old age is regarded as a period of life that is markedly different from the earlier years, and 2) the differences are seen as predominantly, but not entirely, negative. For example, Golde and Kogan, using a sentence completion form, demonstrated that college students' perceptions of elderly people are different from their perceptions of people in general (3). In a later investigation, Kogan and Shelton found that a second sample of undergraduates gave a pattern of sentence completion responses ". . . sufficiently similar to the ethnic prejudice case as to warrant discussion in a minority-group context." (8, p. 15). Although the students did not express harsh sentiments toward elderly persons and did, in fact, express some highly positive sentiments, the general impression was that of a bias against the "quasi-minority group" comprised of the aged. "Younger individuals, perceiving that older persons resent them, attempt to avoid interpersonal contact and partially justify such avoidance by suggesting that older individuals are really more interested in their families and are preoccupied with death. The belief that 'old people' are in need of assistance has a patronizing flavor in the present context, but such a belief may serve to assuage guilt feelings deriving from neglect of old people's emotional requirements" (8, pp. 13-14).

Another college sample was investigated by Calhoun and Gottesman who used a semantic differential form consisting of 25 bipolar adjective pairs with 5 scale point separations between them (2). The subjects were asked to describe four concepts: "myself," "my ideal self," "young people," and "old people." The experimenters defined "young" as "in the 20's," and "old" as 65 to 75. Old people were described as qualitatively different from young people, and in more negative terms. The authors conclude that ". . . there is compelling reason to believe . . . that a stereotype of old age as a period of physical, social, and emotional decline is commonly held in this culture." (2, p. 5). Old people were seen most negatively in regard to their energy, health, activity, strength, attractiveness, happiness, popularity, tempo of behavior and social desirability. On a more positive note, they were regarded as "wise" and "kind." The Kogan-Shelton and Calhoun-Gottesman studies included comparisons between attitudes of young adults and those of elderly adults; these comparisons will be discussed in the following chapter.

Negative stereotypes of old age were found to be prevalent in a group of 147 graduate students despite their acquaintance with psychology (11), and similar results were obtained in a follow-up study by the same investigators, Tuckman and Lorge, when the questions were approached with a slightly different methodology (12).

The generally unfavorable picture of old age that other investigators have reported to be common among young adults becomes complicated somewhat when we consider the present data, particularly AAAT responses concerning the temporal orientation that is attributed to elderly people.

It is worth keeping in mind that the AAAT does not confront the subject with the task of making a direct statement about old age. Rather, attitudes toward old age are expressed in a semi-direct manner, and within a context that does not single out any one particular period of life. The respondent is not called upon to deliberate upon which attitude is most likely to be found among elderly people, but such a decision emerges from his set of responses. Furthermore, the subject is not aware that he will be asked to select one of the characters as his "representative" until he has already dealt with them all. This procedure thus provides an approach that is intermediate between requesting a person to make a self-conscious statement about elderly people, and using a more ambiguous, projective-type technique that might elicit underlying attitudes but be difficult to relate to specific problems. A full understanding of attitudes toward elderly people probably requires the use of a wide-ranging set of techniques, including direct, semi-direct, and indirect modes of acquiring information.

The AAAT was administered to experimental samples B, C, D, and E, a total of 389 respondents. The responses indicate that young adults have a strong tendency to regard elderly people as bound to the past. Moreover, this attributed past-boundedness was considered to be quite alien to the respondent's own outlook. Two quantitative points illustrate this situation rather clearly: 1) in each of the samples, Ted (The Beloved Past) was the character *most* frequently assigned the oldest age, and 2) in each sample, Ted was also the character *least* frequently selected as representing the respondent's own outlook. This latter point is underscored by the fact that only one of the almost four hundred subjects accepted Ted as a kindred spirit.

Examination of what the young adults "replied" to Ted further illuminates their attitudes. Subjects were encouraged to engage in imaginary conversations with each of the characters, as though Harry, Charlie, Phil and the rest had just conveyed their sentiments to the present company, and now were more or less waiting for a response. Here we will consider comments made to Ted by all the subjects who assigned him the oldest age.

Comments to Ted were classified into four independent categories (Table 3). Category I included responses which indicated acceptance of Ted's views with no disparagement or effort to change him. Category II included responses indicating disapproval of Ted's past-bound orientation, but accompanied by persuasive, warning, or encouraging comments intended to induce the old man to adjust on the terms required by today's society. Category III also included responses which expressed disapproval of Ted's attitude, but these responses were accompanied by statements of outright rejection and/or exasperation. Responses in Category III pronounced that Ted was "useless," "washed up," and "out of it." Category IV included responses of a neutral character, conversational ploys that did not express clear-cut approval or disapproval of Ted's past-orientation, but served the purpose of making social responses to Ted.

The finding that elderly people tend to be regarded as past-oriented by young people who do not regard themselves as sharing this orientation merely confirms the obvious expectation. The comments made to Ted, however, indicate that the attitudes are a good deal more complex. If a positive attitude is defined as one which accepts the elderly person on his own terms, then it may be a very small percentage of young adults (2.2% in the combined samples here) who are favorably disposed to the aged. If, however, we add those who seem to have a good will toward the elderly, but impose rather stringent conditions for their acceptance as full-fledged members of society, then the percentage is increased markedly (by 49.33%). Combining Categories I and II would have the effect of suggesting that a little over half of the young adults in this sample are favorably disposed toward elderly adults. Yet one might seriously question this step. It might be

Table 3. AAAT: Comments to "Old Ted"

		I		II		III		IV	
		f	%	f	%	f	%	f	%
Group B	75	1	1.3	33	44.0	30	40.0	11	14.7
C	82	1	1.2	52	63.4	24	29.3	5	6.1
D	41	0	0.0	19	46.3	8	19.5	14	34.2
E	29	3	10.3	8	27.6	3	10.4	15	51.7
B, C, D, E	227	5	2.2	112	49.3	65	28.6	45	19.9

I. Unqualified acceptance

II. Disapproval – effort to change

III. Disapproval – rejection

IV. Neutral

argued that if the older person is not accepted *as he is* (or as he is thought to be), then he is not truly being regarded in a favorable light. If the older person is regarded as non-acceptable, this perception indicates a fundamentally disapproving attitude—whether or not the negative appraisal is accompanied by an attempt to change the older person. Following from this line of reasoning, then, one might combine Categories II and III instead of I and II. The conclusion would now be that about 78% of the young adults have a negative attitude toward elderly people who are thought to be past-oriented. Thus, we may conclude either that young people have a slight tendency to regard elderly people in a favorable light (Categories I and II combined), or a definite tendency to regard them unfavorably (Categories II and III).

It is worth noting that one-fifth of the total sample responded to Ted in a conversational manner that was neither supportive nor critical of his past-orientation (Category IV: 19.9%). The percentage of neutral comments was particularly high for the professional trainees (Group C) and graduate nurses (Group D), who not only were a little older than the other groups included here, but also may have been inclined to filter their responses through their professional roles. The nurses in particular appeared to be smoothly professional in their replies to Ted, seeking to establish a "working relationship" with him that should not be jeopardized by obvious value judgments. One cannot dismiss the possibility that many of the nurses did entertain the goal of redirecting the older person, but had decided that the way to begin was by establishing contact in a matter-of-fact, peaceable manner. Also worth noting is the age trend in respect to purely negative, rejecting attitudes. The percentage of Category III responses declines steadily as we move from Group A through Group E.

Definite conclusions at this point would seem to be premature. Perhaps it is sufficient to note that attitudes young adults have toward elderly adults are probably much more complex than can be determined by the use of any single data-gathering technique. When information obtained from the AAAT is added to questionnaire, sentence completion, and semantic differential data the overall picture is altered. Up to a point, the present data seem to support the impression gained from previous research, i.e., approximately four-fifths of the sample was unfavorably disposed toward Ted's past-orientation. This consensual attitude, however, fragments into decidedly different action-tendencies—while some of the young adults with a negative attitude would abandon the older person, having nothing more to do with him, others, in fact the majority, would exert varying amounts of persuasion and effort to bring the older person around to their own point of view. Expression of a negative attitude thus is not invariably associated with an inclination to withdraw from contact with elderly persons, and studies which are limited to expression of attitude without further indication of action-tendency should be evaluated with this consideration in mind.

Attitudes toward later life

The studies already described were concerned with attitudes that young people hold toward elderly people. Consideration will now be given to attitudes toward the later years of one's own life.

When young people are asked to rate their entire life-span in terms of the "happiest" period or some similar choice, the later years tend to be regarded as promising little satisfaction. Rather similar results have been found by Tuckman and Lorge (13), Kuhlen (9) and Kastenbaum (4). The latter study also analyzed a variety of cognitive productions to reveal the extent and nature of temporal orientation, yielding additional findings and hypotheses. Three general conclusions are relevant here:

"1. The adolescent lives in an intense present; 'now' is so real to him that both past and future seem pallid by comparison. Everything that is important and valuable in life lies either in the immediate life situation or in the rather close future.

"2. Extremely little explicit structuring is given to the remote future by most of the adolescents tested. Those attitudes toward the distal region of the subjective life line that do become manifest are of a distinctly negative character. Most of these 15, 16 and 17 year olds regard their remote time fields as risky, unpleasant and devoid of significant positive values.

"3. More explicit structuring is given to the past than to the remote future, suggesting a greater place for the past in conscious awareness. Curiously, however, the past time fields which can be assessed at a surface level of functioning bear a remarkable similarity to the remote-future time fields which do not lend themselves to such direct observation. The past, too, is seen as a risky, unpleasant place. It is also a vague, confusing place where the adolescent is none too sure of his personal identity." (4, p. 104).

These considerations are incorporated into the hypothesis of a "boomerang effect." It is suggested that the adolescent "remembers himself as confused, inept, undifferentiated, bound to the wishes of others." He attempts to throw away his past but, instead, unconsciously attributes "all the dysphoric and terrifying feelings that have made his notion of the past unacceptable to him" to the remote future which "stands as an unstructured 'temporal ink blot' . . . ready to receive those feelings the adolescent is trying to dislodge from consciousness." (4, p. 111).

The vague and negative outlook toward one's later years of life is thought to be strongly influenced by society's emphasis upon values associated with youth, and its reluctance to contemplate death in a straightforward manner. "The adolescent who develops in this cultural atmosphere is likely to pattern his own subjective life line along the same model, so that his later years contain little to which he can look forward. Because the future is realistically ambiguous, it can to a large measure be shaped by the wishes and fears the individual projects forward; the expectation selects and prepares future experiences. The wheel comes full circle as the behavior of the once-adolescent, now-aging individual influences the next generation in the development of its attitudes toward later life and death." (4, p. 112).

How far ahead a person thinks can be assessed in many ways. Because we have found similar results with a variety of techniques, it may be sufficient here to consider information obtained by one of the simplest procedures, (IY).

At all ages sampled here, there were some people who did not project beyond their present age, i.e., whose "important years" were exclusively in the past and/or present. The percentage of those who report *no* future orientation in this sense increases with age, but the majority of respondents display a future orientation until approximately the mid-point of life. Around the age of 40 a reversal occurs. As can be seen in Table 4, two-thirds of the subjects in the age group 35-39 cited at least one important year in the future, while only about one-third of those in the age group 40-44 did so. That this shift is no "fluke" becomes clear when we note that the reversal not only maintains itself throughout the succeeding age groups, but continues consistently in the direction first revealed around age 40. The percentage of exclusive past orientation continues to increase to age 55, a point at which the percentage of future orientation in the present samples dropped to zero. Included in Table 4 are the 12 over-55 subjects from Sample F, and 49 Cushing Hospital patients whose other responses are considered in the following chapter. None of these 61 men and women cited their present age or any year in the future as an important year.

These findings seem to support and extend the studies summarized above. Unfavorable attitudes toward the later years of life would seem to be associated with a disinclination to *think* ahead to the later years. The present findings are also relevant to the question of whether or not people become "bound to the past" as they age. Recent studies indicate there are some ways in which elderly people do *not* live exclusively in the past. Perhaps one of the frameworks in which people do tend to be absorbed by "pastness" is the framework of one's total life span, as contrasted with a shorter time span, e.g., "tomorrow" and "yesterday" (10), or with the use of temporal categories in the cognitive organization of experience (6).

Data obtained with the IY also suggest that there is a tendency to expand the range of important years as one proceeds from adolescence

Table 4. Important years: Frequency of future projections by age groups

Age groupings	N	Yes f	%	No f	%
13-14	49	47	95.9	2	4.1
15-19	221	196	88.7	25	11.3
20-24	79	63	79.7	16	20.3
25-29	19	12	63.2	7	36.8
30-34	14	10	71.4	4	28.6
35-39	6	4	66.6	2	33.4
40-44	13	5	38.5	8	61.5
45-49	9	3	33.4	6	66.6
50-54	10	1	10.0	9	90.0
55-59	3	0	0	3	100.0
60-64	1	0	0	1	100.0
65-69	(4 + 3*) 7	0	0	4	100.0
70-74	(2 + 10*) 12	0	0	12	100.0
75-79	10	0	0	10	100.0
80-84	18	0	0	18	100.0
85-89	8	0	0	8	100.0

*The added numbers in these groupings and all cases in the last 3 groupings represent Cushing Hospital patients.

Table 5. Important years: Range

	Mean 1st year	3rd year	Range of years
Group A (123)	12.9	34.8	22.4
B (102)	12.4	25.0	13.6
D (63)	12.1	46.2	35.3
E (53)	10.9	38.7	29.3
F (73)	10.4	40.6	30.5

to adulthood (Table 5). It might be said that one's personal realm of affectively structured time enlarges with maturation and experience. Subjects in the youngest sample (Group A) had a mean range of 22.4 years, while the three adult groups (D, E, F) had mean ranges of 35.3, 29.3, and 30.5. The juvenile offenders (Group B) showed the most compressed range (13.6 years), considerably smaller than the slightly younger group of non-delinquent adolescents. Subjects in Group B also had the most limited extension into the future, if we assess future extension in terms of the age cited for the third or oldest important year. These findings support earlier research which indicated that juvenile offenders have a more limited future outlook than do their non-delinquent peers (1).

Inspection of Table 5 suggests several hypotheses concerning the development of past and future orientation over the life span. These hypotheses must be regarded as highly tentative, considering the limited scope of the findings reported here and particularly the drawbacks of a cross-sectional approach. One might cautiously frame the hypothesis that early in adult life there is the formation of a fairly stable notion concerning how much of the total life span one will take into account as being of prime significance. The present data suggest that this figure is in the vicinity of 30 years. But it has already been observed that the tendency to project important years into the future diminishes over the last half of the life span, with a marked shift occurring around age 40. If the range does remain fairly stable, but futurity becomes increasingly foreshortened, then it would appear that stability of the range must be achieved by a compensatory lengthening of extension back to the past. That such a process might be operating is suggested by the slight but regular decline with age in the mean *first* year (Table 5).

The most relevant aspect of these considerations to the present problem concerns the early onset of a tendency to blank out the later years of life. The present study and two previous investigations (4,5) indicate that adolescents in general do not think far ahead (which is not to say that they are not *concerned* about or *oriented toward* the future). The information summarized in Table 5 suggests that from adolescence to adulthood there is an increase in future extension (see mean range of *third* year, Table 5). Concurrently there is an expansion of the subjective range of important years. As previously noted, once this range has been expanded early in adult life, it tends to remain stable.

It is conceivable that a person would always maintain a sort of "psychological center," a subjective location of himself somewhere between the extremes of personal past and personal future. As the person grows older, he would either lengthen his range to "give himself room" for future experiences, or would shift the entire range upward.

Were this the case, then the individual would approach his view of later life in gradual stages, and not be taken by surprise when phenomena of aging emerge without prior announcement. It would be as though one were standing on the bow of a ship, and were equipped with a telescope. One would always be seeing a finite distance ahead. "Old age" would come into sight not because one had obtained a more powerful instrument, but because one's own motion had brought him within the effective range of contemplating his later years.

This fantasy has been presented for the purpose of emphasizing the fact that all the present data go in the opposite direction. Rather early in life people start looking backward, and do not extend the subjective range of important years. One then runs the risk of ramming into "old age" as though it were an uncharted reef (e.g., 7). Furthermore, lack of contemplation of one's own later years would seem to diminish the capacity for empathic identification with persons who are already advanced in years.

Summary

Attitudes of young people toward old age have been explored rather sketchily by summarizing previous research and reporting a few new empirical observations. It has been seen that there is some evidence indicating a predominantly negative appraisal of older people, and also a tendency for young adults not to take the later years of their own lives into consideration. Several hypotheses have been suggested to aid in the interpretation of these findings and in subsequent research.

One of the most interesting problems has not been considered up to this point: the relationship between attitudes of young adults toward old age, and what elderly adults themselves have to say. This comparison will be made in the last section of the following chapter.

References

1. Barndt, R. J., and Johnson, D. M. Time orientation in delinquents. *J. Abnorm. Soc. Psychol.*, 1955, *51*, 589-592.
2. Calhoun, M. K., and Gottesman, L. E. Stereotypes of old age in two samples. Division of Gerontology, University of Michigan (mimeo).
3. Golde, P., and Kogan, N. A sentence completion procedure for assessing attitudes toward old people. *J. Geront.*, 1959, *14*, 356-360.
4. Kastenbaum, R. Time and death in adolescence. In H. Feifel (ed.), *The Meaning of Death*. New York: McGraw-Hill, 1959, 99-113.
5. Kastenbaum, R. The dimensions of future time perspective, an experimental analysis. *J. Gen. Psychol.*, 1961, *65*, 203-218.
6. Kastenbaum, R. Cognitive and personal futurity in later life. *J. Indiv. Psychol.*, 1963, *19*, 216-222.

7. Kastenbaum, R. The crisis of explanation. In this volume.
8. Kogan, N., and Shelton, F. C. Beliefs about "old people": A comparative study of older and younger samples. *J. Genet. Psychol.,* 1962, *100,* 93-111.
9. Kuhlen, R. G. Age trends in adjustment during the adult years as reflected in happiness ratings. *Am. Psychol.,* 1948, *3,* 307.
10. Rosenfelt, R. H., Kastenbaum, R., and Slater, P. E. Patterns of short-range time orientation in geriatric patients. In this volume.
11. Tuckman, J., and Lorge, I. Attitudes toward old people. *J. Soc. Psychol.,* 1953, *37,* 249-260.
12. Tuckman, J., and Lorge, I. The effect of changed directions on the attitudes about old people and the older worker. *Educ. and Psychol. Measuremt.,* 1953, *13,* 607-613.
13. Tuckman, J., and Lorge, I. Perceptual stereotypes about life adjustments. *J. Soc. Psychol.,* 1956, *43,* 239-245.

19

Elderly people view old age

Robert Kastenbaum and
Nancy Durkee

What young and middle-aged people have to say about old age is important because they constitute the largest part of the society in which elderly people live, and because they themselves are candidates for advanced age. What scientists and other trained observers have to say about old age is also important because they presumably have a perspective that promotes analytic and objective evaluation. Yet it is what elderly people themselves have to say about old age that is most relevant, and perhaps most instructive.

Procedure
This chapter is organized around some of the questions that have been put to elderly persons concerning their view of old age. Preference has been given to topics that appear most suitable as an introduction to this area of inquiry.

Findings reported by other investigators are summarized and discussed in connection with each set of questions. New data are also presented. For ease of later discussion, the nature of the subject population and the techniques involved in acquiring this information will be summarized at this point.

The subjects. Studies were made of 49 patients in residence at Cushing Hospital. The sample includes 29 females and 20 males, with a mean age of exactly 80 years. The ratio of females to males and the mean age were both highly representative of the total hospital population at the time of testing. It appears justifiable to regard this set of subjects as a fair sample of the full range of elderly individuals who come to be institutionalized for medical, custodial, rehabilitative and psychosocial reasons at a public facility.

The techniques. Two of the techniques used to obtain information concerning attitudes toward old age in this sample were also used with

Collection of the data reported here was made possible by USPHS research grant MHO-4818.

young adults: "The Age-Appropriate Attitude Technique, Part 1: Six Futures"; and "Important Years." The AAAT presents brief biographical sketches of six persons, each of whom manifests a distinct attitude toward past-present-future. The subject is asked to estimate the most likely age of each character, explain the basis of his decision, offer comments to each character, and select the character whose attitude is most like his own. The IY procedure requests the subject to specify the "three most important years" of life, whether past, present, or future, and share the reasons for his selections.

Analyses reported here also include items excerpted from three procedures not used with the younger populations. These procedures include a research interview format, and two techniques known as "Changes-with-Age" and "Past Futures." The research interview furnishes mental status information, while the other procedures provide information about how the subject presently interprets his situation as an elderly person, and how he regarded "old age" when he was younger. The specific items will be presented in connection with the relevant data.

"Old" or "not old"?

There are some reasons to bemoan the shifting, contradictory, ambiguous uses of the term, "old age." Yet the protean character of this term adds to its value in assessing attitudes toward aging. If there is no single, dominant way in which "old age" is to be defined at present, then there is something to be learned from the particular way in which an individual interprets the term. More specifically, it seems worth determining whether or not elderly persons classify themselves as "old," and what factors are associated with this opinion.

Let us first consider what findings have already been reported in the gerontological literature. Perlin and Butler recently carried out intensive studies of 47 healthy volunteers (mean age: 71). More than a third of these elderly men classified themselves as not old (21). We will return to consider this study in more detail.

Tuckman and Lorge have contributed several investigations concerned with various aspects of self-concept and aging. Most relevant here is their finding that within a population of 99 elderly persons (mean age: 74), "except for the 80's and older with its bare majority classifying themselves as old, the 60's and 70's classify themselves primarily as middle-aged and young rather than old" (28, p. 420). In this same study, three samples of younger adults overwhelmingly classified themselves as not old, e.g., from a total subject population of 1032 individuals, only one person below the age of 60 classified himself as old.

Zola queried 219 members (100 men and 119 women) of that unique organization, the Age Center of New England (30). One-fifth of these volunteer subjects (mean age: 68.6) considered themselves to be old (20% of the men and 21% of the women). Two other studies also have indicated that there is no overwhelming tendency for elderly people to classify themselves as old. Kutner *et al.* found that only 42% of their 500 subjects over 60 years of age classified themselves as old or elderly (17). Approximately half of the 300 subjects over 70 years of age queried by Phillips identified themselves as middle-aged rather than old (22).

Our findings support the general trend noted in all the preceding studies, namely that somewhere between 30%-80% of persons in the retirement range do *not* consider themselves to be old. The present sample of institutionalized elderly persons falls in approximately the middle of the range noted above: 24 subjects classified themselves as old, while 25 classified themselves as not old. Two characteristics of the present sample set them somewhat apart from the subjects studied by the other investigators: 1) our subjects were institutionalized, and 2) they had a higher mean age than any of the other groups. Very generally then, it appears that many persons in their later years of life, whether living independently or institutionalized, whether barely across today's official "disengagement age" or well into their eighth decade or beyond, do not regard themselves as "old."

Correlates of self-classification

The results that have been summarized up to this point have some interest in themselves, but are of more significance in setting the stage for further inquiry. Since some elderly persons consider themselves to be old but many do not, it is appropriate to explore the differential correlates of this self-classification. In its simplest form the question might be put this way: Is it "good" for an elderly person to consider himself as old, or does the wise man "think young"?

Perlin and Butler gave particular attention to the psychiatric aspects of adjustment to aging in their study previously cited (21). They noted that individuals who declined to classify themselves as old tended to have psychiatric diagnoses. Yet a "hypomanic denial of the aging 'role' " in some cases was related to high morale and good adjustment. Perlin and Butler present these observations within the context of an "identity crisis" interpretation of problems encountered by the aged. "Maintenance of a functional sense of identity seemed to be crucial to successful adaptation. For most subjects, finding oneself old was a normative crisis, not an affliction. In 13 subjects experiencing an age-crisis as an affliction, one or more features of identity often substituted for the whole of identity. An apparent alternative to the shattering of functional identity was the acceptance of the stereotyped identity of an aged person." (21, p. 188-189) .

This line of reasoning is in accord with interpretations suggested elsewhere by one of the present authors, and it serves to complicate tremendously the simple question above, "old" or "not old"? (11,12). It would appear that those who declare themselves not to be old do so because of an inability to accept the implications of the age-appropriate role. However, he who "whistles in the dark" in this case seems to have bolstered his spirits sufficiently to achieve what impresses knowledgeable observers as good adjustment. Moreover, Perlin and Butler suggested, in the previously quoted passage, that to *accept* the identity of being an aged person can also have primarily a defensive function. Either choice, then, might be determined primarily by a need to protect one's jeopardized identity.

Correlates of self-classification can be explored further with data obtained from the Cushing Hospital sample. Most of the patients who made an "old"/"not old" decision were tested with the procedures described earlier. Comparison of "old" patients with those who classified themselves as "not old" disclosed three points of difference:

1. There was a tendency for patients who judged themselves as "old" to be better oriented than those who judged themselves "not old."

It had been found from prior analyses that a scale composed of 3 items (knowledge of date, knowledge of age, and interviewer's rating of patient's general contact) behaved statistically almost as well as the larger set of mental status items included in the research interview. Each item was rated 0, 1, or 2, the 0 score signifying complete lack of orientation, and the 2 score signifying perfect orientation. For the 3-item scale then, the lowest possible score was 0, the highest, 6. Patients with scores of 0 to 1 and those with scores of 5 or 6 were distributed asymmetrically between the "old" and "not old" groups, statistical test (Fischer's Exact Test) indicating that the difference was significant at the .05 level.

2. Those who presently consider themselves to be old had a more extensive outlook on the future when they were young than did those presently considering themselves not to be old.

Five items from the Past Futures procedure were combined to yield a scale. Subjects were asked to recall how the future looked to them when they were about 18 years of age and, again, when they were about 35 years of age. From the "age 18" perspective it was determined how much concern they had for the future at that time, whether or not they projected ahead to life at age 35, and whether or not they projected ahead to life at their present age. Data were treated in dichotomous 0 or 1 fashion for each item, providing a range of Past Future orientation from 0 to 5. Patients classifying themselves as "old" had significantly higher PF scores than those classifying themselves as "not old" ($t = 4.70$, $< .05$).

3. As seen from the perspective of the present, the future was regarded as more negative and uncertain by patients who classified themselves as "old" when compared with those who classified themselves as "not old." The "not olds" tended either to report no future outlook at all, or to state simply that everything would be just fine. It was difficult to avoid the impression that many of the expressions of a positive future outlook were rather shallow and empty statements, substituting for, rather than representing, the results of contemplation.

Replies to the question, "How does the future look to you now?" were categorized as negative and/or uncertain, positive, and "null future." "Old" and "not old" patients differed significantly in the manner stated above (Fischer's Exact test, $< .01$).

It might be added at this point that when all of the participating patients are considered as a group, disregarding the "old/not old" classification, there is a positive relationship between having a future outlook when young and maintaining a future outlook when elderly (Chi square: 7.15 $< .01$).

One obvious explanation of the differences between subjects classifying themselves as "old" and those classifying themselves as "not old" might be that the "old" patients were in fact more advanced in years. This possibility definitely can be ruled out. There was no significant difference in chronological age between the two groups, or any tendency toward a difference. A similar finding was obtained by Zola (30).

Both the Perlin-Butler investigation and the present one seem to point in the same direction. Elderly people who classify themselves as "not old" tend to show more psychiatric symptoms than those who classify themselves as "old." Denial of old age, however, often is accompanied by an apparently optimistic outlook on life. Those who identify themselves as "old" tend to have a broader perspective on life, but a perspective frequently colored by uncertainty and the anticipation of unfavorable developments.

How do these findings relate to our initial question? First of all, no support is given to the sentiment that "thinking young" is associated with good mental health in later life—at least, if by "thinking young" we mean that the elderly individual denies that he is "old." Secondly, it may be that we are confronted with a value decision: is it "better" to deny old age and function within a shallow, limited, but reasonably tolerable framework, or to accept one's status as an "old" person and function within what appears to be a richer and more realistic framework, but highly vulnerable to the stressful implications of "growing old"? This value conflict has been explored elsewhere in relation to the use of psychotropic drugs with the aged (3). Thus, the question under consideration here may be involved in many decisions concerning therapy or management, i.e., should an aging person be encouraged to stay reasonably content by denying the implications of "old age," or should he be encouraged to confront his situation in its full complexity and possibly suffer heightened anxiety and/or depression in so doing?

Studies of individual differences no doubt will advance our understanding of the problems considered above. Reichard, Livson, and Petersen, for example, recently reported a study of 87 elderly men in which much attention was given to individual patterns of adjustment (24). Five life-styles were described three of which were associated with good adjustment in later life, and two with poor adjustment. The most relevant point for the present discussion is that there were "accepters" and "rejectors" among both the well-adjusted and the poorly-adjusted groups. Some of the well-adjusted men felt that ". . . their lives had been rewarding, they were able to grow old without regret for the past or loss in the present. They took old age for granted and made the best of it." Others, more passive by nature, ". . . welcomed the opportunity to be free of responsibility and to indulge their passive needs in old age." However, the third group of well-adjusted men were "unable to face passivity or helplessness in old age," and "warded off their dread of physical decline by keeping active." (24, pp. 170-171). Among the poorly-adjusted were the "angry men" who "blamed others for their disappointments and were unable to reconcile themselves to growing old," but also the "self-haters" whose "growing old underscored their feelings of inadequacy and worthlessness."

Kutner et al. have suggested that among those elderly people who do not classify themselves as aged are some who have distorted judgment, and others who "do not wish to admit defeat." (17, p. 99).

Most of the elderly psychologists participating in Aisenberg's study (2) did not consider themselves to be "old" (70%). From the analyses already performed on the psychologists' questionnaire responses it appears as though additional life-style patterns will have to be recognized in order to understand the meaning of this self-classification, the psychologists being different in many respects from the elderly persons studied by Perlin and Butler, Reichard, Livson, and Peterson, and by the present investigators. Thus, it will be increasingly important to take individual life styles into account in understanding the implications of accepting or rejecting "old age" status. In this connection it should be acknowledged that the concept of life style owes much to the pioneering work of Alfred Adler whose observations on the subject merit continued attention (1).

The threshold to old age

What is the nature of the threshold that one passes over when he enters "old age"? Among elderly psychologists there were interesting differences of opinion between men and women (2). "None of the women in the sample felt that simply reaching a particular age (e.g., 65) made them feel old; but 22% of the men did. Also, approximately 6% of the men but no women thought that the attitude or behavior of others made them feel old." The most common description of when one first began to feel old pertained to the onset of illness or physical handicaps, while others started feeling old at retirement. This information is based entirely upon responses from the minority of psychologists who classified themselves as "old."

Tuckman and Lorge (27) asked 88 elderly persons (45 men and 43 women, mean age: 74.8 years), "In your opinion when does old age begin?" The same question was also asked of (27, p. 483) of three samples of younger adults. "One hundred per cent of Undergraduate Students and 97% of Middle Age consider that old age begins at a specific chronologic age but only 58% of Graduate Students and 51% of Older Age do so." Those who considered old age to begin at a specific chronologic age usually specified the beginning or midpoint of a decade. Respondents in the oldest group most frequently mentioned the most advanced beginning date of "old age" (age 70), while the younger subjects chiefly mentioned ages 60 and 65. Tuckman and Lorge conclude that "Chronologic age is a poor criterion of aging since it fails to take into account the existence of wide differences among individuals and in job requirements. Yet the majority of the respondents, more so for Undergraduates and Middle Age than for Graduate Students and Older Age, believe that a specific chronologic age rather than other criteria of aging determines when old age begins and a worker becomes old.... For respondents who use other criteria of aging, Graduate Students believe that the type of work plays an important part in determining when a worker becomes old while Older Age deny that old age ever begins or that a worker ever becomes old." (27, p. 488).

Giese (cited by Jones and Kaplan, 9, pp. 136-137) found that most of his elderly German subjects thought of their aging chiefly in physical terms. They reported that their first awareness of becoming old was associated with physical symptoms such as a breakdown in the locomotor apparatus, nervous difficulties, sense-organ impairment, deterioration in the skin, hair, etc., increased tendency to fatigue and a greater need for sleep. (It should be noted that "nervous difficulties" may well refer to phenomena that are more appropriately considered as psychological than as physical changes.) Giese found that the realization they are no longer young comes upon them rather suddenly. He also noted that educated persons were more likely to mention mental symptoms (perhaps, that is, to use mental terminology instead of speaking more vaguely of "nervous difficulties"). Jones also found that the subjective perception of aging more frequently was associated with physical than with psychological symptoms, again noting that educated persons more frequently reported mental changes (8).

With the Cushing Hospital sample it is possible to compare the interpretations of those who consider that they have crossed the threshold to old age with those who regard themselves as a step or more away. As may be seen in Table 1, approximately half of each group considered that old age is ushered in by psychosocial factors. Physical factors were the second most commonly noted by both groups, being somewhat more frequent for the "olds" (40.9%) than the "not olds" (33%). Approximately one-tenth of each group cited chronologic age as the main indication.

Although the general distribution is highly similar between these groups, further attention to the content reveals a different "twist" to the psychosocial interpretations. The "old" patients spoke of social dislocations that, as it were, forced old age upon them (e.g., compulsory retirement). The patients who considered themselves not to be old opined that age-mates who indeed were "old" had brought this circumstance upon themselves, (e.g., they were "lazy," or had "given up").

The institutionalized patients studied here therefore turned out to be more psychosocially oriented than any of the other samples, including elderly psychologists! The present sample is the only one whose most common account of crossing the threshold emphasizes psychosocial changes, although it is true that physical reasons are not far behind. It is also of interest to note that only 10% thought that chronologic age *per se* had much to do with being old, while the Tuckman-Lorge study found that 51% of their elderly respondents cited chronologic age as the primary factor.

Possibly different criteria are used by elderly persons to define "old age" depending upon the context in which their judgment is made, i.e., the institutionalized patient compares himself with hundreds of

Table 1. Circumstances associated with entry into old age (40 respondents)

	Self-classification:					
	Old		Not old		Total	
	f	%	f	%	f	%
Physical	9	41	6	33	15	37.5
Psychosocial	11	50	10	56	21	52.5
Chronologic age	2	9.1	2	11	4	10

other persons all of whom are "old" by chronologic definition alone, thus this definition becomes less useful for making differentiations, while the elderly person in the community compares himself with a much broader spectrum of society. In the latter case, physical changes may seem more salient, as they emphasize the widening differences between the aging individual and others in the community.

A methodological consideration is relevant here. It might well be that discrepant results in this area of research derive largely from the temporal factor—attitudes toward "old age" have been changing rapidly during the last few years, and it is likely that self-appraisals related to aging have also been in flux. Thus, the relatively high psychosocial sensitivity of the Cushing Hospital patients may in part stem from the fact that this study was conducted in 1963, while the Tuckman-Lorge study was conducted in 1953. Obviously, there is much to recommend continued sampling of similar populations at regular intervals, if we wish to differentiate between current views of aging and whatever may be relatively constant in the self-appraisals of elderly persons.

Appraisals of "old age" by young and elderly adults

It is now appropriate to consider some points of comparison between the views of "old age" that are held by young and by elderly persons. Findings described in the preceding chapter suggested that young adults tend to have a negative appraisal of older people, and tend not to think ahead to the later years of their own lives. Furthermore, elderly people are regarded as being bound to the past, an orientation shared by very few young adults.

A number of studies indicate that many elderly people also regard the later years of life as a relatively difficult and unrewarding aftermath. Landis, for example, interviewed 450 persons over the age of 65 to obtain retrospective evaluations of happiness over the life span (18). Only 5% of the respondents selected middle or old age as the period of greatest happiness. In a similar study, Kuhlen found that happiness ratings declined after the first two decades of adult life (15). Other studies reporting negative views of later life on the part of elderly people include those conducted by Mason (19), Sward (25), Morgan (20), Bloom (4), Tuckman and Lorge (29) and Calhoun and Gottesman (6). After surveying the findings available about five years ago, Kuhlen judged that ". . . the data seem to suggest that consciously or unconsciously the individual, as he gets older, has a less positive attitude toward himself." (16, p. 871).

More recent investigations suggest that this conclusion might require some revision. The data reported by Aisenberg (2) and by Kogan and Shelton (14) yield the impression that some elderly persons have positive or ambivalent rather than predominantly negative outlooks. It is worth noting that both studies drew upon samples of elderly people who exceed the general population in educational and occupational level and probably also in intellectual level. Perhaps individuals who have put outstanding personal resources to effective use throughout the earlier years of their lives are able both to maintain favorable circumstances in their later years and to arrive at favorable interpretations of their circumstances. Thus, for example, the subjects studied by Kogan and Shelton seemed to be alert, independent, financially secure and actively involved in the social scene. Their objective circumstances supported the positive and ambivalent view of old age that characterized their responses to a special sentence completion test. Yet these people also tended *not* to define themselves as "old," i.e., when they were commenting upon old people they were taking the observer's point of view. This observer orientation toward "old age" indicates that these elderly persons avoid a negative self-appraisal not only through the positive features of their objective situation, but also through their tendency to interpret their situation as being distinct from those who are really old. Kogan and Shelton observed that although their subjects did not show a negative attitude toward old age, they did manifest a concern about being set apart, considered different or rejected. A related study by the same investigators led to the similar conclusion that, "it is a positive picture of old people, although a defensively positive one." (25). The tendency for an elderly person to consider himself in a more positive light than he does elderly people in general was also reported by Calhoun (5).

If it is true that there are major variations in the attitudes that elderly people hold toward old age, then it should be possible to discern some of the factors which predispose toward positive or negative appraisals. As already noted, data from the Aisenberg and Kogan-Shelton studies suggest that higher educational, occupational and perhaps intellectual level favor a positive or at least ambivalent outlook. Two studies by Tuckman and Lorge (28,29), and investigations by Davis (7), and Pollack, *et al* (23) raise further possibilities. These studies collectively suggest that elderly persons who are hospitalized have a more negative view than those who live in the community, and that persons who are making a good adjustment to their circumstances, whatever the circumstances might be, are likely to have a more favorable view.

Patients in the Cushing Hospital sample tended to feel that young people do not understand them very well (71%). Many of the respondents found it difficult to elucidate this feeling. The most common explanation was that young people expect too much from the aged, e.g., expect them to do too much or move too quickly (and, perhaps, to answer too many silly questions!).

This rather vague feeling that young people do not really understand the elderly finds support when the AAAT responses of Cushing Hospital patients are compared with those of the young adults reported in the previous chapter. All samples of young adults agreed that an elderly person is most likely to have a past-bound orientation (i.e., Ted and his "Beloved Past"). However, the AAAT character most frequently selected by the Cushing Hospital patients as representing their own outlook was not Ted—it was his most contrasting peer: Sam, the future man. Elderly people thus attributed to themselves an orientation that prefers futurity and novelty to pastness and familiar routine. It is worth adding that although the plurality of Sam choices was not overwhelming (33%), the percentage is higher than in any of the samples of young adults, none of which predominantly favored Sam.

Here, then, is one of the most striking examples of a misjudgment by younger generations of the attitudes held by the senior generation —or is it? The AAAT assesses attitudes; it does not assess future extension *per se*. It will be recalled from the preceding chapter that none of the Cushing Hospital sample (or, for that matter, any adult over the age of 55) cited a single "important year" that projects beyond the present age of the respondent. This finding does not very closely resemble the future-oriented Sam. A previous study drawing upon a different sample of Cushing Hospital patients (10) also indicates a constriction of personal (but not cognitive) futurity, as does the trend of data from the total study from which the present material has been extracted.

Possibly what has been described is another example of the elderly person's awareness that he is the target of a volley of negative stereotypes, and his resulting compensatory or over-compensatory efforts to make himself look more like the "aggressor" than like the "victim." Again, it might be that some elderly persons are in a transitional psychological state characterized by an attempt to develop the new coping techniques seemingly required for successful adaptation, but techniques which cannot easily be integrated with their long-term habits and viewpoints. Both of these interpretations call attention to dynamic rather than static qualities in the life adjustment of elderly people. Elderly people not only are sensitive to the attitudes of others, but they respond to these attitudes by sometimes rather subtle alterations in their own attitudes and behavior. The most illuminating sort of research has yet to be performed, i.e., studies that would enable us to observe the dynamic interaction between young and elderly adults. Attitudinal studies of the type summarized in this chapter have their value, but tend to yield much too static an impression of the ways in which adults of all ages influence each others' views of later life.

References

1. Adler, A. *The Individual Psychology of Alfred Adler*, ed. by H. Ansbacher and R. Ansbacher. New York: Basic Books, 1956.
2. Aisenberg, R. What happens to old psychologists? In this volume.
3. Aisenberg, R., and Kastenbaum, R. Value problems in geriatric psychopharmacology. Presented at Sixteenth Annual Scientific Meeting of The Gerontological Society, Boston, Mass., Nov. 9, 1963.
4. Bloom, K. L. Age and self concept. *Am. J. Psychiat.*, 1961, *118*, 534-538.
5. Calhoun, M. K. Stereotypes of old age and self-esteem in the aged. Division of Gerontology, University of Michigan (mimeo).
6. Calhoun, M. K., and Gottesman, L. E. Stereotypes of old age in two samples. Division of Gerontology, University of Michigan (mimeo).
7. Davis, R. W. The relationship of social preferability to self concept in an aged population. *J. Geront.*, 1962, *17*, 431-436.
8. Jones, L. W. Personality and age. *Nature*, 1935, *136*, 779-782.
9. Jones, H. E., and Kaplan, O. J. Psychological aspects of mental disorder in later life. In O. J. Kaplan (ed.), *Mental Disorder in Later Life*, 2nd edition. Stanford, Calif.: Stanford U. Press, 1956.
10. Kastenbaum, R. Cognitive and personal futurity in later life. *J. Indiv. Psychol.*, 1963, *19*, 216-222.
11. Kastenbaum, R. Multiple personality in later life—A developmental interpretation. *Gerontologist*. In press.
12. Kastenbaum, R. The crisis of explanation. In this volume.
13. Kastenbaum, R., Slater, P. E., and Aisenberg, R. Toward a conceptual model of geriatric psychopharmacology: An experiment with thioridazine and dextro-amphetamine. Paper presented at Sixteenth Annual Scientific Meeting of The Gerontological Society, Boston, Mass., November 9, 1963.
14. Kogan, N., and Shelton, F. C. Beliefs about "old people": A comparative study of older and younger samples. *J. Genet. Psychol.*, 1962, *100*, 93-111.
15. Kuhlen, R. G. Age trends in adjustment during the adult years as reflected in happiness ratings. *Am. Psychol.*, 1948, *3*, 307.
16. Kuhlen, R. G. Aging and life-adjustment. In J. E. Birren (ed.), *Handbook of Aging and the Individual*. Chicago, Ill.: University of Chicago Press, 1959, 852-900.
17. Kutner, B., et al. *Five Hundred Over Sixty*. New York: Russell Sage Foundation, 1956.
18. Landis, J. T. What is the happiest period in life? *School and Society*, 1942, *55*, 643-645.
19. Mason, E. P. Some correlates of self-adjustments of the aged. *J. Geront.*, 1954, *9*, 324-337.
20. Morgan, C. M. The attitudes and adjustments of recipients of old age assistance in upstate and metropolitan New York. *Arch. Psychol.*, 1937, no. 214.
21. Perlin, S., and Butler, R. N. Psychiatric aspects of adaptation to the aging experience. In *Human Aging: Biological and Behavioral Aspects*. Bethesda, Md.: Public Health Service Publication No. 986, 1962, 143-158.

22. Phillips, B. S., A role theory approach to adjustment in old age. *Am. Sociol. Rev.*, 1957, *22*, 212-217.
23. Pollack, M., *et al.* Perception of self in institutionalized aged subjects. 1. Response patterns to mirror reflection. *J. Geront.*, 1962, *17*, 405-408.
24. Reichard, S., Livson, F., and Petersen, P. G. *Aging and Personality*. New York: Wiley, 1962.
25. Shelton, F. C., and Kogan, N. Images of "old people" and "people" in general and in an older sample. *J. Genet. Psychol.*, 1962, *100*, 3-21.
26. Sward, K. Age and mental ability in superior men. *Am. J. Psychol.*, 1945, *58*, 443-470.
27. Tuckman, J., and Lorge, I. The attitudes of the aged towards the older workers. *J. Geront.*, 1952, *7*, 559-564.
28. Tuckman, J., and Lorge, I. Old people's appraisal of adjustment over the life span. *J. Person.*, 1954, *22*, 417-422.
29. Tuckman, J., and Lorge, I. Classification of the self as young, middle-aged, or old. *Geriatrics*, 1954, *9*, 534-536.
30. Zola, I. K. Feelings about age among older people. *J. Geront.*, 1962, *17*, 65-68.

ON THE ORGANIZATION OF
EXPERIENCE IN LATER LIFE

When we set an alarm clock or circle a date on the calendar, we are making use of external systems in the service of organizing our personal experience. When we awaken precisely at 6:30 A.M. *without* benefit of an alarm, then it is apparent we are using an internal system to achieve the same purpose, although this system is difficult to specify. The operations we employ to organize our experience and the purposes they serve are capable of even greater subtlety without loss of precision—for example, we may feel unaccountably sad on a day that marks the anniversary of a tragic event we no longer think about (and whose date we may even have "forgotten").

The organization of experience is a distinctively psychological process or set of processes about which much remains to be learned. Explorations into the organization of experience in later life are handicapped by the limited knowledge available on this topic in general. Yet there can be no doubt about the significance of this topic in later life, for included here are such problems as coming to final terms with the meaning of one's life and death, determining how one's past and future are to be interpreted, and how best to use one's remaining time and resources. Each of the six chapters in this section explores a somewhat distinct set of problems with a common concern for ways in which people attempt to organize and reorganize the meaning of their lives in their later years.

The life review:
An interpretation of
reminiscence in the aged

20

Robert N. Butler

*They live by memory rather than by hope, for what is left to them
of life is but little compared to the long past. This, again, is the
cause of their loquacity. They are continually talking of the past,
because they enjoy remembering.*—Aristotle, Rhetoric, *367-347, B.C.*
Mem'ry's pointing wand, that calls the past to our exact review.—
Cowper, Task IV, *1784.*
*What makes old age hard to bear is not a failing of one's faculties,
mental and physical, but the burden of one's memories.*—Maugham,
Points of View, *1959.*

The universal occurrence of an inner experience or mental process of
reviewing one's life in older people is postulated. It is proposed that
this process helps account for the increased reminiscence of the aged,
that it contributes to the occurrence of certain late-life disorders, particularly depression, and that it participates in the evolution of such
characteristics as candor, serenity and wisdom among certain of the
aged.

Intimations of the existence of a life review in the aged are found
in psychiatric writings (notably in the emphasis upon reminiscence) as
well as in the literature of various historical periods. The nature,
sources, and manifestations of the life review may be studied in the
course of intensive psychotherapeutic relationships (7).

One of the great difficulties that younger persons (therapists) find in
working with the elderly is that of listening (8). The older person is
often experienced as garrulous and "living in the past." The content
and significance of his garrulousness and reminiscence are often lost or
devalued.

Indeed, the prevailing tendency is to identify reminiscence in the
aged with psychological dysfunction and thus to regard it essentially
as a symptom. In fact, the point is made that reminiscence is frequent
in the mentally disordered and/or institutionalized aged. Of course,
many of our prevailing ideas and "findings" concerning the aged, and

aging, stem primarily from the study of such samples of elderly people. Since the adequately functioning community-resident aged have only recently been systematically studied (4,5,24), and intensive study of the mentally disturbed through psychotherapy has been comparatively rare (7,26), these important sources for data and theory have not been contributory to our understanding of the amount, prevalence, content, function and significance of reminiscence in the aged.

Furthermore, definitions and descriptions of reminiscence—the act, process or fact of recalling the past—indicate discrepant interpretations of its nature and function (11,18,23). Reminiscence is, at times, seen as occurring beyond the older person's control; it happens to him; it is spontaneous, nonpurposive, unselective and unbidden. At other times, reminiscence is viewed as volitional and pleasurable; escapism is hinted. Thus is purposiveness introduced; that is, reminiscence occupies the person, filling the void of his late life. And yet, reminiscence is also considered to obscure the older person's awareness of the realities of the present; further, it is held to be of dubious reliability (although, curiously, "remote memory" is held to be "preserved" longer than "recent memory"). In consequence, reminiscence becomes a pejorative; preoccupation, musing, aimless wandering of the mind are suggested by the term; in a word, reminiscence is fatuous. Occasionally, the constructive and creative aspects of reminiscence are valued and affirmed in the autobiographical accounts of famous men (13), but it must be concluded that the more usual view of reminiscence is a negative one.

The life review*

The life review is conceived of as a naturally-occurring universal mental process characterized by the progressive return to consciousness of past experiences, and particularly, the resurgence of unresolved conflicts; simultaneously, and normally, these revived experiences and conflicts are surveyed and reintegrated. It is assumed that this process is prompted by the realization of approaching dissolution and death, and by the inability to maintain one's sense of personal invulnerability. Although the process is initiated internally by the perception of approaching death, it is further shaped by contemporaneous experiences and its nature and outcome are affected by the lifelong unfolding of character.

> A man of 70 describes a dream: "I dreamt that I had died and my soul was going up and when I did reach the top I saw a great, huge statue—or living man—sitting there—and then a second man came over to me and

---

* The term life review has the disadvantage of suggesting that orderliness is characteristic. In fact, the reminiscences of the old are not necessarily more orderly than life itself and older people may be preoccupied at various times by particular periods of their life and not the whole of it.

asked 'What do you want?' I answered, 'I want to get in here.' So the big man said, 'Let him in.' But then the second man asked, 'What did you do in the other world?' I told him a great deal about myself and was asked, 'What else?' I told of an occasion in which I helped an old lady. 'That's not enough. Take him away.' It was God judging me. I was very afraid and woke up."

The significance of death

It may be through the mechanism of the life review that the biological and psychological fact of death plays a significant role in the psychology and psychopathology of the aged.

A 70-year-old retired, widowed mother came to visit her son from another city six months before referral and showed no inclination to return home. The son was anxious about his depressed, irritable mother. She reluctantly accepted a psychotherapeutic relationship. Frightened and guarded—overly suspicious—she continually described her worthlessness; in fact, she considered herself so unworthy that she was not able to attend church. I had two impressions: 1) that she was wrestling over guilt concerning past wrongs, acts committed, acts avoided; 2) that she was afraid of death and judgment.

In one interview, she suddenly appeared to confirm these impressions, which up to then had not been presented to her. She asked about privileged communication, viz. would I testify in a court of law against her if she were indicted for her past misdeeds, an unlikely event, but one she considered likely. Later in the hour: "I am worried about my granddaughter—that something does not happen to her." (What?) "I wonder if she will be able to face her final examinations and graduation day." (Since her granddaughter is an excellent student, she has little reason to worry.) Still later in the hour: "My doctor referred to these black spots on my head as God's subpoenas," she said. She went on to explain that she has been having difficulties getting her hair done properly and perhaps this is because she is contagious. (She was referring to brown, not black, senile freckles on her scalp.)

The significance of death is often inappropriately minimized, reflecting the human tendency to deny the reality of death; it is also potentially side-stepped by some writers through the use of such psychoanalytic constructs as castration anxiety, which has been held to be the basic fear. Fear of death is conceptualized as merely manifest and not authentic (16).

The life review process not only occurs in the elderly but may be instigated at earlier ages by the expectancy of death; for example, in the fatally ill* or the condemned; it may also be seen in the introspection of those preoccupied by death.

---

* The recent Japanese motion picture, *Ikiru,* describes the salvation of a man whose 30 unproductive years as a governmental bureau chief were interrupted by cancer; his redemption is likely rare for those who are thoughtless in their use of life.

It is commonly held that "life passes in review" in the process of one's dying. Certain cultural and literary associations between the life review and insight to death may be noted. One thinks of the matador during the faena in association with the idea of the "moment of truth." The life review may be Janus-like insofar as it involves both facing death and looking back. In both the Bible and in Greek mythology, in the persons of Lot's wife and Orpheus, respectively, the association of looking death in the face, looking back, and insight may be noted.

The life review is more commonly observed in the aged because of the reality of the nearness of life's termination—and perhaps also by the time provided for self-reflection in old age by retirement, in addition to the removal of work as a customary defensive operation.

To the extent to which the more severe consequences of the life review may bear a quantitative relationship to the extent of actual and/or psychological isolation, one must consider the writings of Cannon (9), Richter (27), Adland (1), Will (31) and others suggesting a relationship between isolation, or loneliness, and death. Fromm-Reichmann wrote about loneliness in her old age (14). "The feeling of unrelatedness is incompatible with life in the human being" writes Will (31).

It is understood, then, that reviewing one's life may be a general response to crises of various types of which death would be but one instance of the category. It is also likely that the fact of approaching death varies as a function of individual personality in the degree to which it is a crisis. Intended here, however, is the explicit hypothesis that the biological fact of approaching death independent of (even if reinforced by) personal and environmental circumstances, prompts the life review.

Manifestations of the life review

The life review is not simply to be viewed as looking back, but looking back as set in motion by looking forward to death and potentially but not always, proceeding towards personality reorganization. Thus, the life review is not synonymous with, but includes overt and silent reminiscence; it is not alone the unbidden return of memories, nor the purposive seeking of them, although both may occur.

The life review and reminiscence may not be voiced but may proceed silently without obvious manifestations. In fact, many elderly persons may be only vaguely aware of the experience (before inquiry) as a function of their defensive structure; but alterations in defensive operations do occur. Speaking broadly, the more intense the unresolved life conflicts, the more work there is to be accomplished towards reintegration. Although this process is active, not static, the content of one's life usually unfolds slowly; since time is required for its accomplishment, the process may not be completed prior to death.

The life review may be first observed in stray and seemingly insignificant thoughts about oneself and one's life history. These thoughts may emerge in brief intermittent spurts or be essentially continuous, and undergo constant reintegration and reorganization at various levels of awareness.

" 'My life' is in the background of my mind much of the time; it cannot be any other way. Thoughts of the past play upon me; sometimes I play with them, encourage and savor them; at other times I dismiss them." So spoke a man of 76 years.

In its mild form, the life review is reflected in increased reminiscence, mild nostalgia, mild regret; in severe form, it is reflected in anxiety, guilt, despair and depression. In the extreme, it may involve the obsessive preoccupation of the older person in his past and may proceed to a state approximating terror and result in suicide. Thus, although it is considered to be a universal and normative process it may have varied (including psychopathological) manifestations and outcomes.

Other clues as to its existence range from reminiscence itself to dreams and thoughts of death and of the past to the curious phenomenon of mirror-gazing.

The frequency with which dreams and nightmares have been reported to occur in the aged is a further intimation of the life review process (24). The dreams of the aged appear to principally concern the past and death. There is a suggestion that the life review is, in fact, a highly visual process.* Imagery of past events and symbolisms of death seem frequent in waking life as well as dreams.

"I was passing my mirror. I noticed how old I was. My appearance, well, it prompted me to think of death—and of my past—what I hadn't done, what I had done wrong."

The apparent commonness of mirror-gazing in the aged appears to be related to the life review. One 80-year-old woman, whose husband had died five years before hospital admission, had been discovered by her family to be berating her mirror image for her past deeds and shaking her fist at herself. It was learned that she was preoccupied by her past deeds and omissions in her personal relationships.

Excerpt from nursing notes: "Patient in depths of gloom this morning—looking too unhappy for anything. Patient looked angry. I asked her with whom? She replied, "Myself." I asked, "What have you done that merits

---

* Other sensory process are also involved. Older people report the revival of the sounds, tastes, smells of early life. ("I can hear the rain against the window of my boyhood room.")

so much self-anger so much of the time?" She replied, "Haven't you ever looked yourself over?" In the course of conversation I suggested she might be too harsh with herself. At this she gave a bitter laugh and stuck out her chin again."

Later in her course, she purposely avoided mirrors.

A periodically confused, 86-year-old patient often stood before the mirror in his hospital room and rhythmically chanted either happily or angrily. He was especially given to angry flare-ups and crying spells over food, money and clothes. When angry he would screech obscenities at his mirror image; but he denied the image was himself (in contrast to the first patient). In his rage he would savagely beat his fist upon a nearby table and so the mirror was covered to protect him. When an observer came up beside him and said, "See, this is me in the mirror and there you are in the mirror," he smiled and said, "That's you in the mirror all right, but that's not me."

Adaptive and constructive manifestations

As the past marches in review, as one sees one's life again, it is surveyed, observed and reflected upon by the ego. Reconsideration of previous experiences and their meanings as well as revisions in their understanding and explanation occurs. Such reorganization of past experience may be a more valid picture and give new and significant meanings to one's life; it may also prepare one for death and mitigate one's fears of death.

Most impressive are the occasions in which the life review may be seen to be creative and to have positive, constructive effects.

A 78-year-old man, optimistic, reflective, and resourceful, and who had had significantly impairing egocentric tendencies, became increasingly more responsive in his relationships to his wife, children and grandchildren. These changes corresponded with his purchase of a tape recorder.* Upon my request, he sent me the tapes he had made, and wrote, "There is the first reel of tape on which I recorded my memory of my life story. To give this some additional interest I am expecting that my children and grandchildren and great-grandchildren will listen to it after I am gone. I pretended that I was telling the story directly to them."

The remarkable Swedish motion picture, *Wild Strawberries,* directed by Ingmar Bergman, provides a beautiful example of the life review in its constructive aspects. The visions and dreams of the protagonist-physician concerning both his past and his death are shown; the non-affectionate and withholding qualities of his life are realized by him; feeling re-enters his life (i.e., love); the doctor changes even as death hovers upon him.

---

* Samuel Beckett's one act play, *Krapp's Last Tape,* dramatically illustrates the life review.

Although it is not presently possible to describe in detail either the life review nor the possibilities for reintegration which are suggested, it seems likely that, in the majority of the elderly, a substantial reorganization of the personality does occur. Indeed, this may help account for the evolution of such qualities as wisdom and serenity, long noted in some aged persons. Although a favorable, constructive and positive end result may be enhanced by favorable environmental circumstances such as comparative freedom from crises and losses, it is more likely that successful reorganization is largely the function of the personality; in particular, those features of the personality that are somewhat vague in meaning, including flexibility, resilience, self-awareness.

In addition to the more impressive constructive aspects of the life review, certain adaptive and defensive aspects may be noted as well. One may note the aged who have illusions of the "good past"; those who fantasy the past rather than the future in the service of avoiding the realities of the present; those who maintain their characteristic detachment from others and themselves. Other than maintaining a status quo of psychological functioning, little else is thereby gained.

Psychopathological manifestations
Constructive outcomes to the life review are not invariable. The reviewer may experience many and varied behavioral and affective states some of which have been indicated earlier, such as severe depressions, states of panic, intense guilt, and constant obsessional rumination and, instead of increasing self-awareness and flexibility, one may find increasing rigidity. The more severe affective and behavioral consequences would appear to occur when the process proceeds in isolation in those who have been deeply affected by increasing contraction of life attachments and notable discontinuities, including such psychosocial disruptions as forced retirement and death of spouse. But while environmental circumstances are important, it is in character, and in its lifelong unfolding, that the unfortunate manifestations of the life review mainly originate.

In a recent series of articles on the aged appearing in a national magazine a 70-year-old woman in a mental hospital is quoted: "Some nights when I can't sleep, I think of the difference between what I'd hoped for when I was young and what I have now and what I am" (21). The most tragic situation is that of the individual whose increasing (but partial) insight leads to a sense of total waste: the horrible insight of never having lived occurring just as one is about to die, or seeing oneself—near the end—as one really is. This situation is similar to the terrifying one described by Henry James in *The Beast in the Jungle* (18).

Because the affective consequences are not all readily attributable to definitive losses, the painful accompaniments of the life review are often difficult for the observer to understand. It is often extremely difficult for the reviewer to communicate his insights because of their unacceptability to him. When these insights are communicated, it is also extremely difficult for the observer to comprehend and to face them. The more tragic manifestations are the most difficult, if at all possible, ones to treat. It is believed that this tragic situation is one pathway toward suicide and one contribution to the increased suicide rate found in old age. One is reminded of the concept of anomie offered by Durkheim in 1897 (10).

One group of individuals (i.e., personalities) who seem to be especially prone to anxiety, despair, depression or the extreme kind of total catastrophe outlined above are those who always tended to avoid the present and to put great emphasis on the future. These individuals made heavy investments in and commitments to the future; in the future would come what they struggled to achieve, and it would be free of that which they have strived to avoid in the present. This places a considerable strain upon old age, which often cannot "deliver;" the wishes cannot be met. This idea is clearly stated in the line of the poet, Adah I. Menken, who wrote, "Where is the promise of my years, once written on my brow?"

Another group of individuals who appear to be especially prone to some of the more severe manifestations and outcomes of the life review are those who have exercised the human capacity to consciously injure others. These individuals, in whom guilt is real, can see no way of reversing the process; they do not imagine forgiveness and redemption. Still another group who appear especially vulnerable to the consequences of the life review may be best described as characterologically arrogant and prideful. This group may merge with the previous group described but may not necessarily have undertaken directly hurtful actions. Their narcissism is probably particularly disturbed by the realization of death.

The following case illustration concerns a person whose life and personality probably involves a merger of all of the above features of predisposition towards psychopathological complications of the life review:

> Mrs. E. G., a 69-year-old married woman, developed a depression six months prior to admission; her depression had been unsuccessfully treated by electroshock, tranquilizers, recommended vacations and suggested moving to a new environment. She was agitated, suspicious, delusional, nihilistic ("This is the end of the world."), self-derogatory, self-accusatory, and she revealed suicidal ideas. She was embittered and hostile, particularly towards her husband with whom she was often combative. She was preoccupied with thoughts of death: she had lived for nearly 20 years across the street from

a hospital morgue; her physician had sensed this to be disturbing to her and had therefore recommended moving. In refusing psychological testing, she stated, "Why should I be uncomfortable during the little time remaining." She had a fear of cancer; she once stated, "You can see your funeral go by but still not believe it." She viewed her situation as futile and increasingly refused to talk in any detail about herself to others, including members of her family.

She was in good physical health although she showed increasing preoccupation with her gastrointestinal tract and, upon admission, symptoms suggesting the possibility of a malignancy required investigation. The various examinations were all negative but the patient became increasingly "fixated" upon her lower bowel.

There was no evidence of organic mental changes, including confusion. She became essentially mute several weeks after her admission; she refused to recognize her psychotherapist as a therapist and refused to cooperate with nursing personnel or the ward administrator. She felt no one "could understand." She assaulted others and herself; she would smash her fist at her head and body until she was a frightful sight to behold—with extensive ecchymoses and hematomas all over her body. She refused to eat and continued to lose weight; she also refused liquids; she rarely slept, day or night. Upon the firm insistence of the administrator that she would be sedated and fed intravenously or by tube, she responded by maintaining a minimum intake of food and fluid. Occasional sedation interrupted her sleeplessness. Otherwise, she did not materially change at that time, and continued to be assaultive towards family members and staff, and to be self-abusive. Because of her 69 years and the remarkable amount of self-destructiveness, she created a considerable amount of anxiety and despair on the part of the staff which eventually was reflected in terms of considerable anger and rage at her. It was exceedingly difficult to break through this kind of bind. Her own threat of death made the situation for the professional staff even more difficult. However, during the course of a year, her general manifest behavior improved to some degree so that she was no longer as self-punitive or assaultive.

On one occasion she communicated to the Director of Psychotherapy her concern with "God's wrath" and at various points gave intimations of her severe and intense sense of guilt about past actions but also about past omissions. Her wish to kill herself seemed quite clear in both direct and indirect statements.

Her past history strongly suggested that she had never realized her potentialities as a person and had never achieved an individual sense of identity.

Her pre-morbid personality was characterized by dependency, indecisiveness, self-centeredness, stubbornness and a lack of generosity, despite the fact that she had stayed home to care for her mother and father after the other siblings had married. An attractive woman, she did not marry until one and one-half years after her mother's death, when she was 47; her husband was then 60. Behind a dignified and passive facade lay a formidable character. She was the quiet but potent center of opposing family forces; her gift was the masterly regulation of these forces. Moreover, she had become increasingly isolated in the three years prior to admission.

In addition to whatever irrational and unconscious feelings of guilt the patient may have experienced, it appeared quite clear that she had in fact done or omitted to do things so that it was important to recognize the reality of her sense of guilt. From those indirect intimations and direct communications, it became apparent that she was indeed engaged in a process of reviewing her past life but that despite the presence of professional people she was unwilling to review her life with them.

Her therapist, writing independently of the author, concluded "all of these changes, especially the more restricted life, might have brought on an opportunity for the patient to inquire about herself; that is, to do some introspective thinking. Such introspection might have led to some thoughts about the uncertainty of her future, as well as some unpleasant traits of her personality, and it is this kind of inquiry that might have led to her depression.*

Discussion

It is evident that there is a considerable need for the intensive detailed study of individual aged persons in order to obtain information concerning their mental functioning, the experience of aging, approaching death and of dying. Behavior may be clarified as subjective experience is revealed. Because of the garrulity, repetitiveness and reminiscence of the aged, it is not always easy for investigators or therapists to listen. For those who will listen, there are rewards. The personal sense and meaning of the life cycle are more clearly unfolded by those who have nearly completed it. The nature of the forces shaping one's life, the effects of life events, the fate of neuroses and character disorders, the denouement of character itself may be studied in the older person. Recognition of the occurrence of a vital process (the life review) may help one to listen, tolerate and understand the aged, and not to treat reminiscence as devitalized and insignificant.

Of course, people of all ages review their past at various times; they look back to comprehend what forces and experiences have shaped their lives. However, it is probably a fair, although by no means definite, measure of mental health to determine that the principal concern of most people is the present. One tends to consider the past most when prompted by current problems and crises. The past also absorbs one in attempts to avoid the realities of the present. A very similar point has been made by others in connection with the sense of identity: one is apt to consider one's identity in the face of life crisis; at other times the question of "who and what I am?" does not arise.

At this time we do not know enough about the mental disorders of the aged and how they may differ from the manifestly similar disorders of younger age groups. We do know that late life is the period when individuals are most likely to develop mental disorders, specifically,

* I am indebted to Dr. Ping-nie Pao for making available this clinical data.

organic disorders and depressions. The question arises as to whether the life review relates to the increased occurrence as well as the character and course of these disorders.

The current nosology involving the so-called exogenous or reactive depressions on the one hand and the endogenous depressions on the other may be clarified and explained in part by the concept of the life review. Endogenous depressions, which operationally are those which are least easily comprehensible in terms of environmental variables, may owe their existence to the inner process of life review. The relationships of, and distinctions between, depression and despair need study. The role of guilt especially requires investigation. Recently, Busse (6) suggested, in connection with "so-called normal elderly persons," that "guilt as a psychodynamic force of importance is infrequently seen in our subjects of elderly persons living in the community. It appears that old people become involved in very little guilt-producing behavior." The latter, sanguine idea seems questionable. Not only do older people appear to maintain the human capacities to undertake hurtful actions and to feel guilt but the past is not lost to them and, indeed, comes back forcibly. It is essential to accept the occurrence of real as well as imagined guilt (3).

The oft-stated impression that the aged have relatively greater impairments of recent than remote memory may nonetheless reflect the avoidance of the present as a consequence of the life review. If indeed memory is subserved by the same neurophysiological mechanisms, why should temporal periods of memory be selectively impaired through organic change?

Other writers have offered constructs pertinent to the aged which probably relate to the life review process. The atrophy of the capacity to project oneself into the future, described by Krapf may be another way of discussing the life review but one in which the stress is upon the absence rather than upon the presence of another, but nonetheless active, process (20). Balint has written of the *Torschlusspanik* (German; literally, the panic at the closing of the gate) which may be related to the state of terror already described in the extreme unfolding of the life review and may also be germane to the "time panic" which has been described by Krapf (2).

Intimations of the life review are found in the literature of psychotherapy; indeed, the danger of the older person reviewing his life has been raised as either a contraindication to, or a basis for modification of technique for, psychotherapy in this age group. Rechtschaffen wrote, "Also to be seriously considered in this regard is the emotional price paid when a patient reviews the failures of his past. It must be exceedingly difficult for a person nearing death to look back upon the bulk of his life as having been neurotic or maladjusted." (26). It is this consideration that led Grotjahn to suggest that it was important for the aged person to integrate his past life experiences as they have been lived, not as they might have been lived (17). It is curious, and probably reflective of our own concerns (counter-transference) that the dangers of reviewing one's life in psychotherapy should be raised; underlying is the implication that truth is dangerous.* The existence of a life review occurring irrespective of the psychotherapeutic situation suggests that the aged particularly need a participant observer, professional or otherwise; and that this alleged danger of psychotherapy should be re-evaluated.

Past and current forms of, or views about, the psychotherapy of the aged might well be evaluated in terms of their relation to the life review; e.g., the "Martin Method" (26) may have been successful because of enthusiasm, interest and support provided in this inspirational catechismic form of therapy but perhaps also, because the client was asked to relate his life history in detail including the reporting of seemingly irrelevant side thoughts or images which might come to mind in order to get at "subconscious complexes."

Goldfarb and his associates, on the other hand, propose a technique based upon illusion; namely, creating the illusion of mastery in the patient (15). Goldfarb's brief therapy is not oriented towards insight, or towards discharge, but rather to amelioration of disturbed behavior.

One might speculate upon what relationships there might be of the onset of the life review to the self-prediction of, and occurrence of, death. One might also speculate that, on the one hand, the intensity of a person's preoccupation with the past might express the wish to distance himself from death by restoring the past in inner experience and fantasy, while, at the same time, a constructive re-evaluation of the past may facilitate a serene and dignified acceptance of death.† There may be a relation to our narcissism or sense of omnipotence in the former, for we can recreate persons and events and bring them back.

The phenomenon of mirror-image gazing is of theoretical and practical interest. It might afford one a diagnostic clue to the existence of the life review. From a theoretical standpoint, the idea of an "aging image" has been considered elsewhere (30). The aged undergo bodily and mental changes marked by rapidity, profundity, and multiplicity. The aged may be unusually excellent experimental subjects for the

---

* In the atmosphere of hospital units for the mentally-disturbed aged are to be found the notions that the aged "can't stand the truth;" must be protected from "bad news;" need to be reassured about their "conditions;" and, curiously, that therapy may prove too disturbing." (1) It may be submitted that the hospital aged, already disturbed, need honesty.

† It is not intended that a "serene and dignified acceptance of death" is necessarily appropriate, noble, or to be valued. Some people die screaming, and rage may be as fitting as dignity.

study and further elucidation of the concepts of self and body image, and of the phenomenon of depersonalization.

Certain schizophrenic and neurotic patients are also known to seek out and gaze at their images in the mirror, talk to their images and reveal many behavioral manifestations. The French psychiatrist, Perrier, has stated flatly that the schizophrenic does not recognize himself in the mirror; he considers that this "symptom shows that the patient has neglected and lost his ego." (25). Schulz has described a patient whose depersonalization ceased upon gazing at herself in the mirror; this 25-year-old woman felt her right arm was not connected to her body; she was reassured about her body integrity by looking in the mirror (28). The experience of a probably paranoid schizophrenic observing himself in mirrors is excellently described in a novel by Simenon (29).

Schulz also reported a neurotic patient who would examine himself in the mirror while shaving and experience the recurring inner questions, "Is that me?", "Who am I?", probably illustrating his concern about his identity. In this connection, one observes that adolescents frequently spend time examining themselves in mirrors; and analysands, especially female, often report mirror-gazing in their childhood, especially during pubescence. Certain narcissistic characters describe disrobing before a mirror and deriving great pleasure in self-observation; occasionally there are reports of actual or wished-for orgastic experiences. The theme of the mirror as revealing character is ancient, ranging from the tale of Narcissus, to that of Snow White, to the use of the mirror as a chastity test in *The Arabian Nights*. The possible experimental employment of the mirror is suggested.

Memory is an ego function whose neurophysiological mechanisms remain hypothetical and inconclusively demonstrated. It serves the sense of self and its continuity; it entertains us; it shames us; it pains us. Memory can tell our origins; it can be explanatory and it can deceive. Presumably it can lend itself towards cure. The recovery of memories, the making of the unconscious conscious, is generally regarded as one of the basic ingredients of the curative process. It is a step in the occurrence of change. We tend to operate with the associations of self-awareness and health on the one hand and lack of awareness and morbidity on the other.

Probably at no other time in life is there as potent a force operating towards self-awareness as the time of old age. Yet, the capacity to change, according to prevailing stereotype, decreases with age. "Learning capacity" falters with time. Indeed, it is fair to say, that the majority of gerontological research throughout the country with respect to the aged is concerned, almost enthusiastically so, with measuring decline in various cognitive, perceptual and psychomotor functions (7).

Comparable attention towards studies of the individual, of wisdom, of the meaning of experience, is not ordinary. It has therefore been of interest to notice the positive, affirmative changes reported by the aged themselves as part of their life experience and to find constructive alterations in character possibly as a consequence of the postulated life review (30).

Actually, the relationships of changed functions to aging *per se*, and to diseases, psychosocial crises and personality remain obscure (22). There is at least reason to observe that personality change can occur all along the life span, and that old age is no exception.

The nature of change warrants study. It is not a happening that can be attributed only to professional effort; nor can changes in behavior outside of professional effort and beyond our understanding be casually categorized as either unreal or "spontaneous" change. We need to study the changes wrought in life itself by experience, eventful and uneventful, by brief instances of entering into relation with another human being, in person or through his image obtained in hearing or reading his efforts.

In the course of the life review, the older person may reveal to his wife, children or other intimates, unknown qualities of his character and unstated actions of his past; in return, he may be told unknown truths. Hidden themes of great vintage may emerge and change the quality of a lifelong relationship; revelations of the past may forge a new intimacy, render a deceit honest; they may sever peculiar bonds and free tongues; or, again, they may sculpture terrifying hatreds out of fluid, fitful antagonisms.

Sameness and change may both be manifestations of the active process of ego identity. Erikson writes ". . . identity formation neither begins nor ends with adolescence: it is a lifelong development largely unconscious to the individual and to his society (12). He also writes that "early development cannot be understood on its own terms alone, and that the earliest stages of childhood cannot be accounted for without a unified theory of the whole span of pre-adulthood." Similarly, it may be argued that the life cycle, early life included, cannot be comprehended without inclusion of the psychology of the aged.

Summary
Considered in this chapter is the existence of a universal normal experience of reviewing one's life, observed to intensify in the aged, and occurring irrespective of environmental conditions; its nature (conscious and unconscious), its basis (the sense of impending death), and its function (reintegration of personality and preparedness for death) are suggested. Its considerable significance in the psychopathology of the aged, as reflected in the effects and the outcomes of the reviewing

process, is postulated. The process of the life review offers one explanation for increased reminiscence, its nature, basis and function; for disturbed behavior, including depression and despair; and for certain traits, behaviors and characteristics that have been observed to occur in the aged such as independence, candor, serenity and wisdom.

References

1. Adland, M. L. Review, case studies, therapy and interpretation of acute exhaustive psychoses. *Psychiat. Quart.*, 1947, 21, 38-69.
2. Balint, M. The psychological problems of growing old. In *Problems in Human Pleasure and Behavior*. London: Hogarth, 1951.
3. Buber, M. Guilt and guilt feelings. *Psychiatry*, 1957, 20, 114-39.
4. Busse, E. W. Psychopathology. In J. E. Birren (ed.), *Handbook of Aging and the Individual*. Chicago: University of Chicago Press, 1959, 390-391.
5. Busse, E. W., Barnes, R. N., and Silverman, A. J. Studies in the processes of aging: 1. Behavioral patterns in the aged and their relationship to adjustment. *Dis. Nerv. System*, 1954, 15, 22-26.
6. Busse, E. W., *et al.* Studies in the process of aging: Factors that influence the psyche of elderly persons. *Amer. J. Psychiat.*, 1954, 110, 897-903.
7. Butler, R. N. Intensive psychotherapy for hospitalized aged. *Geriatrics*, 1960, 15, 644-53.
8. Butler, R. N. Re-awakening interests. *Nursing Homes, J. of the Amer. Nursing Assn.*, 1961, 10, 8-19.
9. Cannon, W. B. "Voodo" death. *Amer. Anthropologist*, 1942, 44, 169-181.
10. Durkheim, E. *Suicide*, translated from *Le Suicide*, 1897, by J. A. Spaulding and G. Simpson. Glencoe, Ill: The Free Press, 1951.
11. English, H. B., and English, A. C. *A Comprehensive Dictionary of Psychological and Psychoanalytical Terms*. New York: Longmans, Green, 1958.
12. Erikson, E. H. The problem of ego identity. In *Identity and the Life Cycle*. Psychological Issues 1: 101-164. New York: International Universities Press, 1959, 113 and 121.
13. *Felix Frankfurter Reminisces:* Recorded in talks with Dr. Harlan B. Phillips. Reynal and Company, 1960.
14. Fromm-Reichmann, F. On Loneliness. In D. M. Bullard (ed.), *Psychoanalysis and Psychotherapy*. Chicago: University of Chicago Press, 1959, 325-336.
15. Goldfarb, A. I. The rationale for psychotherapy with older persons. *Amer. J. Med. Sci.* 1956, 232, 181-185.
16. Grotjahn, M. Psychoanalytic investigation of a 71-year-old man with senile dementia. *Psychoanl. Quart.*, 1940, 9, 80-97.
17. Grotjahn, M. Some analytic observations about the process of growing old. In G. Roheim (ed.), *Psychoanalysis and Social Science*, Vol. 3. New York: International Universities Press, 1951, 301-312.
18. Hinsie, L. E., and Campbell, R. J. *Psychiatric Dictionary*, third edition. New York: Oxford U. Press, 1960.

19. James, H. The Beast in the Jungle. In C. Fadiman (ed.), *The Short Stories of Henry James.* New York: Modern Library, 1945, 548-602.
20. Krapf, E. E. On aging. *Proc. Roy. Soc. Med.* (London), 1953, *46*, 957-964.
21. *Life Magazine.* Old Age: Part IV. Time, Inc., August 3, 1959.
22. National Institute of Mental Health. *Human Aging: Biological and Behavioral Aspects.* Bethesda, Md.: Public Health Service Publication, No. 986, 1962.
23. *The Oxford English Dictionary.* Oxford: Clarendon, 1933.
24. Perlin, S., and Butler, R. N. Psychiatric aspects of adaptation to the aging experience. In *Human Aging: Biological and Behavioral Aspects.* Bethesda, Md.: Public Health Service Publication, No. 986, 1962, 143-158.
25. Perrier, F. The meaning of transference in schizophrenia, translated by M. A. Woodbury. *Acta Psychother* (Basel), 1955, *3* suppl. 266-272.
26. Rechtschaffen, A. Psychotherapy with geriatric patients; A review of the literature. *J. Gerontol.,* 1959, *14,* 73-84.
27. Richter, C. P. On the phenomenon of sudden death in animals and man. *Psychosom. Med.,* 1957, *19,* 191-198.
28. Schulz, D. Personal Communication.
29. Simenon, G. *The Man Who Watched the Trains Go By.* New York: Berkley, 1958.
30. Werner, M. *et al.* Self-perceived changes in community-resident aged: "aging image" and adaptation. *Arch. Gen'l. Psychiat.,* 1961, *4,* 501-508.
31. Will, O. A. Human relatedness and the schizophrenic reaction. *Psychiatry,* 1959, *22,* 205-223.

Delay of gratification
in later life:
An experimental analog

21

Kenneth Pollock and
Robert Kastenbaum

Infants are notorious for their fierce devotion to the present moment. Food and comfort must be provided *now,* a message that is communicated through urgent bursts of declamation. Gradually this impetuous creature will be transformed into a child who has a somewhat greater capacity to "wait for what he wants," and then into an adult who is patient enough to postpone the satisfaction of his own immediate needs and desires in order to meet those of his infant.

This synopsis of ego development omits many important elements because of its brevity. One of the most significant omissions, however, must be attributed not to brevity but to a large gap in fact and theory. The course of ego development in later life has received much less attention than its earlier phases. This chapter reports a simple study of one aspect of ego development in later life: the delay of gratification.

Background of the problem

The early years

The importance of delaying capacity in the formation of personality has been strongly emphasized by psychoanalytic theory. Freud considered that the infant responds to its bodily needs by an immediate and restless discharge of motor activity, a simple tendency to ". . . unburden the mental apparatus of accretions of stimuli." (5, p. 16). The next step in development is the formation of the "reality principle." The reality principle or secondary process is aimed at preventing the discharge of tension until an object which is appropriate for the satisfaction of the need has been discovered. The ego formulates a plan for the satisfaction of the need, and then tests the plan. The reality principle gains dominance over the pleasure principle that previously had reigned supreme. Now pleasure or need-satisfaction is somewhat delayed while the developing child engages in adaptive behavior.

This chapter is based upon an honors thesis performed at Clark University (Worcester, Massachusetts) by the senior author with guidance from the junior author.

A shift to the reality principle can come about only if a sense of futurity has been established in the individual. Hartmann observes that ". . . the reality principle . . . implies something essentially new, namely, the familiar function of anticipating the future, orienting our actions according to it, and correctly relating means and ends to each other. It is an ego function and, surely, an adaptation process of the highest significance" (7, p. 43).

Piaget and Inhelder (12) and other developmental psychologists agree that the cross-over from primary to secondary process is a major step in psychosocial maturation. The concensus seems to be that the ability to delay gratification increases from infancy through childhood, and again, from childhood through adolescence to adulthood. In psychoanalytic terms, this sequence is interpreted as the gradual internalization of the delaying mechanism associated with the emergence of the reality principle. Wolff and Precker illustrate this sequence with the changing reactions of the growing child in response to being struck (18). At one stage he responds with a direct counterblow; later he may abuse the assailant verbally and, finally, he may completely inhibit or delay overt response, but conduct various countermeasures in fantasy.

The healthy functioning of the human organism is assumed to rest, to a large extent, on its ability to utilize the secondary process. Thus, the individual who never achieves the ability to delay gratification is considered to be arrested in development, and the individual who reverts to earlier forms of thought and behavior is considered to have regressed to a less adequate mode of functioning.

The later years

According to this point of view then, the ability to delay gratification increases from infancy to adulthood as one of the most important aspects of general ego development. But what happens to this ability in later life? Is the ability to delay gratification retained and perhaps even strengthened—or is it weakened? Both alternatives can be supported by theoretical considerations.

It might be ventured that delay of gratification remains strong in later life for several reasons:

1. Because delay of gratification has been practiced for so many years, it has become a well-established habit and, therefore, should be resistant to change and ensure its own perpetuation.

2. The normal individual will have utilized delay of gratification with success. He knows from favorable experience that patience and planning frequently will bring him what he wants.

3. Many instinctual drives which impel one toward impulsive behavior early in life have passed the peak of their urgency. Furthermore, these drives will have become more or less integrated into the total personality structure. Therefore, in later life one should find it

easier to delay gratification because there is reduced pressure for urgent relief.

One might also predict, however, that delay of gratification will weaken in later life for such reasons as the following:

1. There may be a general decline with age of the sensory and integrative capacities of the individual. Advanced senility would be an extreme case of this decline, but even more moderate impairment might significantly reduce ability to delay gratification.

2. Instinctual drives previously under the control of developmentally higher structures may "break the leash," so to speak, and emerge as urgent goads to direct gratification of needs.

3. The aging individual may perceive that time is running out on him. With this thought in mind (consciously and/or unconsciously) he might decide that there is no point in continuing to delay gratification. It is important to note that if this factor is the dominant one, then the abandonment of the "waiting game" need not be viewed as a pathological regression. Rather, it would represent a realistic adaptation to a new situation in life.

Prior to the data-gathering phase of this investigation, one author (K.P.) predicted that the results would show a decline in delay of gratification. This prediction was based upon the last reason given above. The other author (R.K.) raised all the other possibilities stated above and, by so doing, perplexed himself too much to be able to offer a prediction.

Vicarious channelization

The methods and concepts used in the present study draw upon previous work conducted from psychoanalytic and/or developmental approaches to personality. Of particular relevance is the work of Singer and his colleagues and Werner and his colleagues. In 1955 Singer reviewed the available evidence on the relationship between the delay of gratification and ego development (15). He pointed out that the experimental work of Werner was quite relevant to the Freudian concept of delay.

Werner and Wapner describe perception as a function of the dynamic interaction of externally derived sensations and pre-existing tonic states in the organism (17). Both sensory and tonic events have equivalent functions in the economy of the organism and may serve vicariously as substitutes for each other. When available tonic energy is not released in bodily movement, the tonicity will express itself in perceptual displacement, e.g., illusory motion or movements in the "mind's eye." The process might be regarded as a "transformation of energy" from one sphere to another. This principle of "vicarious channelization" implies that available energy may be released through alternative channels, so that if one mode of response is blocked, activity may be channeled into another mode.

The principle is supported by the work of Goldman (6) who hypothesized that if sensory-tonic energy is blocked from being released through motor channels, then it should find expression in heightened autokinetic motion (6). Contrariwise, if this energy is released through greater motor activity, then the degree of perceptual (autokinetic) motion should be reduced. In Goldman's investigation, subjects observed a fixed point of light under three conditions: 1) immobilization, 2) control and 3) increased motor activity (exercise). It was found that readiness to perceive motion was greatest under the condition of physical immobilization, less under the control situation, and least under heightened physical activity.

In another experiment, subjects were asked to report what they perceived when line drawings of various objects (e.g., baseball players, trains, etc.) were presented tachistoscopically (10). Prior to the presentation of the pictures, the experimental group was required to perform vigorous exercise. A control group went through the identical procedure without exercising prior to the presentation of the pictures. The number of movement responses reported by the experimental group was significantly smaller than that reported by the control group.

Another study supporting the principle of vicarious channelization deals with differences in human movement responses on the Rorschach test (14). Two groups of problem children were chosen. One group was judged to be hyperactive; the other group was judged to be hypoactive. In consonance with the principle of vicariousness, it was found that hypoactive children show a significantly greater number of human movement (M) responses than do hyperactive children.

Singer argues that the most fruitful possibility for operational expression and experimental study of the concept of delay has come in research with the Rorschach M response (15). Rorschach believed that those individuals who produce many M responses tend to be rather imaginative, introverted and creative, but to be relatively stable or inhibited in their motoric activity (13). Singer suggests that Rorschach was working toward a triadic theory encompassing and relating motor inhibition, perception of motion, and imagination or active inner life. This theory seems to fit well as a link between the psychoanalytic concept of delayed gratification (inhibition of motor response) and the sensory-tonic theory of vicarious functioning of motor activity and motion perception.

If the delayed discharge of motor activity results in an increase in M responses, then it could be inferred that this increase is a function of the delay. Such a finding would support the ideas outlined above.

Research in this direction has been performed. In one experiment (16), the M responses of subjects increased following periods of motor inhibition (standing rigidly in awkward postures, and slow-writing tasks). Another study investigated the effects of speeding up or slowing down the tempo of Rorschach response (14), yielding the conclusion that M production is positively related to the tendency to delay response.

Singer felt that the evidence justified the conclusion that there is a linkage between delay of motor discharge, motion perception, and imagination. A more recent investigation by Kurz found additional support for the idea that M is related to the capacity for delayed need satisfaction, in that subjects who like to think of time as passing rapidly produce fewer human movement responses than do those who prefer slow or static images of time (11).

The experimental problem

This investigation attempted to study, in simple form, the complex processes involved in delay of gratification. Specifically, the study was intended to determine 1) whether or not elderly people can (or will) inhibit their motoric activity as well as young people can (or will), and 2) whether or not the effort to inhibit activity will produce as strong a displacement to the perceptual sphere (M response) in elderly people as it does in the young. Performance of a slow-writing task was taken as the operational definition of delay of gratification (as a relatively simple task analogous in some respects to more complex behaviors).

Method

Twenty elderly men (mean age: 72.2 years) and 20 young men (mean age: 19.1 years) participated in the experiment. The younger subjects were college students; the older subjects were members of a local church and had received high school education. All subjects were of middle-class socio-economic status.

Three testing procedures were used:

1. *A measure of spontaneous writing tempo.* The subject was requested to write the phrase, "New Jersey Chamber of Commerce." No other instructions were given. The score was the time elapsed in writing the phrase.

2. *A measure of slow-writing tempo.* A subtest of the Downey Will-Temperament Scale was administered. This procedure calls for the subject to write the phrase, "New Jersey Chamber of Commerce" as slowly as possible without stopping the motion of the pencil or lifting it off the paper. The score here, too, was the time elapsed in writing the phrase.

3. *A measure of interpretive perception.* Rorschach inkblot cards III and VII were administered with the instructions as recommended by Klopfer (8). The cards were presented in counterbalanced order, i.e., half the subjects received Card III first, and half were given Card

VII. The score was the number of human movement (M) responses given to each card.

All subjects were requested first to write the standard phrase. Next, they were presented with one of the inkblots. Ten subjects in each of the populations (young and elderly) were then called upon to perform the slow-writing task. Following this task, the experimental subjects were given the other inkblot.

The remaining ten subjects in each group were used as controls. In place of the slow-writing task they were requested to write, "New Jersey Chamber of Commerce" just as they had in the pre-test of spontaneous or habitual writing tempo. In other words, no delay performance was required of the control subjects.

It should be noted that the slow-writing task performs double-duty: it provides both a measure of delaying ability and an experimental condition for the investigation of M, the second measure of delaying ability.

Results

The young and elderly men differed in two respects prior to the experimental (slow-writing) intervention: 1) The young men's spontaneous writing speed was significantly faster, and 2) they reported significantly more M responses to the first inkblot presented (Table 1). Both of these differences were large (mean tempo of young almost twice as fast, and mean number of M more than twice as great), and in the expected direction. The difference in M responses supports previous research by Klopfer (9) and Davidson (3).

The experimental results were also rather clear-cut (Tables 2 and 3): 1) The young men were better able to inhibit their writing speed than were the older men. A ratio was computed for each individual to compare his inhibition tempo with his own spontaneous tempo. The inhibition ratio difference between young and elderly men was highly significant ($<.001$). 2) The young men in the experimental (slow-writing) group showed a greater increase in M responses than did the elderly men in the experimental group. 3) Young men in the experimental group also showed a greater increase in M responses than did the young men in the control group.

Taken together, this set of findings has the effect of indicating that elderly men are less responsive than young men with respect to both aspects of the slow-writing task: as a measure of inhibition ability, and as a situation generating motor inhibition. That the task does generate motor inhibition is indicated by the difference in M responses (between first and second inkblots) for experimental and control conditions of young men.

From a methodological point of view, it is worth noting that the order in which the Rorschach cards were administered made a differ-

Table 1. Writing times and Rorschach M responses of elderly and young men.

	Experimental groups		Control groups	
	Elderly (10)	Young (10)	Elderly (10)	Young (10)
Mean age	72.2	19.1	73.5	19.7
Mean writing time:				
Pre-test	19"	11"	19"	12.5"
Inhibition	74"	315"	–	–
Mean #M	0.8	1.9	0.1	1.1
Mean net change in M	0.0	+0.8	−0.1	−0.1

Table 2. Analysis of variance for change in M response from presentation of 1st card to 2nd card

	df	SS	MS	F	P
Cells	7	14.7	2.1	6.46	.01
Treatment	1	2.5	2.5	7.69	.01
Age	1	1.6	1.6	4.92	.05
Order	1	6.4	6.4	19.68	.01
Tr. x Age	1	1.6	1.6	4.92	.05
Age x Order	1	0.7	0.7	2.15	
Tr. x Order	1	1.6	1.6	4.92	.05
Tr. x Order x Age	1	0.3	0.3	0.92	
Error	32	10.4	0.325		
Total	39	25.1			

Table 3. Analysis of variance for initial M response

	df	SS	MS	F	P
Cells	3	1.9	0.64	2.92	.05
Age	1	1.25	1.25	5.71	.05
Order	1	0.6	0.6	2.74	
Age and Order	1	0.05	0.05	0.228	
Error	36	7.9	0.219		
Total	39	9.8			

ence. As may be seen in Table 3, the sequence proceeding from Card VII to Card III was more productive of increased M responses than was the opposite sequence. There was no card-sequence effect between ages in the initial production of M responses.

Discussion

Consideration of the results should include not only the quantitative findings, but also the most salient qualitative observations. Often the elderly subject forgot that he was supposed to be inhibiting his speed in the slow-writing task. He would begin at a slowed tempo, and then shift to his regular tempo. When reminded that he was supposed to write as slowly as possible, the subject would often reply, "I forgot what you told me." It would then be typical for the subject to write slowly, but only for an instant—then he would speed up again. When questioned later, the subject would say that he had forgotten the instruction again.

After completing the inhibition task, a number of elderly subjects volunteered introspective remarks such as, "I didn't *want* to slow down—I'm used to doing things quickly," while others said, "I *can't* slow down, even when you ask me to—I think of how little time I really have left!"

The purpose of the study was explained to each subject at the conclusion of all the procedures. At this time a number of the elderly men commented that they could have gone very slowly in the slow-writing task if they "really had wanted to." These subjects were then given the opportunity to try again: they still could not sustain a controlled, slow-writing approach to the task. None of the elderly subjects came close to the mean delaying time recorded for the young group.

Three other points should be considered before a general interpretation is offered.

1. The Rorschach cards were used in this study in order to obtain some information concerning the inner life of the subjects as influenced by the delaying task. If the slow-writing task alone were used, one could not deny that perhaps the differences between young and elderly subjects were related entirely to physical factors. The Rorschach cards therefore constitute a measure of the personality correlates accompanying physical delay.

2. The data do not permit a clear decision between two alternative ways of accounting for the lack of increased M in the elderly subjects following the delaying task. It might be that the mechanism of vicarious channelization does not function as sensitively in the aged as it does in the young (or that it functions on entirely different principles). But, again, it might be that the elderly men did not become sufficiently involved in the delaying task to build up a need for an "energy displacement" from the motoric to the perceptual realm.

3. The slow-writing task appears to be quite different from the types of behavior that might come to mind when one thinks of delay of gratification. Certainly it is a relatively simple behavior (although with an underlying complexity far beyond our present understanding). To exert the amount of control required to perform this task, however, builds up a state of inner tension. One's basic urge would seem to be in the direction of halting the task or racing through it—either of these alternatives would prevent a further augmentation of the tension and permit a pleasurable sense of relief. In this task then, the gratification that is delayed is the sense of completing a difficult assignment and exchanging a feeling of strain for a feeling of relief. The comments made by the elderly subjects indicate that they were particularly anxious to complete the task, i.e., to achieve some measure of "gratification" without suffering too much delay.

There is more than one way to interpret the findings in this exploratory investigation, and no interpretation can be made on completely secure grounds at this time. Yet it appears worthwhile to suggest a line of reasoning that is consistent with the results. As mentioned earlier, one of the authors predicted the correct direction of the findings, and did so on the basis of the aging person's perception of time and death. This point of view regards the reduction with age of delaying ability as a normal adaptation, not a regressive, pathological phenomenon. It is as though the elderly person were saying to himself, "Why slow down, why delay, when there is so little time left to do all that I wish to do? My future is too short to permit myself the luxury of delaying."

Disengagement theory also regards the changed perception of futurity and death as the occasion for a marked reorientation of the aging individual (1, 2). Both lines of reasoning consider the later years of life as constituting a "new reality" that requires a new form of adjustment, at least for many individuals. The two points of view seem to diverge concerning the question of how the individual does adapt himself to the new reality. Disengagement theory emphasizes a process in which society and the individual mutually withdraw from each other, while the present approach emphasizes a reorganization in which the present moment and the immediate future may take on greater significance as the locus of gratification.

Perhaps the most general implication of the present approach is that as the individual ages he may find ample cause to transform his orientation toward life. These transformations may sometimes assume forms that are developmentally more simple and primitive (e.g., living for the moment rather than the morrow). However, one should not hastily conclude that the form serves the same function that it does for the younger individual or that it necessarily represents pathology and deterioration. What the transformation represents is an active adaptation to a new phase of reality, the later years of life. Subsequent research may not only confirm the adaptive, nonpathological nature of this transformation, but may indeed reveal the operation of creative processes by which the aging individual works the materials of his life into a form distinctively suited to his unique qualities.

References

1. Cumming, E., and Henry, W. *Growing Old.* New York: Basic Books, 1961.
2. Cumming, E. Further thoughts on disengagement theory. In this volume.
3. Davidson, H. H., and Kruglov, L. Personality characteristics of institutionalized aged. *J. Consult. Psychol.*, 1952, *16*, 5-12.
4. Freud, S. *An Outline of Psychoanalysis.* New York: Norton, 1949.
5. Freud, S. Formulations regarding the two principles in mental functioning. In *Collected Papers*, Vol. IV. London: Hogarth, 1953, 13-21.
6. Goldman, A. E. Studies in vicariousness: Degree of motor activity and the autokinetic phenomenon. *Amer. J. Psychol.*, 1953, *66*, 613-617.
7. Hartmann, H. *Ego Psychology and the Problem of Adaptation*, translated by D. Rapaport. New York: International Universities Press, 1958.
8. Klopfer, B., and Davidson, H. H. *Rorschach Technique: An Introductory Manual.* New York: Harcourt, Brace, 1962.
9. Klopfer, W. G. Personality patterns of old age. *Rorschach Res. Exch.*, 1946, *10*, 145-166.
10. Krus, D. M., Werner, H., and Wapner, S. Studies in vicariousness: Motor activity and perceived movement. *Amer. J. Psychol.*, 1953. *66*, 603-608.
11. Kurz, R. B. Relationship between time imagery and Rorschach human movement responses. *J. Consult. Psychol.*, 1963, *29*, 273-276.
12. Piaget, J., and Inhelder, B. *The Growth of Logical Thinking from Childhood to Adolescence*, translated by A. Parsons and S. Milgram. New York: Basic Books, 1958.
13. Rorschach, H. *Psychodiagnostics*, translated by P. Leukan and B. Kronenburg. Berne: Hans Huber, 1942.
14. Siipola, E., and Taylor, V. Reactions to inkblots under free and pressure conditions. *J. Pers.*, 1952, *21*, 22-47.
15. Singer, J. L. Delayed gratification and ego development: Implications for clinical and experimental research. *J. Consult. Psychol.*, 1955, *19*, 259-266.
16. Singer, J. L., Wilensky, H., and MacCraven, V. G. Delaying capacity, fantasy, and planning ability: A factorial study of some basic ego functions. *J. Consult. Psychol.*, 1956, *20*, 375-383.
17. Werner, H., and Wapner, S. Toward a general theory of perception. *Psychol. Review*, 1952, *59*, 324-338.
18. Wolff, W., and Precker, J. A. Expressive movement and the methods of experimental depth psychology. In H. H. Anderson and G. L. Anderson (eds.), *An Introduction to Projective Techniques*. New York: Prentice-Hall, 1951, 457-497.

Patterns of short-range time orientation in geriatric patients

22

Rosalie H. Rosenfelt, Robert Kastenbaum,
and Philip E. Slater

It is strange, considering the central role of time experience in our lives, that its qualitative aspects have not been of more interest to research psychologists. Rather, it is the philosophers, historians, dramatists and writers who have studied qualitative aspects of time experience. In a formal or quantitative sense, time has been studied by physicists, musicians and astronomers. Behavioral scientists, however, except for the psychophysicists, have investigated time but little. Psychophysical research has consisted mainly in the analysis of short, quantifiable, microcosmic units of duration. Recently psychologists have shown increased interest in the qualitative aspects of time, considered especially in larger, or macrocosmic, units. For these studies, duration and quantitative concerns are of less salience than personality factors, individual differences and situational circumstances.

Concurrently with expanding interest in time experience, psychologists have turned their attention to the developing field of gerontology. In consequence of the convergence of these interests, psychological reports are beginning to appear about the meaning of time in old age. One such study was conducted by the psychology department of Cushing Hospital, as part of multi-disciplinary research on aging.

Short-range time orientation

Impaired health, advanced age, low energy level, need for hospitalization, and the prospect of imminent death are among the factors which seem to disqualify geriatric patients as subjects of psychological research. Yet these obstacles are more apparent than real when methodology is adapted to the requirements of gerontological research (3). The very difficulties challenge the investigator's curiosity—what is the nature of experience under such conditions? Can general patterns of response be discerned? Are there, in addition, certain patterns unique

An earlier version of this material was read at the Sixth International Congress on Gerontology, Copenhagen, August 16, 1963. The study was supported in part by USPHS grant MHO-4818.

to the geriatric individual, through which he interprets and copes with his world?

In the present study these questions were approached through inquiry into short-range time perspective. Temporal experience has been studied extensively in the form of time *perception,* involving units of a minute, a second, or less, and in the form of time *perspective,* involving units as large as a lifetime. The distinction between these modes of inquiry is obscured by focus on the magnitude of the temporal units involved. The salient difference has to do with whether emphasis is given to the perception itself or to its final integration into the totality of the individual's mental life. It is an artifact of this distinction that eventuates in the assignment of short temporal units to the realm of time perception, while qualitative factors, not easily discerned in small units of time experience, are relegated to time perspective.

This study was undertaken from the point of view of time perspective, although the temporal range investigated is shorter than usual for such studies, being only 72 hours in length. Inquiry was restricted to the time unit one day in each direction from "Today," that is to say, "Yesterday" and "Tomorrow." "Today" constitutes the present, equidistant from the short-range past, which is "Yesterday," and the short-range future, which is "Tomorrow."

The sample

The subjects were patients at Cushing Hospital, a 650-bed general hospital for the elderly, operated by the Commonwealth of Massachusetts. Committable neuropsychiatric cases or those involving the terminal phase of acute illness are not usually accepted for admission. Most patients are supported wholly by public funds, but a number have private means of support.

There were 57 subjects, 28 males and 29 females. Age range was 66-94 years. The mean age for males was 76.7 years; for females, 79.9 years. Educational range was 0-15 years. Sixteen subjects, 10 males and 6 females, had been institutionalized previously in state hospitals or schools, most of them for substantial periods of time. The mean length of stay at Cushing Hospital was 0.8 years for males, and 1.4 years for females. Within a year and a half following the research interview, 15 subjects had died: 8 male and 7 female.

An independent sample of 24 subjects was studied, using a slightly altered stimulus, for comparison of results. This group comprised a somewhat narrower and higher range of age, had a proportionately greater number of females and a greater discrepancy between the educational levels of males and females. More information about the samples is contained in Table 1.

Table 1. Description of subjects

	Original sample			Second sample		
	Males: 28	Females: 29	Total: 57	Males: 9	Females: 15	Total: 24
Age (years)						
range	66-94	66-90	66-94	73-89	71-90	71-90
mean	76.7	80.0	78.4	81.9	81.3	81.5
Marital status						
married	7	2	9	2	3	5
widowed	12	20	32	6	9	15
single	9	7	16	1	2	3
divorced	0	0	0	0	1	1
Education						
range (years)	0-14	9-15	9-15	0-9	3-16	0-16
mean (years)	8.8	8.9	8.9	7.2	9.5	8.6
Cushing Hospital stay						
range	4.1 days to 4 years	4.1 days to 4 years		6 mos. to 5.5 years	7 mos. to 5.7 years	
mean (years)	0.8	1.4	1.1	2.7	2.8	2.7
Total institutionalization						
longest (years)	43.4	29.1		13.2	48.7	
mean (years)	5.1	4.1	4.6	4.9	6.3	4.7
Expired after interview:						
within 9 months	4	0	4	3	1	4
within 19 months	9	6	15	*	*	*

*The table was compiled nine months after the second sample interviews were completed.

It should be noted that the samples studied represent a group of aged, institutionalized patients, whose number, both proportionately and absolutely, is great. This group is very old, in frail health, beset with severe emotional problems, socially inadequate, often in straitened economic circumstances. Institutionalization is at present the accepted mode of coping with the difficulties presented by these people—mentally deteriorated, behaviorally regressed, likely to die within a short time and, certainly, as seen in the hospital, reacting to the stressfulness of their condition in life. At one time the possibility was considered of restricting this investigation to patients conforming to certain standards of intelligence, cooperativeness and alertness. The decision was reached, however, not to eliminate from the sample any one capable of responding, however minimally, to the test tasks. Consequently, the subjects embrace a wide range of mental ability and physical condition. The sample includes individuals transferred from state hospitals and state schools as well as the holder of a graduate degree from Columbia University. Heart disease, arthritis, arteriosclerosis, cerebral vascular accident and diabetes are among the physical disorders encountered.

Procedure

As part of more extensive psychological study, subjects were asked in an interview, "What did you do yesterday?" and "What would you like to do tomorrow?" Verbatim responses were analyzed in terms of 53 variables, on which high interjudge reliability was obtained.

The variables were organized into seven categories. *Structure of the statement* included such variables as the number of words used and the number of actions or emotional states differentiated. *Social setting and background of action* classified the kinds of activity mentioned, such as work, body-concern, service to others, eating and so forth. *Value and affective response* covered variables such as meaningfulness, affirmativeness, fearsomeness—expressive of the subject's evaluation of, and affective reaction to, the actions or emotional states mentioned in the response. *Quality of action* was concerned with evaluation of the response from the observer's point of view and included such dimensions as: goal-directedness, creativity, grandiosity, routineness and destructiveness. *Role of the subject* grouped variables that described how the subject saw himself with respect to the action in his response: agent, instrument, recipient, or none of these. *Patterns of relationship* dealt with relationships between the subject's report about "Yesterday's" actions and those anticipated "Tomorrow." These variables were: similarity, contrast, improvement, deterioration, expansion and contraction.

In the second study the futurity stimulus was changed to provide a broader basis for inference. This group of subjects was asked, "What did you do yesterday?" and " What are you going to do tomorrow?" The change from "like to do" to "going to do" was not without effect. Nevertheless, the findings from the two studies were more alike than different. The results reported here were confirmed, at least as to direction of trend, by the second study.

Results

The general findings indicate these aged subjects could make realistic discriminations between the certainties of the past and the contingencies of the future. "Tomorrow" was viewed as significantly more subject to contingency than "Yesterday." Similarly, wished-for activities were regarded as being more vulnerable to interference from the environment or by circumstances "Tomorrow" than "Yesterday." Statements about "Yesterday" were made with a more affirmative quality, and more subjects answered, "I don't know," in response to "Tomorrow" then to "Yesterday."

Another general finding pertains to the geriatric patient's view of himself as being either the agent or instrument of action. The subjects tended to ascribe to themselves the role of agent for past actions, that is to say, for what happened "Yesterday," but less frequently assumed responsibility for "Tomorrow," the future. The reverse occurred with respect to perception of the self as an instrument by which others act—more subjects viewed themselves as instruments of others "Tomorrow" than "Yesterday."

The common-sense observation that people tend to be consistent was supported by correlations between many kinds of response to "Yesterday" and "Tomorrow." These included routineness, self-centered activity, avoidance of action or feeling through the defense mechanism of denial or withdrawal, expressions of creative interest, goal-directedness of action, locale of action being outside the hospital, meaningfulness, enjoyability, recreation and work.

Although there were other general findings, we will turn now to some indications of individual differences. Male and female subjects were remarkably similar in their responses; such differences as were found were few and of small degree.

Length of institutionalization proved to be inversely related to length of verbal communication: i.e., the longer a person had been exposed to institutional life, the fewer words he had to offer about either "Tomorrow" or "Yesterday." As used here, length of institutionalization refers to total time a subject spent in any institution.

Among patients whose admission to Cushing Hospital had been the first experience of institutionalization, a comparison was made between the "old timers" and the "newcomers." Those who had been institutionalized for a relatively shorter period of time expressed more awareness of the routine quality of their daily existence, and they more frequently voiced apprehension that "Tomorrow" would bring some restriction of a planned or hoped-for action. We might infer from these two findings that institutional life seems to decrease communication and lessen concern about the monotony of daily existence.

These findings, however, constituted only the beginning of a search for individual patterns of short-range time perspective. Next it was important to determine if there was sufficient variability in the responses to indicate that individual patterns had not been obscured by age, illness and hospitalization. The first such indication was the finding that the subjects were divided about evenly on the dimension of diurnal continuity. That is to say, for approximately half the subjects "Tomorrow" and "Yesterday" were essentially the same, while the other half gave reports that indicated pronounced differences between past and future experiences. This diversity in outlook might in itself serve as a useful means of distinguishing between two types of institutional experience: the expectation that one's days will be all alike, and the expectation that they will vary, as life brings changes.

This line of analysis was supplemented by a profile analysis based on statistical evidence. Nine operationally defined patterns of short-range time perspective were found, by means of which subjects expressed the diversity of their feelings about "Yesterday" and "Tomorrow" and the relationship between short-range past and future. In other words, even in this small sample of institutionalized geriatric patients, there were divergent interpretations of the linkage between "Tomorrow" and "Yesterday."

There was little support for two frequently heard generalizations: first, that elderly people "live in the past," and, second, that geriatric patients are insensitive to time. Rather, the results suggest that geriatric patients experience short-range units of time in diverse patterns of orientation, and that most of these patterns include clear distinction between past and future. Generalizations about temporal experience in the aged, it would seem, must not overlook the broad spectrum of individual interpretation.

One of the patterns, as might be expected, was that some subjects expended much more feeling, interest and attention upon "Yesterday" while showing less or no interest in "Tomorrow." Other subjects, however, showed equally pronounced one-sidedness in the other direction. If this difference is meaningful, perhaps we can use the *direction* of short-range temporal orientation as the basis for differential predictions about the life course of individuals. Further research should be undertaken to investigate this possibility.

Evidence from an earlier study indicates that old people are able to use both past and future as cognitive categories and that they are fully as capable as young people (and in some respects more capable) of functioning within the mode of cognitive futurity (2). In the sphere of personal futurity, however, older subjects proved to be more limited than the younger; that is to say, older subjects, when the futurity examined resides within the personal framework of reference, appear more restricted than younger subjects. These results do not contradict the cultural dictum that "old people live in the past." Rather, they limit its range of applicability to the personal frame of reference and exclude such "living in" as occurs in the cognitive dimension alone.

The current study illuminates further the question of old people's living in the past. Clinical impression suggests that, in some sense, they certainly *do*. The study referred to above leads to the inference that, to the extent the aged live in the past, it is the past of personal experience that preoccupies them. If we grant the validity of this inference, which is well supported by clinical observation, the essential question becomes: within what *temporal* framework does the manifest past-centeredness exist? The present study demonstrates that the temporal framework of geriatric past-centeredness even for institutionalized, deteriorated subjects is *not* the time span bounded by "Yesterday" and "Tomorrow." Almost certainly, in this connection, it is larger temporal segments that pertain to the temporal orientation process in old age. Increasing the span of time investigated by small amounts, in serial replication, should provide pertinent information about this topic.

What is chiefly lacking is a body of normative information against which these results and others related to them can be compared. We would like to know, for example, how this sample differs from the non-institutionalized of the same age, from younger persons who are institutionalized and from the elderly in other societies.

From the methodological viewpoint, the present study indicates that cooperation and meaningful responses can be secured from subjects, who seem to be grossly handicapped physically, mentally and socially, by the use of a set of simple questions, such as might be included in an interview format.

Disengagement and time orientation

The disengagement theory of aging, proposed by Cumming and Henry, excites the interest of gerontologists and developmentalists, because it is the most highly elaborated and articulated theory of personality in later life yet to have been presented (1). It would seem appropriate to discuss the findings of the study described above in relation to the implications of disengagement theory.

In terms of this theory, it is the awareness of the imminent approach of death that colors the experience of time in middle and in old age, although in different manners for the two periods. In old age the knowledge that life is virtually over is a major element fostering the process of disengagement, the mutual severing of ties between an individual and those in his society. The proponents of disengagement theory say:

> "If the individual becomes sharply aware of the shortness of life and the scarcity of the time remaining to him, and if he perceives his life space as decreasing, and if his available ego energy is lessened, then readiness for disengagement has begun.
>
> "It seems probable that disengagement would be resisted forever if there were no problem of the allocation of time, and thus no anticipation of death. Questions of choice among alternative uses of time lead to curtailment of some activities. Questions of the inevitability of death lead to introspective reflections on the meaning of life." (1, pp. 216-217).

One might infer that individuals not partaking of the disengagement process (or not yet partaking of it), when confronted with the Yesterday-Tomorrow stimulus, would ascribe as much importance and interest to the short-range future as to the short-range past, or even weight the future more heavily. Disengaged people would be expected to show a backward-reaching time perspective or to manifest reduced interest in both short-range past and future.

Within our samples, prolonged institutionalization was associated with a peculiarly laconic quality of responding. A disengaged attitude toward life, entailing boredom and disinterest in time, could certainly be inferred from the responses of this group of long-term patients. Conversely, relatively shorter institutionalization was associated with apparently keener awareness of the value of time and the uncertainties of the future and also with dissatisfaction with the routineness enforced by hospital life.

In other words, the findings presented above do not lend unequivocal support to a theory of disengagement which proposes a process activated by forces endogenous to the aged individual. Our results suggest that, within the circumscribed sphere of experience studied, such observed behavior as could be interpreted as part of a disengagement process appeared to be set in motion primarily by forces exogenous to the aged person. (It is open to question, perhaps, whether being institutionalized is wholly the consequence of social action, exogenous to the individual. It may be that the societal response is stimulated by behavior, on the part of the future patient, which proceeds from conditions endogenous to him.) This is not the place to elucidate the fine distinctions inherent in the act of institutionalization. What is of significance is that orientation to time in old age, in the case of hospitalized, geriatric patients, does not appear, within short-range temporal units, to reflect an age-induced process of disengagement but, rather, to reflect a more diffuse process, in which institutionalization is the mediating variable, the connection with advanced age being more tenuous.

The clarification of this problem through further studies of time orientation in old age, with careful control of the institutionalization variable, would be highly valuable to the further development of personality theory.

References

1. Cumming, E., and Henry, W. E. *Growing Old.* New York: Basic Books, 1961.
2. Kastenbaum, R. Cognitive and personal futurity in later life. *J. Individ. Psychol.*, 1963, *19*, 216-222.
3. Rosenfelt, R. H., Kastenbaum, R., and Kempler, B. "The Untestables": Methodological problems in drug research with the aged. Paper presented at 16th annual scientific meeting, Gerontological Society, Boston, Mass., November 9, 1963.
4. Rosenfelt, R. H., Kastenbaum, R., and Slater, P. E. Patterns of short-range time perspective in geriatric patients. Paper presented at Sixth International Congress of Gerontology, Copenhagen, August 16, 1963.

23

On the meaning and function of reading in later life

Frederick E. Whiskin

Whenever we speak of the "meaning" of *anything* to *anyone,* be it event, object or activity, we must clarify whether we intend its *conscious* or *unconscious* meaning to the individual. This chapter will attempt to explore some of both in relation to the older reader.

There are only a few contributions in the psychoanalytic literature related to reading; perhaps the most comprehensive was the one by James Strachey which emphasizes the importance of oral components in reading (4). "Reading," he says, "is actually a method of taking someone else's thoughts inside oneself. It is a way of eating another person's words." He adds that difficulties in reading arise principally when gratifications are related to the ambivalent oral phase in which reading may have an unconscious aggressive meaning, creating guilt and resultant inhibitions.

As to symbolic meanings of the printed page, Strachey quotes Freud's statement that books and papers are female symbols (1). Next, he quotes Jones' interpretation that books and other printed matter are symbols for feces (2). Strachey relates the latter to the widespread habit of reading in the bathroom and mentions one case where defecation was impossible without reading. He suggests that a coprophagic tendency lies at the base of all reading, and agrees with Jones that coprophagy may represent not only a gratification of early, unintegrated component instincts, but also a regressive gratification of genital impulses that have been repressed.

When thinking of the older reader, one might hypothesize that because of the very considerable regression which has been observed particularly in hospitalized persons, individuals who had previously been able to use reading in a sublimatory way now would experience inhibition because of the threatened break-through of aggressive and coprophagic fantasies connected with reading. The methodology of

Based upon a presentation at the workshop on "The Meaning and Function of Reading in Later Life," Second Annual Symposium on Old Age, Cushing Hospital, Framingham, Massachusetts, May 21, 1963.

the present study does not lend itself to an assessment of this possibility but it is an area worth considering.

Subjects for this study were the patient population of Cushing Hospital, a geriatric hospital of 650 beds, with a patient age range of 65 to 98 and an average age of 80 years. Data were obtained by direct observation and interviewing a number of patients and personnel. The hospital librarian was able to contribute significantly to our stockpile of information about the reading habits of Cushing patients. A summary of the above information was compiled by Rosalie H. Rosenfelt from which most of the following findings are derived (3).

It was noted that only a small proportion of Cushing patients are habitual readers. Factors precluding reading were mental retardation, physical illness, and lack of motivation relative to lower class background. The latter factor was found to be more important than poor vision, even though visual difficulties undoubtedly contribute to the problem. Relative to this, it is interesting to note that the New England Council of Optometrists recently launched a "Books for Tired Eyes" project through which volumes printed in at least 12 point type will be made available to those with limited vision.

A small number were found to be *en rapport* with contemporary authors. These tended to read the daily paper and other periodicals in an attempt to keep abreast of current events. Others were noted to read mostly out of habit, rather than appreciating much of what they scanned. One day, I observed a patient looking intently at the newspaper. On being asked what he was reading, the patient pointed to a picture of the world series and said "He is bald, too." Obviously, this patient was not able to understand much of what he read, at least in the usual sense.

A number of patients seemed to enjoy re-reading best sellers of vintage 1900. The motivation here may be akin to that in reminiscence where pleasant events and associations are reviewed in an attempt to escape the unpleasant present memories. Biographies of important figures are also popular with the patients. The relationships of this preference to the patient's feeling of insignificance need only be mentioned in passing.

The sweet, tender love story, where all ends well, and tales of adventure are favorites of older women and men, respectively, in the population studied. Religious works, the Bible itself, are widely read; whether this is related to the older person's fear of death is not established as yet.

Leanings toward genuine intellectual challenge were found to be lacking in our subjects. Wit, humor, drama held little appeal. This lack of interest may be more on the basis of cultural differences than the age factor. Contemporary frankness in discussing sexual matters was generally offensive to the older readers. This could be related in part to their own strict early training, and also a general feeling that older people should not be interested in sex.

One interesting facet that came to light in talking with the hospital librarian was the difficulty she had in discarding extra copies of books. Once, several books were thrown into the trash can only to reappear a week or so later, arranged neatly on a shelf. Apparently, older patients do not like to see books discarded. Is this because they do not care to see objects of *any* kind cast aside, as they feel themselves to be?

A colleague brought out an interesting point in relation to his elderly mother-in-law, an intelligent, well-read person who had experienced considerable anxiety in interpersonal relationships all her life. He had observed that, although she could not remember what people said to her in social relationships, she could recall in detail what the characters said in the books she was reading. His thesis was that the stress of interacting with people involved so much of her ego-energies that there was not enough left for her to "absorb" what was happening in her relationship with others while, in the quietness of her study, there was no such stress and hence she could remember.

An experienced interviewer at the Age Center of New England (Boston) reported to me that many of the elderly people she has met read very widely. However, the interesting point she brought out was that authors are viewed by older people as friends who come to replace lost loved ones and companions, "And these friends never die," one older person said. Apropos, also, of the present discussion was the fact that the conversation was taking place in the reception room of the Age Center, and listening to it quietly was the receptionist, himself a 93 year old. It was apparent from what he said that he was still reading very widely and obviously retaining a good deal of it. More significant, though, was his statement that he was in the process of moving and that it involved a good deal of book packing. One of the people present facetiously asked, "Why don't you throw the books away?" He answered, "Oh, I wouldn't do that. They're my friends. Where I go, they go!" Moreover, he added that he had willed them to a young man of his acquaintance, as if he wanted them cared for after his demise. Thus, it appears that books, for the elderly, become personalized and are seen as old friends who stand by steadfastly while, around them, friends and relatives disappear one by one.

It is my feeling that those individuals who had established adequate reading habits in earlier life may find adjustment to later life easier because of the satisfactions gained through reading. As mentioned, these satisfactions would vary with each individual. Some have carried a keen interest in a particular subject into later life and continue to read widely in this area. Such an individual can find post-retirement years fruitful because of the increased time for research and reading. On the other side of the coin, should organic impairment or visual difficulties make it difficult or impossible for the individual to keep up with his reading, his sense of loss is more marked than, say, the person who never read much anyway.

Reading is seen to function as a valuable substitute for the gradually diminishing social contacts of many older people. In reviewing the cases of patients admitted to Cushing, time after time one finds the story of a spouse dying, the subject living alone for a while, becoming confused and unable to care for himself or herself, being taken in to live with a son or daughter, becoming more and more seclusive, and, finally, being admitted to Cushing, either because they felt they were in the way or because the son or daughter felt they could no longer care for them. Throughout this process there is a continuing, progressively increasing isolation, some of which might be combatted if the subject were able to turn to his books for stimulation and satisfaction, thus helping prevent the deadly, deteriorative sitting-and-ruminating which becomes a way of life for so many elderly people.

Even reading the daily paper can be a valuable way of keeping a degree of orientation. So many of the patients at Cushing do not know the day's date or even the month, not so much because of organic deterioration but because they have no place to go, nothing to look forward to. Their motivation and need to know the date is much less than that of the individual who has to remember, say, that he has an appointment somewhere with someone.

Reading the newspaper would not only keep the individual oriented in terms of world events but also in terms of *time*. However, unfortunately, one cannot say to the older person, "Start reading the daily papers. It will help you to make sense out of the world that seems far away from you now." If he does not "feel like" reading, he will not do so. The only possible solution here, and this is assuming that basically he is capable of reading, is to sit down with him a few times, or many times, and find out what directions his life has taken in the past few years, the losses he has sustained, and his unexpressed griefs.

It is my feeling that many older people are experiencing what is akin to a traumatic state of the ego. Recent years have been filled with the loss of loved ones and friends which has put such a load on the age-threatened ego that adequate working through of grief reactions is impossible for them. Thus, they sit grieving, insulated from the painful reality around them, giving up some of the available satisfactions they used to enjoy. One of these satisfactions might be reading. I would think that whenever we see a person of good vision who used to read regularly markedly reduce his reading habits, we should think, among other things, of unresolved grief, and/or depression before jumping to the conclusion that the individual has become "senile."

In summary, the subject of reading in the elderly is a complex and interesting one as yet little studied. Findings of a preliminary clinical study and a few ideas related to the meaning and functions of reading for the older person have been outlined. There is a need for further research in this area, the result of which might have important implications in our efforts toward the furtherance of "successful aging."

References

1. Freud, S. *New Introductory Lectures on Psychoanalysis.* New York: Norton, 1933.
2. Jones, E. Anal erotic character traits. In *Papers on Psychoanalysis.* New York: Beacon, 1961.
3. Rosenfelt, R. H. Observations on the reading behaviors of elderly hospital patients. Unpublished paper.
4. Strachey, J. Some unconscious factors in reading. *Int. J. of Psychoanal.,* 1930, *11,* 322-331.

Artistic expression in later life

24

Stephen Durkee

Man has communicated his thoughts and feelings through artistic means for thousands of years, whether expressed in the sophisticated art of the Golden Age of Greece or in the sculpture of so-called primitive tribes. The word "art" has encompassed such a rich variety of productions that it is difficult to select any single interpretation as the "one-and-only true definition." This chapter will be limited to a consideration of art as a visual expression of individual experience. Particular attention will be given to drawing and painting.

By "art" I mean visual interpretation, and not imitation. The word is often attached to copy work, but this usage misses the significance of personal, intuitive expression. A complete work of visual art is a personal expression that communicates the intuition, originality and uniqueness of its creator through the elements of point, line, plane, color, texture, mass and form; it embodies the principles of balance, emphasis, rhythm and proportion.

The qualities of a line and its relationships with the other elements and principles are virtually infinite. When one thinks of the variety of tools and materials available, the visual possibilities of countless environments, the different philosophies and techniques of the artists, the unpredictable intuitive and creative developments, and the diverse experiences undergone by any one artist, then one is impressed by the uniqueness of a work of art. Art has as many faces as there are individuals who use it as a form of expression.

Art can make an important contribution to the lives of people at any age. This chapter will explore the relevance of artistic expression to old people. The writer's experience has included patients residing in Cushing Hospital, both in individual and group sessions, and work with a variety of persons outside the institutional setting. Concurrent experience with college freshmen and the aged has revealed that both age groups have rather similar interests and attitudes toward art. Although the emphasis in this chapter is on the aged, the intention is not to exaggerate differences between age groups, but to explore artistic expression as a natural and vital aspect of life for individuals at all ages.

Do aged people express themselves by artistic means?

The answer seems to be that the aged in our society generally do not express themselves by artistic means—largely because the aged are but one part of a general population that does not engage in artistic modes of expression. From colonial times our society has measured progress in terms of production and economic growth. Attitudes, education and mores have been related to this goal of "progress" with relatively little energy directed to the "non-productive" area of art.

Our educational system has largely ignored the cultivation of individual expression in the visual medium. The first state-supported art school, Massachusetts School of Art, was established to improve product design, not to encourage individual expression in the fine arts. Art still is not a required subject in most high schools, but is tolerated in the curriculum as an elective. In many instances, art functions as the school administrator's last resort for unmotivated students who do not succeed in other subjects. Virtually no liberal arts college requires an art *experience* in its four-year curriculum. Some colleges require an art appreciation course, but this typically consists of slides and lectures surveying the history of art. The student *views* the work of master artists, but has no opportunity to experience a personal involvement with materials with which he can communicate his ideas to others in visual form. The possible result of this lack of visual education will be discussed later.

Other examples of cultural attitudes toward art are the stereotyped ideas that prevail about art and artists. The beard and the beret are well-known symbols. Artists are frequently considered to be eccentrics rather than responsible citizens contributing something of value to their environment. Art is for women, for children, for people who have nothing to do; for the sick, perhaps, or the convalescing to while away long hours. Art is frivolous and a luxury. It is for those *not* participating in the mainstream of life. Moreover, non-objective and abstract art is incomprehensible because of inadequate art education, and this further alienates the artist from his community.

Another current attitude is the general desire to have things the "instant" way—instant coffee, instant mashed potatoes, instant oil paintings; the do-it-yourself variety of painting appears to be highly popular and requires only that one buy the set, then follow the numers in order to achieve a finished product that can be identified to friends as "my own" or "an Utrillo." Furthermore, contemporary man has little need to work with his hands. He need not make his own bread, furniture or clothing, and there is little room left for artistic expression or even for the feel of craftsmanship in the impersonal, assembly-line manufacturing process. Self-identification with the product is shallow and often non-existent.

For all such reasons, the society in which our aged people live does not have a core interest in visual art. Then there are additional reasons for non-participation in art activity that are more specific to the aged themselves. For one thing, when the aged of today were in school, art was chiefly "mechanical drawing" and copy-work. This emphasis must have been frustrating to those who did not have the aptitude to produce a skillful copy of a prescribed design or picture. This type of "art education" did not contribute to their understanding of art, nor did it contribute to developing their total sensory awareness of the richness and variety in the environment around them.

Present attitudes toward the aged also tend to inhibit artistic expression. Our cultural accent is on youth. The older person can hardly help but be aware that he is discriminated against. When he enters the minority group of "over 65'ers" he is likely to suffer a decline in self-confidence that is likely to hinder the beginning of any new experience. This deteriorating self-image is especially detrimental in art because the result of the art effort is visual, and this visual record is exposed to comments and criticism from uninformed, insensitive self-appointed critics. "What a critic will look for will depend upon his preconceptions of what he ought to find, and these preconceptions naturally will depend on his total education." (4). The total education in our culture generally produces people who are ill-equipped for the role of art critic. The aged person, having lost many of his earlier defenses, is most vulnerable to negative criticisms and may discontinue an enjoyable experience because of the rejecting or ridiculing attitude of others.

On the brighter side is the fact that some aging persons do participate in creative art activity. Those who do so are aware of its values. Adult education is the main avenue bringing art activity to the aging; indeed, several large centers have been established to function for this age group exclusively. The movement is rapidly expanding because of the need to extend the meaning of life to accompany the success of medical science in extending life itself. One noteworthy example of elderly persons' participation in arts and crafts can be found at the Sharon (New Hampshire) Art Center. Director Kenneth Wilkins states that the type of person attracted to this center needs no "motivational" help; only equipment, materials and guidance are necessary.* The people come there to explore their capabilities in an art medium; many come with previous experience, but develop new techniques and refurbish old ones. Their approach is serious, and the tenacity with

_____
* Private communication.

which they grasp the experience of artistic creation is sufficient evidence of their involvement in self-expression. There are other places throughout the country which are serving some elderly people in this vital way.

Is there any "good reason" for an aged person to participate in art?

Let us now consider some of the "good reasons" for artistic expression in the lives of elderly individuals.

There appears to be some disagreement among gerontologists as to the psychological condition of the inactive aged. Cumming and Henry indicate that life after a successful "disengagement" is usually a happy one (1). Levin questions this opinion, and suggests that there is much apathy and depression caused by a variety of external as well as internal factors (2). The writer's personal observations are more in accord with Levin's views, at least with respect to institutionalized elderly patients. Withdrawal from activity seems to allow adults of any age to dwell upon themselves. If people are inactivated socially and psychologically over a prolonged period, as is the case with many aging persons, the inactivity can itself lead to depression. If the hypothesis is valid that older people tend to dwell upon themselves and their past, then art can be seen as a positive means of aiding the older person to organize his past experiences and establish new concepts about his present life.

Activity in the visual arts has a number of qualities that are especially suited for elderly persons. In the realm of social functioning one can note the following possibilities:

1. The more vividly and openly one communicates with his environment, the more fertile are the resources for personal interpretation and expression of experience. The entry into a new activity often is accompanied by the formation of new associations with others who have similar interests. These new associations are possible avenues to new techniques and ideas, or totally new activities and interests. The gradual decrease in social interaction, noted by many researchers, can be reversed through artistic endeavors.

2. The common visual language might be a further link to communication between all age groups. A child ten years old can understand the visual language of an adult of seventy-five and respond in a mutually enriching manner.

3. Similar to symbols in drawing, a piece of hand-woven fabric communicates something to those who are aware of its quality. It tells something about the person who created it. It has an intrinsic value of its own which develops in the creator a sense of contribution to the world outside the self.

4. The blind or near blind have the sense of communicating in a new form when they produce a sculptured piece. Blind people can communicate with each other through their sculpture and weaving.

5. Since the majority of the aged population have not had a handicraft or artistic experience, it becomes a new form of expression for them—one which has been well documented as an emotional outlet. Loss of loved ones, physical loss, financial restrictions and gradual isolation are common conditions which prevail among the aging and which slowly eliminate avenues of emotional outlet. By objectifying his past through art experiences, a person may integrate his entire life. In this way his art and his life become more meaningful to him.

6. The monetary value of "something made" establishes a new relationship between the person who made it and the person who may buy it or receive it as a gift. The aged person feels he can produce something of value; thus, in a symbolic sense, he re-establishes himself in the economic flow. The sense of usefulness which may have deserted him returns when he sees that he has something to offer that is desired by others.

There are few areas of art that require physical exertion. The non-ambulatory, the deaf, the feeble, the blind and the mute can find a particular activity to utilize their remaining physical facilities. Any art endeavor increases and prolongs cognizance—the very act of participating in this kind of activity necessitates a new visual and/or tactile awareness. Involvement in good learning experiences nutures olfactory, gustatory and auditory sensitivity since these senses are strongly related to art expression.

How are we to interpret art produced by the aged?

It is necessary to establish a point of view before commenting on examples of visual expression. The orientation of the contemporary art educator is toward the individual and his self-identification. "An essential quality of art is that it places a high premium on uniqueness and individuality." It is a matter of accepting each person as someone who has unique personal experiences that can be shared through art. The educator's primary function is to help the aged person recall experiences in which there can be an emotional involvement strong enough for him to wish to tell about it visually. The degree of skill is subordinate to the act of expression just as the rendition of the subject matter or the final product remains subordinate to the process of expression. Even becoming aware of the visual possibilities of the art elements and principles is subordinate to the development of innate expression. Untainted by formalized training, innate expression can be beautiful and sensitive; naive symbolism has an aesthetic quality. Until the individual himself feels a need for learning procedures and techniques, the art educator's function is to help find meaningful activities, offer a few suggestions and then—*observe.* The teacher-observer must achieve an identification with the person who is actively involved in artistic expression. This attitude is fundamental to the understanding of the person and the expression intended. Sensitivity both to the feelings of the older person and to the possibilities and limitations of the material being used is required of the art educator.

Persons participating in an art activity usually can be classified as *uninhibited* or *inhibited.* Both categories can be subdivided into types which have different visual characteristics.

The self-taught uninhibited. This kind of artist would be typified by "Grandma" Moses, a person who did not have formal training in art. John Pickett, John Kane, and Guy Pène du Bois are other well known American folk-art painters. "Primitive" is a word sometimes used to describe this type of artist.

The naive uninhibited. This type of artist is less aware of spatial relationships. He draws as though verbally telling about the picture. The motivation to show specific things has an emotional basis, but the drawing itself is utilitarian, a direct diagrammatical plan to communicate an idea. Line is usually the art element used, and color is added only when it has particular significance. No conscious consideration for any art principle or element is in evidence.

Drawing #1 was executed by Mr. S., a man 73 years of age. He seldom conversed with staff members or his fellow patients. Once a week art materials were made available to him and several other men on his ward. Each week a subject for drawing was suggested, and each week different materials were made available. "The first house that you remember" was suggested at the fifth session, and drawing #1 was the result. Up to this point, the patient had not participated in the art activity, nor had he communicated in any way except for shaking his head when asked if he would like to participate.

This time, however, he became interested in telling about his first home, one he had helped to build. After a few minutes of discussion, paper and crayons were put before him and he was asked to show what his home had been like. There was no hesitation. He seemed to realize that his words were not adequate. As he drew, Mr. S. explained how the house had been constructed and what materials had been used. The color of crayon used to draw the house was selected arbitrarily. Color was not a consideration until Mr. S. was asked what was in the front yard. He symbolized the grass by making long, vertical green lines.

This drawing seems to be purely functional in nature, not evidencing any conscious thought of aesthetic criteria. The only purpose Mr. S.

appeared to have in executing the drawing was to communicate something that he could not communicate in any other way. The objective was to "diagram" the verbal story. His treatment of the well and bucket helps to substantiate this point. When asked what was to the left of the house, Mr. S. drew the well and an X-ray view of the bucket located inside the well. Drawing #1 thus provides an example of X-ray percepts. Both "outside" and "inside" views appear in the same picture, a circumstance that seems to be regarded as quite natural and unremarkable by the artist. Children and "primitives" also are known to use X-ray perceptions in their drawings.

The skilled and experienced uninhibited. These people have participated in art for most of their lives. Their work usually has the flavor of the art school or teacher from which they learned. There is often a well-established style that does not change. Compositions are very similar to established or traditional concepts of landscape, still life and so forth. Often the aim is to paint the subject matter "exactly" as they see it. In this general category also belongs that rare artist, the one who develops new visual forms.

The completely inhibited. Perhaps 90% of the aged population could be classified here. People in this group will not participate at all because of inhibitions dating back to childhood. Many young adults have similar inhibitions which prevent any form of artistic self-expression. Self-confidence has deteriorated because of the emphasis on technical perfection rather than human values.

The partially inhibited: the copiers. The "post card and calendar" group is dedicated to exact reproductions of a particular photograph or picture previously created by someone else. There is a desire for approval, for technical perfection, for photographic representation. The post card is an enjoyable crutch that challenges the painter to reproduce it but requires nothing else of him. Because of prevalent misconceptions about art, this type frequently is appreciated by the public while a noncommittal or negative reaction greets the more fundamental uninhibited types. Unfortunately, many people in a situation to introduce art to the aged are promotors of post card copying. Once this introduction is made and the aged person becomes dependent on copying, it is difficult to break away and develop a personal visual communication.

There are variations within this classification. The design or composition of a picture can be copied, yet the technique of painting can remain individual. Mr. B., age 73, (painting #2) became intrigued by the possibilities of the brushes and paint. His original goal of an exact copy was intuitively altered. A personal technique developed over a period of time, if combined with copied compositions, can produce the illusion of paintings by professionals. This painting is a good example. His work is admired by staff and patients, and he has at times produced via the assembly line method, painting several copies of the same composition at one time.

The motivation to copy a picture results from an over-concern for "aesthetics" which are beyond the capabilities of the copier, but are instilled by a well-meaning teacher. The technique of Mr. B. (painting #2) is the creative contribution and provides more validity as a work of art than painting #3, the purpose of which was to copy precisely every detail of the photograph. It was painted by a woman 74 years old who spent a few hours each day for approximately six weeks to complete it. She said it was "very difficult and tiring work." The procedure she used was to completely finish one section and slowly and methodically work across the canvas. The selection of the picture to be copied was made not by the patient herself, but by a staff member. This external control had the effect of eliminating any sentimental or aesthetic preference the patient herself might have expressed.

There might be some value in copying pictures. Copying might launch a person, who would otherwise not attempt to paint, into independent interpretation; if not, then the painted result is at least appreciated by others, and positive personality changes could be a by-product. Nevertheless, art educators in general, and this writer in particular, would never encourage copying. The copiers are outside the definition of art we are using and are included here only for the purpose of the classification of all types of "artists."

Mr. B. became very interested in the hospital administration building and made a pencil sketch which he transferred onto canvas to paint it (painting #4). The technique, space concepts and composition are naive. He was so involved in the subject that his established techniques were "forgotten." He had had little experience developing his own compositions and space concepts. The result of his effort shows primitive qualities.

Because artistic expression is often quite personal it is therefore sensitive to positive and negative comment. Too much negativism on the part of observers can result in complete inhibition and an end of creative expression. The drive, determination and complete individuality of now-famous artists has often been told. Paul Cezanne, Paul Gauguin, Henry Rousseau, Vincent Van Gogh and many others were ridiculed and unappreciated throughout their lives. Such strength in adversity is rare. The average person depends upon support and approval. A person of any age who has amateur status in art will have some frustrations in trying to solve technique problems. Negative comments by others or standards imposed by an insensitive teacher would only increase the frustrations.

Change, new thoughts, the unfamiliar, the new invention often receive discriminatory comment. The creative child and the creative adult often experience negative reactions—by other people—to their art work. This is perhaps the nature of man. Lowenfeld describes the clinging to the old as a manifestation of insecurity, a reluctance to face, accept and identify with the present (3). Whatever the reason for criticism, the observer who volunteers unsolicited comments shows his insensitivity. It is a puzzle why laymen "authorities" often feel obliged to tell creative people what should or should not be done to a painting which is a personal expression of what the artist sees or feels. There is usually some quality in the art endeavor that can be sincerely complimented—color, an interesting line, a warm, lively or gay feeling or an unusual texture. It is better to comment on a specific quality rather than make a general statement such as "it's pretty, it's nice," and so forth. The role of evaluator belongs to the teacher whose goal is to learn what further awareness might be developed in the participant.

Visual stagnation:
fact and challenge
The similarities found among the self-taught uninhibited type, the uninhibited naive type, and art produced by children suggest that perceptual growth for many people terminates between the ages of 6 and 12. The curiosity and wonder of a young child and the ability to absorb the visual knowledge of his fresh new world are often responsible for his life-long perceptions. Developing perception beyond the point of functional utility in everyday life is not considered a necessity in our society and thus not encouraged by formal or informal education. We are made aware of objects by their use or function. Visual qualities are rarely mentioned separately, and then only to help identify the object. There is very little planned visual education or learning-by-observation. By contrast, children spontaneously observe. A child in the second grade did not finish his assigned work. When asked why, he replied, "I was watching a fly on my desk. It was cleaning its wings and rubbing its legs together—I heard them rub!"

"The inlet is situationed in the mind of the individual, and we may say that at birth and throughout childhood it is wide open. But it gradually silts up with the dust of our practical activities, and the verbal mucous excreted from the rationalizing mind until, long before the individual becomes an adult, he is deaf and blind to all sensitive experiences, incapable of bringing new passions to expressive shape." (4, p. 63).

Is it necessary—or possible—to counteract this visual stagnation? Millions of Americans see functionally, and are not visually perceptive beyond the requirements of necessity. There does not seem to be any easily identifiable dire consequence of this visual stagnation, but might not this stagnation be a contributing factor to the apathy and passive resistance of so many of our population when they become aged?

If the aged became involved in a program in which they were visually "re-awakened" to the textures, shapes, colors, lines, rhythms, harmonies and variations of the world around them, a renaissance could occur in their lives. A former carpenter might explore the visual qualities of his own trade. Revelations would come because he probably had never "looked" at the changing light and shadow on a partially-framed house, nor been aware of the textures, colors and shapes of his tools and materials. Women whose prime function had been in the job of homemaking could explore the use of functional and decorative textures. A variety of textures could be assembled and consciously experienced. Every occupation could be explored, and all of the senses could be alerted and activated in the search. The process of exploration could go on indefinitely.

Aged people in the year 2000 will be greatly different from those of the mid-twentieth century. This is a statement made hopefully and with the premise that the new American education now slowly emerging, including the contributions of adult education, will make learning a central lifetime function, a natural part of daily life. The impact of this concept as a "natural resource" of our nation is staggering to contemplate. Because of earlier retirement and longer life, it is possible to be retired for as long as 30 years, a period of time equal to the number of working years. The 30 years of retirement would not be lost in isolation and "killing time," but would provide the opportunity to revitalize interests that perhaps were set aside during the earning years, or to initiate new interests from the background of continuous learning that has occurred.

References

1. Cumming, E., and Henry, W. *Growing Old*. New York: Basic Books, 1961.
2. Levin, S. Depression in the aged: The importance of external factors. In this volume.
3. Lowenfeld, V. *Creative and Mental Growth*. New York: Macmillan, 1961.
4. Read, H. The shaping spirit. *Boston Univ. J. of Educ.*, 1963, *145*, 61-64.

25

The crisis of explanation

Robert Kastenbaum

"The objects with which he has identified, and to which his behavior is normally tuned, have been removed. He has been suddenly shorn of much of the support and assistance of a culture and a society upon which he depends and from which he draws sustenance; he has been deprived of the instrumentalities by which he has manipulated his environment; he has been, in effect, castrated, rendered impotent, separated from all sources of support, and left naked and alone, without a sense of his own identity, in a terrifying wilderness of ruins.

"The response to the assault of this realization is withdrawal from perceptual contact with this grim reality and regression to an almost infantile level of adaptive behavior characterized by random movement, relative incapacity to evaluate danger or to institute protective action, inability to concentrate attention, to remember, or to follow instructions. Such individuals appear to be 'dazed,' 'shocked,' 'stunned,' 'apathetic.' Actually they are far from being indifferent; it is the intensity of the previously-felt anxiety which has prompted this blocking of perception and this regression" (8, pp. 127-128).

In the passage quoted, Anthony Wallace has described and interpreted the behavior of normal adults who have experienced a disaster situation. The Worcester (Massachusetts) tornado of June 9, 1953 provided the specific occasion for his analysis, but it appears applicable to other disaster experiences as well.

It will be suggested here that similar dynamics may operate in the lives of men and women who experience the advent of "old age" as a disaster. Certainly, the behavioral description offered by Anthony will be familiar to many people who have observed geriatric patients. This paper will take seriously the apparent parallel between the behavior of disaster victims and geriatric patients, offering a tentative theoretical rationale and illustrating the phenomenon with the rather limited empirical information presently available.

This chapter is based in part upon observations made during the course of an investigation supported by USPHS research grant MHO-4818.

Old age as an
"unexpected misfortune"

It does not seem easy for a young person to understand that some day he might *really* be old, or that his grandfather (or father) once *really* was young. The immediate situation and one's own limited experience provide strong evidence that "I am young" ("I have never been old") and "Grandfather is old" ("I have never seen him young"). By implication, then: "I will *always* be young," and "he has *always* been old."

This formulation could be generalized to state that it is exceedingly difficult to realize, with full intellectual and emotional involvement, that a situation which contradicts our present state of knowledge and feeling can actually exist. So, for example, it is not easy to recapture the realization that there is such a state of feeling as urgent, desperate hunger when one has just finished an ample meal—even though one may have had previous experiences of intense hunger. How much more difficult it must be to feel oneself into an appreciation of advanced age when one has never had the experience of being old.

As reported elsewhere in this volume, young adults do not often seem to become involved with the prospect of their own later years (3). Furthermore, in at least one population of elderly men and women self-report information indicates a strong tendency *not* to have thought ahead to their present advanced age when they were young adults (4). Additional investigation is required to determine the extent to which these findings can be generalized. But the evidence now on hand (particularly from diverse samples of adolescents and young adults) clearly suggests that it is not common for persons in our society to give serious prior consideration to their possible situation in later life.

For many people, then, "old age" may be encountered *as if* unexpected (unconscious appreciation of the fact of personal aging might be operative, of course, but this possibility has not been tested). Unexpected events are seldom tolerated by our cognitive systems: either we find some way to explain them, or forget or distort the events so that they do not sound a continuing note of cognitive dissonance. Bartlett and Murphy are among those investigators who have emphasized the motivational aspects of cognition, the propelling force of the need to know or the "effort after meaning," in Bartlett's apt phrase (1,7).

The "effort after meaning" is likely to have a particular urgency behind it when one is confronted by an event that is not only unexpected, but also has the character of a misfortune. It will be useful at this point to emphasize some distinctions among three terms that are often used interchangeably: *stress, misfortune* and *crisis*.

Stress is considered to be present when the defensive reactions of the organism are called into operation. Misfortune refers to an unfavorable occurrence that, by connotation, takes one somewhat by surprise;

expectations have been upset. Thus, misfortune and stress are not necessarily identical. A mountain climber or astronaut, for example, will be well aware that he is likely to encounter stressful conditions. When the conditions do in fact develop, the individual may experience them as stress, but not as misfortune.

One can endure stress up to a point. If stress continues beyond that point, severe injury or death may result. Yet a person may suffer injury and death without experiencing a crisis situation. Crisis occurs when an individual's way of life, his very nature, is in jeopardy, not necessarily when his life alone is endangered. On this view, a person who is slowly dying of an insidious disease but does not recognize it as such would be involved in stress reactions on a physiological level, but not involved in a crisis situation. Similarly, a person who decides to fast in support of a cause to which he is intensely devoted may endure severe stress, but not crisis, so long as his devotion is unshaken. Crisis is experienced by the person who recognizes that he is in a situation whose outcome may alter the core of his value structure—i.e., it is the person who must yet decide which set of conflicting beliefs to support at the critical moment who is in a crisis situation.

To be struck by misfortune is to suffer more than the specific stress of the occasion: it is also to have a shock to one's view of life, an intimation that perhaps one really cannot cope with the world.

Sometimes the doubt is speedily resolved, and one then reacts chiefly to the specific stress. However, sometimes the misfortune has a severe impact upon the individual's confidence in his general grasp upon life. It challenges his belief that he can correctly interpret his experience. "If I was so wrong this time, how can I depend on my judgment next time?"

When misfortune turns into crisis it is because the individual cannot find an acceptable explanation for what has happened. This *inability to explain the misfortune,* rather than the misfortune itself, constitutes the crisis. This will be termed the *crisis of explanation.*

The crisis is resolved when the individual can convince himself that he understands the conditions responsible for the misfortune and, preferably, that these conditions do not involve a drastic downward re-evaluation of his own resources. Misfortunes can be explained in a number of ways that satisfy the "effort after meaning" without damaging the self-confidence necessary to continued activity. Thus, the misfortune was the result of "bad luck," or "the odds were against us;" perhaps it was brought about by "somebody else's error" or failure, or it could be that "somebody had it in for us" and took unfair advantage.

If this line of explanation does not meet criteria for acceptance, then it might be determined that we ourselves were at least partially responsible for the misfortune, perhaps as a function of our ignorance, sinfulness or error. Yet again, it might be that we had been in a gruel-ling struggle and emerged as an honorable loser.

Explanations of this second type are infinitely preferable to no explanation at all. Even if we did not or could not prevent the mis-fortune, we demonstrate the power to label and contain it within a mental framework that is larger than the misfortune—"over there is the misfortune, and here I am, looking at it, and integrating it into my entire view of life." Once the misfortune has been put into a per-spective, we can continue to function with a measure of confidence and self-esteem.

It would appear that for some people "old age" not only comes as an unexpected event, but also as a profound misfortune. The indi-vidual is faced with the exceedingly difficult task of explaining to him-self (and others) how it has come to pass that he is "not what he used to be." The observations reported below are presented as possible illustrations of what will be termed the "crisis of explanation;" they provided the first material that suggested this formulation.

Regression as a consequence of symptom removal

The present report is in the nature of a summary and reconsideration of observations reported in a previous paper (2). The observations were noted during the course of clinical and research activities of the Department of Psychology at Cushing Hospital. The availability of test data on patients participating in a psychotropic drug investigation made it possible to compare the cases noted here with a sample of their peers. Two of the "crisis" patients participated in the drug study, but the phenomena summarized here occurred at a later time.

The typical patient was approximately 74 years of age, which was 6 years younger than the mean age of Cushing Hospital patients. Dif-ficulty in walking or sensory deficit were likely to be the symptoms which engaged the primary attention of both patient and staff. The physician would find that the presented symptoms had an organic basis, and the psychologist would observe that the patient was genuinely distressed by his or her symptoms. A vigorous treatment program would then be instituted by the physician, sometimes involving tem-porary transfer to a special rehabilitation unit. The increased atten-tion and accelerated action concerning the symptom would seem clearly to have conveyed to the patient the determination of the hospital staff to provide relief for his or her distress.

Sometimes, of course, this program would fail in its aim, and some-times there were degrees of success which were accompanied by a brightening in the patient's mood. At other times, however, the treat-ment of what had almost come to be regarded as a chronic, irreversible condition had a rather sudden success that was followed by a transient state of panic. The patient would become confused and unsettled. There might be a marked withdrawal from previous relationships and activities, or a rapid alternation between withdrawal and urgent requests for emotional support. Previously "reliable" patients would lose their self-control, becoming provoked to tears or anger with little or no obvious reason. Whatever form the behavior took, the patient would appear to be in a state of high anxiety. (Sometimes direct observations by psychologists or psychiatrists were not made until the peak of panic reaction, according to descriptions of ward personnel, had passed.)

In those cases in which therapeutic intervention was delayed, ineffectual or omitted, the patient tended to sink into a profound apathy. This state was described earlier in terms of deterioration (2). However, thus far it has not been possible to obtain further information that would clearly support the implications of the term "deterioration;" it would appear to be more accurate, then, to characterize the end state as regression. The patient came to function on a level markedly below the level of adjustment before the symptom had been treated.

This sequence of behavior might be understood in terms of the following considerations:

1. These patients, by their self-report, had not given serious conscious attention to the prospects of later life at any time prior to their current situation. While Cushing Hospital patients in general did not conceptualize "old age" when they were young adults, the patients referred to here still had not thought of themselves as "old." This finding is suggestive of the observation that persons threatened by a disaster frequently ignore signs of impending danger (6, 9).

2. These patients held the implicit attitude that "old age" was a "misfortune." In partciular they had a negative attitude toward other elderly patients *for being elderly,* and seemed to have followed a life plan which relied upon the achievements, resources, and affiliations of the early years, with little provision for developing new goals or techniques of coping.

3. Eventually, the patients came to perceive that this "misfortune" of "old age" was upon them. They did not come to this realization easily, and pulled up short of accepting the self-designation of being an "old" person. However, they did perceive and react to specific self-changes that, added together, would suggest the operation of the aging process. The patients generally had attempted and abandoned one or more of the usual explanations of "misfortune." They were in the dilemma of being able neither to accept their aging with equanimity nor attribute their condition to "bad luck," "sinfulness," or other familiar interpretations of misfortune.

Here it is relevant to point out that these patients were in good contact and of average intellectual ability or better. In reluctantly abandoning routine interpretations of misfortune, they seemed aware that being transformed from a young into an aged person was a remarkable process, one that could not be assimilated within their characteristic view of life. It was common for these patients to express astonishment at their own aged appearance—"Is this me? I can't bear to look at these hands."

For these individuals, then, "old age" not only increased the stress of life, but also threatened to obliterate their identity. It was exceedingly difficult to act as though one were still "the old self," and the present self was exceedingly difficult to accept, or even to explain. To put this interpretation another way: *it may be that the reason some aged people do not do much or plan much is because they literally do not know what has happened to them, cannot explain to themselves where they are or who they are, and cannot determine in which direction to move and for what purpose.*

4. The symptom became the explanation. It was no longer the case that the individual had been struck by a cruel, unexpected misfortune that he could not understand—rather, he "had a bad leg" that required him to curtail his activities. The patient thus rescued himself from the brink of catastrophic anxiety by pinpointing a symptom that he could consider to be apart from his "true self." The "true self" could now be regarded as having been battered by the world, but not mysteriously enveloped by "old age."

5. When the symptom was removed, the patient was thrown into a state of confusion. Unable to find any explanation that would permit him to retain self-consistency and integration, he withdrew to a markedly lower level of functioning. Elliot Luby might well have been describing such a patient when he wrote (of psychosomatic reactions) that "Because he can neither make instrumentally valid responses nor psychotically withdraw, he remains trapped in a chronically stressed state with all its tissue-destructive consequences. These may result from the exhaustion phase of the general adaptation syndrome . . . (Such patients) have utterly retreated, profoundly reducing affective arousal and physiological responsivity. . . ." (5, p. 5) .

Summary and implications

The present chapter is an exploration into the meanings that "growing old" may have for the individual, and the implication of these meanings for adjustment in advanced age. No advice on the management of elderly patients is intended, although, hopefully, some of the material might be of use to clinicians in coming to their own conclusions.

It has been suggested that parallels can be observed between the behavior of disaster victims and the behavior of some geriatric patients. Furthermore, it is hypothesized that similar dynamics also prevail. The person who has never considered and psychologically prepared for the later years of life—and who regards "old age" as a profound misfortune that is totally incongruent with his self concept—may in advanced age be "deprived of the instrumentalities by which he has manipulated his environment . . . left . . . without a sense of his own identity, in a terrifying wilderness of ruins. The response to the assault of this realization is withdrawal from perceptual contact with this grim reality and regression to an almost infantile level of adaptive behavior . . ." (8, p. 128). Some elderly patients appear to defend themselves against what has been termed "the crisis of explanation" by organizing their lives around a fairly specific disability. So long as this disability is not challenged—or removed—the individual can use it as an explanation for his objective and subjective difficulties. The alternative is either to admit that one is "old" (without being able to explain or accommodate this fact), or to regress.

No doubt there are many other ways by which individuals come to terms with the self-perception of aging phenomena. "Old age" has not yielded itself to easy explanation by all the gerontological sciences; it is not surprising that individuals may also have difficulty in making sense out of "growing old." As Stephen Vincent Benet* writes:

> "A stone's a stone
> And a tree's a tree,
> But what was the sense of aging me?
> It's no improvement
> That *I* can see."

The particular difficulty that has been explored in this chapter may represent a special case of a more general phenomenon that has long been familiar to physicians and psychologists. The general phenomenon is, of course, that physical symptoms may serve the psychobiological function of defending the individual against a "something worse" than the symptom itself. What is the "something worse?" Many observers now believe that the fate-to-be-defended-against is the loss of ego-integrity. Thus, perceptive physicians sometimes will permit a symptom to persist, within tolerable limits, in order to support the patient's hard-pressed defensive efforts.

Here it has been suggested that a crisis of explanation can stimulate the development of such somatic defenses—furthermore, that the in-

---

* Excerpt from "Old Man Hoppergrass." *Selected Works of Stephen Vincent Benet*, New York: Holt, Rinehart, and Winston. Copyright, 1936, Stephen Vincent Benet. Reprinted by permission of Brandt and Brandt.

ability to explain one's "growing old" can be the specific precipitating factor. This interpretation raises the following question: is it possible that such phenomena as apathy, regression, lack of future perspective, and "disengagement" in some elderly individuals might be understood *not* as natural corollaries of the so-called "aging process," but, rather, as *normal* reactions to *crisis?*

References

1. Bartlett. F. C. *Remembering.* Cambridge: Cambridge U. Press, 1932.
2. Kastenbaum, R. Deterioration as a consequence of symptom removal. Paper presented at Sixth International Congress on Gerontology, Copenhagen, August 16, 1963.
3. Kastenbaum, R., and Durkee, N. Young People View Old Age. In this volume.
4. Kastenbaum, R., and Durkee, N. Aged People View Old Age. In this volume.
5. Luby, E. D. An overview of psychosomatic disease. *Psychosomatics,* 1963, *4,* 1-8.
6. Moore, H. E. *Tornadoes Over Texas: Waco and San Angelo in Disaster.* Austin: University of Texas Press, 1958.
7. Murphy, G. *Personality: A Biosocial Approach to Origins and Structure.* New York: Harper, 1947.
8. Wallace, A. F. C. *Tornado in Worcester.* Washington, D.C.: National Academy of Sciences-National Research Council, 1956.
9. Wolfenstein, M. *Disaster: A Psychological Study.* Glencoe, Ill. The Free Press, 1957.

INDEX

325